THE CAUSES OF
ANTI-SEMITISM

THE CAUSES OF ANTI-SEMITISM

A Critique of the Bible

Revised Edition

Arthur Blech

SelectBooks, Inc.

A previous edition of the book was published in 1997.

The Causes of Anti-Semitism: A Critique of the Bible
Revised Edition
©2005 by Arthur Blech

This edition published by Selectbooks, Inc. For information address Selectbooks, Inc., New York, New York

Revised Edition.

ISBN: 1–59079–068–5

Library of Congress Cataloging-in-Publication Data
Blech, Arthur.

The causes of anti-semitism : a critique of the Bible / Arthur Blech.--
Rev. ed.
    p. cm.
"A previous edition of the book was published in 1997."
Includes bibliographical references.
ISBN 1-59079-068-5 (hardcover : alk. paper)
1. Antisemitism--History. 2. Bible--Controversial literature. 3. Jews in the New Testament. 4. Jews--Persecutions. 5. Jews--History. 6. Christianity and antisemitism. I. Title: Causes of antisemitism. II. Title.

DS145.B56 2005
261.2'6'09--dc22

2004022449

Printed in the United States of America

10 9 8 7 6 5 4 3 2 1

This Book is dedicated to the Memory of my Father Jakub, my Mother Anna, and my Sisters Susan and Liane who were murdered at Auschwitz-Birkenau in March 1944.

Contents

Publisher's Note

This is a unique and important book which sheds light on the mystique of the biblical version of events—for all to see and judge. Many a reader will find the content disturbing and leading to unbelief; others will find it thought-provoking; still others will discover stimulating emotional visions that validate religious convictions not experienced before. But no reader's faith, beliefs, comprehension or comfortable ideas of the Old and New Testaments will remain unaffected after reading through this unrelenting examination of the Scripture by the author.

Most of the established ideas of the Bible are based on superficial reading, tendentious accounts feeding repugnant views, and a good dose of fictional presentation of Hollywood movies—such slipshod and superficial understanding will not suffice to confront and ward off the ever menacing fundamentalist religious ideologies presently challenging the accepted traditions and cultures of mankind, and may continue to do so for the rest of this century.

We must always be mindful that, not so long ago, corruption and falsification of the Bible's message led to unspeakable suffering, persecution, bloody conflicts and the murder of untold millions of innocents. Such tragedies must not be repeated because of devout ignorance.

Prologue

This book will arouse its share of controversy for it will disturb many comfortable religious notions. I made it my aim to write about subject matters I knew were suppressed by tendentious historians, doctrinaire researchers and dogmatic theologians. It is well to remember that it was not so long ago any discussion of controversial subject matters concerning religion was interdicted and the offender exposed to serious injury or worse. Nowadays, any discussion of religion and of ancient religio-historical subjects which goes against the current will arouse the opprobrium of iconoclasts for disturbing the tranquil and comfort level of dominant preconceived beliefs.

The lack of critical analysis in the past—proscribed by religious authorities some of whom even decreed that it was a sin to possess a Bible—resulted in the building up of layer upon layer of falsehoods, untruths, inventions and myths which became accepted in time not to be questioned; regarded as hallowed and venerable on account of their longevity and durability. An idea is not true just because it has been so considered since antiquity nor is an idea on that account true because a great majority of the public is of this opinion.

Judaism and Christianity cannot both be true; one of them has to be untrue or they both could be false; the contradictions within and between them are irreconcilable. The Hebrews were in Egyptian slavery either 400 years or for 4 generations only—or not at all—; it had to be one or the other or they could both be false. God gave the Israelites good laws or bad laws; found animal sacrifices pleasing or condemned them; accepted human sacrifices or considered them abominations; commanded murder or issued injunctions against it; commanded stealing or legislated against it: These appear in the Scripture of the Jews. Some of the Christian Scripture contradictions: Christ was crucified at the third hour or the sixth hour; he was crucified or hanged on a tree; there is one God or two Gods; baptism was ordered or not commanded; Christ was for nonresistance or demanded resistance; the infant Jesus was taken in flight to Egypt or not taken. As to the contradiction between the two religions, the Jews claim an eternal exclusive Covenant with God and to be his Chosen People to fulfill his plan on earth. The Christians believe in Jesus Christ, the heavenly sent Messiah, the Redeemer, who died for the sins of mankind so that those who believed in him may have everlasting life. There is no community of beliefs between the two faiths and any claim put forward that they are different aspects of the same idea is absurd.

They both jealously guard their claims to originality and special revelation with Christianity asserting the unique claim to be the fulfillment and successor of Judaism. That claim is made in the belief that Judaism had a divine foundation—they were once God's chosen—and that the Old Testament laid the groundwork for the New Testament. That claim was unreliable for it took for granted that Judaism rested on true revelation; if that assumption turned out to be false then Christianity's claim to be the fulfillment of the Old Testament is of no theological help to it; on the contrary, it absorbed and was heir to the flawed foundation of Judaism. For Scripture tells us that the God of the Israelites cannot be worshiped outside the Promised Land and gave them laws that were not good and observances by which they could never live; that Jesus and his Apostles left no written or oral instructions for the establishment of a new faith or a Universal Church; that Christ, the Messiah, could not be the one predicted by the Old Testament prophets; that Jesus was accused of blasphemy and therefore had to be tried and sentenced by the Sanhedrin and not by Pontius Pilate; that the Christ Jesus of Paul and Jesus of the Gospels were not one and the same.

Both religions claim to be the guardians of man's craving for redemption and salvation; of his need for the supernatural and healing power of piety. The Good News was proclaimed with the angels' trumpets blaring but most of the Bible prophecies were false. If the New Testament (which preached a hatred of Jews that turned into anti-Semitism) and the Old Testament (which preached contempt and rejection of non-Jews that was fully reciprocated and aroused feelings inimical towards Jews) were written by profane authors and not the result of divine revelations, then the hatred and contempt they preached have irreparably misled and mistaught Christians and Jews alike; then the curse of anti-Semitism is kept alive by inventions and myths—artificial props to the corrupt and unnatural. This book will analyze these views, the validity of their divine sanction and the causes of bitter and unending mutual hostility.

Introduction

1. When as a young man after World War II, news of the state sponsored mass extermination of Jews surfaced, news about extermination camps, transport trains, mass murder of innocent men, women and children for no other reason but the accident of birth, searing and agonizing questions began to haunt me. Why did this happen and to what purpose? This was done to Jews by Christians in Christian Europe! With the exception of a number of selfless, praiseworthy and noble Christians who could not remain silent, who assisted in alleviating the suffering of Jews and did their small part in frustrating the extermination process, the majority remained silent or worse. Significantly and inexplicably the great majority of Christian Churches, bishops, priests and above all Pope Pius XII and the Curia remained silent and on the sidelines.

2. Jews were persecuted and murdered in Europe for centuries prior to World War II. The process was never relentless, uncompromising and without alternate choices. In most of the cases there was a way out, a window of opportunity to cheat death. Those who died for the "Sanctification of the Name" made their solemn choice. The World War II atrocities were state organized, merciless, the end result inevitable, no choices given and the victims doomed. The murderers were for the most part church-going Christians, none of them were read out of the Church, denied communion or excommunicated.

3. The authority of any religion can only be sustained if it represents a socially necessary force in propagating morality and ethics, in teaching respect for human beings of all faiths. A religion, whose churches indoctrinate their adherents with teachings that Jews were accursed and rejected by God; that they bear a damnable guilt, that hatred of them is a virtue—

such a religion is responsible for centuries of church-inspired anti-Semitism. The end result was mass murder and the difference between World War II atrocities and those of prior centuries is technological. Such a religion needs to critically reexamine its fundamentals. Christians were fighting Christians from very early on for doctrinal reasons. Later on the Bible and sword joined in partnership as Christian nations fought for economic and political reasons. The butchery and mass murders committed knew no bounds; the persistent hatred carries on to the present. Jews too were fighting Jews in innumerable fratricidal and internecine wars pitting one segment against another—rivers of blood flowed to soak up the madness so that the winner could enjoy the spoils and privileges. What of the Ten Commandments? What of love of one's neighbor? It took the Roman military might to put an end to this corruption.

4. This mind-poisoning record of bloody bigotry leads one to the inevitable question: Did religion constitute any sort of restraining force? Did it make any difference? The sharp dagger was just as deadly whether applied in the name of monotheism or polytheism and the victims were just as dead. Today, we see actual or potential anti-Semitism branded into the psyche of most Christians. A calumny often repeated takes on a life of its own and we become ignorant of its causes. Very early on the evangelizing propaganda frustrated in its efforts to convert Jews on a massive scale, turned its efforts to pagans with successful results. The early Christians appropriated the Tanak (Old Testament) as their own, termed their new creed the "New Covenant," declared themselves the real "Israel" and Jesus the Messiah foretold by the Israelite prophets and fulfillment of the Tanak. The religious duty to uphold all the laws of Moses was abrogated to make conversion of pagans less difficult. According to Paul, Judaism and the Torah were no longer valid. Paul, whose writings preceded the earliest Gospel by more than thirty years, encountered increasing opposition in his activities from Jews. He laced his preaching with anti-Judaic sentiments in his effort to bolster the conversion of pagans. This attitude was later adopted by the Gospel writers and Church theologians with increasing virulence to the point of pathological hatred so as to distort the teachings of Jesus, their Messiah, whose preaching centered on love, humility, mercy and forgiveness.

5. The Jewish uprisings against Rome (from Vespasian to Hadrian) particularly the major last one by Bar Kokhba, in which the Romans prevailed

with difficulty and at great cost, disposed the Romans to view the Jewish religion the cause of unending incitements to rebellion and divisiveness. Aware of the Roman anti-Jewish sentiments, the Gospel writers and Church theologians in their effort to preserve the nucleus of the newly founded religion (after separation from Judaism) and to promote its rapid propagation, adopted increasingly more hostile anti-Judaic teachings which resulted in extreme intolerance, hatred and persecution of Jews. But not only Jews. By the 4th century, with the help of secular rulers, the Church by then called "Catholic", persecuted a great number of Christian "heretical" sects to extinction in the power struggle for primacy and exclusivity. The anti-Judaic references in Paul and the Gospels formed the theological roots of anti-Semitism.

Paul I Thessalonians 2:15–16
"… the people (Jews) who put the Lord Jesus to death, and the prophets too. And now they have been persecuting us, and acting in a way that cannot please God and makes them the enemies of the whole human race…"

Luke 21:24
"… and Jerusalem will be trampled down by the pagans until the age of the pagans is completely over."

Luke 10:16
"… and those who reject me (Jesus) reject the one who sent me (God)."

Matthew 23:13
"Alas for you, scribes and Pharisees, you hypocrites!"

Matthew 23:33
"Serpents, brood of vipers, how can you escape being condemned to hell? …"

Matthew 23:37
"Jerusalem, Jerusalem, you that kill the prophets and stone those who are sent to you! …"

Matthew 27:26
"… And the people (Jews), to a man, shouted back 'His blood is on us and on our children!'… He (Pilate) ordered Jesus to be first scourged and handed over to be crucified."

John 16:2–3

"They will expel you (Christians) from the synagogues, and indeed the hour is coming when anyone who kills you will think he is doing a holy duty for God. They (the Jews) will do these things because they have never known either the Father or myself (Jesus)."

John 18:6

"Pilate said, 'Here is the man (Jesus).' When they saw him the chief priests and the guards shouted, 'Crucify him! Crucify him.' "

6. What mind-poisoning bigotry, what a flood of incriminating statements! The following reactions of the early Church Fathers, bishops, priests—many of them elevated to sainthood—can be summarized in a few sentences. It must be understood that these views follow as a logical consequence from the anti-Judaic statements found in Paul, the Gospels and the early "orthodox" (i.e. Catholic) Church's struggle for pre-eminence and exclusive leadership: The Jews were condemned by God to eternal slavery as retribution for causing the death of Christ. Formerly Jews were a nation loved by God but now they are his enemies. Christ has shed his blood for the Jews, yet they refuse to recognize him as their Savior. Until Jews become Christians, there can be no messianic peace on earth. The Jews are perfidious murderers of Christ. It is incumbent upon all Christians to hate Jews. Jews worship the devil. For killing of God no expiation is possible. Jews are a perverse people forever accursed and Christians may never cease vengeance. Jews are the assassins of prophets.

7. It is not hard to assess the lasting impact of such vitriolic utterances upon the ordinary followers of Christ, upon the uneducated laity. The effect of such a crescendo of vituperation upon the educated princes and theologians of Christianity centuries later is set in concrete, such as:

Pope Innocent III (1198–1216)

"The Jews ... are doomed to wander about the earth as fugitives and vagabonds ... They are under no circumstances to be protected by Christian princes but, on the contrary, to be condemned to serfdom."

Martin Luther (1483–1546)

In a pamphlet written in 1543, he accused the Jews of poisoning the wells, murdering Christian children. He urged Christian princes in one of his sermons,

"... If the Jews refuse to be converted, we ought not to suffer them or bear with them any longer".

And in his pamphlet "Von den Juden and ihren Luegen" (About the Jews and their lies) he wrote,

"... Jews should be banned from the roads and markets, their property seized ... In the last resort they should simply be kicked out for all time!"

8. These are only the barest of examples. The future belonged to those who understood the method of mass conversion and related propaganda. If it were not for Christian hatred and persecution of Jews, the Jewish people would have long ago merged with other nations. The hatred and hostility toward Jews became essential to Christianity in holding Jews collectively responsible for Jesus' death. For if the Jews were comfortable and prospering, the Church's teachings about Jesus were questioned. On the other hand, if the Jews were made to suffer, the teachings about Jesus were justified. It was the essence of Christian theology to oppress and persecute Jews in order to proselytize them. But it never intended to eliminate the Jews altogether, since Jesus' prophecy of his second coming—so fundamental to Christianity—would have been theologically frustrated (Matthew 16:28 reference to "some of these standing here" was interpreted to mean as referring to the Jewish people and not solely to the individual listeners). So the Catholic cardinals, bishops and priests desired the Jews not to disappear, only to be humbled and to suffer for their rejection of Christ. This would forever be testimony of the truth of the Gospels.

9. Anti-Semitism (anti-Judaism, anti-Jewishness: those terms will be defined later in this book), however, did not start with Paul and the Gospels. Centuries before, when the Jews began to settle among other nations principally in cities like Rome, Alexandria, Antioch and Babylon, where they attained large numbers, they carried with them the biblical and priestly injunctions. They felt favored above all other nations because of the Covenant with God; that they were the Chosen People of God and therefore had to maintain their separateness and exclusivity. From these followed their special distinctiveness, autonomous ethnic communities, separate entities, prohibition of marriage with foreigners, i.e., non-Jews, separate cemeteries, refusal to participate in communal events, exemption

from appearing in Courts on the Sabbath, exemption from serving in the army because of dietary laws, tax advantages and economic privileges, the right to send the annual Temple tax to Jerusalem (on which account they requested exemption from secular taxation), the right to export gold in support of the Temple in Jerusalem and special animal slaughtering privileges. Coupled with their understandable refusal to participate in ceremonies that involved worship of local deities and emperors, all these resulted in bringing forth envy, contempt, hatred and opposition from the rest of the population. The situation was tailor-made for Jew haters; the various pogroms, persecutions, anti-Jewish agitation and uprisings were the result. Their divine laws made them slaves to a system of thought which provoked from within an attitude odious to the Gentiles and branded their personality and behavior. Claudius, the Roman Emperor (41–54 A.D.), of friendly disposition toward Jews, had to warn the Jews of Alexandria not to seek more than their due.

10. The Tanak itself put words into the mouths of the enemies of Jews which was a treasure-trove for future anti-Semites. A few samples will suffice:

Numbers 14:12 (God speaking to Moses about the Israelites)
"I will strike them with pestilence and disown them. And of you I shall make a new nation, greater and mightier than they are."

Numbers 14:34–35 (God speaking to the Israelites)
"… for forty years you shall bear the burden of your sins, and you shall learn what it means to reject me."

Numbers 26:4 (God speaking to Moses about the Israelites)
"Take all the leaders of the people. Impale them for Yahweh, here in the sun …"

Jeremiah 3:25
"Let us lie down in our shame, let our dishonor be our covering for we have sinned against Yahweh our God."

Jeremiah 7:9–11
"Steal, would you, murder, commit adultery, perjure yourselves, … follow alien gods that you do not know? … Do you take this Temple that bears my name for a robbers' den?"

Jeremiah 19:4–5

"… have offered incense here to alien gods … They have filled this place with the blood of the innocent. They have built high places for Baal to burn their sons there …"

Ezekiel 7:2–4

"The Lord Yahweh says this to the land of Israel: 'Finished! The end is coming for the four quarters of the land. Now all is over with you; I mean to unleash my anger on you … for all your filthy practices. I mean to show you no pity, I will not spare you; …' "

Ezekiel 22:27–28

"Her leaders in the city are like wolves tearing their prey, shedding blood and killing people to steal their possessions. Her prophets have white-washed these crimes with their empty visions and lying prophecies."

Deuteronomy 28:15 and 28:29–30

"But if you do not obey the voice of Yahweh your God nor keep and observe all those commandments and statutes of his that I enjoin on you today, then all the curses that follow shall come up with you and overtake you."

"You will never be anything but exploited and plundered continually, and no one will come to your help."

Deuteronomy 28:63–65

"For not obeying the voice of Yahweh your God, … you will be torn from the land which you are entering to make your own. Yahweh will scatter you among all peoples from one end of the earth to the other; … Among these nations there will be no repose for you, no rest for the sole of your foot …"

11. The priestly sect and scribes were responsible for the redaction of the Torah, full of contradictions, historical errors and written many centuries later than the events they described. These priests wrote their own charter imposed on their flock by claiming divine sanction whose terms were elitist, aristocratic; their office hereditary and who wrote laws to perpetuate their monopoly of power; living the life of privilege on tithes claimed to be divinely sanctioned; considered religious unity and monopoly indispensable to the maintenance of supremacy. Death was the penalty decreed by the Torah for refusal to obey the decision of priests. The essence of the Mosaic

books, i.e., the Torah, was to place unlimited power in the hands of the priesthood who made themselves indispensable by claiming exclusive efficacy of their oracles, administration of Temple rituals and performance of sacrifices. As long as their elaborate legal codes and rituals were not interfered with, the oracles were favorable. But as soon as the Israelites worshiped at "high places", sacrificed at other shrines and refused to regard the Jerusalem Temple as the central sanctuary—as when Jeroboam authorized sacrifices at Dan and Bethel—Israelite blood flowed in streams. This was the true religion? Not according to Isaiah 1:11,where the prophet quoted God: ' "What are your endless sacrifices to me?' says Yahweh. 'I am sick of holocausts of rams and fat calves. The blood of bulls and of goats revolts me." ' Instead Isaiah 1:16–17 quoted God as wishing: "Take your wrongdoing out of my sight. Cease to do evil. Learn to do good, search for justice, help the oppressed, be just to the orphan, plead for the widow." (But then the First Isaiah knew nothing of Moses and his laws!) The observance of these admonitions would have spelled economic ruin of the priestly sect; it therefore never happened.

12. Such a religion needs to critically re-examine its fundamentals. But there are no prophets today. The prophet Habakkuk in vain asked the right questions, "Your eyes are too pure to rest on wickedness, … why do you look on while men are treacherous, and stay silent while evil man swallows a better man than he?" (Habakkuk 1:13). And again: "Yahweh … For all your wrath, remember to be merciful." (Habakkuk 3:2) He received no answers.

13. I shall question in this book the nature of the Bible. I am disturbed by the content of both Testaments in that they appear to incline the mind toward unintended directions, namely hatred, envy, intolerance and other socially damaging views. I shall inquire whether the lofty ethical pronouncements in the Testaments were not more than nullified by other contradictory views propounded. I shall inquire about the significance of the commandment "You shall not kill" in light of the divinely sanctioned mass murders of innocent men, women and children. I shall inquire whether certain fundamental views expressed in the Testaments are in fact original or copied from non-biblical writers and documents. I shall inquire whether the venal and power-hungry priestly sects were the guiding hand of the Scriptures. I shall inquire whether the attribution to God of the worst

human passions such as jealousy, anger, vengeance, desire for cruel punishment, could have had a divine guiding hand. I shall inquire whether fathers, who willingly slit the throats of their children rather than have them confess another faith, were brain-damaged murderers or acting out of misguided piety. I shall inquire whether the constant harping about the need for salvation encourages egotism and self-centeredness, inimical to vital social and moral forces essential to the well-being of mankind.

Introduction:
Chapters 1–15

As one of my aims in this book, I set out to question the validity of the Bible with particular attention devoted to the Torah (the Pentateuch, the five Books of Moses) and the influence it had (and the other books of the Tanak) on the mind-set of the Jewish people. Throughout this book I quoted extensively verses from *The Jerusalem Bible* (copyright © 1966 by Darton, Longman & Todd, Ltd. and Doubleday, a division of Bantam Doubleday Dell Publishing Group, Inc. Reprinted by permission) since it was the main source of my critique; I let the Bible tell its own version of events. The Bible chosen is concise and crisp in its language; in my view it is the most reliable English translation of the original Hebrew, Aramaic and Greek texts. The reader must bear with my extensive recitals of the Bible verses and the pointed repetition of some of them where necessary. For it is mainly in the context of some of the quoted verses that the Bible fails the test of authenticity.

Chapter 1

The Sumerians and Babylonians

1. Sumer, part of Mesopotamia, the south-eastern portion of present day Iraq, mainly between the two rivers Euphrates and Tigris, was first settled about 5000 B.C. The first settlers were non-Semitic who, after struggles with the Semites from the north and west, produced a Sumerian people and achieved the first and most unique civilization known to history. Sumerian influence on the Hebrews came indirectly through the Babylonians (and possibly Canaanites); when we first hear of the Hebrews, Sumeria faded into history. The Sumerians had reached a high level of civilization by 3500 B.C.

2. The claim of the Jews to be in possession of sacred books of first impression shatters when we learn that much which is foundational in the Torah (Pentateuch) derives from Sumerian and Babylonian (and Egyptian) civilizations and religions much more ancient than the time of the Hebrew Patriarchs and Moses. "One of the main achievements of archaeological activity in 'Bible lands' is that a ... revealing light has been shed on the background and origin of the Bible itself" (51–141). In Genesis 10:10–11 there appears a reference to Sumer, "First to be included in his empire were Babel, Erach and Accad, all of them in the land of Shinar (Sumer)." The Sumerians had a written code of laws around 2500 B.C., received details and specifications from their gods; had Temples, the planning and materials to be used were communicated by their gods; the Temples acted as depository of treasures and records; had a highly developed priesthood with a high-priest, where priests ruled as priest-kings; managed to centralize their religion; the priesthood amassed great wealth and kept clay tablets of records of business transactions; their gods are represented as standing upon a mountain. The Encyclopaedia Judaica (53–516, Vol. 15) describes the derivation eloquently:

3

"… the literary motifs, themes, patterns, and ideas that go back to Sumerian prototypes: the existence of a primeval sea; the separation of heaven and earth; the creation of man from clay imbued with the breath of life; the creative power of the divine word; several "paradise" motifs; the Flood story; the Cain–Abel rivalry; the Tower of Babel and confusion of tongues; the notion of a personal, family god; divine retribution and national catastrophe; plague as divine punishment; the "Job" motif of suffering and submission … not a few of the biblical laws go back to Sumerian origins and in such books as Psalms, Proverbs, Lamentations, and the Song of Songs there are echoes of the corresponding Sumerian literary genres."

3. Since the beginning of civilization the priesthood raised its head, a class apart, living in opulence, interposed between mankind and gods, drawing privileges unto itself, preying upon the fear of mankind, creating self-serving laws and ordinances to preserve its aristocratic and exclusive position. The Sumerian priest, long before Abraham and Moses, was already expert in this field. "Man was created for the sole purpose of serving the gods and supplying them with food and shelter, hence the building of temples and offering of sacrifices were man's prime duties. Sumerian religion, therefore, was dominated by priest-conducted rites and rituals …" (53–514, Vol. 15).

4. Even though a great number of different gods were worshiped (each city had its own god or gods), various priesthoods were involved; military conflicts between cities were common, however, one thing stands out remarkably: there prevailed a great deal of religious tolerance. It was not until 2000 year later, long after the Sumerians passed from history, that the politically inspired priest-made monotheism subverted the previously accepted henotheism. I lay the blame for the tragic history of the Jewish people primarily at the doorstep of a corruptible and corrupt Israelite and Jewish priesthood, whose priests and scribes formulated certain Torah laws, precepts and commandments which exercised a reason-perverting power in spreading intolerance, hatred and vindictiveness. And so with the Christian priesthood that followed. More about that later.

5. The first known examples of writing on clay tablets date from about 3300 B.C. They were found near the ancient city of Uruk, in Sumer. There

must have been many previous stages of development going back to a more ancient past as the clay tablets contain a complete system of writing with more than 700 signs. The infrastructure of the city-state was of an advanced nature as their economic and administrative needs necessitated their writing skills.

6. In the view of the Sumerians, the major components of the universe were heaven and earth, surrounded on all sides by a boundless sea. The earth was flat and heaven in the shape of a vault. See Genesis 1:1, 1:6–8. Their cosmogony followed with the creation of light-giving astral bodies, followed by plant, animal and finally man. See Genesis 1:11–12, 1:20–22, 1:24–25, 1:26. Man was created by the gods for their pleasure; only the gods are immortal, man's final destiny is death. "Kings and rulers constantly boasted of the fact that they had established law and order in the land; protected the weak from the strong, the poor from the rich; and wiped out evil and violence … protected the widow and orphan, … regulated weights and measures to ensure honesty in the market place … practically all the major deities of the Sumerian pantheon are extolled in Sumerian hymns as lovers of the good and the just, of truth and righteousness" (50–102). A very advanced civilization indeed!

7. Old Testament biblical scholars consider the Book of Job so different in style and content from the other books of the canon as to attribute authorship to a non-Hebrew. We have to turn to the Sumerians for guidance. "The proper course for a Sumerian 'Job'… was not to argue and complain in the face of seemingly unjustifiable misfortune, but to plead and wail, to lament, and to confess his inevitable sins and failings. … It was to … his personal deity, that the individual sufferer bared his heart in prayer and supplication, and it was through him that he found his salvation" (50–105). Similarly with the Old Testament Book of Proverbs. The Sumerians compiled proverbs and sayings in written form nearly 4000 years ago.

8. The purpose of this chapter is to show that if Moses lived around 1200 B.C., there were advanced civilizations a thousand or more years before his time which had written clay tablets of their laws and religions; that the author/authors of the Torah and other books of the Old Testament drew heavily upon those ideas and were greatly influenced by them; that many

of these clay tablets were stored in royal libraries of Babylonian and Assyrian cities readily accessible to Israelite scribes and scholars; that no originality can attach to those ideas taken from the ancient writings and that no divine revelation can attach to such copied ideas. But more about that later. With the above in mind, I shall combine in this Chapter Sumerian and Babylonian (and Assyrian) religious, ethical and legal ideas in so far as they predate the putative time of Moses. Sargon I, King of neighboring Akkad (founder of its Semitic dynasty) conquered Sumeria about 2800 B.C. Hammurabi, greatest king of the first dynasty of Babylon, conquered Sumeria around 2100 B.C. Each copied and added to civilization.

9. Below are listed some of the mind-inspiring ideas which stoked the imagination and religious concepts of Bible writers. The source and influence are unmistakable:

(a) "… the Ebla (located in present-day Syria) and Mari tablets contain administrative and legal documents referring to people with … names such as Abram, Jacob, Leah, Laban and Ishmael; …" (5–12).

(b) "The Mari tablets … give examples of the legal ritual of confirming a covenant by slaughtering an animal, just as Abraham confirmed his covenant with God in Genesis 15:9–10" (5–13).

(c) Sargon I, King of Babylon (ca. 2600 B.C.) had a beginning that calls to mind the story of Moses:

" 'My humble mother conceived me; in secret she brought me forth. She placed me in a basket-boat of rushes; with pitch she closed my door.' Rescued by a workman, he became a cup-bearer to the king, grew in favor and influence, rebelled, displaced his master, and mounted the throne …" (4–121).

His father is not named and his mother was a temple prostitute. (See Exodus 2:1–6.)

(d) "Sacrifices of animals were made, libations poured out, and incense burned. Priests wore special dresses, ablutions were strongly insisted upon, clean and unclean animals were carefully distinguished, special festivals were kept in harmony with changes of the seasons and the movements of heavenly bodies. Religious processions, in which gods were carried about in arks ... were common. A Sabbath was observed for the purpose of assuaging the wrath of gods, that their hearts might rest. Every indication points to the existence of a powerful priesthood whose influence was felt in all spheres of social and national life ..." (45–104). (See Leviticus)

(e) "They gave the Jews the mythology which the Jews gave to the world. Babylonia became the Eden of Semitic legend ... the Euphrates is one of the four rivers which according to Genesis (2:15) flowed through paradise" (4–218).

(f) The Sumerian poem "Dilmun" was the source material for the biblical story describing the fashioning of Eve from the rib of Adam. (See Genesis 2:22.).

(g) "... the Biblical deluge story is ...(taken)...(from)... the eleventh tablet of the Babylonian *Epic of Gilgamesh* ... The Babylonian deluge myth ... is of Sumerian origin" (50–148).

The gods decided to bring the flood and destroy mankind. The counterpart of the biblical Noah (Ziusudra) is pious and god-fearing; the flood raged for seven days and nights; the sun then dries up the water and Ziusudra in gratitude for being spared prostrates himself before the sungod and offers sacrifices. (See Gen..6:13 ff)

(h) "The priests are judges, scribes, and authors. Writing is first employed in the service of the gods" (45–99).

(i) "In the center of each city is the temple, with its ruling and protective deity ... and the temples ... are centers of mercantile activity; they are the banks, the granaries and the seats of exchange" (45–105).

(j) The Assyrian kings requested oracles before battles.

"The Assyrian plan is laid before the god for his approval; an oracle as to the outcome of the king's policy or of the enemy's reported movements is requested in a fashion which ... is in essence similar to that employed by the kings of Israel. (I Sam 30:8, 1 Kings 22:5, 22:15)" (45–292).

(k) The Sumerian "King Ur-Engur proclaimed his code of laws in the name of the ... god Shamash, for government had soon discovered the political utility of heaven ..." (4–127).

(1) In many Mesopotamian cities the temple of the city god was superimposed on a ziggurat, which was a series of superimposed platforms.

"Temples set on platforms are found as early as ... 5000 B.C. ... The same plan was used for the most famous ziggurat of all, that of the god Marduk at Babylon, which gave rise to the story of the Tower of Babel. Begun in the 18th century B.C. ... (it was described as) the temple of the foundation of heaven and earth" (51–104). (See Gen. 11)

(m) Hammurabi, from an Amorite tribe, founded the first Babylonian empire (the date of inception of his rule varies between 2123 B.C. and 1792 B.C.) ruled as king for 43 years; he is remembered primarily for his Code of Hammurabi, a set of secular laws for his people. The Book of Covenant (Exodus 20:22 ff) shows affinity with the Code of Hammurabi. At the head of this Code, like that of Moses, we see the figure of Hammurabi receiving this set of laws as a gift from Heaven from Shamash, the Sun-god, who promised to establish Babylon an "everlasting kingdom." Hammurabi made strenuous efforts

"to cause justice to prevail in the land; to destroy the wicked and evil, to prevent the strong from oppressing the weak ... to enlighten the land and to further the welfare of the people ... who helped his people in time of need; who establishes in security their property in Babylon; ..." (4–219 ff).

Further the Code states in the epilogue:

"... In my bosom I carried the people of the land of Sumer and Akkad; ... in my wisdom I restrained them, that the strong might not oppress the weak, and that they should give justice to the orphan and the widow ... Let any oppressed man who had a cause, come before my image as king of righteousness! ..." (4–220).

What a thrill to learn that at a time in history and for at least 3800 years thereafter, when royalty, aristocracy and priesthood fattened and battened on their subjects, a divinely inspired Hammurabi went against the current of ethical barbarity and devised a Code that would do honor to a present-day social reformer. And all this without the benefit of monotheism, reward of eternal life after death and salvation of soul!

(n) Under Babylonian law a "creditor could seize the debtor's slave or son as hostage for an unpaid debt, and could hold him for not more than three years" (4–229). (See Deut. 15:2–13)

(o) Long before the time of Hammurabi, in an episode reminiscent of Moses, a stele from Ur shows the King Ur-Engur receiving instructions from the Moon god to build him a temple. (See Exodus 26)

(p) In Deuteronomy 19:21 we read: "Life for life, eye for eye, tooth for tooth, hand for hand, foot for foot." In Exodus 21:25 there is added to the former: "... burn for burn, wound for wound, stroke for stroke." This equal punishment or equivalent retaliation is known as the "Lex Talionis."

"In the Code of Hammurabi the law of retaliation also appears, where it applies to injuries inflicted by a man of the aristocracy, the seignior, upon another member of the same class" (3–221).

Later, a monetary fine was substituted for the retaliatory measure and the fine became the sole punishment; the Torah, however, did not relent. In Hammurabi's statute 206 we read:

"If a man wound another accidentally in a quarrel with a stone or his fist, and oblige him to take his bed, he shall pay for the loss of his time and for the doctor" (3–170).

For the same offense the law of Moses reads in Exodus 21:18–19:

"If men quarrel and one strikes the other a blow with a stone or a fist so that the man ... must keep his bed, the one who struck the blow ... must compensate him ... for his enforced inactivity, and care for him until he is completely cured."

(r) "The Babylonian story of creation consists of seven tablets (one for each day of creation)... ; they are a copy of a legend that came down to Babylonia ... from Sumeria" (4–237) (See Genesis 2:1–2).

(s) In the Babylonian legend, the burnt offerings were pleasing to the gods.

"The gods snuffed up the odor, the gods snuffed up the excellent odor, the gods gathered like flies above the offering" (4–237).

In Exodus 29:10 ff, God commands Moses about the procedures of offerings. It is God speaking to Moses when he says:

"This will be a burnt offering whose fragrance will appease Yahweh; it will be a holocaust in honor of Yahweh" (Exodus 19:18).

In Leviticus 1:9 God speaks to Moses: "This holocaust will be a burnt offering and the fragrance of it will appease Yahweh." Similarly in Leviticus 1:13, 1:17, 2:2–3, 3:5, 6:22, 17:6.

(t) The Sumerian word for the Hebrew Sheol is Kur, which is the place below earth's crust to which went all the dead; none of them saw the light of day again. To the Sumerians, the idea of personal immortality as a reward from the gods was unknown. The reward for pleasing the gods was a good life on this earth; the punishment for displeasing the gods were all kinds of diseases and sufferings on this earth. The views expressed in the Torah are similar. Deuteronomy 32:22, "Yes, a fire has blazed from my anger, it will burn to the depth of Sheol." The descent of the dead to Sheol is wrapped in mystery and no clarification can be offered. The writer was familiar with the Sumerian and Babylonian legends and saw no reason to change them. In the Torah, rewards and punishments are on this earth and the impact is immediate. In Leviticus 26:3 ff, God is speaking:

"If you live according to my laws, if you keep my commandments ... I will give you the rain you need ... the earth shall give its produce and the trees ... their fruits; ... You shall eat your fill of bread and live secure in your land."

If, however, the laws and commandments of God are not kept, then God says, in Leviticus 26:21 ff:

"If you set yourself against me and will not listen to me, I will heap these plagues on you in sevenfold punishment for your sins... ."

(u) "The striking resemblance of many paragraphs of the Book of the Covenant (Exodus 21:22 ff) to sections of the Babylonian Code of Hammurabi resolves for us the enigma of the origin of the Israelite Code. This code is an offshoot of the Babylonian law ..." (46–96).

Chapter 2

The Egyptians

1. The Egyptians created a magnificent civilization by 3500 B.C., which is about 2300 years before the time of Moses as accepted by most biblical scholars. They created a rich literature in the area of religion and many themes parallel the literature of the Torah; a faith of much complexity with prayer, ritual, sacrifices, temples and most importantly, a powerful and wealthy priesthood. I shall quote a few citations which affected the Torah author/authors:

2. "The Egyptians tried to promote health ... by circumcision of males; even the earliest tombs give evidence of this practice" (4–183).

There are records of Egyptian operations in Egyptian reliefs before 2500 B.C.

"The rite was ... common to most Semites (although it was not practiced by the Babylonians) and many other non-Semitic peoples ... the Phoenicians, and the Syrians in Palestine, acknowledge that they learned it from the Egyptians ..." (42–136).

The Edomites, Moabites, Ammonites and Canaanites used it. The Hebrews adopted it and the Torah with great fanfare made it a central theme in God's Covenant with Abraham as if it were a pristine innovation peculiar to the Hebrews. In Genesis 17:10–11, God is speaking:

"Now this is my Covenant between myself and you, and your descendants after you: all your males must be circumcised."

And again, God is speaking in Genesis 17:13–14:

"My Covenant shall be marked on your bodies as a Covenant in perpetuity. The uncircumcised male, whose foreskin has not been circumcised, such a man shall be cut off from his people: he has violated my Covenant."

3. Certain striking parallels to the Decalogue in Exodus 20:1 ff appear in the Egyptian "Book of the Dead," consisting of about 2000 papyrus rolls, some dating from 2500 B.C. and earlier; scrolls written by priests in the very "handwriting" of the god Thoth. The dead man, in the presence of the god Osiris and his court, declares in a "Negative Confession," among other items:

"... I have not committed evil, ... I have not stolen, ... I have not defiled the wife of a man, ... I have not robbed, ... I have not killed men, ... I have not uttered falsehood ... I have not blasphemed against my local god. ... I have not oppressed the poor ... I have done no carnal act within the sacred enclosure of the temple ..."

For the confessor to recite such confessions in the negative, there must have been known to him direct laws of prohibition, scrolls either lost to us or as yet not unearthed.

4. Throughout human history the gods had to be appeased and propitiated, which required special knowledge and ability to mediate the contacts and relation between man and god. Such men were called "priests" who in time became the privileged class of experts, claiming secret knowledge of the means of mediation between the divine and profane. The Egyptian priesthood appears to be the first to have perfected this craft into an art. They had priests and high-priests, elaborate ceremonies, rituals, prayers and sacrifices, much as the Israelites did later on. They were supported by tithes and income from properties; jealously guarded the temple treasuries against royal or other encroachments; lived on sacrificial food and drinks; resided in the temples; were the beneficiaries of a hereditary system; were obsessed with ritual cleanliness; wore special garments and ornaments; were circumcised; all this thousands of years before the alleged time of Moses and much as the Israelites did later on. The resemblance to the priesthood as outlined in the Torah is unmistakable. Referring to the Egyptian priesthood:

"... a class had to arise adept in magic and ritual, whose skill would make it indispensable in approaching the gods ... the office of priest passed down from father to son and a class grew up which ... became in time richer and stronger than ... the royal family itself. The sacrifices offered to the gods supplied the priests with food and drink; the temple buildings gave them spacious homes; the revenues of temple lands and services furnished them with ample incomes ..." (4–201).

Will Durant, quoting Herodotus (4–202), speaking of Egyptian priests:

"They are of all men the most excessively attentive to the worship of the gods ... They wear linen garments, constantly fresh washed ... They wash themselves in cold water twice every day and twice every night."

Reference will now be made to Israelite priests and priesthood.

"The priests are called ministrants of God ... and their function in the temple is called service—holy service, they stand before God to minister to Him ..." (53–1069 Vol. 13) "While every man of Israel was entitled to offer sacrifices on individual altars (i.e., altars without a temple) without the intermediation of authorized personnel, the cultic service associated with the altars attached to the temples ... was always reserved for regular priestly families ... their (priests') natural place is only in a house of God ..." (53–1072 ff Vol. 13). "The primary ... cultic function of the priests was the offering of the sacrifices on the altar which stood in the Temple court. ... The priest blessed the people in the name of God ... the priests also proclaimed blessings and curses to the people ... A distinct function of the priests was to carry the ark ... whenever the ark was carried out to the battlefield. ... (Other) activities included the burning of frankincense on the inner altar, the care of the lamps, and the setting out the shewbread on the table. ... These activities simultaneously performed by the high priest inside the temple complement one another. They provide ... food (bread), drink (the libation on the table), aroma (frankincense), light (candles), sound (bells), and arouse the memory (the stones on the vestments). ... This inner system of ceremonies is rooted in the primal conception of the Temple as God's dwelling place, in which He, as it were 'lives' His life, and in which all His needs are to be satisfied. The Israelite religion inherited the system of ceremonies as a fixed and crystallized pattern of divine worship" (53–1076 ff Vol. 13). "The priests, being essentially servants of God, enjoy greater holiness than the rest of the people. ... This right is seen in the Bible basically as divine grace extended to a chosen tribe, or part of it. The holiness of the priests is agreed upon in all biblical sources, ... A blemished priest (one who is physically handicapped) cannot approach the altar or enter the temple in order to serve there, in the same way that a sacrifice has to be ... without taint" (53–1080 Vol. 13). "The period of temples in Israel began after the conquest of Canaan ... the Israelite priesthood began with the settlement. ... Its real activity began with the message of

Moses (the Torah) ... From that time the priesthood became one of the faithful bearers of this religion and the preserver of its cultic rites. The rites themselves were generally taken over from the pagan culture which preceded Moses, but the Israelite priesthood used them as raw material ..." (53–1082 Vol. 13), to found a system of rites, rituals, laws of hygiene and diet, curses and exclusivity, which were to serve with disastrous consequence and results in the future years of the Jewish people.

5. One of the most fundamental claims of Jewish religionists is that the Torah gave monotheism to the world. Not so. (Whether the Torah in fact taught monotheism, as such, will be treated in a later chapter.) The Egyptian King Amenhotep IV (Ikhnaton) (1380–1362 B.C.)—who lived before Moses' alleged time and in an age when every nation, city and tribe worshiped a distinct deity—announced that there was but one god. He brought forth the concept of a naturalistic monotheism, of one invisible god belonging to all the nations. This was an idea far ahead of its time and the conceiver paid the price which all innovators and radical reformers paid throughout history; those who dared to go against the current and take on the Establishment: in this case the powerful Egyptian priesthood. This courageous young man with his idea of a compassionate and caring one god quickly faded, consumed by a crafty priesthood whose livelihood depended on cultic idolatry. The wear and tear of priestly opposition brought him to an early grave (age 30) or he was possibly killed during the priestly-promoted revolution against him. After he was gone the priesthood quickly "normalized" matters. What did Amenhotep teach? He attempted to change the people's polytheistic religion; pronounced that all these many gods were idolatry; attempted to teach the people a religion of one invisible god; that there was but one god "Aton," the Egyptian Sun-god.

Chapter 3

The Early Religion of Israel

1. The purpose of this chapter is to review the early religion of Israel with a view of demonstrating that its religion was polytheistic and in no way monotheistic; that Israel was not the recipient of a sudden revelation but developed its early religion along with its neighbors (the break did not occur until the 9th century B.C. as a result of prophetic activity and during King Josiah's Temple discovery in the late seventh century B.C.—the complete break not till after the Babylonian Exile); that it included the cults of various Canaanite deities and was Canaanite in character. The cult of Baal, Asherah, high places, sacrifice of children and other practices later abandoned and condemned formed part of Israel's early religion; was typical of the region and did not differ materially from that of its neighbors.

2. By 4000 B.C., Canaanites were well settled in towns and villages in what was known later as Palestine: By 2000–1600 B.C., the Semitic Amorites became dominant; the Hittites, Hurrians and Habiru (identified by a majority of scholars as the original Hebrews) also penetrated. The Moabites, Ammonites, Edomites, Horites, Midianites, Perizzites, Hivites, Jebusites and later the Phoenicians and Philistines intermingled with the population of Canaan and formed its immediate neighbors.

3. A series of tablets discovered near the site of ancient Ugarit (Syria), known today as the "Ugaritic text" dating to about 1500 B.C., provided extensive information about Canaanite religion. The principal god was El; his consort Asherah; Baal the Storm-god and Astarte the goddess of fertility. "Israelite religion in its earliest form did not contrast markedly with the religions of its … neighbors in either number or configuration of deities … the number of deities in Israel was … typical for the region" (40–25). "… the monarchy permitted religious devotion to Baal down to its final days

(Jeremiah 2:8, 7:9, 9:13, 12:16). From the cumulative evidence it appears that on the whole Baal was an accepted Israelite god, that criticism of his cult began in the 9th or 8th century ... There is no evidence that prior to the 9th century Baal was considered a major threat to the cult of Yahweh" (40–47). In the Book of Judges there are clear references: "After Gideon's death, the people of Israel again began to prostitute themselves to the Baals, and took Baal-Berith for their god. The Israelites no longer remembered Yahweh their God ..." (Judges 8:33–34). "So they (the Israelites) gave him (Abimelech) seventy shekels of silver from the temple of Baal-Berith, ..." (Judges 9:4). After rebelling against the murderous Abimelech, the Israelites of Migdal-Shechem "took refuge in the crypt of the temple of El-Berith" (Judges 9:47). The Old Testament treats Baal and El interchangeably. The word Baal is recognizable in biblical names, as in "That day Gideon was given the name Jerubaal, ..." (Judges 6:32); "a son of King Saul ... Saul father of ... Eshbaal ..." (I Chron. 8:33) and "Saul's son Jonathan was father of Meribbaal." (See I Chron. 8:34).

4. Asherah, a Canaanite goddess, the wife of El, according to Ugaritic tradition, but the consort of Baal in Palestine. In the Bible the noun "Asherah" is used with more than one meaning: both as a Canaanite goddess and a wooden cult object which can be built and is placed near the altar; a sacred pole representing her. This was pagan idolatry pure and simple! This is Yahweh speaking to Gideon: "Take your father's fattened calf, and pull down the altar belonging to your father and cut down the sacred (sic) post at the side of it" (Judges 6:25–26). Again, Yahweh speaking to Moses: "You are to tear down their (the various nations of Canaan) altars, smash their standing stones, cut down their sacred (sic) poles." (Ex 34:13). And again: "... cut down their sacred (sic) poles, ..." (Deut. 12:3). Asa, King of Judah (911–870 B.C.) "did what is right in the eyes of Yahweh" and "He even deprived his grandmother of the dignity of queen mother for making an obscenity for Asherah; Asa cut down her obscenity ..." (1 Kings 15:13). The cult of Asherah was so widespread among the kings of Judah that Manasseh (687–642 B.C.) "did many more things displeasing to Yahweh" and provoked Yahweh's anger: "He placed the carved image of Asherah which he had made in the Temple" (2 Kings 21:7). It was as late as Josiah (King of Judah 640–609 B.C.) who ordered his priest "... to remove all the cult objects that had been made for Baal, Asherah and the

whole array of heaven" from the Jerusalem Temple (2 Kings 23:4). In recognition of the widespread use of the "sacred" poles of Asherah, and in an attempt to purge pagan elements from worship of Yahweh, Deut. 16:21–22 solemnly intones: "You must not plant a sacred pole of any wood whatsoever beside the altar that you put up for Yahweh your God; ..."

5. Baal was worshiped in the open and under trees. The belief in trees as places of divine presence was widespread in Canaan; the tree was the Canaanite symbol of the goddess Asherah; Hebrew jar inscriptions from Kuntillet Ajrud raise the problem of Yahweh's relationship with Asherah; these inscriptions associate Yahweh of Samaria with Asherah; the Asherah may have been carved from wood or a living tree planted to represent the symbol. "The sons of Israel did what displeases Yahweh and served the Baals. They deserted Yahweh ... to serve Baal and Astarte" (Judges 2:11–14). Again, in I Samuel 12:10 "We have sinned, for we have deserted Yahweh; we have served the Baals (sic) and the Astartes (sic)." In almost every area in Palestine where excavations have been made, terracotta figurines were found, representing a nude woman, probably associated with the fertility goddess, widely worshiped by the Israelites. The question of Yahweh's consort is one of the most puzzling in light of the Elephantine papyri documents, dating from the fifth century B.C. A colony of Jews in the Upper Egyptian city of Elephantine had a temple where Yahweh (pronounced Yahu) was worshiped along with two goddesses, Ashimah and Anath, the latter appeared to be Yahweh's consort. The children of Israel could not desist from the Baal worship and according to the Bible, Yahweh responded with savage punishment. In Numbers 25:1 ff we read: "Israel settled at Shittim. The people gave themselves over to debauchery with the daughters of Moab. These invited them to the sacrifices of their gods ... With Israel thus committed to the Baal of Peor, the anger of Yahweh blazed out against them. Yahweh said to Moses, "Take all the leaders of the people. Impale them for Yahweh, here in the sun; then the burning anger of Yahweh will turn away from Israel." Moses said to the judges in Israel, "Every one of you must put to death those of his people who have committed themselves to the Baal of Peor." The preceding excerpt illustrates that the anger of Yahweh could be appeased with human sacrifices! Yahweh accepted the existence of other gods but instructed the children of Israel to desist prior to their entry into Canaan. In Ex. 23:32–33

we read: "You must make no pact with them (the people of Canaan) or with their gods. They must not live in your country (Canaan) or they will make you sin against me; you would come to worship their gods, …" Again and again Yahweh has to remind the children of Israel that he is a jealous God and refers to other gods:

"You shall bow down to no other god, for Yahweh's name is the Jealous One; he is a jealous God. Make no pact with the inhabitants of the land or, when they prostitute themselves to their own gods and sacrifice to them, they may invite you …" (Ex 34:14–16). The faith of the children of Israel in their one God was thin indeed.

6. The conduct of worship at "high places" (I Sam. 9–10,1 Kings 3:.4–5, 2 Kings 23:8 ff) by the Israelite priests was pervasive, and it was not until the time of King Josiah (640–609 B.C.) that the sacrifices at "high places" by Israelite priests were proscribed. But not for long, for after Josiah's death the old customs were re-established. Israel's neighbors practiced their religion in "high places" and was the custom in the land. "Monotheism was not a feature of Israel's earliest history … The cult of Baal, the symbol of the Asherah, the high places … belonged to Israel's ancient past, its Canaanite past … thanks to the evidence that Genesis 49 provides … polytheism was part of the religion of Israel prior to the tenth century, and in the case of the 'Queen of Heaven' and … other minor deities, afterward as well" (40–154, 155, 165).

7. The worship of pillars of stone was also an early cult of Israel, in common with the pagans, and later developed into the stone altar at sanctuaries, used for animal sacrifices, a sacred visible symbol of the presence of the deity. In Genesis 28: 20 ff, Jacob made a vow: "… and if I return home safely to my father, then Yahweh shall be my God. This stone I have set up as a monument shall be a house of God, …" In 1 Kings 7:21, speaking of King Solomon "He set up the pillars in front of the vestibule of the sanctuary; he set up the right-hand pillar and named it Jachin; he set up the left-hand pillar and named it Boaz." Monolithic pillars of stone are mentioned in the more ancient parts of the Bible as standing at sanctuaries; the idol represents the presence of God; the sacrificial shedding of blood by the stone made it a legitimate sacrifice. Joshua is speaking: "See! This stone shall be a witness against us because it has heard all the words that Yahweh has spoken to us: …" (Josh. 24:27). Joshua took the stone and set it up

under the oak in the sanctuary of Yahweh. In I Samuel 7:12 we read: "Then Samuel took a stone and erected it between Mizpah and Jeshanah and gave it the name Ebenezer, saying 'Thus far has Yahweh aided us.' " That the stone pillar was widely used in the place of worship is evident from Hosea 3:4 (ca 775 B.C.) "For the sons of Israel will be kept for many days without a king, without a leader, without sacrifice or sacred stone ..."

8. Each tribe worshiped a local deity whose power was confined to the land inhabited. The power of the deity did not extend to the land of the neighbor's god. If a man travelled to the land of a neighboring god, he abandoned the worship of his former god and transferred his worship and allegiance to the local deity; and so with Israel. The power of Yahweh was limited to a certain area inhabited by the tribe of Israel. Their God was a national deity, co-extensive with the land inhabited and had no claim to allegiance outside Israel's habitat. When David was forced out of his land by the jealous fury of King Saul, David regretted not being able to serve Yahweh, for in 1 Samuel 26:19–20 we read: "... for now they (Saul and his men) have driven me (David) out so that I have no share in the heritage of Yahweh. They have said, 'Go and serve other gods'. So now, do not let my blood fall to the ground out of the presence of Yahweh; ..."

9. The animal sacrifices described in the Book of Leviticus are based on an old tradition and differed not from those of the neighboring nations. The use of animal sacrifice as an atonement for sin brought the priestly sect into its own. The more complicated and ritualistic the rules of sacrifice, the greater the power of the priests, the Shamans and workers of magic. In the early religions all worship took the form of sacrifice, mainly animal sacrifice; a ritual to appease the wrath of gods and earn their goodwill. Originally, the animal sacrifice was fully consumed by fire, i.e., a holocaust consumed by the deity. As things developed, the worshippers and the gods shared in the sacrificial meal; a social fellowship between worshippers and the deity. No rules, no magic, just ordinary animal sacrifices and sharing of meals. The complications set in with the inevitable rise of the priesthood who, with the proven taste for power, did set rules for the necessarily complex rituals of sacrifice which required divine insight. If a sacrifice did not follow all the complex rules, it lost its efficacy and worshippers were out of luck, or worse, committed a sin: a neglect of ritual obligation. The only sin during the early times was that of violating the

rules of ritual sacrifice. To cure it, there was used for sin-offering another sacrifice, which could only be performed by priests and required additional ritual.

Soon the priests, as representatives of the deity began to share in the meals and claimed for themselves the portion reserved for the deity; and to perpetuate the cycle, more complex rituals were needed to assure the priests a constant source of meals, gifts and riches. Burnt-offerings, animal blood, wine and cereal, all formed part of the offerings. The above represents a brief statement of the sacrifice-cultus common to the Semitic and non-Semitic peoples of the land of Canaan and its environs. So when the Torah of Moses proclaims that Yahweh instituted the practice of sacrifice, holocaust and sin—offerings, and the elevation of a special select group to exclusively attend to such duties, we know that (1) the proclamation that Yahweh eats the flesh of bulls and drinks the blood of goats was not an innovation but a rehash of ancient practices; (2) the selection of the priestly sect by Yahweh to administer exclusively to such duties—and ordering his "Chosen People" to maintain them in the level of comfort to which they were entitled by order of Yahweh—was not a divine revelation but paralleled priesthoods of more ancient nations, many of them non-Semitic. Let me turn to the Book of Leviticus for source quotations. Yahweh speaking to Moses about holocaust: "When any of you brings an offering to Yahweh, he can offer an animal from either herd or stock. If his offering is a holocaust of an animal ... He is to lay his hand on the victim's head, and it shall be accepted as effectual for his atonement. Then he must immolate the bull before Yahweh, and the sons of Aaron, the priests, shall offer the blood. They will pour it out on the borders of the altar ... Then he must skin the victim and quarter it ... This holocaust will be a burnt offering and the fragrance of it will appease Yahweh" (Lev 1:1 ff., And so with Lev. 1:13, 17, 2:2–3, 2:13, 3:5.) Yahweh speaking: "Then this is what he is to offer as a burnt offering for Yahweh: the fat that covers the entrails (of a goat), all the fat that is on the entrails, the two kidneys, the fat that is on them and on the loins, the fatty mass which he will remove from the liver and kidneys ... All the fat belongs to Yahweh. This is a perpetual law for all your descendants, wherever you may live: never eat either fat or blood" (Lev. 3:14–17).

For sins committed by the community, the rules are more complex. Yahweh speaking: "If the whole community of Israel has sinned inadvertently (sic), and without being aware of it has done something that is forbidden by the commandments of Yahweh, the community is to offer a young bull as a sacrifice for sin, an animal of the herd without blemish, when the sin of which they have been guilty is discovered ... the elders of the community shall lay their hands on the bull's head and it must be immolated before Yahweh. Then the anointed priest is to carry a little of the blood of the bull into the Tent of Meeting. He is to dip his finger in the blood and sprinkle the veil before Yahweh seven times. Then he must put a little of the blood on the horns of the altar that stands before Yahweh inside the Tent of Meeting, and then pour out all the rest of the blood at the foot of the altar of holocaust at the entrance to the Tent of Meeting. Then he is to remove all the fat ... ; and when the priest has performed the rite of atonement over the people, they will be forgiven" (Lev. 4:13–20). If a man is guilty of touching something "unclean," according to Yahweh's instructions revealed to Moses "he will have to confess the sin committed, and must bring to Yahweh as a sacrifice of reparation for the sin committed a female (sic) of the flock (sheep or goat) as a sacrifice for sin; and the priest shall perform the rite of atonement over him to free him from his sin" (Lev. 5:3–6). Yahweh's instructions go on and on. Besides the sin and guilt offerings, there are the dedicatory, burnt, meal, libation, fellowship, peace, votive, freewill and ordination offerings. In case the worshipper is still confused about the portion to be allocated to priests, Yahweh supplements the instructions given to Moses: "As with the sacrifice for sin, so with the sacrifice for reparation—the ritual is the same for both. The offering with which he has performed the rite of atonement is to revert to the priest. The skin of the victim ... shall revert to the priest. Every oblation baked ... shall revert to the priest who offered it" (Lev. 7:7–10).

Lastly, I shall cite from Leviticus Yahweh's lesson to the children of Israel in exchange-rate valuation and profit add-on computations. "If anyone is guilty of fraud and sins inadvertently by not observing Yahweh's sacred rights, he is to bring to Yahweh as a sacrifice of reparation an unblemished ram from his flock. This ram is to be valued in silver shekels according to the rate of the shekel of the sanctuary. This is a sacrifice of reparation. He must restore what his sin subtracted from the sacred rights, adding one-fifth to the value, and give it to the priest. The priest shall perform the rite of atonement over him with the ram for sacrifice of reparation and he will be forgiven" (Lev. 5:15–16). In 2 Kings 17:10 ff, the fall of the kingdom of Israel is attributed to, "They set up pillars and sacred poles for themselves on every high hill and under every spreading tree. They sacrificed there after the manner of the nations that Yahweh had expelled before them …" Prayer was of no use. Dropping on one's knees and asking for forgiveness was of no redeeming value; it did not engage the priest nor benefit him. Not one ounce of spirituality in all these sacrifices. The instructions about sacrifices are a direct revelation by Yahweh to Moses; it is the Torah; the only part of the Scripture directly revealed. See Numbers 12:8, God speaking to Moses "face to face," "plainly and not in riddles." To others God spoke not as to Moses but "in a vision," not plainly. So when the prophets spoke out violently against the cult of sacrifices it was not because of a more perfect opinion of the Torah, but because either (1) They knew nothing about the Torah. Or (2) They rejected the Torah. I concluded that it was the former. When the First Isaiah (ca 740 B.C.) attacked the corrupt national life in the kingdom of Judah and said: "Hear the word of Yahweh, … 'What are your endless sacrifices to me? … I am sick of holocausts of rams and fat calves. The blood of bulls, and of goats revolts me … Bring me your worthless offerings no more' " (Isaiah 1:11), but instead Yahweh admonished "Cease to do evil. Learn to do good, search for justice, help the oppressed, be just to the orphan, plead for the widow" (Isaiah 1:16–17), then Isaiah could not have known the content of Leviticus. Nor could the prophet Amos (ca 760 B.C.) when he recited the words of Yahweh: "I reject your oblations, and refuse to look (sic) at your sacrifices of fattened cattle" (Amos 5:22). Nor could the prophet Jeremiah (ca 650–585 B.C.) when he recited the words of Yahweh: "Your holocausts are not acceptable, your sacrifices do not please me" (Jeremiah 6:20). The above quotations from the Prophets notwithstanding, Yahweh's revelation to Moses at the conclusion of Part I of the Book of Leviticus "The Ritual of Sacrifice" intones "… this is a perpetual law for all their (Israel's) descendants" (Lev. 7:36).

Chapter 4

Sacrifice of Children— Human Sacrifices

1. It is with understandable great lamentations and embarrassment that the Old Testament (Tanak) apologists treat the subject of human sacrifices, the sacrifice of children, the first fruit of the womb. The cult of human sacrifice conjoins the Hebrew religion with that of the pagans; the barbaric custom was viewed with great horror by the prophets who condemned the cult without exception. The Israelites did not adopt the cult of child sacrifice in Egypt; the cult was prevalent among the various nations in Canaan and its neighbors and the Israelites assimilated the custom. Yahweh spoke to Moses in Lev. 18–21: "You must not hand over any of your children to have them passed to Molech, nor must you profane the name of your God in this way." (This is a euphemism for child-sacrifice.) The Torah, which scorns those "former practices", was revealed by God to Moses soon after the flight from Egypt. In what period of time could they have "profaned" their God by handing over their children to have them sacrificed to Molech? It is apparent when the Book of Leviticus was written.

2. In the present state of our culture the subject of child sacrifice is incomprehensible; it must not, however, be judged by today's standards. The religion of the Israelites was formed in an era and in an area where the mind-perverting influence of the custom was acceptable; it is one more criterion that the religion of the Israelites up to the time of the Babylonian Exile was related in origin and allied in quality with the religions of its neighbors, the influence of the great prophets notwithstanding. The other nations had their prophets too. The Torah is a composite of various writings from different periods redacted during and after the Babylonian Exile. So when Yahweh commanded Moses: "Consecrate all the first-born to me, the first issue of every womb, among the sons of Israel. Whether man or beast,

this is mine" (Ex 13:1–2) and again, Yahweh speaking: "You must give me the first-born of your sons; you must do the same with your flocks and herds" (Ex. 22:29–30) the meaning is unmistakable, the command is clear, there is no room for misunderstanding. Who but the priestly writers could have attributed such words to Yahweh? With such chilling predictability!

3. Later Israelites were so filled with consternation by the practice of child sacrifice, that they corrupted the text by changing the name of the god from Yahweh to Moloch, Molech, Milcolm, Malik/Muluk, as though child sacrifices had been offered only to a foreign deity. Moloch is a misvocalization of the Hebrew word Melekh, "king." The Septuagint (the Greek translation of the Tanak in the 3rd century B.C.) translates Molech as "king." It is also plain in Isaiah 30:33, "For in Topheth (the place outside of Jerusalem where children were sacrificed) there has been prepared beforehand, yes, made ready for Molech, a pit deep and wide with straw and wood in plenty. The breath of Yahweh, like a stream of brimstone, shall set fire to it." Isaiah relates the above quoted verses with equanimity, as if reporting an accepted Judean practice in the name of Yahweh.

4. As the story goes in Genesis, Abraham was willing to sacrifice his son to show his fear of God; for this the Hebrew God Yahweh told Abraham. "I will shower blessings on you, I will make your descendants as many as the stars of heaven …" (Genesis 22:17). The writer was obviously ignorant of the number of stars of heaven (billion billions) or Yahweh did not keep his promise. The style of writing about the intended sacrifice of Isaac at the command of Yahweh was as if reporting a common event, for God said to Abraham: "Take your son, your only child Isaac, whom you love, …(and) offer him as a burnt offering, on a mountain I will point out to you" (Gen. 22:2). After an angel of Yahweh called to Abraham from heaven asking that Isaac not be harmed, Abraham sacrificed a ram instead and called this place "Yahweh provides." Whether the story is fiction or history, and whether there is a moral to the story is not relevant for the language used does depict the mores of the times and is addressed to people who would not be astounded. But we should be astounded that Abraham called the place "Yahweh provides," for in Ex. 6:2–3, God spoke to Moses: "To Abraham … I appeared as El Shaddai; I did not make myself known to (him) by my name Yahweh." According to the Torah, this is about six centuries after Abraham.

5. The story of Jephthah in Judges 11:30 ff is interesting from two points of view, revealing the common acceptance of human sacrifices in the period of Judges. (1) Jephthah making a vow to Yahweh that if he returned victorious over the Ammonites he would sacrifice to Yahweh the first person to meet him from the door of his house; (2) when that person turned out to be his only child, a daughter (still a virgin), and Jephthah was downcast, it was the victim who urged him to keep the promise made to Yahweh. Jephthah kept his promise. No angel of Yahweh called from heaven and no ram was sacrificed in her stead. The story would have some elevation had the father sacrificed his life to Yahweh and saved his daughter.

6. The idea of child-sacrifice is to offer one's best, choicest and most cherished possession to appease the wrath of the deity; this would be performed in times of national crisis. Thanks to the institution of monarchy and priesthood, there never was a dearth of crises. The Tanak says of King Ahaz of Judah (736–716 B.C.), "He followed the example of the kings of Israel, even causing his son to pass through fire, copying the shameful practices of the nations which Yahweh had dispossessed for the sons of Israel" (2 Kings 16:3); and again about King Manasseh of Judah (687–642 B.C.), the anointed son of King Hezekiah, "He caused his son to pass through the fire" (2 Kings 21:6). When the war went badly for King Aram of Moab (middle of ninth century B.C.) "… he took his eldest who was to succeed him and offered him as a sacrifice on the city wall" (2 Kings 3:27). After the deportation of the Israelites of the Northern Kingdom by the Assyrians (ca 722 B.C.), the area was repopulated by the King of Assyria with various people from other lands, among them the people from Sepharvaim, who complained to the king that they did not know how to worship the god of the country. The king obliged and sent them an Israelite priest, "… he taught them how to worship Yahweh" (2 Kings 17:28). Nevertheless, "… the Sepharvites burned their children in the fire in honor of Adramelech and of Anammelech, gods of Sepharvaim. They worshiped Yahweh as well, …" (2 Kings 17:31–32). The Psalms, referring to the Israelites, "They did not destroy the pagans as Yahweh had told them to do, but, intermarrying with them, adopted their practices instead" (Psalms 106:34–35). And what was the consequence of not "destroying" the pagans? The Israelites were "Serving the pagans' idols, … sacrificing their own sons and daughters to demons. They shed innocent blood, the blood

of their sons and daughters, offering them to the idols of Canaan, they polluted the country with blood" (Psalms 106:36–38). So not long after the Covenant and Decalogue at Sinai, after Yahweh descended the mountain of Sinai in the sight of all the people, and after Moses gave the sons of Israel "The Book of the Covenant," what is the stark reality and baleful legacy? Paganism, idolatry, child-sacrifices! Isaiah speaking of the unworthiness of the leaders of Judah and alluding to their human sacrifice cults, intoned: "Lusting among the terebinths (a certain kind of tree), and under every spreading tree, sacrificing children in the wadis and in rocky clefts" (Isaiah 57:5). According to rabbinic interpretation, the biblical references of passing children through fire and delivering them to the pagan priests is akin to an initiation rite; that is meant to dismiss the subject! This squalid debasement of the biblical text ravages reason and does injustice to the vaunted rabbinic biblical scholarship which, by such reasoning, must be brought into question.

7. So far I have addressed only positive statements from the Tanak which referred to child-sacrifice. I shall now cite the prohibitions and widespread condemnation of the practice, which would give clear indication how widespread among the Israelites, the Judah monarchy in particular, this plague could be found. "Yes, the sons of Judah have done what displeases me—it is Yahweh who speaks. … they have built the high places of Topheth in the Valley of Ben-Hinnom, to burn their sons and daughters; a thing I never commanded, a thing that never entered my thoughts." (Jerem. 7:30–32). Yahweh said to Jeremiah to go towards the Valley of Ben-Hinnom and to proclaim to the kings of Judah and the citizens of Jerusalem: "… I am bringing down such a disaster on this place … This is because they … have profaned this place, have offered incense here to alien gods (sic) which neither they, nor their ancestors … ever knew before. They have filled this place with the blood of the innocent. They have built high places for Baal (sic) to burn their sons there, which I had never ordered or decreed, …" (Jerem. 19:3–5). It is interesting to note that Yahweh refers to "alien gods" and "high places for Baal." Ezekiel speaks more forcefully: "You have even—it is Lord Yahweh who speaks—taken the sons and daughters you bore me and sacrificed them as food to the images. Was it not enough for you just to be a whore? You have slaughtered my children and handed them over as a burnt offering to them, …"

(Ezek. 16:20–22). And again, "As for the children they had borne me, they have made them pass through the fire to be consumed" (Ezek. 23:37, it is Yahweh who speaks). Ezekiel is instructed by Yahweh to say to the House of Israel: "The Lord Yahweh says this: Since you insist on defiling your-selves by behaving like your fathers, … by offering your gifts and by burn-ing your children as sacrifices, …" (Ezek. 20:30–31). Jeremiah citing Yahweh: "… They have built the high places of Baal in the Valley of Ben-Hinnom, there to make their sons and daughters pass through fire in honor of Molech—something I never ordered, …" (Jerem. 32:35). Lastly, King Josiah (640–609 B.C.) in a remarkable effort to reform the idolatrous reli-gion of Judah, determined to desecrate "the furnace in the Valley of Ben-Hinnom, so that no one could make his son or daughter pass through fire in honor of Molech" (2 Kings 23:10–11).

8. Enough has been said about the subject to convince the reader about the crass reality of the cult of child-sacrifice and Moloch worship practiced by the Israelites up to the latter part of the seventh century B.C. The Moloch cult was an established institution. The cult was no different than that prac-ticed by the pagan and idolatrous neighbors. These matters must all be con-sidered when discussing to what extent the revealed religion of Moses had an impact on the "children of Israel" prior to the Babylonian Exile.

Chapter 5

Bull and Calf Worship

1. It is the author's intent to show in this book that monotheism was not a feature of the early history of the Israelites; that on the contrary—until the Babylonian Exile—they were pagan idolaters, polytheists, believers in spirits, practiced the cult of Baal and child-sacrifice, worshiped in high places, etc. Their beliefs were not distinguishable from those of the other nations residing in Canaan. If it were not for the claim of the Jews that their God was superior on account of his invisibility, as opposed to the gods of the pagan idolaters, this chapter would not be necessary. Yahweh and Baal were at times indistinguishable. The evidence from the Torah shows that their religion could not have been revealed in one short, swift dramatic period at Mt. Sinai; that instead, it developed slowly by the free assimilation of concepts from more ancient religions, the priests and scribes, and finally the purifying influence of the prophets which gave it singularity.

2. It is a false claim of the Jews that Yahweh, their God, is invisible; evidence from the Tanak speaks to the contrary: face to face dialogues, hands, fingers, back, sitting on a throne (Isaiah writes in 6:1–2, "In the year of King Uzziah's death I saw the Lord Yahweh seated on a high throne; …" and the prophet Micaiah "I have seen Yahweh seated on his throne; …") (1 Kings 22:19), an aged figure, the attribution of many human passions, the enjoyment of pleasing odors of animal sacrifices, lapses of memory, walking, resting and many other anthropomorphic features. The Bull and Calf worship by the Israelites will be treated in this chapter.

3. Throughout this book the Jewish people will be referred to as follows:
(1) As "Hebrews" prior to Exodus from Egypt.
(2) As "Israelites" after the Exodus and up to the Babylonian Exile (587 B.C.). After the destruction of the Kingdom of Israel (722 B.C.), the

inhabitants of Judah will be referred to either as "Israelites" or as "Yahuds" or "Yahudim".

(3) As "Jews" in the Babylonian Exile and thereafter.

4. The Egyptians paid divine honors to the Apis bull and considered him the living image and representative of Osiris—one of the most important gods of ancient Egypt—he was also god of fertility and the power that caused the growth of vegetation and the cause of the vital annual floods of the Nile. The bull was later called Osiris-Apis, a clear sign of divine symbolism (cf the Hellenistic god Sarapis). As Israelites have taken up farming they began to regard their God as a fertility deity, who brings rain indispensable to survival of farmers, fertility to their flocks, good growth of corn, wine and oil. Same as the god Baal. The bull concept is common in Near Eastern iconography where it appears as cult object, as symbol of Baal, the storm god; the latter sometimes standing on top of a bull serving as Baal's pedestal.

5. As the Israelites took up agricultural trades, they began to view Yahweh as a fertility God and worshiped him as such, sometimes symbolically in the form of a bull or calf. The Torah is full of uncanny and oblique references that Yahweh was worshiped as Baal under another name, the latter at times worshiped in lieu of Yahweh as a symbol of the God of the Israelites. The first known reference of calf-worship is in Exodus 32. The Israelites had left Egypt a few weeks before, where they as slaves for hundreds of years built cities for the Egyptians and from what is known were not engaged in agriculture. A god of fertility should have had no meaning for them. Let me quote in full, the Israelites speaking to Aaron: "Come, make us a god to go at the head of us; … Aaron answered them, 'Take the gold rings out of the ears of your wives and your sons and daughters and bring them to me.'… He took them from their hands and, in a mould, melted the metal down and cast an effigy of a calf. Here is your God, Israel, they cried who brought you out of the land of Egypt! … Aaron built an altar before the effigy. 'Tomorrow,' he said, 'will be a feast in honor of Yahweh' " (Ex. 32:1–5). Compare this with 1 Kings 12:28–32, speaking of King Jeroboam—several hundred years after the Aaron golden calf episode, after the death of King Solomon and division of the kingdom—"So the king thought this over and then made two golden calves; he said to the people, '… Here are your gods, Israel; these brought you out of the land

of Egypt!' ... he set up the temple of the high places (altars) ... also instituted a feast ...", almost identical verbiage with the one in the Aaron episode. The Aaron story was before the Decalogue. The Jeroboam story was several hundred years later. By then, the worship of the calf-symbol of fertility and strength was commonplace; the matter-of-fact statement of Jeroboam and the prompt acceptance by the northern Israelite tribes is evidence of that; by then the Israelites were deeply involved in agriculture as their main livelihood. Although the Aaron story appears to be an anachronism, in speaking of the connection between the worship of calf, altar and feast just like in the Jeroboam story, it points out nevertheless that the injunction of the Decalogue "You shall have no gods except me" and "You shall not make yourself a carved image ..." (Ex. 20:3–4) and also "You shall make yourself no gods of molten metal" (Ex. 34:17), made no impact on the worship of the Israelites—until King Josiah, the latter part of the seventh century B.C.

6. King Jeroboam set up one golden calf in a temple built on a "high place" at Dan, and another one at Bethel; built altars to them and appointed priests to both temples; he sacrificed to the calves he had made. King Jeroboam (931–910 B.C.) was succeeded by his son Nadab (910–909 B.C.) as King of Israel: "He did what is displeasing to Yahweh; he copied his father's example ..." (1 Kings 15:26), a euphemism for calf-worship. All the succeeding kings of Israel, Baasha (909–886 B.C.), Elah (886–885 B.C.), Zimri (885 B.C.), Omri (885–874 B.C.), Ahab (874–853 B.C.), Ahaziah (853–852 B.C.), Jehoram (852–841 B.C.), all these had one particular common trait: they did what was displeasing to Yahweh and copied Jeroboam's example. Finally, Yahweh caused a disciple of the prophet Elisha to anoint Jehu King of Israel; Jehu then proceeded systematically to massacre the royal families of his predecessors, the adherents of Baal, and even massacred the princes of Judah, all in an orgy of the grossest butchery. And what does Yahweh say to Jehu, according to the writers of the Tanak? "Since you have done properly what was pleasing to my sight ... your sons shall sit on the throne of Israel down to the fourth generation" (2 Kings 10:30–31). And what was Jehu's response after he dutifully rid Israel of Baal? "Even so, Jehu did not give up the sins into which Jeroboam ... had led Israel, the golden calves of Bethel and Dan ... But Jehu did not follow the law of Yahweh ..." (2 Kings 10:28–31). And so the history of the

monarchy goes on. Similarly, the kingdom of Judah fared no better, right at the start with Rehoboam (931–913 B.C.), son of Solomon, "He did what is displeasing to Yahweh, …" (1 Kings 14:22). What conclusions can be drawn from this benighted conduct of the Israelites and Yahudim? They were all cast of the same common clay; they displayed not the slightest acquaintance with the laws of Moses and the Decalogue, nor the Covenant with Yahweh, but were out-and-out idolaters, worshippers of calves and high places; they set up pillars and sacred poles on every high hill and under every spreading tree!

7. The golden-calf Aaron story quoted above (Paragraph 5) was a reflection of the various gods worshiped by the Israelites and shared with the pagans among whom they lived; it is to these various gods that Joshua, toward the end of his life, must be making reference when he says in Joshua 24:14 ff. "… put away the gods that your ancestors served beyond the river and in Egypt, and serve Yahweh. But if you will not serve Yahweh, choose today whom you wish to serve, whether the gods that your ancestors served beyond the River, or the gods of the Amorites in whose land you are now living. As for me and my House, we will serve Yahweh." This is an admission that throughout the period of the Canaan conquest under the leadership of Joshua, the Israelites, or at least most of the tribes, were serving not Yahweh but other gods. Joshua is referring to the religious worship of the Israelites under his command, admonishing them to put away the gods of their ancestors "beyond the river," i.e., the river Jordan. This is a most astounding statement in light of Yahweh's promise to Joshua, "As long as you live, no one shall be able to stand in your way: I will be with you as I was with Moses; I will not leave you or desert you" (Joshua 1:5). This despite the fact that the Israelites did not keep the Covenant: they were not circumcised until later on the "Hill of Foreskins" (Joshua 5:2–3); despite the anger of Yahweh which "flared out against the Israelites" (Joshua 7:1); despite Joshua's plea to Yahweh, "Alas, Lord Yahweh, why did you bring this nation across the Jordan only to deliver us into the power of the Amorites and destroy us? …" (Joshua 7:7); lastly, despite the severe punishments Yahweh always inflicted on the Israelites for serving other gods and bowing to idols! What are we to make of the incredible statement, at the conclusion of the Book of Joshua: "Israel served Yahweh throughout the lifetime of Joshua and the lifetime of those

elders who outlived Joshua and had known all the deeds that Yahweh had done for the sake of Israel" (Joshua 24:31)? The writers of the verses cited were either totally uninformed of the actual history or hastily redacted bits and pieces of various documents without regard to internal consistency.

8. Speaking of the northern Israelites, the Tanak in 2 Kings 17:14 ff summarizes the reasons for their fall and disappearance at the hands of the Assyrian conquerors: "But they would not listen, they were more stubborn than their ancestors had been who had no faith in Yahweh their God. They despised his laws and the covenant he had made with their ancestors, and the warnings he had given them … They rejected all the commandments of Yahweh their God and made idols of cast metal for themselves, two calves; they made themselves sacred poles, they worshiped the whole array of heaven, and they served Baal." During the reign of 19 kings of Israel (931 B.C.–722 B.C.), after exposure to prophets like Elijah, Amos, Hosea and others, 500 years after Moses and the Covenant at Mt. Sinai, there was nothing that even remotely resembled Judaism.

Chapter 6

The Temple, Tabernacle and Ark

1. Yahweh spoke to Moses: "Build me a sanctuary so that I may dwell among them (the sons of Israel). In making the tabernacle and its furnishings you must follow exactly the pattern I shall show you" (Ex.25:8–9). This was said to Moses on the mountain to which he ascended following Yahweh's command. Then follow detailed instructions about the materials to be used and dimensions. "Further, you are to make me a throne of mercy, of pure gold, … For the two ends of this throne of mercy you are to make two golden cherubs; … The cherubs are to have their wings spread upwards so that they overshadow the throne of mercy. They must face one another … You must place the throne of mercy on the top of the ark. Inside the ark you must place the Testimony that I shall give you. There I shall come to meet you, …" (Ex. 25:17–22). These were to be placed in the Holy of Holies, measuring about 17 ft x 17 ft, about one third of the Tabernacle proper. The Tabernacle proper measured about 50 ft x 17 ft, the grounds of the Tent of Meeting measured about 167 ft x 83 ft; a very modest structure considering that the Israelites at that time numbered in excess of 2 million people. The Israelites needed a center for religious activities and the God of Israel desired to dwell among the sons of Israel. "The cloud covered the Tent of Meeting and the glory of Yahweh filled the tabernacle …" (Ex. 40:34). During the stationary period the cloud rested on the tent. Lifting of the cloud from the tabernacle was an indication for the sons of Israel to resume their march (Ex. 40:36–37). It was here that God spoke to Moses. This all sounds very original, innovative and Yahweh's new experiment with the sons of Israel. The first problem arises from Ex. 33:7–11 where the Torah speaks of a Tent of Meeting pitched outside the camp where Yahweh would speak with Moses face to face; where the pillar of cloud would come down and station itself at the entrance of the Tent and all the

people would rise and bow low—this Tent appears to be of a wholly different character from that of the Tabernacle; it is depicted as an ordinary tent; it is situated outside the camp; the pillar of cloud descended at the door of the tent and did not rest on it. In Ex. 25:9 where Yahweh tells Moses of his intent to dwell among the sons of Israel, he now says to Moses: "I shall not go with you myself—you are a headstrong people—or I might exterminate you on the way" (Ex. 33:3–4); instead, Yahweh would send an angel to go in front of the Israelites. But there are other problems (apart from the cherubs and the people bowing to the cloud—a violation of Yahweh's commandment about "images" and bowing to them), namely, that the authenticity of the Torah account about the Tabernacle is questioned by most biblical scholars who maintain that it never existed. Little is heard of the Tabernacle after the settlement in Canaan; there was nothing uniquely Yahwistic about the Tabernacle and the ark; most ancient nations and peoples long before the time of Moses had their own Tabernacles and arks which contained sacred testimonies; the Egyptians had similar portable canopy-like structures for more than a thousand years before Moses; the same can be said of the Chaldeans and Babylonians; finally, the depiction of the Tabernacle was meant to serve as a forerunner of Solomon's Temple, described and designed by priests during and after the Babylonian exile to attach to the First Temple (and the Second) the concept of divine and ancient origin.

2. In Ex. 26:1, Yahweh issues his divine command to Moses: "The tabernacle itself you are to make with ten sheets of fine twined linen, of purple stuffs ..." Yet in 2 Samuel 7: 4–13, about 200 years later, "... the word of Yahweh came to Nathan: 'Go and tell my servant David, ... Are you the man to build me a house to dwell in? I have never stayed in a house from the day I brought the Israelites out of Egypt ..., but have always led a wanderer's life in a tent ... I will preserve the offspring of your body ...(It is he who shall build a house for my name, ...)." So Solomon, the son of David, after he became king sent a message to Hiram, the King of Tyre (not an Israelite), "... I therefore plan to build a temple for the name of Yahweh my God ..." (1 Kings 5:19); and continuing in the message Solomon says: "So now have cedars of Lebanon cut down for me; ..." (1 Kings 5:20). In other words, out went the tent, twined linen and all other detailed instructions given to Moses; in comes Solomon with the cedars of Lebanon,

retains a foreign king, gives him no plan of construction, makes a financial arrangement with him and leaves it up to Hiram to design and proceed with the construction. After four years the Temple was completed and Yahweh spoke to Solomon: "This house you are building ... And I will make my home among the sons of Israel, and never forsake Israel my people ..." (1 Kings 6:12–14).

3. Solomon's Temple was of modest size; rectangular shape, of 124 ft x 55 ft and 52 ft high; contained a Holy of Holies in which the ark was placed guarded by two Cherubs with wings spread out so that they met in the middle of the chamber; the Main Hall and Porch (Entry). "Most biblical scholars today recognize an affinity between the Temple of Solomon and the Canaanite and Phoenician cultures current in Palestine in the second part of the second millennium and beginning of the first millennium B.C.E. These cultures had a strong influence on the culture and art of the Israelites" (53–946 Vol. 15).

4. Solomon's Temple, which took four years to build for which construction 30,000 Israelites and 150,000 Canaanites were conscripted as laborers, was just an annex to the much greater palace Solomon built next to it; a palace for his family which took eleven years to build, the expenses bled the nation white, created irreconcilable dissensions among the social classes of the population and sowed the seeds of a future split of his kingdom after his death which was never to heal the animosity between Judah and Israel. Jewish religious writers who grow ecstatic over the glory of Solomon's kingdom, the Temple, the palace, his wisdom ("Yahweh gave Solomon immense wisdom and understanding ... The wisdom of Solomon surpassed the wisdom of all the sons of the East, ... men from all nations came to hear Solomon's wisdom ..." 1 Kings 5:29–34), cannot point to a single historical document, archaeological finding, epigraphic evidence or any other writings outside the Bible that would in the remotest sense establish the historicity of the biblical accounts. The neighboring nations such as the Phoenicians, Arameans, Moabites, Ammonites, Philistines and others, left numerous inscriptions, but not one single reference to Solomon, or David, or the Temple, or the palace. None exists.

5. Solomon was not a monotheist; he was a crude idolater, "... his heart was not wholly with Yahweh ... became a follower of Astarte ... and of

Milcolm ... He did what was displeasing to Yahweh, and was not a whole-hearted follower of Yahweh ... built high places for Chemosh the god of Moab ... and the Milcolm the god of the Ammonites ..." (1 Kings 11:4–7). In his time monotheism was unheard of. Besides, Solomon was a murderer, who commissioned the murder of his brother Adonijah just to get him out of the way. Despite all this, the Tanak says that Yahweh accepted "This house you are building ..." (1 Kings 6:12) and agreed to make his "home" there. "I consecrate this house you have built: I place my name there for ever; my eyes and my heart shall be always there" (1 Kings 9:3).

6. But the Temple was not a Yahwistic concept. Before 3000 B.C. in Mesopotamia, the principal centers for religious activities were the temples. The gods were present in the temples in the form of statues. King Hammurabi (about 1700 B.C.) built various temples and set up his law stele in the temple of Esagila in Babylon. King Gudea of Lagash (about 2200 B.C.) in Sumeria, built a temple in accordance with detailed specifications and materials to be used which he received from his god in a dream. The temple of RE (the Sun-god) at Heliopolis (Egypt) was planned by the god Toth who specified the actual ground area, dimension of the temple and its enclosure. The Egyptians, a thousand years before Moses, had built many temples to serve various gods, had a highly developed priesthood, rituals and offered sacrifices in their temples. Closer in time and geography is evidence derived from excavations of temples of the late Bronze period (1500–1200 B.C.). Several temples in Palestine at Lachish, at Beth Shean, at Hazor show, several centuries before Solomon, the main elements of the later constructed Temple of Solomon: the Holy of Holies, the Main Hall and the Porch. A temple discovered at Tell Tainet in northern Syria indicates that the architectural plan used in the construction of the temple was widely used in the area around the tenth century B.C. and shows a close resemblance to Solomon's Temple.

7. The following are quotations from an article written by Volkmar Fritz "Temple Architecture" in the July/August 1987 issue of BAR. "The Bible makes no mention of a sanctuary at Arad, although places of worship are mentioned outside Jerusalem at Shiloh, Bethel, Gilgal, Beer-Sheva ... This temple at Arad is the only Israelite temple discovered so far. It seems clear that the Israelite God Yahweh was worshiped here. The plan of the temple, however, bears no resemblance to Solomon's Temple as described in the

Bible (The Bible's description of Solomon's Temple is inexact, lacks all detail except for a brief notice concerning the windows—1 Kings 6:2–4) ... The temple plan of Arad probably goes back to the house architecture of early Israel and must therefore be considered as an authentic Israelite temple form ... When Solomon wanted to build a house for Israel's God ... he looked not to available Israelite proto-types, but to Phoenician exemplars, which ... we can now trace back to ... temples in northern Syria ..."

8. The Temple was not originally intended to serve as a place of prayer but as an abode of the ark; it was considered to be a place of the revelation of the Divine Presence. "According to Israelite belief, God did not dwell in His Temple. The Temple was no more than a place wherein he chose to have his Divine Presence rest, in order to prevail upon man to direct his heart to his God" (53–947 Vol. 15). But if the Tanak has any credibility, this was not the belief of the Israelites; this is pure sophistry by later scribes, priest and rabbis who by then, much later however, understood the meaning of divine omnipresence, the invisibility of Yahweh and the immensity of the universe—concepts unknown to the original writers of the Tanak—who nevertheless engaged in intellectual double-talk in all of its splendor. What of the "house to dwell in"; the pillars of cloud; the cherubs; the testimony placed in the ark; dwelling among the sons of Israel; Yahweh's throne of mercy on top of the ark; Moses speaking to Yahweh face to face in the Tabernacle; Yahweh complaining to the prophet Nathan that he was leading a wanderer's life; Yahweh complaining that he never stayed in a "house" but only a "tent"; Yahweh's eyes and heart dwelling in the Temple? Are all these to be understood as poetic verbiage? Did they have difficulty reconciling Yahweh's instructions to Moses, David and Solomon concerning the Tabernacle, Ark and Temple with their more advanced understanding of divine omnipresence? What of the first Jerusalem Temple—that culmination of pride in the glory and splendor of Solomon's Temple of the later Jewish people who, in their many dark moments of their tortured history, hoped for a rebirth—built by Solomon, an outright idolater, debaucher and murderer who—if biblical history is correct—by his depraved autocratic rule despoiled his people in order to support a life of opulence and self-aggrandizement, causing the break-up of his kingdom after his death which resulted in many destructive internecine wars? What of the non-Yahwistic nature of the Tabernacle, the Ark and the Temple

originating hundreds of years before Yahweh's instructions to Moses, by the ideas of Babylonians, Chaldeans, Egyptians and Phoenicians, which the Israelites assimilated and claimed as their own? The answers are painful.

9. The Ark of Covenant containing the original tablets of the Ten Commandments disappeared with the destruction of Solomon's Temple by the Babylonians in 587 B.C.; so did the cherubs; not a trace of the First Temple remained. The Second Temple's Holy of Holies had no ark and no cherubs; in fact it had nothing in it. The Israelites were religious barbarians when they were marched off into Babylonian Exile. When about 70 years later a minority returned (referred to henceforth as "Jews"), they were a changed people who have assimilated some of the worldly civilization of the Babylonians and the high spiritual visions of that imposing figure: the prophet Ezekiel. The Jews were fortunate that the political and moral debauchery of the monarchy founded by David came to an end, only to be revived by the Hasmoneans over three centuries later. They were unfortunate in that the priesthood usurped the governing function, so far as allowed by their foreign overlords.

Epilogue to Chapter 6

In Chapters 1–6 of this book, I endeavored to show that there was nothing original or unique in the concepts presented by the Torah that would have required divine revelation. A concept or idea, which required divine revelation, could not by its very nature have been pre-existing and known to other nations or peoples hundreds or thousands of years before. The Hebrews, Israelites and Jews managed selectively to assimilate from the prevalent religions ideas and concepts, couched them in new language and versions and claimed them as their own. Modern biblical scholars go through painstaking efforts to attribute one or other segments of the Torah to the E, J, P, D writers and periods. Is it really relevant other than to reinforce the idea that the Torah was not divine revelation? Moses did not write it. Moses did not receive it orally as divine revelation to be passed on from generation to generation until written down in the Mishnah exactly and literally without emendations, additions or deletions. The Torah by its content totally contradicts this approach. The Jews, the people of the Book, preserved the written Torah which in turn preserved them. The priest-made and priest- preserved concept of the "Chosen People" with whom God made an exclusive "Covenant," became the bane of the Jewish people which led to its painful history: In this respect the Torah can be said to be unique.

Chapter 7

Priests and Priesthood

1. "From among the sons of Israel summon your brother Aaron and his sons to be priests in my service" (Ex. 28:1); "They are to make sacred vestments for your brother Aaron and his sons to be priests in my service" (Ex. 28:4–5); "You will put these on your brother Aaron and his sons. You will then anoint and invest and consecrate them to serve me in the priesthood." (Ex 28:41–42); "You are to bring Aaron and his sons to the entrance of the Tent of Meeting and they are to be bathed." (Ex 29:4–5); "And by irrevocable ordinance the priesthood will be theirs. This is how you are to invest Aaron and his sons" (Ex. 29:9). In all the above quotations it is Yahweh speaking to Moses. Further, Yahweh speaking of the breast and thigh of a ram investiture offering to be made to Yahweh, "This, by perpetual law, will be the portion that Aaron and his sons are to receive from the sons of Israel ... from their communion sacrifices, the portion they owe to Yahweh" (Ex. 29:28); "Aaron's sacred vestments are to pass to his sons after him ... The son of Aaron who succeeds him in the. priesthood and enters the Tent of Meeting to serve in the sanctuary must wear them ..." (Ex. 29:29–30). These are Yahweh's instructions to Moses on the establishment of the priesthood in the service of Yahweh. No definition of priesthood is offered and Moses understood the term; he asked no questions. From those few superficial instructions a most intricate priestly order evolved in time to affect the Israelites and Jews in all their pursuits; a priestly order, hereditary and absolutist by Yahweh's instructions, which in time became the governing aristocracy, plutocracy and even royalty in a theocracy engaged in almost continuous power struggles seeking the selfish interests of its ruling priestly families; a power struggle which ended with several priestly induced fatal uprisings against Rome.

2. Moses did not have to ask for any definitions. Whether the narrative is historical or the fiction of later priestly authors, the existence of elaborate priestly orders, performing the same services to gods as described by Yahweh to Moses, were already institutionalized by the Egyptians, Sumerians, Babylonians (and by many other nations) for several thousand years predating the time of Moses. The Canaanite term for priest is identical with the Hebrew one in the Torah: Kohen.

3. Priesthood is the institution that mediates between the sacred (gods) and the profane (people); they are the ritual experts and are proficient in the technique of divine worship. The priests are the functionaries in divine services. For the Israelites the priests were the interpreters of God's will; the experts in ritual sacrifices whose punctilio must be followed rigorously to have the desired efficacy; blessed the people in the name of God; had the sole function to carry the ark (before it was lost); administered and officiated in the Temple exclusively; dealt with ritual impurities and diseases; the givers of oracles; instructors in the law; acted as judges in disputes; keepers of the Temple treasury; writers of historical traditions; custodians of historical traditions; and through the chief of the priesthood, the High Priest—the most important person in the post-exilic Jewish community and president of the Sanhedrin, the ruling council of the Palestine Jews from about the second century B.C.; the chief representative of the Jewish people to the foreign powers, Seleucid and Roman—who ruled Palestine. All the ingredients of priest-made and priest-preserved accumulation of power, prestige and wealth were in place. Add to this the divinely ordained hereditary nature of the priesthood to the exclusion of all others, as the Hasmoneans found out in time to their sorrow—you have a select group of people who grew fat and worldly on account of the power wielded by divine edict, who in time were corrupted. In their effort to preserve their superior status, they gave the Israelites and the Jews rules and ordinances of a most unnatural and unique nature, many of them preserved to this day, to which can be attributed the tragic history of the Jewish people and the opprobrium to which they have been exposed.

4. Among the primitive people, the priest had his precursor in the tribal medicine man who manipulated the sacred power. Also, the tribal shaman who was the visionary, medicine man and cult leader performed the priestly functions. No divine revelation was required. The position of the sacred

men was attained by displaying occult powers, supernatural insight and knowledge of spirits. The altars and temples came much later in history and with them the priesthood—in Egypt and Mesopotamia in particular. There the priesthood attained the zenith of development. In Egypt the occupant of the throne, the Pharaoh, was regarded as a god incarnate; he alone was the intermediary between mankind and the gods. Under the influence of the priesthood the sacred kingship was given solar significance; the Pharaohs were represented as the sons of the Sun-god RE. The Pharaoh was the high priest of every god, but for practical purposes he delegated his temple functions to the particular local priesthood. In time, the priests shared in his powers and privileges. Every temple had its high priest who performed the sacred ritual functions assisted by a large retinue of priests who, in time, became so numerous, powerful and wealthy as to ultimately usurp the throne. "The priests of Egypt were the necessary props to the throne. A class had to be raised adept in magic and ritual in approaching the gods. The office of priest passed from father to son, and a class grew up that became in time richer and stronger than the feudal aristocracy or the royal family itself. The sacrifices offered to the gods supplied the priests with food and drink; the temple buildings gave them spacious homes; the revenue of temple lands and services furnished them with ample incomes, and their exemption from forced labor, military service and ordinary taxation left them with prestige and power" (4–201). "The road to eternal bliss led not through a good life but through magic, ritual and generosity of the priests" (4–204). Under Rameses III (1204–1172 B.C.) the priests attained such power and wealth that they became a state within a state. "… the priests had 107,000 slaves (1/30 of Egypt's population), held 750,000 acres (1/7 of all arable land), owned 500,000 head of cattle, received revenues from 169 towns in Egypt and Syria, …" (4–214). The Egyptian priests, however, did not flaunt their wealth; they were anxious to establish a reputation for learning and piety, of humility and self-denial. Their food was plain since they paid special attention to the quality of their food. They paid special attention to their bodily cleanliness, bathed twice a day and twice a night and a great ceremony of purification was held before major feasts.

5. In Mesopotamia, as in Egypt, a powerful priesthood was already fully established after the fourth millennium B.C., discharging the same function as the priests in Egypt. The temples were the centers of sacred learning,

they promoted the study of astronomy, medicine and jurisprudence. The priesthood was hereditary; the priests had specialized functions; included diviners and magicians; were exempt from taxes and military service; had large land holdings and slaves which belonged to the temples; exercised a monopoly of sacred knowledge of rituals and ceremonies. Similar characteristics were found in all other priesthoods of the Near East.

6. The Torah priestly writers had ample ancient precedent to draw from in compiling the privileges and duties of Israelite and Jewish priesthood. The peculiarities of the first priestly investiture of Aaron and his sons as presented by Yahweh are worth noting since they are draped in mystic ritual, level with the times and parallel with the Egyptian and Babylonian cults. As outlined in Ex. 26:40 ff, 29:1–21, Yahweh instructs Moses that Aaron and his sons must wear special garments to give them "dignity and magnificence" to set them apart as priests from the other people. Then Moses is to take one bull and two rams without blemish, a term that Moses apparently had no difficulty in understanding. Aaron and his sons must be bathed, put on the prescribed vestments, be anointed with special oil; then they are to lay their hands on the head of the bull, which is then to be immolated before Yahweh. Then Moses is to take some of the bull's blood and with his finger put some of it on the horns of the altar and the rest of the blood to be poured at the foot of the altar. Next Moses is to take one of the rams and Aaron and his sons are to lay their hands on its head; then the ram is to be immolated and its blood poured out on the area around the altar. Next Moses is to take the other ram and Aaron and his sons are to lay their hands on its head; then the ram is to be immolated and some of its blood put on the lobe of Aaron's right ear, on the lobes of his sons ears, the thumbs of their right hands, and the big toes of their right foot and the rest of the blood poured out around the altar. Then Moses is to take some of the blood that remains on the altar and sprinkle it on Aaron and his vestment and on Aaron's sons and their vestments. This procedure assures Aaron and his sons that all their vestments will be consecrated.

Yahweh commands Moses: "This is what you are to offer on the altar: two yearling lambs each day in perpetuity. The first lamb you must offer in the morning, the second between the two evenings. With the first lamb you must offer one-tenth of a measure of fine flower mixed with one quarter of a hin of purest oil and, for a libation one quarter of a hin of wine. The second lamb you must offer between the two evenings; do this with the same oblation and the same libation as in the morning, as an appeasing fragrance, an offering burnt in honor of Yahweh. This is to be a perpetual holocaust from generation to generation, ..." (Ex. 29:38–42). The type of sacrificial ritual outlined is not peculiar to the Torah; it is similar to the ritual practices of religions during that historical time among the nations and tribes of Canaan, in Egypt and among the people of Mesopotamia. The sacrifice of bulls and rams, the ritual bathing, sacred garments, blood on and around the altar, four horns of the altar, anointing with sacred oil poured on the head in priestly investitures, morning and evening sacrifices, appeasing fragrances, all these rituals were practiced by other nations long before the time of Moses. The Egyptian priests wore garments that were like those prescribed by Yahweh (Ex. 28:30) complete with the Urim and Thummim worn during the giving of oracles. Whatever comments one could make of the divinely revealed priestly investiture cited above, two points are clear: (1) They caused no harm to anyone then or in subsequent times; such ceremonies evoked tribal loyalties and in this respect performed useful functions; i.e., they were a good "show." (2) They required no divine revelation since they were known to and practiced by other nations long before then. The Yahwist priesthood, however, in an effort to protect their special privileges and dominant status, indulged in burdening the children of Israel with injunctions, prescriptions and proscriptions for which they claimed divine authority in order to facilitate enforcement and obedience—they were immeasurably harmful. The Yahwist priests unburdened themselves of ideas which have been harmful to the Jewish people to this day, affected their social relations with other peoples, ostracized them and had a mind-perverting influence upon them. Most importantly and unfortunately, the Yahwist priests served as the prototype to that most avaricious, power-seeking, self-aggrandizing and corrupt (presently greatly reformed and acclimated) of all man-made institutions: the Catholic priesthood. When Christianity absorbed the Tanak (the Old Testament, which it declared as divinely inspired and binding) into their canon, they also absorbed the Torah injunctions (such as the burning of witches, heretics and blasphemers) which served as divinely inspired justification for the commission of all kinds of crimes against humanity. That subject will be treated in later chapters.

7. I am listing a few of the Yahwist priesthood injunctions (treated more fully in the next chapter) which proved harmful to the mind-set of the Jewish people. Yahweh speaking to Moses "The man who profanes it (the Sabbath) must be put to death; whoever does any work on that day shall be outlawed from his people" (Ex. 31:14). Yahweh speaking to Moses "Make no pact with the inhabitants of the land (Canaan)..." (Ex. 34:15). "... yet he (Yahweh) lets nothing go unchecked, punishing the father's fault in the sons and in the grandsons to the third and fourth generation" (Ex. 34:7–8). "If the daughter of a ... priest profanes herself by prostitution ...(she) must be burnt to death" (Lev. 21:9). "No descendant of Aaron the priest must come forward to offer the burnt offerings of Yahweh if he has any infirmity; ... he must not come forward to offer the food of his God" (Lev. 21:21). "Any man who curses his God ... The one who blasphemes the name of Yahweh must die; ..." (Lev. 24:16). "... to the sons of Levi I (Yahweh) give as their inheritance all the tithes collected in Israel, in return for their services, ..." (Num. 18:21). "The Levitical priests, ... they shall live on the foods offered to Yahweh and on his dues" (Deut. 18:1–2). "For failing to serve Yahweh your God ... He will put an iron yoke on your neck until you perish" (Deut. 28:47–48). "If your brother, ... or your son or daughter, or the wife you cherish, or friend with whom you share your life, if one of these secretly tries to entice you, saying 'Come, let us serve other gods,' ... you must show him no pity, you must not spare him, you must not conceal his guilt. No, you must kill him; ..." (Deut 13:7–10). Everything seemed to be ordained to insure benefits to the priests; placed them in the center around which the Jewish people orbited; cloaked their commands with divine sanction and planted in the people's mind the dark propaganda: Keep the laws and covenants of Yahweh so that your life may be joyful, and failure to do so will earn you all the curses.

8. The Tanak represents the priestly view of a sequence of events aimed to serve and benefit the priestly aristocracy. That effort is very transparent in the divinely prescribed ordinances of the Torah. Who else but the priests could benefit from the constant harping about ritual purity, perpetual laws, irrevocable ordinances, kingdom of priests, holy conditions, sacrifices to Yahweh reverting to priests, binding tithes for the support of priests, blemishes, purifications, payment of census ransom, punishment of death for disobedience of priests, exclusive right to conduct sacrifices—originally

permitted to laymen—hereditary right to priesthood to the absolute exclusion of laymen, obsession with pedigree, exclusive servants of God, cloaked in greater holiness than the rest of the people, holiness of priests to be equal to the holiness of the house of God? The priests wrote these ordinances for their own welfare. They had no fear of detection; they could write self-serving laws and ordinances and wrap them in the aura of divine authorship. They could read and write better than the laymen and had ample time to devote to alterations, revisions, interpolations and emendations of texts. Centralization of worship in Jerusalem stood for centralization of animal sacrifices, aided the profitable trade in sacrificial animals, brought funds into the central treasury by eliminating competition. The priest could not inherit property but that was an idle rule of no consequence; they received tithes from harvests and money support for the Temple maintenance which included support for priests—for life. In sin-offerings that part of the flesh that was not burned belonged to the priests; sin-offerings were too holy to be eaten except by priests; money offered in expiation of sin to the Temple was appropriated by the priests. The Jerusalem priesthood claimed that only their ceremonies and not those of other Temples had efficacy and divine sanction. The split between Rehoboam and Jeroboam was not only about taxation but, very importantly, also about the lucrative pilgrimages. It is therefore apparent that the Tanak presents priestly views.

9. Those who refused to accept the decision of the priests were to be put to death. Aaron and sons, and those who came after them, were to carry out their priestly duty in the Tabernacle; any layman who came near it was to be put to death. "You must add nothing to what I command you, and take nothing from it, but keep the commandments of Yahweh your God just as I lay them down for you" (Deut. 4:2–3). Anyone sacrificing to other gods or anyone practicing proscribed cults was to be put to death. The priests had full power of expropriation: they could place any object under the ban and thereby acquire exclusive right to claim it. These ordinances were aimed at enslaving the children of Israel to the priestly rule. To maintain the priesthood, priest-made ordinances placed unlimited power into their hands. In the priestly view, idolatry or worshipping other gods was a crime greater than murder or rape; worshipping other gods would undermine their economic base whereas murder and rape had no

effect. To obtain forgiveness of sin, prayer and repentance were of no use—such conduct was of no benefit to priests. Instead, strict priestly sin-offering rituals had to be followed.

10. Were the priestly writers of the Torah successful in giving the children of Israel a religion worth its name? Did they give them a system of beliefs and worship of God which had divine authority and affected the views and conduct of their adherents towards other human beings? —a force of harmony and benefaction? Did all the sacrificial rituals, dietary laws, laws of impurity and cleanliness citing impurities, contamination, purification, nocturnal emissions, menstrual blood, impurities of semen, body discharges, non-seminal discharges—did all these laws and ordinances inspire the people to piety and harmony? If the events described in the Torah are history, the answer must be in the negative. What kind of people were the children of Israel, chosen by God as his people, selected from all other nations for an exclusive covenant with God, promised unending prosperity as long as they adhered to God's laws and commandments, yet continually relapsing and choosing other gods, idolatry and acting the same as their "banned" neighbors? They displayed in their conduct, ethics and beliefs not the slightest influence of the Decalogue. Yet according to the priestly writers they were privileged to witness the acts of Yahweh, their God, and solemnly promised to obey his decrees. "Israel witnessed the great act that Yahweh performed against the Egyptians, and the people venerated Yahweh; they put their faith in Yahweh and in Moses, his servant" (Ex. 14:31). And again, Moses went and told the people all the commands of Yahweh and all the ordinances. In answer, all the people said with one voice, "We will observe all the commands that Yahweh has decreed" (Ex. 24:3–4). Moses took the Book of Covenant and read it to the listening people who vowed, "We will observe all that Yahweh has decreed; we will obey" (Ex. 24:7). When the people came before the Tent of Meeting and observed how a flame which leaped forth from before Yahweh and consumed the holocaust, "At this sight the people shouted for joy and fell on their faces" (Lev. 9:24). Yahweh promised the children of Israel that if they kept his laws and commandments, "I will be your God and you shall be my people" (Lev. 26:13) and that Yahweh is "… the faithful God who is true to his covenant … for a thousand generations towards those who love him and keep his commandments, …" (Deut. 7:9–10). But if the people did not

listen to Yahweh and did not observe his commandments, he would heap curses upon them, inflict terror and consumption, they would waste away and exhaust the breath of life. He would punish them sevenfold for their sins. "I will send out the sword against you, to avenge the Covenant" (Lev. 26:25). Any other people, one would think, would have humbly fallen on their knees and conformed, just out of practical self-interest. That is, if the Torah is true history and not the priestly version of it; no people could behave like this. This went on from the time of Moses till after the return from the Babylonian Exile, or about 700 years. Thereafter other problems arose, dealt with in another chapter. Suffice it to say that after the return from Babylonian Exile, after the clearest demonstration of God's punishment inflicted upon the Israelites and Jews, and after Ezra read the Law of Yahweh to the people, it was only by forced conformity imposed by the priesthood that the Jews were kept in line. This time it was not the threat of Yahweh's punishment but the political and military power of Artaxerxes, King of Persia, which turned the tide. For the king's orders, as related by Ezra, thundered: "If anyone does not obey the Law of your God—which is the law of the king—let judgment be strictly executed on him: death, banishment, confiscation or imprisonment" (Ezra 7:26). The message was clear; the bearer of this message—Ezra—was a priest and a scribe, skilled in the law of Moses.

11. I have often wondered why the priesthood did not preach the doctrine of personal immortality of the soul, life after death in whatever form. To the Egyptians, a belief in life after death was part of an elaborate design of magic rites performed by the priesthood. They believed that the body had a "soul" and that the blessing of priests would lead the soul to salvation and eternal life. A good and virtuous life was no assurance to eternal rewards; the soul had to overcome many tests and the priest knew the ways of passing these tests; they were the "Book of the Dead" and the "Negative Confession," which contained prayers and formulas all devised by the priesthood to guide the dead and achieve eternal salvation, all no doubt, at a price and economic gain to the priesthood. All these were known at the time of Moses, yet the Torah is silent on the subject of personal immortality. For the Israelites and Jews, the good and bad descended to Sheol, the subterranean abode of the dead, a place of darkness, total inactivity, a region of dark and deep, forever enclosed, a place of no return. Jacob, on

hearing of Joseph's death, said to his sons and daughters: "... I will go down to Sheol beside my son" (Gen. 37:35). Again Jacob, refusing to let his youngest son Benjamin accompany his brothers for fear of his life: "... you would send me down to Sheol with my white head bowed in grief" (Gen. 42:38). When Abraham died the Torah relates, "... and he was gathered to his people" (Gen. 25:9). When Jacob died, the Torah relates, "... and breathing his last was gathered to his people" (Gen. 49:33). Yahweh predicting Aaron's death," Aaron must be gathered to his people ..." (Num. 20:24). Yahweh predicting Moses' death, "Die on the mountain you have climbed, and be gathered to your people, ..." (Deut 32:50–51). Commenting on David's death, "So David slept with his ancestors ..." (1 Kings 2:10); "Then Solomon slept with his ancestors ..." (1 Kings 11:43); "Then Joash (King of Israel) slept with his ancestors ..." (2 Kings 13:13); "Then Menahem (King of Israel) slept with his ancestors, ..." (2 Kings 15:22) and so on. There is not the slightest reference to immortality in the Torah; the subject just does not exist. Even the Old Babylonians, thousands of years before the time of Moses, believed in immortality—not as explicit as the Egyptians—since drink and food were placed with the dead in their graves.

The prophet Ezekiel, a priest active among the Exiles in Babylon (6th century B.C.), was the first to hint on the subject of resurrection, not of immortality. "The Lord Yahweh says this: 'Come from the four winds, breath; breathe on these dead; let them live!' I prophesied as he had ordered me, and the breath entered them; they, came to life again and stood on their feet, a great, an immense army" (Ezek. 37:9–10). Yahweh speaking to Ezekiel: "Say to them, 'The Lord Yahweh says this: I am now going to open your graves; I mean to raise you from your graves, my people, and lead you back to the soil of Israel ... And I shall put my spirit in you, and you will live, and I shall resettle you on your own soil; ...' " (Ezek. 37:12–14). Ezekiel was greatly influenced by Babylonian theology and mysticism; his elaborate visions anticipated those of the prophet Daniel, whose composition was falsely attributed to the Babylonian Exilic period. The evidence is clear from the text that it was written shortly before or during the Maccabean period, i.e., around 167 B.C., a time when the Wisdom literature was in full bloom. The aim of Daniel was to sustain the hope among the Jews during the persecutions by Antiochus Epiphanes, the

Seleucid king. "Of those who lie sleeping in the dust of the earth many will awake, some to everlasting life, some to shame and everlasting disgrace. The learned will shine as brightly as the vault of heaven, and those who instructed many in virtue, as bright as the stars for all eternity" (Daniel 12:2–3). This language is light-years distanced from the Torah. It speaks of "everlasting life," "the learned" and "virtue"; the first glimmer of the concept of immortality. But then Daniel was not a priest.

Then there is the reference to a ghost in 1 Samuel. King Saul consulted Yahweh but Yahweh would not respond. So he decided to consult the dead Samuel. Saul approached a woman necromancer, "Conjure up Samuel" (1 Sam. 28:11). The woman responded "I see a ghost rising from the earth" (1 Sam. 28:13–14). After describing the ghost, Saul knew it was Samuel, who chided him for disturbing his rest. This kind of "consulting," predicting of future events by occult means was the turf of priests, who jealously guarded this privilege; they lumped it together with divination, witchcraft, magic, and necromancy, and the penalty for the "infringement" was as expected: Death.

We read in Ex. 22:17,"You shall not allow a sorceress to live." Immortality as a religious concept implies the doctrine of rewards and punishment respectively for good and bad actions, a degree of adherence to God's commands and ordinances during life on earth. Simply put, there is a divinely ordained just and equitable balancing scale for man's deeds and misdeeds in relation to reward and punishment on earth and after death. The virtuous are not necessarily rewarded on this earth and the evil-doers are not necessarily punished. This is not divine justice. The authors of Ecclesiastes, Job and Habakkuk were painfully aware of this. In Ecclesiastes and Job, the searing question is asked: do virtue and vice get their rewards on this earth? The answer is "no." Why must the bad be punished by the worse? The prophet Habakkuk (6th century B.C.) had the courage and audacity to challenge God: "Why do you look on while man swallows a better man than he?" (Hab. 1:13).There was no answer but to postulate the immortality of the soul, life after death, with the consequent concept of rewards and punishment. Then why did the priests ignore the subject of the immortal soul?; reward and punishment after death as a requirement for dispensing divine justice? The priest were very intelligent and had time to contemplate on the subject in Babylon. There must have been a good reason! It was essential to the economic prosperity and survival of the priests, maintenance of their privileges and stranglehold on the Israelites and later on the Jews, that compensation for obedience to Yahweh's laws and ordinances was rewarded with tangible evidence of success, prosperity and good life on earth; that tangible punishment for disobedience would be meted out promptly on earth. There was no point telling the obedient believer who encountered misfortune to suffer in silence, and that just compensation would be dispensed after death. How long would he listen to the priests and believe in Yahweh's power, particularly, since it was the people of Israel who received reward or punishment? The individual gained in importance through the influence of the message of the prophets which took several hundred years to seep through. How much easier to tell the suffering individual or Israel that he or they violated some sacrificial ordinance or prostituted themselves to other gods? Or infringed upon some sacred priestly rights? The priests wanted to convince the people of the superiority of the Yahwist religion by promising tangible earthly rewards exclusively provided by the grace of Yahweh; that the world is ruled by a just and wise God who rewards the good and punishes the wicked here on earth—swift retribution. Experience, however, did not bear it out. The perceived injustice led not only to Isaiah, Ezekiel, Job and Habakkuk, but also to the idea of a Davidic Messiah, who would rise up from among the people and remedy matters by military force, if necessary, establish justice on earth, defeat the enemies of Israel, liberate the Jewish people, continue and/or re-establish the privileges and power of the priesthood and the Temple, and establish a kingdom on this earth where righteousness would be dispensed to all. There was no room for the doctrine of immortality. Priestly laws and ordinances as expressed in the Torah and priestly machinations and encouragement caused the Jewish militants and religious zealots, led by messianic pretenders, to bring about innumerable reckless uprisings against the occupying powers; the major last three against the Romans in 66 A.D., 115 A.D. and 132 A.D. (treated in a later chapter) bled the Jewish people white, decimated the flower of Jewish manhood and caused the final dispersal of the Jewish people throughout the world. The priestly grown and nurtured tree bore its poisoned fruit: not only the destruction of Jerusalem, the Temple and the Second Jewish Commonwealth, but also the destruction of the priesthood. The priestly spirit of the Torah survived, the rabbis became its teachers, the spiritual leaders and shepherds of the Jewish people. In response to the fire-storms and havoc caused by the defeat of the Jewish militants in these uprisings and also as a result of the influence of Christianity, they propounded the doctrine of personal immortality (which had no trace of divine sanction), and of after-life rewards and punishment. The priesthood was dead; the priestly teaching and priest-made laws and ordinances survived only to subject the Jewish people to mental servitude. But for the fatuous uprisings, one can only speculate how much the history of the Jewish people would have differed.

Chapter 8

The Mind-perverting Influence of the Priestly Torah and the Historical Books of the Tanak

1. It is well known that surroundings affect conduct and views; that such conduct and views are affected by healthy or diseased bodily conditions, economic well-being, climate, acceptance by society, age, the extent of fortune and misfortune encountered in life and a host of other internal and external causes. It follows that such conduct and views are not fixed, but are determined by changing internal and external causes. The mores and prevalent ideas of society, of a people, and of a nation similarly affect the conduct and views of individual members who for the most part feel constrained to seek peer approval by an attitude of conformity. It is the exception that certain individuals choose to challenge established conduct and views of their peers thereby drawing attention to themselves or worse. The same would apply to a group of people within a larger group in the normal course of everyday development. If, however, an individual or group of people within a larger group are determined to defy the established conduct and views in order to remain separate and distinct regardless of changing conditions and regardless of the effect of such conduct upon the larger group of people, then one of the following consequences would result in time:

(a) The conduct and views of the smaller group would be progressively acclimated to the conduct and views of the larger group, in a natural process.

(b) The conduct and views of the smaller group would be forcibly assimilated to that of the larger group, the latter enforcing conformity.

(c) The conduct and views of the smaller group would defy, resist .and obstruct the challenges of the larger group, with the result that the surrounding conditions of the larger group would deteriorate in proportion to the persistence and power of the smaller group to enforce its conduct and views upon the larger group.

This chapter will be concerned with the implications of the third consequence.

2. The essence of all human activity is the continuous effort to preserve one's existence and enhance it to its fullest potential and development. Anything that promotes that effort is called "good"; anything that hinders that effort is called "bad." That effort encompasses the field of all ideas and all bodily aspects of human activity, i.e., the totality of all causes and effects. It follows therefore that:

(a) An individual would no more choose a lesser "good" over a better "good" than choose a worse "bad" over a lesser "bad."
(b) The nature and consequences of the "good" and "bad" are only perceived as such by the mind of the individual, and no two individuals would have identical perceptions.
(c) The mind of an individual may be mistaken it its determination of "good" and "bad", i.e., cause the individual to act in a manner contrary to the best interests of preservation and enhancement of existence.
(d) It follows, therefore, that whether the "good" or "bad" are the real and true "good" or "bad" is irrelevant, i.e., the mind of the individual is the only arbiter.
(e) When the mind of an individual chooses a lesser "good" over a better "good" ; or a worse "bad" over a lesser "bad" as a result of outside causes disposing the mind to such choices, such causes are defined as "mind-perverting."
(f) The above applies equally to a group of individuals, a people, a society, a nation.

3. The aim of religious laws and ordinances should be to promote harmony, amity, well-being, a coming together among individuals, society, people and nations. If it promotes and strives to achieve these results, in addition to teaching piety, promoting virtue and civility, a better and peaceful relationship among its adherents of this and other peoples and nations, such a religion can be called a "social force." The prophet Isaiah wrote about a vision concerning Judah and Jerusalem, Yahweh is speaking, "… Your hands are covered with blood, wash, make yourselves clean. Take your wrongdoing out of my sight,

cease to do evil. Learn to do good, search for justice, help the oppressed, be just to the orphan, plead for the widow" (Isaiah 1:15–17). And again, "... Woe to the legislators of infamous laws, to those who issue tyrannical decrees, who refuse justice to the unfortunate and cheat the poor among my people of their rights, who make widows their prey and rob the orphan" (Isaiah 10:1–2). What imperatives of justice; what lyric warmth; what nuggets of truth! But then Isaiah the First (preached ca 740–701 B.C.) did not have even a nodding acquaintance with the laws of Moses, for he writes, quoting Yahweh, "What are your endless sacrifices to me? ... I am sick of holocausts of rams and the fat calves. The blood of bulls and of goats revolts me ... Bring me your worthless offerings no more, the smoke of them fills me with disgust" (Isaiah 1:11–13). The thoughts of Isaiah are a powerful "social force." It is the consensus among modern biblical scholars that there were three, perhaps four different authors of "Isaiah," Isaiah (chapt. 1–35), unknown (chapt. 36–39), Second Isaiah (chapt. 40–55), Third Isaiah (chapt. 56–66).

4. Rabbi Hillel, who lived near the end of the first century B.C., considered the greatest of the sages of the Second Temple period, replied to a heathen who came to him to be converted on condition that he teach him the entire Torah while standing on one foot: "What is hateful to you, do not unto your neighbor; this is the entire Torah, all the rest is commentary." But the rabbi was wrong; there is much more to the Torah than that! He did not live to see the tragic influence of the priestly Torah: the priest-fomented fatuous uprising against Rome in 66 A.D.; the rise of the messianic pretenders and their many disastrous rebellions; the rabbi-induced Bar Kokhba rebellion against Rome in 132 A.D. which decimated the Jewish people in Palestine, caused their impoverishment, expulsion, repression and sale into slavery for most of the remainder.

5. I indicated in prior chapters that it was the priests, and the priests only, who benefited from the multiplicity of sacrificial laws, tithes, sin-offerings, Temple cults, vestments, oracles; it was the priests who derived economic benefits, prestige and power from these laws. It therefore follows that the priests also passed laws and ordinances designed to preserve their monopoly of power, the status quo, and expended every effort to enhance their extraordinary privileges and station. The Temple treasury grew in wealth to such an extent that it became the most power-dispensing institution in the land, both politically and economically. In the last century of its existence

it controlled the destiny of the Jews. These privileges were jealously guarded against intruders and dissipation. Only Levites could become priests in accordance with the Torah, descent from Aaron was an essential further limiting factor, and only a small circle within this small circle were wealthy enough to buy and sell the office of the High Priest. Corruption was rampant and learning was of no consequence; sometimes the High Priest was so inexperienced that he was unable to conduct Temple services allocated to his function without help from the lower order. When the Jews were later ruled by the Seleucids and Romans, especially the latter, the High Priest was appointed by the ruling foreign power with a view of maintaining order, pacifying the Jews and assuring tribute. In this the office of the High Priest and priesthood were allied with the foreign power with which it shared a common interest, i.e., the maintenance of its power in exchange for assurance of the collection of the assessed tribute. Inevitably, the interests of the Jews clashed with those of the priesthood.

6. The prophet Ezekiel—apparently embarrassed by the interminable apostasies of the Jews and the infidelities towards Yahweh in spite of the Torah and Moses, and "because they kept their eyes fastened on their ancestors' idols" (Ezekiel 20:24–25)—came up with the most mystifying statement, quoting Yahweh: "I even gave them laws that were not good and observances by which they could not live; and I polluted them with their own offerings, … which was to punish them, so that they would learn that I am Yahweh" (Ezekiel 20:25–26). However, as will soon be apparent, it was the priests who unwittingly gave the children of Israel laws that were not good and observances by which they could not live. These laws and observances were instituted to keep the people in check and place a yoke around their necks so they would better serve the priestly cause. Instead, these laws and ordinances tended, in time, to confuse the children of Israel, debased their instincts, polluted their minds, made them unable to get along with their neighbors, unable to make treaties of friendship with their neighbors, unable to govern themselves peacefully, unable to be governed without plotting reckless rebellions, made them outcasts among nations, made them demand special privileges not accorded others which engendered envy and hostility, fostered exclusivity and intolerance, hatred for other people, made them institute for the first time religious persecution and forced conversions; in short, perverted their minds causing them to act against their best interest.

7. Laws must be clear to be enforceable. Laws imposed by a higher authority must, in time, be understood by the people to be enforceable. Only those laws should be instituted which can be enforced, otherwise the system would be corrupted. Laws regulating opinions cannot be enforced for an extended period—and are subject to various interpretations and abuse—and should therefore not be imposed. Laws and ordinances instituted which run counter to the interests of the majority of the people would have to be maintained, in time, by force; as such, they would create resentment and invite circumvention. To enforce compliance, the severity of punishment would increase by degrees, until the ultimate penalty, i.e., death, would be imposed. The severity of punishment would compel compliance for a time if the authority has the power of punishment. The lesser the power, the greater the need for severe penalties. The power of the priests rested not in their numbers but to the extent to which they succeeded in imposing their opinion of a supernatural deity—full of wrath and angered by disobedience to his laws and ordinances—inflicting severe punishment on violators. The divine laws and ordinances served to perpetuate the power of the priests and sustain them in their effort of self-preservation. Since punishment for law and ordinance violations was reserved for the people—the Torah is silent as to any punishment of the Aaronite priests except in a vague case "he is to offer to Yahweh a young bull" as a sin-offering—the interests of the priests and the people were not identical; as such, the laws and ordinances which were "good" for the priests did not necessarily serve the interests of the people. They were not clear but subject to varying interpretations and misinterpretations, confusion, manipulation, vindictiveness, contradictions, corruption; many of them exercised a perverting influence upon the conduct of the Jews. "... I will set you apart from all these people ..." (Lev. 20:26) became a self-fulfilling prophecy, as spoken by Yahweh.

8. In order to maintain and strengthen the hold upon the Jewish people, the priests passed laws and ordinances which made the Jews dependent upon them, were injurious to true religion and left no stone unturned in accentuating the separateness, difference and the feeling of superiority over other people. The severity of some of the laws (by the prevailing standards) and ordinances had the unintended effect of contributing to that aim. It is Yahweh speaking:

(a) "Any man or woman who is a necromancer or magician must be put to death by stoning; ..." (Lev. 20:27).

(b) "You shall not allow a sorceress to live" (Ex. 22:17).

(c) "You must keep the Sabbaths carefully ... The man who profanes it must be put to death" (Ex. 31:12–14).

(d) "Any man who curses his God... The one who blasphemes the name of Yahweh must die; ...stranger or native, if he blasphemes the name, he dies" (Lev. 24:16–17).

(e) "A human being laid under ban cannot be redeemed, he must be put to death" (Lev. 27:29).

(f) "If anyone presumes to disobey either the priest ... or the judge, that man must die" (Deut. 17:12).

(g) "But the prophet who presumes to say in my name a thing I have not commanded him to say, or who speaks in the name of other gods, that prophet shall die" (Deut 18:20).

(h) "That prophet or that dreamer of dreams must be put to death, for he has preached apostasy from Yahweh your God ..." (Deut. 13:6).

(i) "If there is anyone, man or woman, among you in any of the towns Yahweh your God is giving you ... who goes and serves other gods and worships them, ... you must stone that man or woman to death" (Deut. 17:2–6).

Referring to a young wife who is unable to prove her virginity,

(j) "But if the accusation that the girl cannot show the evidence of virginity is substantiated, ... her fellow citizens shall stone her to death ..." (Deut. 22:20–21).

(k) "If a man has a stubborn and rebellious son who will not listen to the voice of his father or the voice of his mother, and even when they punish him he still will not pay attention to them, ... Then all his fellow citizens shall stone him to death" (Deut. 21:18–21).

(1) "No bastard is to be admitted to the assembly of Yahweh. No Ammonite. or Moabite is to be admitted to the assembly of Yahweh; not even their descendants to the tenth generation may be admitted to the assembly of Yahweh, and this is for all time; ... Never, as long as you live, shall you seek their welfare or their prosperity" (Deut. 23:3 ff).

(m) "Anyone who curses father or mother must die" (Lev. 20:9).

Criticism

(a) (b) What definitions apply to necromancers, magicians or sorcerers? What is the range of limits? At what point does one cross the fatal line? Totally unclear, confused and corrupt; nothing but transparent priestly turfmanship; primitive stupidity at its worst. It was the priests' prerogative to engage in magic and sorcery, yet the penalty for the outsider's encroachment was death. We do not know the number of victims of these mind-perverting laws up to the destruction of the Second Temple—which event terminated the power and hence the activity of the priestly sect—but we do know to what use Christianity put these laws and for the same reason: fear of subversion of faith in priesthood. Pope Gregory IX (1227–1241) was the first Pope to issue orders that "witches" (sorcerers) should be burned; no mercy was shown to these poor wretches because of the commandment in the Scripture even to the point of sheer exercise in lunacy, in that denial of the existence of witchcraft was treated as heresy, calling for the extreme penalty. This scourge had a life span of over 500 years; the last burning took place in 1793. Well over 300,000 convicted "witches" were burned in Europe; most of them confessing under torture. What a testimonial to the power of priesthood; the condemned knew up to their last moments the falseness of the accusation.

(c) How does one keep the Sabbath "carefully"? At what point does one "profane" it? Totally unclear, confused and corrupt; in the Mishnah, which is the core of the Talmud—written by rabbis several centuries after the Babylonian Exile—we find hair-splitting rules on Sabbath observances and prohibitions; the writings were man-made, profane and carried no divine sanction. Yet the penalty was death. These priest-inspired laws place more power in their hands; more judging; more arbitration; more functions. It also fulfilled the priestly aim to set the Jews apart from other nations. The brain-damage caused by these laws prevented the Jews from militarily defending themselves on the Sabbath and fell easy victims to aggressors rather than save their lives at the risk of profaning the Sabbath. The Roman General Pompey figured this one out. This attitude almost spelled the undoing of the Maccabees in the early stages of their uprising until they began to defend themselves on the Sabbath.

(e) (f) Items collected under the ban pass to and are reserved for the priests. Property confiscated due to noncompliance with an administrative order or decree belong to the priests. "All in Israel on which the ban is laid shall be yours" (Numbers 18:14–15, Yahweh is referring to the priesthood). "Everything in Israel put under the ban shall be for them (priests)" (Ezekiel 44:29). "Anyone who eats blood ... shall be outlawed (placed under ban) from his people" (Lev. 7:27). It is all too apparent that the laws regarding "ban" were written by priests for priests; the rapacity and plunder shine through; they had the supreme power to lay any human being under "ban"; so did the Catholic Inquisition many centuries later. For anyone who "presumes" to disobey, i.e., to question, argue or countermand the priest, the penalty is death. Totally unclear, confused and corrupt laws; the aim was to establish privileges for the priests which were jealously guarded.

(g) (h) How is anyone to judge whether a prophet is conveying the wish of Yahweh? At best, Yahweh appeared or spoke to him in a vision or dream (Numbers 12:6); was the prophet—an interpreter of signs and social critic—mistaken in his evaluation? If so, did it earn him the death penalty? The only official interpreters of signs and oracles were the priests; to them exclusively was given that function as part of their priestly duty—they would allow no interference. The accusation of speaking in the name of "other gods" or "preaching apostasy from Yahweh" was to silence the prophets; it was the priests' response to a challenge that could not go unpunished: the verdict was death. Pre-Exilic kings and prophets were replaced in post-Exilic times by High-Priests and scribes; activities of prophets were still widespread, those inspired men who claimed to speak in the name of God. Just like there was conflict between kings and prophets, so later there were hostile confrontations between prophet and priest. Prophets were social reformers who lamented the harsh fate of the poor and oppressed, the false pride of the wealthy, and who undercut the position of the priestly order by severely criticizing the multiplicity of sacrificial laws and Temple rituals—a criticism that had to be anathema to the priestly interests. The two cited laws are totally unclear, confused and corrupt, designed not to clarify but to obfuscate and to leave priests sufficient elbow-room to remove such undesirables permanently.

(i) This priestly law dealt with non-conformists; demanded denunciation of one's neighbor; terrorized the Jewish people as the Spanish Inquisition terrorized the New Christians. The priestly sect required religious unity; all nascent opposition had to be rooted out at the early stages. It was a bad law because it failed miserably in its avowed aim. At best, it recalls the insecurity of the priests; at worst, their intolerance, fear of dissenters and the drastic manner of dealing with them. It justified forcible conversion of non-Jews, a terror which came to haunt the Jews of Christian Europe centuries later. John Hyrcanus, the Hasmonean king and High-Priest (134–104 B.C.), considered the whole of Palestine as the divinely ordered inheritance of the Jews. He forcibly converted the Edomites to Judaism, extirpated foreign cults and those who refused conversion were slaughtered. He also destroyed the Jewish temple of the Samaritans on Mt. Gerizim; an action that was hailed by the Jerusalem priests as the elimination of a competitor. His son Aristobulus (104–103 B.C.), also king and High-Priest, forced the Arab tribe of Itureans to embrace Judaism and slaughtered those who refused. His brother-successor Alexander Jannaeus (103–76 B.C.), also king and High-Priest, expanded the territory of the Jewish kingdom from the sea to the desert and in the process forcibly Judaized the inhabitants of conquered land, slaughtering or expelling those who refused. He understood the principle that a people professing the same religion contributed to political unity; a subject which was dear to the heart of the Jerusalem priests. The Hasmoneans ruled for about 100 years and bled the Jewish people white. The law was unclear, confused and corrupt; it corrupted those who placed their own selfish interpretation upon it; it ill-served and weakened the Jewish people.

(j) This law almost parallels the one about sorcery in its absurdity. A girl must show evidence of virginity, and if she cannot, she must die. One must assume that what the law meant is that if the girl, i.e., bride, did not bleed upon first sexual contact with the groom, she was not a virgin. This is medicinally totally absurd and, even by today's standards of great knowledge about the subject, a gross common misconception. No, virgins do not always bleed on first sexual intercourse! The hymen which partially or completely covers the vaginal opening may rupture for various normal and medically explainable reasons, other than sexual intercourse. This is priestly lunacy at its worst; it is as if priests intentionally passed laws that were subject to such varying interpretations as to increase the need for their services (marriages were, of course, common) of judging the extent to which the law was violated. The law is unclear, confused and subject to corruption; it would corrupt all parties trying to enforce it and as such is mind-perverting.

(k) The Torah speaks of the obligation of a son (or daughter) to his father and mother; "Honor your father and your mother so that you may have a long life in the land that Yahweh your God has given to you" (Ex. 20:12). This is a majestic commandment of highest ethical value, worthy to be termed a "social force." No culture required a grown son (the reference obviously is not to a minor) to listen to the advice of his parents, any more than to be punished for disregarding such advice; let alone cause his death for such an act. What if the son is more intelligent, more worldly, more experienced, more productive in farming the land than his parents? What if the parents are not "compos mentis"? What if he listened to the voice of his mother and not that of his father? It is obvious that this is another one of the intrusive priestly laws designed to interfere in family matters, act as judges in family disputes—which like nowadays were common—and thereby enhance their economic gain. What of a parent that would demand the death of his/her son for disobedience? Even in the face of such a law? This law is totally unclear, confused and corrupts anyone coming in contact with it.

(1) No blemished animals were acceptable as sacrifices. The priests had a fetish about blemish, uncleanliness and pollution. Yahweh commanded Moses that no one was permitted to offer the food of his God if he had an infirmity such as blindness, lameness, deformity, injured foot or arm, if he was a hunchback or dwarf, had a running sore, disease of the eyes or the skin. The same applied to priests (Lev. 21:17–21). His infirmity would profane Yahweh's holy things (Lev. 21:23), "A man whose testicles have been crushed or whose male member has been cut off is not to be admitted to the assembly of Yahweh" (Deut. 23:2–4). A descendant of an irregular union (intermarriage; bastard is the term used in the quoted text) was not to be admitted to the assembly of Yahweh (Lev. 23:4). The drift of this kind of thinking is clear. Humans, just as sacrificial animals, had to be unblemished—not of character or spirit but of physical appearance—to be acceptable. Another standard for aloofness, exclusivity, divisiveness, setting people apart. Since most mature people had some ailment in those days, it was again up to the priests to be the arbiters, interpreters and loophole-

finders deflecting the impact of the law and be rewarded with appropriate gifts. Irregular unions were defined as mixed marriages with non-Israelite or non-Jewish partners; this must have affected the majority of the people because the Israelites and Jews intermarried with a great number of foreigners, resulting from forced colonization. The aim was not so much maintaining purity of the race (of which there was none) but preventing the "whoring" after foreign gods and sacrificing to them, a matter of prime importance to the priests. "No Ammonite or Moabite is to be admitted to the assembly of Yahweh; not even their descendants to the tenth generation ... and this for all time ..." (Deut. 23:4–5). The Ammonites and Moabites were descended from the ancestors of the Hebrews through Lot, nephew of Abraham; therefore they were not a foreign people; the family of David was of Moabite extraction (Ruth 4:17, 4:22); in Deut. 2:9 Yahweh commanded Moses, "Make no attack on Moab. ..." The apparent reason for the prohibition was that the Israelites adopted for a time the cult of the Moabite Baal of Peor, an abomination to the priests. "The people gave themselves over to debauchery with the daughters of Moab ... and bowed down before their gods" (Numbers 25:1–3). Again, it can be seen how the priests spun a cobweb around the children of Israel; there were no values except what benefited the priests. No mercy was shown; instead, exclusion beyond the tenth generation (because of some irrelevant narrative about Baalam, a "seer" of Pethor in Aram-Mesopotamia and Balak, King of Moab), a handicap to be later adapted by the Spanish Catholic clergy who excluded "New Christians", i.e., Jewish converts to Catholicism, from equality with "Old Christians" until passage of six generations. The obsession with unblemished, swarthy and good-looking physical appearance extended to the views of Jews of the 16th and 17th century who considered it one of the "signs" of the pseudo-Messiahs, scoundrels the likes of David Reubeni, Solomon Molko and Sabatai Zevi, all favorably endowed by nature. Further on we read, speaking of the Ammonites and Moabites, "Never, as long as you live, shall you seek their welfare or their prosperity" (Deut. 23:7). The Ammonites and Moabites were damned forever even though David's ancestors descended from the Moabites. The priestly redactor was confused. He was even more confused, as we read on that the Israelites were not to regard the Egyptians as "detestable" because they were once "strangers" in Egypt (Deut. 23:9). (Note the use of the term "strangers" and not "oppressed slaves").

Unlike the Ammonites and Moabites, whose misdeeds were insignificant, the Egyptians mistreated the Hebrews for over 400 years, yet, "The third generation of children born to these may be admitted to the assembly of Yahweh" (Deut. 23:9). This relatively mild treatment of the Egyptians (so soon after the Exodus), raises serious doubts, among others, concerning the nature of the sojourn of the Hebrews in Egypt as "oppressed slaves." The priests, writing with a clenched soul, excluded from the assembly of Yahweh those with crushed testicles, those whose male member had been cut off, those of mixed marriages, the Ammonites and Moabites, even though they were related to the Hebrews. Virtue, piety, love of Yahweh were of no consequence. Such laws and ordinances were highly discriminatory, contributed to exclusivity and contempt for foreigners and handicapped. All this so that the power, importance and economic welfare of the priests would be enhanced. Such laws and ordinances were not clear, were confused and corrupted those who followed them. It is with great joy and relief to find that the Tanak contains passages which boldly controvert and call into question some of the mind-perverting, discriminatory, socially damaging priestly laws and ordinances. Out of the provincial and mind-debasing particularism there rise the imperatives of justice, sweetness and light; a universalism which removes all the bile and narrow-mindedness, for the Third Isaiah proclaims with a forthright voice: "Let no foreigner who has attached himself to Yahweh say, 'Yahweh will surely exclude me from his people.' Let no eunuch say, 'And I, I am a dried-up tree.' For Yahweh says this: To the eunuchs who observe my sabbaths, and resolve to do what pleases me and cling to my covenant, I will give, in my house and within my walls, a monument and a name … ; I will give them an everlasting name that shall never be effaced." (Isaiah 56:3–5). Isaiah continues, "Foreigners who have attached themselves to Yahweh to serve him … all who observe the sabbath, not profaning it, and cling to my covenant—these I will bring to my holy mountain. I will make them joyful in my house of prayer. Their holocausts and their sacrifices will be accepted on my altar, for my house will be called a house of prayer for all the peoples." (Isaiah 56:6–7).

(m) In simple terms, a "curse" is the opposite of "blessing." The former brings pain, suffering, punishment to the accursed, whereas the latter brings joy, reward and benediction. A curse once bestowed cannot be retracted except by Yahweh, as in Deut. 23:4–6, where Yahweh refused to listen to

Baalam's curse and turned it into a blessing for Israel. A "curse" is also an invocation to Yahweh to punish and bring suffering to the accursed. Curses were uttered by priests in Mesopotamia and Egypt in a ritual casting of a spell by sorcerers and magicians. This connotation of "ritual cursing" is also evident in Israelite priestly magical rites, as in Num. 5:12–22, where a wife suspected of infidelity by her husband is brought before a priest to be tested by drinking "water of bitterness and cursing"; if she did deceive her husband, "... May Yahweh make of you ... a curse among your people, making your thigh shrivel and your belly swell ... and shrivel your organs!" (Num. 5:21–22) as pronounced by the priest, i.e., her pregnancies would abort. However, if she did not deceive her husband, she would go unscathed and able to bear children. This divinely sanctioned ritual ably served the Catholic priests in the Middle Ages who practiced "trial by ordeal" in resolving doubts about the guilt of the accused. Noah cursed his son Ham, Canaan's ancestor, who unwittingly saw his father's nakedness, "Accursed be Canaan, he shall be his brothers' meanest slave" (Gen. 9:25). Joshua curses the Gibeonites, "From now on you are accursed, and you shall never cease being serfs (i.e. slaves) ..." (Josh. 9:23). The prophet Elisha, offended by the insults of some small boys (hardly worthy of a prophet, if the story is historical), cursed them in the name of Yahweh, and two she-bears came out of the wood "and savaged forty-two of the boys" (2 Kings 2:25). David cursed those who drove him into exile; speaking of his tormentors, "... may they be accursed before Yahweh" (1 Sam. 26:19). It is clear that a "curse" involved some ritual of magic, or invoked Yahweh's spell to harm, punish, inflict pain and suffering upon the accursed. Noah cursed his son with impunity; apparently the cursing of one's children was no violation. Yahweh's command to honor one's father and mother referred only to reward of a long life and invoked no punishment for failure to do so. This command does not state "Love your father and mother", although "love" is given a higher rank than "honor" as in, "If a stranger lives with you in your land ... love him as yourself' (Lev. 19:33); Yahweh "... who loves the stranger and gives him food and clothing" (Deut. 10:18); "Love the stranger then, for you were strangers in the land of Egypt" (Deut. 10:19–20); "You must love your neighbor as yourself' (Lev. 19:18); this command states only to "Honor your father and mother ..." (Ex. 20:12). Yahweh commands love of neighbor and stranger; both are equated with love of oneself. It is difficult to comprehend love of oneself as a virtue; love of one's neighbor and stranger are virtues of universal application. The priestly authors did not reconcile this confusion. The cursing of one's father or mother involves casting a spell; it involves the practice of witchcraft, sorcery and magic. To do so violated clearly stated prohibitions; "You must not practice divination or magic" (Lev. 19:26); "You shall not allow a sorceress to live" (Ex. 22:17). The practice of divination, sorcery and magic were the jealously guarded prerogatives of the priests and an outsider could not usurp this privilege with impunity. The hand of the priests is only too visible; they injected themselves into family disputes to arbitrate and judge. Were the Israelites such idolaters that they believed so strongly in the efficacy of sorcery and magic as to condemn son or daughter to death? This is a bad law, unclear, confused and corrupt in its implication of setting father and mother against son or daughter; a law difficult to enforce, because it required a parent to accuse and to testify against son or daughter and be instrumental in their death. Who but the priests could have conceived such a law?

Conclusion to Chapter 8

It is only right and befitting that the priestly aristocracy promoted its interest; one should not be squeamish about a basic law of human nature; it is there, forever, and no one should fault them for following survival instincts: They chose a higher "good". But the priestly pursuit of a higher "good" did not always promote the self-preservation instincts of the rest of the Jewish people. On the contrary, many of the priestly laws and ordinances imposed upon the Jewish people caused them to choose a lesser "good" and a worse "bad". The test of divine laws and ordinances regulating human conduct and social behavior must be their attribution to an omniscient being; nothing that existed, exists or will exist can be outside the divine omniscience. Laws and ordinances which display ignorance of fact and ignorance of the consequences resulting from them cannot be divine. It follows that such divine laws and ordinances must be clear and readily understood by human minds to which they are directed even though they may require interpretation by more intelligent minds—in this case the priests—particularly those which mandated "death" for violators.

The laws and ordinances regarding necromancers, magicians, sorcerers, display complete ignorance of fact: Such people never existed; those that claimed such gifts were charlatans and deceived the people; an omniscient

God could not be deceived by such spurious claims and could not ordain such laws and ordinances; the over 300,000 victims accused of the alleged crime of "witchcraft" went to their death fully aware of the falsehood and monstrosity of the charges; yet the Torah ordains the penalty of death for the violators. Only ignorant priests—reflecting the mores of the times and totally provincial and idolatrous—could conceive such laws and ordinances. The man who profanes the Sabbath must be put to death. "Whoever does any work on that day shall be put to death" (Ex. 35:2–3). This commandment is unclear and confusing. It confused Moses; in Numbers 15:32–35 we read that a man caught gathering wood on a sabbath day was brought before Moses, who kept him in custody, because the penalty "... he should undergo had not yet been fixed. Yahweh said to Moses, 'This man must be put to death.' " Moses was not sure that the man deserved death; Yahweh clarified it for him. We read in Ex. 16:29 "... Yahweh has laid down the sabbath for you;" and in Num. 28:9 ff "On the sabbath day, you must offer two yearling lambs ... The sabbath holocaust is to be offered every sabbath, in addition to the perpetual holocaust, ..." This would confuse any Israelite. It should confuse everyone because the commandment concerning the sabbath is stated in the Torah in three places; two give different explanations and one offers none. "For in six days Yahweh made the heavens and the earth and the sea ... but on the seventh day he rested; that is why Yahweh has blessed the sabbath day and made it sacred" (Ex. 20:11). "Observe the sabbath day and keep it holy, as Yahweh your God has commanded you ... You shall do no work on that day, ... Remember that you were a servant in the land of Egypt, and that Yahweh your God brought you out from there ... ; because of this, Yahweh your God has commanded you to keep the sabbath day" (Deut. 5:12–15). The third reference to sabbath offers no explanation, "For six days you shall labor, but on the seventh day you shall rest, ..." (Ex. 34:2 1). Who but the priests could be the authors of such confusion; and the penalty for violation was death. These are confused laws and ordinances; bad and unclear; mind-perverting; could not therefore be divinely ordained. The laws and ordinances regarding prophets, or dreamer of dreams, who falsely presume to speak in Yahweh's name display gross ignorance of fact: no one but God knew when such violations occurred; no priest or human could be the judge. An omniscient God could not ordain such a law, yet the penalty was death for violators.

The prohibitions regarding serving other gods and worshipping them are unclear and confusing: it required denunciation of one's neighbor; led to forcible conversions of non-Israelites and non-Jews; it failed miserably in its application for despite all the hectoring, the Torah constantly reproaches the children of Israel for "whoring" after other gods. And the penalty for violators was death. The Decalogue declares, "You shall have no gods except me" (Ex. 20:3, Deut. 5:7). Further, "You must keep my laws" (Lev. 19:19); "Do not follow other gods ... for Yahweh your God is a jealous God; his anger could blaze out against you and wipe you from the face of the earth" (Deut. 6:14–16); "... if you refuse my laws ... I will inflict terror on you, ... I will turn against you and you shall be defeated by your enemies" (Lev. 26:14–17). It is clear from the above that it was Yahweh alone who would punish the violators.

Death for a bride that could not prove her virginity? This rests on total ignorance of fact: an omniscient God could not ordain such punishment; ignorant priestly authors could.

Laws and ordinances which condemn a son (what about a daughter?) to death for disobeying his father or mother; condemn to death anyone who cursed a parent—a curse which necessarily involved the practice of sorcery; precluded a "bastard" from admission to the assembly of Yahweh, were of ignorant and mind-perverting priestly authorship, anti-social and of no redeeming value. The laws and ordinances outlined in this chapter were mind-perverting; had unintended consequences; were man-made; most mandated the death penalty despite being unclear, confused and corrupt; reflected priestly ignorance and rapacity; led to corruption and ill-served the interests of Israelites and Jews. The priestly sect, the smaller group within the larger group, challenged the established conduct and views of Israelites and Jews, the larger group; defied customs shared with neighbors; imposed views that, in time, ostracized the larger group; set them apart from all other peoples; caused apostasies, civil wars, major fatal uprisings; polluted their minds; caused them to act against their best interest; passed laws regarding beliefs and opinions which could not be enforced and thus led to corruption; passed laws and ordinances which ran counter to the interests of the majority which needed to be maintained by force: the penalty was death and other punishments. All these in order to enhance the economic benefits of the smaller group, the priests. The insecurity and survival instincts of the smaller group, the priests, were forced in time to join cause with foreign powers in violation of their own laws and ordinances—in opposition to the interests of the people of Israel; the consequences were unintended and fatal:

(a) The destruction of the priesthood.
(b) The military massacres and dispersion of the Jewish people.

"... You are not to give yourself a foreign king who is no brother of yours" (Deut. 17:15).

In the next chapters, all the bad "stars" of the people of Israel will come into alignment.

Chapter 9

The Fateful Covenant
and the Consequences

1. The sabbath, sacrifices, sin-offerings, burnt offerings, priests, communal meals, circumcision, temple, ark, laws written on tablets, laws of purity, forgiveness of sin, priestly dues, prophets, human sacrifices, monotheism: these were not Israelite innovations but adaptations from culture, cults and rituals of more ancient peoples (as outlined in prior chapters). In one respect, however, the religion of the Israelites was unique—it was the idea of a covenant with a deity. The covenant was a solemn ritual agreement, spoken or written, between two parties not necessarily equal, which bound them mutually to certain obligations which could not be retracted and included curses for the party violating the covenant. The idea of a covenant itself between king and people, ruler and ruled, is also ancient and pre-Israelite, as for example in the Hittite treaty structure and the pattern of treaties in the ancient Near East. The Hittite treaty of covenant frequently referred to the land given the subject by his sovereign and the subject was urged to take possession of the land. It is the covenant with the deity, as described in the Torah and referenced in the other books of the Tanak, that is unique and of first impression.

2. Yahweh made a Covenant with Abram (later called Abraham), "To your descendants I give this land, from the wadi of Egypt to the Great River, the river Euphrates, ..." (Gen. 15:18–19). (It is not made clear why God chose Abram at the time when the world was populated with many great nations.) Yahweh also said to Abram that his descendants would be exiled to a land not their own where they would be slaves and oppressed for 400 years; that they would be liberated and would leave "with many possessions" (Gen. 15:15). No reason was given for their slavery and Abram did not enquire, although, as it appears from the narrative, he conversed freely

with Yahweh. Later, Yahweh said to Abram, "Bear yourself blameless in my presence, and I will make a Covenant between myself and you, and increase your numbers greatly" (Gen. 17:2). After informing Abram that henceforth his name would be Abraham, Yahweh disclosed to him, "I will make you most fruitful. I will make you into nations, ... I will establish my Covenant between myself and you, and your descendants after you, generation after generation, a Covenant in perpetuity, to be your God and the God of your descendants after you" (Gen. 17:6–8). Yahweh promised that he would give Abraham and to his descendants the whole land of Canaan, "to own in perpetuity, and I will be your God" (Gen. 17:8). In return Abraham, for his part of the Covenant and binding on all the descendants after him must, as a sign of the Covenant, agree that all males would be circumcised. Any male not circumcised shall be cut off from his people for he violated the Covenant. (As mentioned in a prior chapter, circumcision was practiced long before by other peoples, e.g., the Egyptians). Later on, as the narrative continues, for his willingness to sacrifice his only son Isaac as a burnt offering to Yahweh—which he was directed to do by Yahweh—Yahweh promised to shower him with blessings and that he would make his descendants as numerous as the stars of heaven and the grains of sand on the seashore (Gen. 22:2 ff). In a previous chapter it is stated that Yahweh made a Covenant with Noah, "But I will establish my Covenant with you ..." (Gen. 6:18), promised to save Noah and his family from the flood, and saying to Noah and his sons, 'Be fruitful, multiply and fill the earth" (Gen. 9:1–2). Yahweh imposed on Noah the obligation of not eating the blood of animals and the prohibition against homicide. For his part Yahweh promised:

To Noah:
— that there would be no more floods to destroy the living on earth;
— never to curse the earth because of man.

To Abraham:
— to give him and his descendants the whole land of Canaan, in perpetuity;
— that Yahweh would be their God;
— that his descendants would be as numerous as the stars of heaven and the grains of sand on the seashore.

Both were to be fruitful and multiply. In return for these generous benefits: Noah and his descendants were prohibited from eating the blood of animals and committing homicide; Abraham and his descendants were mandated to have all males circumcised. The Covenants arose from the election of Yahweh and not from the merits of Noah and Abraham; therein was their uniqueness. For the purpose of drawing deductions from the institution of the Covenants and their influence, it matters little whether the election narratives—and that of subsequent Covenants—were authentic; what matters is that the people of Israel believed them to be authentic.

3. A few months after the Exodus from Egypt, the Israelites camped near Mt. Sinai; Yahweh called Moses from the mountain and commanded him to tell the sons of Israel, "… if you obey my voice and hold fast to my covenant, you of all nations shall be my very own … I will count you a kingdom of priests, a consecrated nation" (Ex. 19:5–7). As can be seen, the Covenant in the narrative is getting more explicit as to the promises of blessings to be bestowed by Yahweh; the ever-present hand of the priests is visible in the phrase "a kingdom of priests", i.e., a government by priests, i.e., a theocracy. In order to make room for Israel in the Promised Land, Yahweh would drive out from there and exterminate the Amorites, Hittites, Perizzites, Canaanites, Hivites and the Jebusites. "You must destroy their gods utterly and smash their standing-stones" (Ex. 23:25). "You must make no pact with them or with their gods. They must not live in your country …" (Ex. 23:32–33). The people of Israel were ordered to worship Yahweh who would give them "your full term of life" (Ex. 23:26). Moses related to the people of Israel all the commands and ordinances of Yahweh and the people answered with one voice, "We will observe all the commands that Yahweh has decreed (Ex. 24:3–4). Moses put all the commands of Yahweh into writing, calling it the "Book of the Covenant"; no trace of this most important book was ever found; it is lost to history. The children of Israel are warned not to follow the laws of the nations that Yahweh expelled to make room for Israel; these nations, we are told, practiced rituals for which Yahweh had come to detest them and hence their expulsion. Did Yahweh instruct them or give them laws prohibiting such rituals? We are not told how they violated his laws, but simply that they "did" these things. Yahweh declared that he set Israel apart from these peoples; they were not to mix with them or they would be defiled, "… and I will set you apart from all these peoples so that you may be mine" (Lev.

20:26). Israel is further commanded, "You must lay them under ban. You must make no covenant with them nor show them any pity. You must not marry with them ... (for) the anger of Yahweh would blaze out against you and soon destroy you ... (you must) tear down their altars, smash their standing-stones ... and set fire to their idols. For you are a people consecrated to Yahweh your God; it is you that Yahweh our God has chosen to be his very own people out of all the peoples on the earth" (Deut. 7:2–6); this was the exhortation of Moses. To make sure there would be no doubt who the real consecrated people were, this kingdom of priests, set apart from all other peoples, forbidden to mix with them for fear of defilement, for whom ancient indigenous nations would be expelled and exterminated to make room for Yahweh's own and chosen, Yahweh told Moses, "I myself have chosen the Levites from among the sons of Israel, in place of the first-born ... these Levites therefore belong to me. ... They are mine; ..." (Num. 3:12–13). The hand of the priestly authors left its mark, reminding Israel not to forget the covenant by making carved images of anything forbidden by Yahweh; to do what is right in the eyes of Yahweh so that they would prosper and take possession of the rich land which Yahweh swore to give their fathers; to keep and observe all the commandments of Yahweh. They reminded Israel to make no covenant with the Gentiles of Canaan; not to intermarry with them; to tear down their altars and burn their idols; to show them no pity and devour all the people whom Yahweh delivered over to them; to destroy their gods and to forbid them to live with them. The priestly tree was well planted.

4. Lastly, Yahweh made a covenant with David, a descendant of Ruth, the Moabitess. The word of Yahweh came to Nathan, the prophet,in a dream. Nathan told David that Yahweh would give him "fame as great as the greatest on earth" (2 Sam. 7:9–10); that he would provide a place for Israel to dwell never to be disturbed again; give them rest from all their enemies; that David's son (Solomon) would build Yahweh a house to dwell in; that Yahweh would make the royal throne secure forever and "your throne be established for ever" (2 Sam. 7:10 ff). On hearing this, David, "seated before Yahweh" (2 Sam. 7:18) praised Yahweh, ... "there is none like you, ...": (2 Sam. 7:22). No mention was made why David merited these great blessings except that his son, at some future date, would build a house for Yahweh to dwell in. Nathan's prophecy was false: Israel was disturbed again and did not get rest from their enemies; the royal throne

was not made secure forever and the throne was not established forever. Nathan's "revelation" (2 Sam. 7:17), regarded as the unerring word of God by future generations of Jews (later on by Christians),had a mind-perverting influence upon them and was the cause of unfathomable calamities, grief and false hopes. Nathan's false prophecy became the curse of the Jewish people. Speaking of Yahweh and David, "I will be a father to him and he a son to me" (2 Sam. 7:14).

5. It must be taken as axiomatic that Yahweh would not break his solemn Covenant with Israel; but if the children of Israel violated the Covenant by not observing each of Yahweh's commandments, a veritable inferno would overtake them, this kingdom of priests, this consecrated nation, Yahweh's very own people chosen from among all other peoples. They would be utterly destroyed; scattered among other peoples; beasts would kill their children and destroy their cattle; reduce their number until their roads would be deserted. Yahweh would punish them sevenfold for their sins, their fields and trees would remain barren; he would send the sword against them; and pestilence; deliver them into the hands of the enemy and take away their bread; they would eat the flesh of their own sons and daughters; pile their corpses on the corpses of their idols; reduce their cities to ruins and make their land a waste; they would perish among the nations and the land of their enemies would swallow them (Lev. 26:14 ff).

If Israel did not obey the voice of Yahweh their God and keep his statutes, they would be accursed in the town and accursed in the country; accursed would be the fruit of their body and produce of their soil. Yahweh would infect them with the plague, consumption, fever, inflammation, burning fever, drought, blight, mildew. Their carcasses would be carrion for all the birds and beasts; struck down with Egyptian boils, swelling of the groins, with scurvy and itch for which they would find no cure; struck down with madness, blindness and distraction of mind. They would be exploited and plundered continually and wear an iron yoke on their necks until they perished. Yahweh would scatter them among all the peoples from one end of the earth to the other; among these nations there would be no repose for them and life would be a burden to them; night and day they would go in fear, uncertain of their life and living in terror (Deut. 28:15 ff). "In anger, in fury, in fierce wrath Yahweh has torn them from their country and flung them into another land where they are today" (Deut. 29:27–28).

6. The litany of horrors was to befall and strike all guilty and innocent alike; no distinction was to be made; no pity shown. The opponents of Jews, particularly Christians in the Middle Ages, had a ready-made catalogue of sins to charge the Jews with by just citing the Torah; God abandoned the Jews; they were a people accursed in God's eyes, to dwell among other nations to be exploited and harassed. When the voice of prophets, apart from the priestly authors, joined in the condemnation, the charges gained added credibility. All Israel was punished and no mention is made of sparing the innocent. Were there any innocent? How about the children, the aged and the sick? Even Abraham chided Yahweh not to think of doing such a thing to sinful Gomorrah, i.e., to kill the just with the sinner and treating the just and sinner alike, "Are you really going to destroy the just man with the sinner?" (Gen 18:23–24), and finally obtaining Yahweh's promise that if there were even only ten just men he would not destroy Sodom and Gomorrah. The violation of the Covenant contained no such dispensation: Israel was condemned. Similarly, Jeremiah 5:1 states, "Rove to and fro through the streets of Jerusalem, ... search her squares; if you can find a man, one man who does right and seeks the truth, then I will pardon her, says Yahweh." Who but the priestly authors could deploy such curses against Israel for violating the divine commandments and breaking the covenant? Who but the priests would transfer their blazing vindictiveness and vengeance as passions attributable to Yahweh? Why were the priests so full of hate and fury? Why such brutal punishments? Was it because their status and livelihood were threatened by Israel sacrificing to other gods and not paying the tithes to them and for the support of the Temple? Why were the children of Israel continually breaking the Covenant? Did the priests properly discharge their function of interpreting the divine laws and ordinances to them? Did the priestly privileges invite defection? Did the priestly wealth invite envy and hatred? Did the priests know the law? The prophets, who were known to oppose the priests, had such thoughts. The prophet Jeremiah, who was active about 650–585 B.C., condemned the priests. "How dare you say: We are wise and possess the law of Yahweh? But look how it has been falsified by the lying pen of the scribes!" (Jer. 8:8).

The prophet Ezekiel, who was active in the 6th century B.C., was much harsher, "The word of Yahweh was addressed to me as follows, '... Her priests have violated my Law and desecrated my sanctuaries; they have drawn no distinction between sacred and profane, they have not taught people the difference between clean and unclean; they have turned their eyes away from my sabbaths and I have been dishonored by them. Her leaders in the city are like wolves tearing their prey, shedding blood and killing people to steal their possessions. Her prophets have whitewashed these crimes with their empty visions and lying prophesies' " (Ezekiel 22:21–28). The prophet Hosea, who was active during the reign of Jeroboam II (783–743 B.C.), hurled accusations against the priests with bone-chilling directness, "... listen to the word of Yahweh, for Yahweh indicts the inhabitants of the country: there is no fidelity ... no knowledge of God in the country, only perjury and lies, slaughter, theft, adultery and violence, murder after murder ... it is you, priests, that I denounce. Day and night you stumble along, ... you are the ruin of your people. My people perish for want of knowledge. As you have rejected knowledge so do I reject you from my priesthood; you have forgotten the teaching of your God ... They feed on the sin of my people, they are all greedy for their iniquity ... I will make them pay for their conduct, ..." (Hosea 4:1–9). Hosea accused the priests of still worse crimes, "... a band of priests commits murder on the road to Shechem—..." (Hosea 6:9). The prophet Micah, who was active around 721 B.C., accused the priests of venality, "her priests take a fee for their rulings, ..." (Micah 3:11).

Such charges against the priests are mind-boggling: They are accused of Israel's ruin! But worse was still to come. The prophet Malachi, who was active around 464–424 B.C., the last of the minor prophets, to whom came the word of Yahweh, inveighed against the priests, "And now, priests, this warning is for you. If you do not listen, if you do not find it in your heart to glorify my name, says Yahweh Sabaoth, I will send the curse on you and curse your very blessing ... it is I who have given you this warning of my intention to abolish my covenant with Levi ... it stood for life and peace ... The teaching of truth was in his mouth, falsehood was not to be found on his lips; he walked with me in integrity and virtue; he converted many from sinning. The lips of the priest ought to safeguard knowledge ... But you have strayed from the way; you have caused many to stumble by your teaching. You have destroyed the covenant of Levi, ... And so I ... have made you contemptible and vile in the eyes of the whole people ..."

(Malachi 2:1–9). The First Isaiah, who was active around 740–701 B.C., condemned the priests and their Temple prophets, "Priests and prophets are reeling from strong drink, they are muddled with wine; strong drink makes them stagger, they totter when they are having visions, they stumble when they are giving judgment" (Isaiah 28:7).

7. The prophets were fiercely independent and uncompromising in their condemnation of injustice, as they saw it. The "lying" prophets they condemned with the priests were those attached to the Temple and to the royal court who also played an official part in the worship; the priests needed prophets to counterbalance the anti-priestly message of the divinely inspired prophets. How were the people to recognize the true prophets of Yahweh and avoid the message of the false prophet? There were two criteria: (1) the fulfillment of a prophecy, (2) the prophet's message was in agreement with the commandments and ordinances of Yahweh. In this respect the prophet Nathan, who prophesied to David, was a false prophet: His prophecy to King David that Yahweh would not withdraw his favor from him, that King David's royal throne would be secure forever, and David's throne would be established forever—this prophecy was false. This false prophecy was the cause of misconceptions and failed hopes on an immense historical scale; it inflicted lasting wounds. To the criteria of recognition of a true prophet as outlined above must be added a third: The prophet's message must constitute a social force, i.e., an aid in the people's struggle for self-preservation and conducive to the choice of a better "good."

8. In Paragraph 6 of this chapter I quoted from the writings of the three major prophets: Jeremiah, Ezekiel, First Isaiah and from the writings of three minor prophets Hosea, Malachi and Micah. Their activities spanned 400 years, from the 8th to the 5th centuries B.C., a most turbulent, historically critical and eventful period which marked the destruction of the kingdom of Israel, the expulsion and disappearance of its population; the destruction of the kingdom of Judah, the Babylonian Exile, the return from Exile back to Jerusalem, the building of the Second Temple in Jerusalem. There was every reason for the prophets to exhort Israel to return to the observance of the basic commandments and ordinances of Yahweh as reflected in the Sinaitic Covenant through Moses; to be sufficiently verbose in reminding Yahweh's chosen that compliance would bring prosperity and that breach of the Covenant would invite punishment and curses.

Yet incredibly, these prophets, as can be gathered from their writings, displayed total ignorance of some of the fundamentals of the Covenant. Jeremiah did not mention Moses, Aaron's priestly sect, the tabernacle, the ark, the Decalogue and Sinai. His reference to Exodus is limited to, "For when I brought your ancestors out of the land of Egypt, …" (7:22); his reference to the Covenant is limited to, "cursed be the man who will not listen to the words of this covenant which I ordained for your ancestors when I brought them out of the furnace of iron, out of the land of Egypt" (11:3–4). Ezekiel, one of the major prophets, did not mention Moses, the Exodus, the Covenant, Aaron's priestly sect, the tabernacle, the ark, the Decalogue and Sinai. The First Isaiah (Chapters 1–35) did not mention Moses, the Covenant, Aaron's priestly sect, the tabernacle, the ark, the Decalogue, Sinai; he mentioned only briefly the Exodus, "… to make a pathway for the remnant of his people left over from the exile of Assyria, as there was for Israel when it came out of Egypt" (11:16). The Third Isaiah (Chapters 56–66), who wrote after the Babylonian Exile, made only mention of Moses in Chapter 63, "They remembered the days of old, of Moses his servant" (63:11), and a brief reference to the Exodus, "… who divided the waters before them … who made them walk through the ocean as easily as a horse through the desert?" (63:12–13). Hosea made no reference to Moses, Aaron's priestly sect, the tabernacle, the ark, the Decalogue, Sinai. His most limited reference to Exodus, "When Israel was a child I loved him, and I called my son out of Egypt" (11:1); and the Covenant, "… because they have violated my covenant and rebelled against my Law" (8:1). Malachi, who wrote about 100 years after the return from the Babylonian Exile, when the Torah was fully redacted, made a brief reference to the Covenant, "Why, then, do we break faith with one another, profaning the covenant of our ancestors?" (2:10–11) At the end of his book, in the "Appendices," consisting of three verses, "Remember the Law of my servant Moses to whom at Horeb I prescribed laws and customs for the whole of Israel" (3:22–23), are the briefest of references to Moses, laws and customs; at that it appears to be a later interpolation. Malachi did not mention the Exodus, Aaron's priestly sect, the tabernacle, the ark, Sinai. The prophets Joel, Obadiah, Jonah, Nahum, Habakkuk, Zephania and Zechariah made no mention of Moses, the Exodus, the Covenant, Aaron's priestly sect, the tabernacle, the ark, the Decalogue and Sinai. Amos made only this reference, "It was I who brought you out of the land of Egypt …"

(2:10); no mention of the other seven subjects. Micah did not mention the Covenant, the tabernacle, the ark, the Decalogue and Sinai. He made references to Moses, Exodus, slavery and Aaron, "I brought you out of the land of Egypt, I rescued you from the house of slavery; I sent Moses to lead you, with Aaron and Miriam" (6:4). No mention was made of priestly sacrifices, sacrifices which were pleasing to Yahweh and mandatory punishment of death for certain violations. Instead, Micah spoke out against the tyranny of the rich, against those who plotted evil, seized the fields which they coveted, seized the cloak of the innocent, robbed the children, loathed justice, perverted all that was right. Instead his God pardoned crime, his anger did not last forever, showed mercy. And what is it that Yahweh asked of Israel?, "only this, to act justly, to love tenderly and to walk humbly with your God" (Micah 6:8). What promises did Micah hold for the future of Israel?, "they will hammer their swords into ploughshares, their spears into sickles. Nation will not lift sword against nation, there will be no more training for war" (Micah 4:3). This religion was a mighty social force; but Israel did not listen.

9. The prophets were inspired men who, claiming to speak in the name of God, were the bearers and interpreters of God's message to man and interpreters of current events. Their message taught morality and justice; they were social revolutionaries who taught ethical conduct far ahead of their time; that was their interpretation of God's word. The priests taught obedience of the Sinaitic Covenant as handed down by Moses; the prophets' interpretation of the covenant was life and peace, the teaching of truth, integrity and virtue, the safeguard of knowledge. In the eyes of the prophets, the priests violated the law, dishonored Yahweh, desecrated the sanctuaries, did not teach the people properly, acted like wolves in the cities, shed the peoples' blood and stole their possessions, displayed no knowledge of God, were guilty of perjuries, lies and theft, God denounced them, they were the ruin of the people, rejected knowledge, forgot the teaching of Yahweh, fed on sins of Yahweh's people, did not glorify Yahweh, would be cursed by Yahweh and caused Israel to stumble by their teaching. These condemnations were uttered by divinely inspired prophets who were in constant conflict with the priests. No wonder the children of Israel were accused of violating the Covenant. From the pages of the Torah and the prophets, it appears that such violations were almost continuous;

Israel was not helped by the "lying pen of the scribes" and by the "laws that were not good and the observances by which they could never live."

10. These priests hurled venomous imprecations against Israel; punished the violators of their privileges and prerogatives; commanded the death penalty for sorcerers, magicians, necromancers, violators of the sabbath; provided for the death penalty for disobedience to priests, false prophets, worshipping of other gods, for brides unable to prove virginity, for stubborn and rebellious sons; for children cursing father or mother. These priests insisted on sacrifices for holocausts, sins and reparation; sacrificing of unblemished animals; they were obsessed with purity; blemish and physical contamination; purification of women after childbirth and menstruation; sexual impurities of men and women; the holiness of priesthood. The priestly Yahweh expected his Chosen People to follow these rules, ordinances and commandments so that the people would receive his blessing; the priests—whom the prophets accused of murder, theft, ignorance of Yahweh's laws, who falsified the law and desecrated sanctuaries, misleading the children of Israel and the cause of their ruin—were the teachers, judges, interpreters of commandments, ordinances for which they claimed divine sanction.

How did the prophetic Yahweh respond? He contradicted most of what the priestly Yahweh found "pleasing." Isaiah apparently knew nothing of Leviticus when he wrote, " 'What are your endless sacrifices to me?' says Yahweh. 'I am sick of holocausts … fat of calves. The blood of bulls … Bring me your worthless offerings no more, …' " (Isaiah 1:11–13). Instead of the sacrificial ritual, Yahweh demanded, "Take your wrong-doing out of my sight. Cease to do evil. Learn to do good, search for justice, help the oppressed, …"(Isaiah 1:16–17); and promised Israel, "If you are willing to obey, you shall eat the good things of the earth" (Isaiah 1:19).

The prophet Jeremiah knew nothing of Leviticus 3:17, "All the fat belongs to Yahweh. This is a perpetual law for all your descendants, …" and, "This holocaust will be a burnt offering and the fragrance of it will appease Yahweh" (Lev. 1:9). The voice of Yahweh came to Jeremiah for he relates a completely different view of what Yahweh demanded, "Your holocausts are not acceptable, your sacrifices do not please me" (6:21). Incredibly, he quoted Yahweh as denying all the commandments about holocaust and sacrifice, "For when I brought your ancestors out of the land of Egypt, I said nothing to them, gave them no orders, about holocaust and sacrifice" (7:22–23). The prophet Hosea summarizes beautifully what Yahweh demanded, "... since what I want is love, not sacrifice; knowledge of God, not holocausts" (6:6). The prophet Amos, that true son of the desert who demanded of Israel a morality worthy of God's chosen, an implacable enemy of social injustice, wrote a stinging rebuke, "I hate and despise your feasts, I take no pleasure in your solemn festivals. When you offer me holocausts, I reject your oblations, and refuse to look at your sacrifices of fattened cattle ... But let justice flow like water, and integrity like an unfailing stream. Did you bring me sacrifice and oblation in the wilderness for all those forty years, House of Israel?" (5:21–25).

11. There was a virtual state of "war" between the priestly and prophetic Covenant; the former preached and espoused the law as contained in the books of Exodus, Leviticus and Deuteronomy; the latter taught high principles and standards of morality which they considered central and which reached far beyond the Torah. This conflict led, in time, thanks to the prophets, to the development of the first universal concepts of God and away from the parochial, national and particularistic concept of Yahweh. The Israelites were continuously violating "both" Covenants; they did more than that: they ignored them. It strains credulity that all the people would violate both Covenants; that factions did not fragmentize the people into opposing camps, (the split between Jeroboam and Rehoboam after Solomon's death does not fall into this category since the reasons for the break-up were economic, geographic and priestly greed. The first serious split occurred around 200 B.C. as a result of Greek and Seleucid influence and in the Second Commonwealth under the rule of the Maccabees when, the office of king and High Priest was combined) one camp believing this and the other one that. The priests and prophets seemed to preach in a vacuum with little attention paid to them by the people although they did influence the kings of Israel and Judah and their courts. The prophets were historical personages: the three major and twelve minor ones can be placed in a historical time-slot. But what about the Sinaitic Covenant? When was it really known? When were the books containing it amalgamated and redacted and made known to the people? More about that later.

Is it any wonder that the children of Israel were confused? The divinely ordained priests, wrapped in holiness and purity, condemning "false" prophets to death and the divinely inspired prophets accusing the priests of misunderstanding Yahweh's laws, causing Israel's ruin and interpreting Yahweh's laws as they saw fit. It is not surprising that the Israelites, exposed to these constant conflicts between prophets and priests, mostly ignored both and were strongly influenced by the simple rites of surrounding peoples. The priests and prophets, however, did find common ground: The priestly curses were equaled, if not exceeded, by the severity and directness of the prophetic curses.

12. A covenant was a solemn ritual agreement between two parties not necessarily equals; an exchange of promises to fulfill certain obligations which were mutually acceptable; spoken with ritual solemnity. It was not necessarily a voluntary compact, i.e., it could be imposed by the stronger on the weaker; involved curses upon the party violating the terms; could not be rescinded or retracted. Isaac made a covenant with Abimelech, "Let there be a sworn treaty between ourselves and you, and let us make a covenant with you" (Gen. 26:28–29); Abraham made a covenant with Abimelech regarding water rights, "… and the two of them made a covenant" (Gen. 21:27–28).

These were ordinary business transactions using the solemnity of the covenant for added enforcability. Yahweh made a covenant with Noah where he demanded that Noah must not eat the blood of animals and commit homicide; in exchange, Yahweh promised not to destroy mankind again by a deluge (Gen. 9:4 ff). Yahweh made a covenant with Abraham, a covenant in perpetuity, to be his God and the God of his descendants and increase his numbers greatly. God demanded of Abraham that all males and their descendants be circumcised (Gen. 17:2 ff). These covenants were made with individuals. The Sinaitic Covenant was imposed upon the Israelites and bound them and their descendants to observe the Law, Commandments and ordinances; the Israelites were to become Yahweh's possession out of all the peoples of the earth; a kingdom of priests; a holy nation (Ex. 19:5 ff). There were to be terrible curses upon them and their descendants for violating the Covenant. The Hebrews were slaves in Egypt for 400 years; soon after their liberation by Yahweh through his servant Moses, the Sinaitic Covenant was imposed upon them unlike the ones with Noah and Abraham: the Sinaitic Covenant was read to the assembly of the whole people and they gave their assent. The Israelites and their descendants were bound forever to the terms of the Covenant; were given no opportunity to opt out; were to suffer collective punishment for violations; were to be cursed and threatened with extinction. They became indentured slaves; could not abandon the Law; an object of derision, envy and hatred by their enemies and neighbors. The observance of the Covenant itself nursed an attitude of contempt for Gentiles and a contempt for peoples who worshiped other gods and observed different customs. They were cursed by the priests and by the prophets, even though it is clear that they shared different views of the obligations imposed by the Covenant. The constant lamentation due to their violations of the Covenant resulted in constant curses, even though the Covenant was not mentioned by the prophets Isaiah, Ezekiel, Joel, Amos, Obadiah, Jonah, Nahum, Habakkuk, Zephania and Zecharia. However, the prophetic curses were ear-splitting, even though there did not seem to be any evidence of any effect upon the conduct of the people. "... I have made my decree and will not relent: because you have rejected the Law of Yahweh and failed to keep his precepts ... I am going to hurl fire on Judah, and burn up the palaces of Jerusalem" (Amos 2:4–5). Because of sins committed, "I sent you a plague like Egypt's plague; I slaughtered your young men with the sword, ... and yet you never came back to me" (Amos 4:10); "I mean to break their heads, every one, and all who remain I will put to the sword;" (Amos 9:1). "Now, my eyes are turned on the sinful kingdom, to wipe it off the face of the earth" (Amos 9:8); "I am going to bring such distress on men that they will grope like the blind (because they have sinned against Yahweh)" (Zephaniah 1:18); "A third of your inhabitants shall die of plague or starve to death ... ; a third shall fall by the sword ... a third I will scatter to every wind, ... My anger will be satisfied;" (Ezekiel 5:12–13). "... your inhabitants are going to be cut to pieces and thrown down in front of your idols, ... Throughout your territory the towns will be destroyed and the high places wrecked ... so you will learn that I am Yahweh" (Ezekiel 6:4–7); "I mean to show you no pity, I will not spare you; ... Now disaster is going to follow disaster ... Soon I am going to pour out my fury on you and exhaust my anger at you;" (Ezekiel 7:4–8); "I shall slaughter them all ..." (Ezek. 7:16); "The man who has sinned is the one who must die;" (Ezek. 18:20); "Listen to this priests, attend, House of Israel, listen, royal household, ... They are entrenched in their deceitfulness and so I am going to punish them all" (Hosea 5:1–2); "Israel has rejected the good; the enemy will hunt him down" (Hosea 8:3); "... in the house of his God enmity awaits him. These men are steeped in corruption ..." (Hosea 9:8–9); "They will have to go back to Egypt, ..." (Hosea 11:5); "I have therefore begun to strike you down, to bring you to ruin for your sins. You will sow but never reap, ..." (Micah 7:13–14); "Yahweh is a jealous and vengeful God, Yahweh avenges, he is full of wrath ... Most surely Yahweh will not leave the guilty unpunished" (Nahum 1:2–3); "Since the days of your ancestors, you have evaded my statutes and not observed them. Return to me and I will return to you, ... The curse lies on you because you, yes you the whole nation, are cheating me. Bring the full tithes and dues to the storehouse so that there may be food in my house, ..." (Malachi 3:7–10).

Lastly, I will cite from Jeremiah, that master of imprecations, who was not only prophet to the people of Israel but prophet to other nations as he received the call from Yahweh (1:5) and prophesied the restoration of Egyptians, Ammonites, Moabites and Elamites. Speaking of the sinful inhabitants of Jerusalem, it is Yahweh who speaks, "And death will seem preferable to life to all the survivors of this wicked race, wherever I have driven them—..." (8:3); "I am going to hand you over to terror, you and all your friends; they shall fall by the sword of their enemies;" (20:4); "I am going to scatter them throughout nations unknown to their ancestors or to them; and I am going to pursue them with the sword until I have exterminated them" (9:15–16); "Cursed be the man who will not listen to the words of this covenant ..." (11:3); "And I will smash them one against the other, father and son together—it is Yahweh who speaks. Mercilessly relentlessly, pitilessly, I will destroy them" (13:14); "Yes, even prophet and priest are godless, I have found their wickedness even in my own House— it is Yahweh who speaks. ... For I will bring disaster down on them when the year comes for me to deal with them—" (23:11–12); "Since you have not listened to my words, ... I will lay the ban on them and make them an object of horror, of scorn, of lasting shame" (25:8–10); "For the sons of Israel and of Judah have done nothing but displease me from their youth up ... this city has been such a cause of anger and of wrath to me that I mean to remove it from my sight, ..." (32:30–32); "I will make you an object of horror to all the kingdoms of the earth" (34:18).

13. Individual true prophets claimed to have received the word of Yahweh; the selection was direct and the claim is based on the message they preached; we do not read about their sons succeeding them—unlike

the priests who held office by virtue of birth. The ancestors of priest were summoned by Yahweh, speaking to Moses "... summon your brother Aaron and his sons to be priests in my service" (Ex. 28:1), and later the Levites, his own tribe, was chosen, "... you have won yourself investiture as priests of Yahweh ..." (Ex. 32:29; Deut. 33:8–11). This preference of Moses' tribe and the selection of Aaron, his brother, as High Priest caused the first resentment among the Israelites since they were forced by divine commandment to support the livelihood of priests, which was perceived as keeping them in idleness. Priests lived off the ritual sacrifices and the more sacrifices the more affluent the priests became, who naturally had a vested interest to introduce such rituals to make themselves indispensable and powerful. To maintain such privileges, the priests left no stone unturned to keep the Israelites under control; they passed laws and ordinances—under the guise of revelation—prohibiting worship of other gods, nursing an attitude of utter contempt for other religions and other nations, forbidding intermarriage with other peoples, regarding other nations as God's enemies, regarding only their land as holy and other lands as defiled and unclean, considered as "pious" hatred of enemies and demanded their merciless destruction and extermination. Further, they taught the children of Israel that they were God's chosen, a kingdom of priests, a consecrated nation, who were the beneficiaries of an eternal Covenant with God, given a "Promised Land" inhabited by many other nations which, by Yahweh's command, were to be exterminated to make room for them, a people apart, admonished to follow strict dietary laws which set them further apart (this may have been the aim), taught them cleanliness to the point of obsession, taught them not to tolerate other people living among them, not to show other people any pity. Finally, they taught them not to tolerate foreign dominion which led them to many futile and reckless uprisings (waiting for a tragedy to happen). Such teaching could not help but permeate the people's nature, pervert their mind and poison their attitudes, all to be reciprocated by other nations which in turn spiraled the whole process. We learn from the prophets that the priests did not obey the voice of Yahweh, forgot the teachings of God, were corrupt, full of lies and greed, unable to teach the Law, caused the people to "stumble", falsified the Law and were the ruin of Israel. Unlike the priests, each prophet earned his reputation by individual effort and merit; therefore, one would think, they would exercise greater influence upon the people. Neither the priest nor the prophet received such attention; according to their writings, the Israelites were continuously straying from the Covenant, displeasing Yahweh and experiencing or threatened with punishment. Were they a stiff-necked people? Was there any time that Yahweh was pleased with them? They did "nothing but displease him from their youth up" and followed the idolatrous path of their ancestors; i.e., the Covenant was continuously ignored by the Israelites from day one. Based on the contradictory statements emanating from the priests and prophets, it is no wonder the people were confused and failed in their obligations: when they followed the priests they offended the prophets and vice-versa; in either case earning the opprobrium of the other. Strict obedience to the Covenant could not succeed; many of its statutes were contrary to human nature and enslaved the people again—this time there was no redeemer. Was Yahweh pleased with David and Solomon? He bestowed upon them riches, success and fame: a sign of approval. But they were idolators, who "whored" after other gods and did not pay attention to the Covenant; the Tanak historian thought them untouchable: "David said to Nathan 'I have sinned against Yahweh' " (2 Sam. 12:13); Nathan said to David, "Why have you shown contempt for Yahweh, doing what displeases him?" (2 Sam. 12:9). Speaking of Solomon, that arch debaucher, oppressor, conniver and murderer, "He did what was displeasing to Yahweh, and was not a wholehearted follower of Yahweh, …" (1 Kings 11:6). When Yahweh rewarded Joshua with military victories in the conquest of the Promised Land? That military conquest is no longer accepted by most biblical scholars—there is no archaeological evidence of it and the story is faulted; instead they speak of gradual infiltration or worse. During the Babylonian Exile? No, there is no record of a single house of worship or any obedience to the Covenant. What of the remnant that stayed behind in Jerusalem? There is no record or biblical account of any compliance with the Covenant. The Covenant was simply ignored as if it did not exist. The royal Houses of Israel and Judah ignored it until King Josiah (640–609 B.C.); a book "discovered" in the Temple by one of his priests was acclaimed as the lost book of Deuteronomy. Josiah was intent upon making his people comply with the Law and instituted radical religious reforms, "He did what is pleasing to Yahweh, …" (2 Kings 22:2); he caused the extirpation of all foreign cults. Without seeking any oracles from Yahweh—nor receiving any through his priests or prophets—he recklessly engaged Pharaoh Necho, King of Egypt, in a battle and was killed at

Meggido (2 Kings 23–29). His successor Jehoahaz (609 B.C.) did what was displeasing to Yahweh, "just as his ancestors had done" (2 Kings 23:32); the reforms were soon forgotten as if they never existed, and so with the rest of the kings until the Babylonian captivity, with the exception of Hezekiah (716–687 B.C.). Hezekiah, who should have benefitted from Isaiah's counsel (although he mostly ignored it),instituted religious reforms; destroyed the places of Baal worship and attempted to make Jerusalem the cult center, an action that must have pleased the priests. The story of his life is a stormy one and does not bespeak of Yahweh's blessings. His son and successor Manasseh (687–642 B.C.) rebuilt the high places that his father destroyed and worshiped "the whole array of heaven" and served it. Thereafter, nothing but idolatry except in the case of Josiah, as related before.

14. One would have expected the leaders of the people, above all the other people, the royal Houses of Israel and Judah—the anointed, rich, living in luxury, literate and surrounded by the prophets and priests—to have absorbed some of the precepts of the Covenant. Of the 19 kings of the House of Israel, from Jeroboam (931–910 B.C.) to Hoshea (732–722 B.C.)—a period of over 200 years—without a single exception, not a single one listened to the voice of Yahweh, "He did what is displeasing to Yahweh," a euphemism for idolatry. Of the 19 kings and one queen of the House of Judah from Rehoboam (931–913 B.C.) to Zedekiah (598–587 B.C.)—a span of about 300 years—the following is the information taken from the historical books of the Tanak: 13 were outright idolaters; included in the 13 is Rehoboam (931–913 B.C.), son of Solomon, "He did what was displeasing to Yahweh" (1 Kings 14:22), built high places, set up pillars and sacred poles, set an example for the other 12. Asa, Jehoshaphat, Amaziah, Uzziah, and Jotham "… did what was right in the eyes of Yahweh …" but the authors of 1 and 2 Kings were mistaken because all 5 of them did not abolish the high places and the people were still offering sacrifice on the high places, i.e., practiced idolatry. This leaves Hezekiah and Josiah as the only two kings who "did what was pleasing to Yahweh," yet fate was unkind to them. If we include Saul, David (to whom Yahweh promised not to withdraw his favor regardless of any evil deeds!) and Solomon, namely, a total of 42 kings (including one queen), only 2 of them went against the current and tried to abolish idolatry. How is this possible?

We are not dealing with semi-literate, poor and mostly exploited people of the land whose going astray, though lamented, is explainable. There are only two possible explanations for the events up to the Babylonian exile:

(a) Either the Covenant was not known or not treated as anything superior to the idolatrous worship and customs of the "heathens"; the Israelites and Jews blended with their neighbors.
(b) Or the Covenant, as such, did not exist and was injected and implanted into the Tanak narrative after the Babylonian Exile.

In either case, it was necessary for Nehemiah, appointed by Artaxerxes, King of Persia, to be governor of Judah, to form another covenant—this time in writing—around 445 B.C., almost 100 years after the return from the Babylonian Exile (537 B.C.) and about 70 years after the dedication of the Second Temple (515 B.C.) The covenant was signed by the leaders of the Jerusalem community (Levites, priests and nobles) and contained the following main pledges:

(a) To observe the Sabbath
(b) To abstain from foreign marriages
(c) To support the worship of the Temple
(d) To contribute to the support of the Levites (priests)
(e) To walk according to the Law of God given through Moses
(f) To observe the practice of all the commandments of Yahweh

Nehemiah used autocratic and forceful methods to effect compliance of the latest covenant. That it was necessary to conclude a new covenant is highly suggestive; that it was necessary to use force for its enforcement, such as attacking the violators publicly, beating them and plucking out their hair speaks loudly in what low esteem the Jews held it. Nehemiah had the power of Artaxerxes behind him and he used it.

What matters, for the purposes of this book, is that after the redaction of the Tanak (from hereon referred to as the Old Testament), the literalists accepted the written word as the revelation of God, absolute truth, and the people's nature, mind and conduct were greatly influenced by its content.

15. Ezra, a priest-scribe "versed in the Law of Moses which had been given by Yahweh, ..." (Ezra 7:6), an officer of the Persian court, sent to Jerusalem by the Persian King Artaxerxes (the date of Ezra's mission and

during the reign of which King Artaxerxes—there were three—is in doubt, probably around 458 B.C.; the exact date is not material) to impose the Law of Moses upon the Jewish community in Jerusalem. He brought with him a written book of the Law which was read to the people. Ezra carried with him an edict from Artaxerxes to be read to the people of Israel, one which demanded obedience to the Law of Moses, "If anyone does not obey the Law of your God—which is the law of the king—let judgment be strictly executed on him: death, banishment, confiscation or imprisonment" (Ezra 7:26). Again, as with Nehemiah, no sweet persuasion was applied. Both Ezra and Nehemiah terrorized the people into submission, applied brute force, threatened them with curses and—would you believe it—exile. It suited Ezra, the priest-scribe, to raise a wall between the Jews and the rest of the world; to prohibit mingling with foreign tribes; to repudiate their foreign wives and their children. We see the first concrete example of racism based on religious teachings and priestly greed, when Ezra held that Jews suffered desecration by mingling with non-Jews; that converts who accepted the Law were not to be treated as equals with born Jews; that they were to live apart and insisting upon the exclusion from the community of all who were not of Jewish ancestry. Those Jews who were dissatisfied with the severity of the new orders had to leave the community. The High Priest Joshua usurped the power of sovereignty and thus combined for a time the title of High Priest and secular sovereign. Enmities were aroused, new sects formed by those who felt rejected, the priesthood became more powerful than before. The Law of Moses began to permeate the life of the Jews and create divisions among them; prescribed strict separation from non-Jews who were considered polluted; incited hatred for non-conformers and implanted seeds of future disasters.

16. Even after the return from Exile, a most propitious moment in the history of the Jews, news was brought to Nehemiah (before he embarked on his first mission to Jerusalem) that people there "... are in great trouble and humiliation" (Neh. 1:3). Nehemiah took this as punishment for the sins of Jews who did not follow the Law (we are back where we were many times before) after their return to Jerusalem. He pleaded with Yahweh on behalf of the sons of Israel, "We have acted very wickedly toward you: we have not kept the commandments, laws, and customs you laid down for Moses your servant" (Neh. 1:7–8). After the return from Exile to

Jerusalem—an event that should have inspired the Jews since it was a ful-fillment of the prophetic dreams and despite its influence or because of it—backsliding from the Covenant occurred again, as it did so many times in the past. Nehemiah set out for Jerusalem, instituted reforms and a new covenant as described in Paragraph 14 above. He returned to Persia in 432 B.C. after serving as governor of Judah for 12 years. No sooner did Nehemiah depart from Jerusalem, the High-Priest Eliashib, objecting to the strict rules imposed by Nehemiah regarding mixed marriages, began to backslide and was joined by Jews of similar leanings. The "Nehemiah exiles" were allowed to return and Nehemiah's strict rules against mixed marriages began to disintegrate. "A corrupt priesthood had established itself, preying on all who could be cajoled and terrified" (5–86). This reads like a dream, that incessant pounding of lamentations and variation on the same theme: The Jews did not keep the Covenant etc. Nehemiah returned to Jerusalem the second time (between 430–424 B.C.) and discovered that the Levites abandoned the Temple because the tithes were not collected for them (The Levites had a right to serve in the sanctuary, they were inferior to the priests, the latter performed sacerdotal functions, the former assisted the priests: the tribe of Levi was the origin of both); he restored the col-lection of tithes and dismissed some of the execrable priests. He pursued his obsession against mixed marriages and demanded again their dissolu-tion: The recusants were sent into exile. The people violated the Sabbath (as if they were totally ignorant of it) and Nehemiah insisted upon strict observance of the Law—as had occurred so many times before. There were violations of the Covenant by the children of Israel up to the Babylonian Exile (587 B.C.) and during the Exile up to 530 B.C. and after the return till Nehemiah's time (between 430–424 B.C.). It is only the succeeding periods that saw the emergence of the influence of scribes—the forerun-ners of the Pharisees—that the written Law, the Torah, gradually gained in prominence among the Jews. The key phrases were: the Torah must be strictly observed; the Jews must remain a separate people; the Jerusalem Temple to be the only cultic center; the priests to be the only administra-tors of the cult; foreign customs and influence to be strictly avoided; com-pliance with the Law the only promise of peace and prosperity; non-compliance a sure road to disaster. In the 5th and 4th centuries B.C. the scribes—learned in the words of the commandments of Yahweh—the High-Priests and priests became the leading forces behind the development of Judaism, despite Jeremiah's indictment that the Law of Yahweh, "… has been falsified by the lying pen of the scribes!: (8:8)

Many modern biblical scholars question whether Ezra, the priest and scribe, the restorer of the cult, the lawgiver and second Moses, was in fact historical. There are no traces of him in the Old Testament after the 5th century B.C. despite his notoriety: in fact they are totally ignorant of him. "… What strikes me … is that Ben Sirach (a Jewish Wisdom writer ca 190 B.C. who in his book mentioned all the prominent heroes of Israel's past) not only ignores Ezra but gives Zerubbabel and Joshua the credit for having restored the cult: that means that the author is ignorant of the law promulgated by Ezra" (36–152). Be that as it may, there was no shortage of "falsifiers." I am concerned only with what influence such writings exercised upon the beliefs and actions of the Jews. Judaism began with Ezra and Nehemiah.

The hope, "held out by the prophets, that Judah might yet become a mighty power, to whom kings and nations would bow, …" (54–361) was false prophecy but was enough to cast suspicion that they plotted for independence from Persia and "… thus caused unfavorable decrees to be issued against them at court" (54–361), with the result that mixed marriages were "in" again and the unfavorable Persian decrees made their lives increasingly more difficult. Despite Deut. 17:15, "you are not to give yourself a foreign king who is no brother of yours," the Jews never revolted against Persia; the priests had not yet attained their riches and power; the Jews were too divided and their numbers few: But they made up for this lapse with a vengeance in the not too distant future.

The Samaritans, half-Jews, who later worshiped Yahweh and adopted the Torah and the Book of Joshua as their sacred writings, offered help in the reconstruction of the Temple. Zerubbabel rejected the offer since he feared pollution of the Jewish race. The Samaritans were the descendants of Israelites who survived the Assyrian deportation and the people from various Assyrian communities who were resettled there. This was the cause of ongoing enmity between Jews and Samaritans; when the latter built their own Temple to Yahweh on Mt. Gerizim—the breach became irreparable. Thus a people settled on approximately 20 square miles of land, needing all the help they could get from their neighbors, particularly from those who wished to adopt the worship of Yahweh—even though they accepted the help of pagan Sidonians and Tyrians—invited the irreparable enmity of the Samaritans when they rejected their help due to the fear of priests that their power would be diluted, as it was in the time of the Jerusalem First Temple and the one in Bethel.

17. When Yahweh led the Israelites to the Promised Land, he issued a commandment forbidding marriage with Hittites, Girgashites, Amorites, Canaanites, Perizzites, Hivites and Jebusites, "seven nations greater and stronger than yourselves" (Deut. 7:1). "You must not marry with them; ..." (Deut. 7:3), for this would turn them away from worshipping Yahweh. Marriages were not forbidden with other tribes and nations. Therefore, both Ezra and Nehemiah went beyond the Law and did not follow Yahweh's commandments respecting foreign marriages. They added to the list of forbidden marriages the Moabites, Egyptians and Ammonites. David's ancestor was a Moabitess; Solomon chose Rehoboam as his successor even though he was the son of his union with an Ammonite woman; Moses commanded the Israelites to spare the lives of young Midianite girls "who have not slept with a man, and take them for yourselves" (Numb. 31:18–19). "From the days of our ancestors until now our guilt has been great; ..." (Ezra 9:7); Ezra bemoaned the Promised Land as unclean because of the "foulness" of foreign wives, the abominations with which the impurities have infected it. He cursed not only the people of Israel but also some of the priests and Levites who were likewise guilty. After the return from Exile, Ezra and Nehemiah perceived mixed marriages as a threat to the religious community; the obsession with mixed marriages was the result of priestly fear of competition from foreign priests and to keep the Jews from backsliding. One cannot help wondering in what low esteem Judaism was held that required such drastic measures as the break-up of long-standing marriages and abandoning of children. Ezra and Nehemiah were probably right in finding mixed marriages the prime cause leading to non-compliance with the Covenant. They were devoted men and desired to lay a sound foundation for a national and religious rebirth. In choosing this path, however, they were fatally ignorant of the forces set in motion, which once started could not be controlled. It was not the separateness and related ordinances which preserved the Jews; it was the reciprocated hatred of other peoples and nations that this separateness evoked which preserved

the Jews as a people despite monumental obstacles. From that time on, it was the priestly inspired hatred of anything "foreign" that progressively affected and perverted the mind of the Jews. The contradiction between seeking secular benefits and fear of violating priestly ordinances invested with divine authority became more pronounced with time and adversely affected the basic human instincts of self-preservation. The priests were the keepers of religious records and could alter them as they saw fit without fear of detection. By then priests opposed contacts with foreign nations; concluding any treaties and alliances with them; forbade mixed marriages; aimed to keep Israel apart and separate from other nations so as not to be "polluted" by them; had no qualms about justifying the extermination of other nations which stood in their way; made a virtue of religious intolerance and denigrating the gods of other nations; taught Israel to show them no pity and usurped the secular power. All the separateness of the Jewish people was the design of the priests to tighten dominion over them; in this they were progressively successful after Ezra and Nehemiah.

18. The Jews were confused by the mixed teachings of prophets and priests; their curses for violating the Covenant competed in harshness and vindictiveness. Their secular leaders, the kings of Israel and Judah—except for two of them—continuously violated the Covenant; it took the Assyrians and Babylonians to remove this scourge and clear the way for Ezra and Nehemiah; it took Roman military power to defeat many bloody Jewish uprisings mostly stirred up by priests or priestly influence in the 1st century B.C. and 1st and 2nd century A.D.; to extirpate Yahweh's commandment from the Jewish psyche: "… you are not to give yourself a foreign king who is no brother of yours" (Deut 17:15); it enabled rabbinical Judaism to take the leadership in preparing the Jewish people for a life outside the Promised Land.

That the Jew held his non-Jewish fellowman and his religion in contempt was not the fault of the Jew, but was the fault of the priestly mind-perverting laws implanted in his nature.

Chapter 10

The Priestly Authors
and the Lost Books

1. The settlement of the 12 Tribes poses a problem. It has always been assumed that the tribes in the north numbered 10; the tribes in the south numbered 2; this is incorrect. The south was settled by Judah and Benjamin. The tribe of Reuben settled on the north-east side of the Dead Sea, but ceased to exist as a distinct tribe; it always remained outside the history of Israel and was absorbed by the tribe of Judah. The tribe of Simeon was completely dispossessed of the land assigned to it and settled under the patronage of Judah in the Negeb, i.e., south of Judah—it was completely absorbed by Judah. The tribe of Levi, destined to be Yahweh's own for the priesthood, was not assigned any land. The Song of Deborah (Judges 5) lists 5 tribes who assisted Deborah and Barak: Zebulun, Issachar, Benjamin, Ephraim and Machir; 5 others are listed as not assisting: Reuben, Dan, Naphtali, Asher and Gilead; this makes a total of 10 tribes. Manasseh, Simeon, Judah and Gad are not mentioned. The census in Numbers 1 lists the tribes of Israel: Reuben, Simeon, Judah, Zebulun, Issachar, Dan, Gad, Asher, Naphtali, Benjamin, Ephraim, Manasseh, a total of 12. After Solomon's death the tribes split as follows: The kingdom of Judah under Rehoboam: Judah, Benjamin, Reuben and Simeon, all merging in the tribe of Judah; The kingdom of Israel under Jeroboam: Ephraim, Gad, Manasseh, Issachar, Asher, Naphtali, Zebulun and Dan, a total of 8 tribes. So much for the myth of the 10 lost tribes after dispersal by the Assyrians. At the peak of Solomon's building activity (Temple and palace) he introduced forced-labor throughout Israel, exempting Judah; he also introduced heavy taxation to pay for the projects from which Judah was also partially exempt. This was bound to cause great discontent particularly among the tribes who did not directly benefit from their efforts: Judah was the main beneficiary. Why did Solomon, with all his vaunted wisdom,

prefer the tribe of Judah (Yahuds) to the detriment of the northern tribes who were treated as slaves? And why did his son Rehoboam, when asked by the northern tribes to "lighten your father's harsh tyranny," respond that he would "make it heavier still"? "My father beat you with whips; I am going to beat you with loaded scourges" (2 Chronicles 10:11). This is not a dialogue with a free people but with slaves. Was the king or his advisors versed in the Law of Moses? The Yahuds treated the northern tribes as if they were any other subjugated people; in vain does one look for evidence of fraternity; instead one finds reckless hostility. Upon his return to Jerusalem, Rehoboam mustered the whole House of Judah and the tribe of Benjamin, 180,000 picked warriors to fight the House of Israel and regain the northern kingdom. He was dissuaded from this enterprise by the prophet Shemaiah, who received the word of Yahweh, "Do not go to fight against your brothers; … for what happened is my doing" (1 Kings 12:24). One must marvel at the audacity of the author who attributed to Yahweh the second half of the quoted sentence; such utter blasphemy. This was a direct command by Yahweh to desist from fraternal wars; it was soon forgotten and ignored—no priestly laws were violated; war between them raged almost continuously. We are not told of the casualties.

2. The battles between the two kingdoms (under later kings) reached such ferocity as to boggle the mind. Rehoboam's successor Abijah (913–911 B.C.) fielded 400,000 picked men against Jeroboam's 800,000 picked men. He inflicted a crushing defeat on Jeroboam and killed in the process 500,000 of his men in the battle (2 Chronicles 13:13 ff). Asa, King of Judah (911–870 B.C.) and Baasha, King of Israel (909–889 B.C.) "were at war with each other as long as they lived" (1 Kings 15:16–17). No casualties were listed but they must be considerable since they waged war for about 25 years. Joash, King of Israel (798–783 B.C.) battled Amaziah, King of Judah (796–781 B.C.), defeated him, razed to the ground the walls of Jerusalem, sacked the Temple and took hostages. Ahaz, King of Judah (736–716 B.C.), took the field against Pekah, King of Israel (732–732 B.C.), was thoroughly defeated, suffered 120,000 killed, "all stout fighting men" and the Old Testament narrates "this was because they deserted Yahweh" (2 Chronicles 28:6–7); the Israelite took 200,000 men captive, with their women and children, quantities of booty and carried everything off to Samaria. Judah and Israel were bled white and so weakened by their

senseless fratricidal wars as to become easy prey to hostile neighbors. To understand the magnitude of these losses in manpower one has only to realize that during the Babylonian Exile, a total of between 10,000–20,000 Yahuds were marched off into exile. How did the "chosen" differ from other peoples? In their foolish rush to kill each other and steal the other's treasures, women and children, did they pay any attention to the Laws of Moses? or do we see the machinations of the Jerusalem Temple priests who resented the newly established sanctuaries at Bethel and Dan and employment of priests not of Aaronite descent? One can detect a similar detachment in the author's hand when narrating the commanded bellicosity and wars of extermination in other parts of the Old Testament. In the conquest of the land of King Heshbon, the Amorite, whom Yahweh delivered over to the Israelites, "Then we captured all its cities, and laid whole towns under ban, men, women, children; we spared nothing. but the livestock which we took as our spoil, as also the plunder from the towns we captured" (Deut. 2:33–36). Speaking of the conquest of Jericho: "They enforced the ban on everything in the town: men, women, young and old, even the oxen and sheep and donkeys, massacring them all" (Josh. 6:21). "When Israel had finished killing all the inhabitants of Ai ... all Israel returned to Ai and slaughtered all its people" (Josh. 8:23 ff); "... Joshua took Makkedah ... He delivered them over to the ban ... and let no one escape; ..." (Josh. 10:28); Joshua took Libnah, "... struck every living creature with the edge of the sword, and left none alive, ..." (Josh. 10:30); Joshua took Lachish and put every living creature to the sword "... until not one was left alive" (Josh. 10:33). Joshua took Eglon and every living creature was put to the sword (Josh. 10:35); Joshua took Hebron "... he left not a man alive" (Josh. 10:37), and killed every living creature in it. Joshua took Debir, "He left none alive" (Josh. 10:39). Why did all these cities battle the Israelites rather than surrender peacefully? Even with the limited system of communication in those days, the word must have reached some cities. The Book of Joshua answers the question: "For Yahweh had ordained that the hearts of these men should be stubborn enough to fight against Israel, so that they might be mercilessly delivered over to the ban and be wiped out, as Yahweh had ordered Moses" (Josh. 11:20). These murders and massacres all in the name and at the command of Yahweh go on ad nauseam. People were massacred for defending their homes; their misfortune was living on the land given by Yahweh to the Israelites. If all this is history! But the effects were there; the reader believed it and acted on that knowledge. Yahweh, of course, could never have uttered such words. The priestly authors, who excelled in cruelty and intolerance, polluted the Old Testament with such vicious abominations written centuries after the alleged facts, accommodated that purpose in depicting a cruel, pitiless, vengeful and war-like Yahweh, who aided the Israelites in their battles as long as they followed his commands, but would turn on them with the same swiftness and ferocity if they departed from the straight path. The priestly writers instilled a numbing mind-perverting attitude toward such brutalities that the end justified the means. This acclimated, unbending and uncompromising zealotry of the Jews would later on place them on a collision course with their neighbors. And so the horror goes on.

3. David committed a grave sin for taking a census; Yahweh, through David's prophet Gad, gave David three choices to propitiate Yahweh's anger. David chose three days of pestilence in the country. So "Yahweh sent a pestilence on Israel ... and the plague ravaged the people, and from Dan to Beersheba 70,000 men ... died" (2 Sam. 24:15). All this for one man taking a census. David desired to marry Saul's daughter Michal. As a settlement from David—who was poor—and possibly to set him up to get killed, Saul demanded a hundred foreskins of the Philistines. David took up the challenge "... and killed two hundred Philistines ... brought back their foreskins and counted them out before the king ... Saul then gave him his daughter Michal in marriage. Saul now realized that Yahweh was with David, ..." (1 Sam. 18:27–28).

Samuel, who anointed Saul king over Israel, related to him Yahweh's command to strike down Amalek (the Amalekites were always at war with Israel), "... put him under the ban with all that he possesses. Do not spare him, but kill man and woman, babe and suckling, ox and sheep, camel and donkey" (1 Sam. 15:3). Saul defeated the Amalekites, took their King Agag alive and put the rest to the sword. Saul also spared the best of the sheep and cattle ... "and all that was good"(1 Sam.15:9). This disobedience started the downfall of King Saul, for he was on that account rejected by Yahweh. "The word of Yahweh came to Samuel, 'I regret having made Saul king ...'" (1 Sam. 15:10).

"When Yahweh your God has annihilated the nations whose land

Yahweh your God gives you, and you have dispossessed them and you live in their towns and in their houses, ..." (Deut. 19:1–2). The inhabitants of Canaan were slaughtered by orders of Yahweh. These orders were to permeate the attitudes of the Israelites.

A prophet at the request of Elisha anointed Jehu King of Israel (844–814 B.C.) at the command of Yahweh. Jehu was further commanded, to strike down the family of Ahab; he managed to kill Jehoram, King of Israel, (852–841 B.C.) and Ahaziah, King of Judah (841 B.C.), Jezebel the widow of Ahab, seventy sons of Ahab, everyone who was of the House of Ahab surviving in Jezreel, all his leading men, his close friends, his priests—he did not leave a single one alive, 42 brothers of Ahaziah—the murdered King of Judah; he killed all the survivors of Ahab's family in Samaria, as Yahweh told Elijah it would happen. "Thus Jehu rid Israel of Baal" (2 Kings 10:28). After all these regicides—anointed kings of Judah and Israel—murders and massacres directed against the worship of Baal and at the command of Yahweh, Jehu still did not follow the Law of Yahweh faithfully in that he maintained the golden calves in the temples of Bethel and Dan, nevertheless, Yahweh said to Jehu, "Since you have done properly what was pleasing in my sight ... your sons shall sit on the throne of Israel down to the fourth generation" (2 Kings 10:30–31). Amaziah, King of Judah (796–781 B.C.), sent word to Joash, King of Israel (798–783 B.C.), both anointed kings, "Come, make a trial of strength" (2 Kings 14:9). Joash defeated Amaziah, took him prisoner, demolished the city walls of Jerusalem, emptied the Temple of all its gold, silver and furnishings and took hostages (2 Kings 14:8 ff). We do not know how many lives were wasted in this action of two lunatics since no casualties were cited.

A Levite and his attendants stayed as guests of a resident of Gibeah in the territory of Benjamin. Some scoundrels of the town forced themselves upon the guest's concubine and raped her to death. This outrage was communicated to the Israelites, who assembled 400,000 foot-soldiers to punish Gibeah for the infamy. They did more than that. In the battle that ensued, after consulting Yahweh on two occasions, the Israelites lost over 40,000 fighting men almost wiping out the whole fraternal tribe of Benjamin who lost in excess of 50,000 fighting men and putting the whole population of Gibeah to the sword—men, women and children. All because the Benjaminites, despite the demand to do so, refused to hand over to the Israelites for punishment the guilty scoundrels (Judges 19:ff, 20:ff).

4. The reader must be numb by now by all these distressing events. The Joshua exploits could be understood within the confines of the customs of the times, which were barbaric; self-preservation was at stake no matter the means. In the conquest of Canaan, 31 local kings and over 1 million native people were exterminated in the process: The Hittites, Amorites, Perizzites, Hivites, Jebusites, etc.; but some 700 years later, upon return from Babylonian Exile we still find in Canaan the Hittites, Amorites Perizzites, Jebusites. Despite detailed and vivid descriptions of Joshua's successful exploits in the conquest of Canaan as described in the Book of Joshua, and despite "ancient Egyptian and Chaldean inscriptions, parts of the works of ancient Egyptian and Persian writers on tablets of clay or papyrus, the monuments of kings, and finally the works of the scribes who wrote the story of earlier traditions ... it is a remarkable fact that, except in the Bible, not one hint or suggestion has anywhere been discovered of an Israelite invasion of Canaan, ..." (29–103).

I have intentionally dealt with some of the vicious episodes which were of no redeeming value despite detailed descriptions; but one must not be weak-hearted about these episodes. The priestly authors, who could have excluded from the text anything they chose to, had a definite purpose in including them. They stood as related for their truth could not be challenged and the reader of the Scripture, however morally inclined, was assured that these deeds carried the divine imprimatur; that Yahweh's punishment of the violators was swift, relentless and final; that terrorizing the minds of the people was the surest way to dominate them; and that in the fulfillment of Yahweh's promise, his actions were "just" no matter what the method. The effect of such actions and the effect of the written word could not but permeate the attitude of the Israelites and their descendants toward their neighbors for countless generations to come. The priestly authors, whenever faced with doubts about the thread that bound the narrative or historical version, could always take refuge by referring to a book that was lost, despite the alleged claim of handing down the oral law over countless generations without additions or deletions. We have incomplete histories of the Kings of Judah and Israel, the priestly authors picked and chose what to reveal or not even though they had knowledge of the whole story, such as: "The rest of the history of Jehoram, his entire career, is not all this recorded in the Book of the Annals of the Kings of Judah? Then Jehoram slept with his ancestors ..." (2 Kings 8:23–24). We are never told what is in the Annals; this is repeated in the case of almost all the Kings of Judah and Israel. So with other narratives which refer to books now lost to history: "The Book of the Wars of Yahweh" (Numb. 21:14); "The Book of the Just" (Josh 10:13); "The Book of the Law of God" written by Joshua (Josh. 24:26); "Book of the Annals of the Kings of Judah" (1 Kings 14:30); "Book of the Annals of the Kings of Israel" (1 Kings 15:32); "Book of the Acts of Solomon" (1 Kings 11:42); "The Book of the Covenant" written by Moses (Ex. 24:7); "The Book of the Law" from which Ezra read to the people assembled in Jerusalem—most likely written by Ezra (Neh. 8:8); "The Book of the Law" (different from the one which Ezra read to the people) found by the High-Priest Hilkiah in the Temple during the reign of King Josiah (640–609 B.C.). All these nine books named in the Old Testament, were shrouded in a cloud of mystery, the contents never revealed and the books lost to history.

Chapter 11

Lack of Evidence

1. We know hardly anything about Hebrew history from independent sources other than what is in the Old Testament, which would corroborate the source of the biblical events. "The empire of David and Solomon, the powerful northern kingdom, the long-lived southern kingdom with its Davidic dynasty have left not a single document relating to their existence; not one of the forty kings ... has left a direct trace of his name; we do not even have any votive inscription from the famous Temple of Solomon, as we do for all other temples of antiquity" (36–17). We do have the stele of the Moabite King Mesha from the 9th century B.C., which speaks of the Israelites and says that Moab was oppressed by Israel for 40 years in the time of Israel's King Omri (885–874 B.C.) and one of his sons who is not named. The other nonbiblical reference is the Merneptah Stele, erected by the Egyptian Pharaoh Mernepthah (ca 1224–1211 B.C.) as a victory monument whose inscription relates a won battle in Canaan, in which "... Israel is laid waste. ..." This is the first mention by any nonbiblical source of Israel; it does not help the story of Joshua's conquest of Canaan. In the El-Amarna Letters (over 350 such letters were discovered in 1887 in the ruins of Akhetaton in Egypt) contained the correspondence from the chancery of Amenophis III (1413–1377 B.C.) and Amenophis IV (1380–1362 B.C.) to and from foreign rulers, among them the petty kingdoms of Canaan, which bear quite different names of the kings who ruled the cities of Jerusalem, Gezer and Lachish from those listed in the Book of Joshua. There is no mention of the Hebrews or Israelites; the Hittites and Amurru (Amorites) are mentioned. The Phoenicians, Arameans, Moabites, Phillistines and Ammonites have left inscriptions; the Hebrews and Israelites left none. This is all the more astounding since there were no major cultural or ideological differences between these peoples.

2. The Israelites were mentioned by the Assyrians and Babylonians after they conquered them. "... the Israelites did not make much of an impression on those who knew them ... Hebrew inscriptions are attested only between the eighth century and the first decades of the sixth century B.C. ... in a very limited area of Palestine ... (the) boundaries contrast with the Old Testament narrative, but confirm the decidedly secondary role the extra-Hebraic evidence assigns to the Israelites" (36–19). The situation did not improve after the Babylonian Exile, "... After the exile there is not a single extra-Jewish source which speaks of the Jews before the times of Alexander the Great; ..." (36–19). Is there any explanation for such lack of epigraphic (inscriptions on buildings or similar) evidence? Were the Jews that unimportant? Was their reputation and influence not worth mentioning? Or were the priestly redactors intent upon selectively eliminating any historical references which would conflict with their biblical narratives? Did they create history so as to give meaning and cohesion to the biblical episodes and personalities? The historiographers of those days (6th and 5th centuries) had little fear of detection, particularly if divine authority was invoked to add credibility to their narrative. Jewish historiographers were not busy either and the period from about 430 B.C. to 330 B.C. must have been uneventful and not worth writing about; or the Jews were content under the Persian rule and nothing of much importance occurred. The historical evidence of Moses, Joseph, Joshua, David and Solomon, the latter with all his reputation as the wisest among the wise, was not corroborated by outside sources. Solomon's reputed wealth and splendor of his Temple failed to make any impression outside the Old Testament. How many writings were lost, how many of the books referred to in the Old Testament and mentioned in the previous chapter owe their disappearance to the priestly authors and redactors because they did not fit their scheme of things? What about the Mosaic Laws and monotheism? "If we accept Josiah's reformation as a fact, it must follow that there was nothing but idolatry in Canaan as far back as history can go and that nothing was known about Moses, nor about any code of laws he had given to the forefathers ... But as far as the King of Judah was concerned, he only heard of Moses and his laws for the first time from Hilkiah's book"(29–13). What about the Exodus? There is not one clue by Egyptian historians abut the Exodus of the Hebrews. Considering that the Egyptian population at that time numbered 5–6 million and the Hebrews about 2½ million (600,000 men of military age, plus

women, children and elderly), such an absence of documentation by Egyptian historians is incredible. What about the Decalogue? There are three different versions in the Old Testament: Ex. 20:1–17, Ex. 34:14–16, Deut. 5:6–21; which is the right version? What about Mt. Sinai, the dwelling of Yahweh? The prophets Amos, Hosea, Zechariah, Micah and Habbakuk knew nothing of God dwelling on Mt. Sinai; they thought of God dwelling on Mt. Zion. What about the conquest of Canaan? There is not one nonbiblical source that made any reference to this monumental event. The Egyptian Pharaohs during Exodus? The Old Testament named not a single one; even Yahweh referred to the King of Egypt as "Pharaoh" and did not identify him by another name, "But I shall win glory for myself at the expense of Pharaoh and all his army, and the Egyptians will learn that I am Yahweh" (Ex. 14:4). Yet it names two lowly Hebrew midwives: Shiphrah and Puah. The reason is obvious: the Egyptians were notoriously accurate keepers of annals of the Pharaohs, etc, and any mention of a specific name would identify the date the events occurred—precisely what the priestly writers wanted to avoid. Yet Yahweh frequently referred to various other non-Egyptian kings by name, as in dealing with King Og of Bashan, Yahweh advised Moses, "Deal with him as you dealt with Sihon, King of the Amonites" (Numb. 21:34–35). What about the cosmology of the priestly authors? They knew nothing about the earth orbiting the sun, that the earth was round and of the immensity of the galaxies.

3. During the Exodus when the Israelites saw the miracle of Yahweh returning the waters, drowning the pursuing Egyptians and rescuing the Israelites from Egyptian grasp, "… the people venerated Yahweh; they put their faith in Yahweh and in Moses his servant" (Ex. 14:31). Later on, Moses sent out scouts to report back the conditions in Canaan and some of them reported that "Every man we saw there was of enormous size" (Numb. 13:32). On hearing this, the whole community said that they, their wives and children would all fall by the sword, "Should we not do better to go back to Egypt?" (Numb. 14:3–4). Moses warned them not to rebel against Yahweh; we soon hear Yahweh speaking to Moses; "How long will this people insult me? … I will strike them with pestilence and disown them" (Numb. 14:11–12). From that time on, the Israelites were violating Yahweh's commandments, ordinances, worshipping the idols of neighbors and sacrificing to them. They forgot the miracles Yahweh performed for

them in the past and for their violations they were regularly punished. For some 700 years till the Babylonian Exile, with some short-lived exceptions under Hezekiah and Josiah, monotheism did not exist. Until the discovery by Hilkiah of a book in the Temple of idolaters, nothing was known of Moses or his laws, Judaism as a religion or monotheism was yet unknown. It rested on the shoulders of Ezra, or someone like him who remains unnamed to this day (the historicity of Ezra is seriously in doubt),to introduce the Torah to the Jews of Jerusalem upon their return from Exile. It was only after the return from Exile that the priests acquired real power and established a priestly hierarchy. Great effort was exerted by the priestly authors to camouflage the historical setting of the Exodus. Why was it necessary? Was it that difficult to assign a time slot to these events? If the Exodus did not take place as described in the Torah, the Sinai episode would lose its foundation. God appeared on Mt. Sinai on a momentous occasion, yet Mt. Sinai cannot be located. There is not the slightest description of the locale to help place the mountain. If it was the mountain of God where he dwells, a holy mountain, would not a single believer in antiquity make a journey to visit that sacred place? The Conquest has no historical source of reference. The Conquest is narrated totally within the context of the Bible; it has no other source and in vain do we search archaeological sources consistent with time and geography of the terrain. Monotheism did not exist until Ezra (or someone in his stead) returned from Exile and brought the Torah with him. The Yahuds were deported into captivity by the Babylonians; when they returned Ezra called them "Israelites."

4. Before the Israelites conquered the land of Canaan, each town or city worshiped its own god or gods who was/were worshiped in that particular locality. When a worshipper crossed over to another city, he worshiped the deity of that other city. There was no detriment in worshipping another deity and later returning to the former. The deities were not jealous, were tolerant of each other and did not punish apostates: there were thousands of gods, some more and some less important and crossing over from one to another was not viewed with trepidation; polytheism, by its nature, did not generate any wars or massacres of whole peoples.

The first commandment addressed to the Israelites assembled at Mt. Sinai read: "You shall have no gods except me" (Ex. 20:3). The Israelites were required to worship only Yahweh, who brought them out of the land of Egypt; the non-Israelites were not so commanded. Further, the Israelites were prohibited from making a carved image or any likeness of anything in heaven or on earth, water or under earth and serve these images or bow to them. "For I, Yahweh your God, am a jealous God and I punish ... those who hate me; but show kindness to ... those who love me and keep my commandments (Ex. 20:5–6). A number of conclusions can be drawn from Exodus chapters 19 and 20:

(a) Yahweh is speaking only to those whom he brought out of Egypt, out of the house of slavery. If, as stated in Paragraph 1 of this chapter, some children of Israel were defeated in Canaan by Pharaoh Mernepthah in the late 13th century B.C. and had to be well settled to merit royal mention, not all Israelites were slaves in Egypt and not all Israelites were liberated by Yahweh. Further, in Ex. 12:38 we read that during the departure from Egypt, the sons of Israel were joined by non-Hebrews, "People of various sorts joined them in great numbers; " who may not have been liberated from slavery.

(b) Yahweh requires the Israelites to worship him, but does not identify himself except as their God who brought them out of the land of Egypt.

(c) The Israelites remember God as fire, a dense cloud, a pillar of fire; that he dwelt on Mt. Sinai and talked with Moses or otherwise communicated with him with peals of thunder; that Yahweh could ascend and descend from the mountain in the form of a fire, and that when he did so the mountain shook violently. Thunder and lightning flashes were also a sign of Yahweh's presence.

(d) The Israelites were forbidden from making any carved, i.e., hand-made image of anything that would be visible to the senses, serve and bow to them. It follows that this prohibition did not apply to nature-made or God-made images which man could serve and bow to. Nature-made images are Yahweh's creation and he could not be jealous of his own creations, such as trees, mountains, rivers, lakes, clouds, pillars of fire; see Leviticus 9:24 "at this sight the people shouted for joy and fell on their faces," i.e., prostrated themselves.

(e) The use of the plural "gods" in "You shall have no gods except me" implies the existence of other gods, i.e., it did not exclude the existence of other gods, nor did it imply a lower status of the other gods, nor did it imply that non-Israelites could not worship such other gods.

(f)   Yahweh speaking to Moses, "… because on the third day Yahweh will descend on the mountain of Sinai in the sight of all the people" (Ex. 19:11–12). It follows that all the people assembled at Mt. Sinai witnessed the "sight" of Yahweh.

(g)   Israelites worshipping a god other than Yahweh is identified as "hate" of Yahweh, i.e., rewarded with punishment. This is placed in the man/woman relationship; if a man is "jealous" of his wife he "hates" her by natural instinct. Similarly, "… I show kindness to thousands of those who love me and keep my commandments" (Ex. 20:6). Worshipping Yahweh only is to love him and Yahweh will show kindness to those who love him; just like a man would show kindness to a woman who loved him, and this by natural instinct. This is the sum-total of the theological doctrine regarding the essence of Yahweh as outlined in the Decalogue. In vain does one search for any evidence of "Monotheism," which is defined as the belief in the existence of one God only and exclusive worship of this one God. But here the existence of other deities is not denied; what is affirmed here is simple "henotheism" or "monolatry" (the worship of one god when other gods are recognized as existing). No real definitions are offered, no attributes of omniscience, omnipresence or omnipotence are submitted, except that Yahweh is a jealous God, who punishes and shows kindness. It is not specified how he is to be worshiped until we get to the altar of earth that is to be made for Yahweh and sacrifice on this the holocausts and communion sacrifices, i.e., until we get to the priests and the description of every facet of their ritual functions. But this is not monotheism. It is uninspiring to read with what intellectual awkwardness the priestly authors tackle primitive theology and with what alacrity and fluency they move in the ritual field. At the time when the Greeks were setting thoughts on fire, when Socrates, Pythagoras, Empedocles and Parmenides were soaring high above with compelling ideas, the priestly authors and redactors in the 6th and 5th centuries B.C.—probably totally ignorant of the above cited Greeks or for that matter of any Greeks—talked about God on the level of jealousy, the tabernacle furnishings, fabrics, the altar of holocaust, priestly vestments, the ephod, robe, diadem, clothing and anointing, sacred meals and the altar of incense.

5. God said to Moses, "I am Yahweh. To Abraham and Isaac and Jacob I appeared as El Shaddai; I did not make myself known to them by my name Yahweh" (Ex. 6:2–4). But the priestly authors were mistaken, for in Gen. 15:2 we read: "My Lord Yahweh, Abram replied ..." (Abraham was formerly known as Abram) and in Gen. 28:13 we read that when Jacob had a dream about a ladder reaching to heaven, Yahweh spoke to Jacob saying, "I am Yahweh, the God of Abraham your father, and the God of Isaac." The God of the fathers was known by another name, El Shaddai, and Israel's ancestry had worshiped other gods, as is evident from Joshua 24:14: "So now, fear Yahweh ... ; put away the gods that your ancestors served beyond the River and in Egypt, ..."

6. At Mt. Sinai, three months after the Exodus from Egypt, Yahweh through Moses concluded the Covenant with the children of Israel, issued his commandments, statutes and laws which they pledged to observe, "We will observe all the commands that Yahweh has decreed" (Ex. 24:3). Notwithstanding the preceding pledge and many generations earlier, Yahweh spoke to Isaac that he would fulfill the oath he swore to Abraham, that he would make his descendants as many as the stars of heaven, "... in return for Abraham's obedience; for he kept my charge, my commandments, my statutes and my laws" (Gen. 26:5–6). The latter obviously could have no reference to the commandments, statutes and laws given the Israelites at Mt. Sinai. What was Abraham's obedience? We know that he was willing to sacrifice his own son as commanded by Yahweh and Yahweh made promises to him saying, "You have not refused me your son, your only son" (Gen. 22:12–13). Which of Yahweh's commandments, statutes and laws did Abraham keep? We do not have the slightest clue. We do now know from the Old Testament that such rites existed. Therefore, since it was Yahweh's statement, instructions though unknown to us in fact existed, affected Abraham and other people, merited Yahweh's praise and were totally unknown or ignored by the priestly writers/authors. There was another theology and we were kept in ignorance. A little light is shed in the Melchizedek episode. Melchizedek was a King of Salem (the later Jerusalem) and also a priest of God Most High. After Abraham (then known as Abram) came back from a military victory, Melchizedek came to meet him, bring bread and wine (we have here some form of priestly function performed by Melchizedek) and pronounced this blessing: "Blessed be

Abram by God Most High, creator of heaven and earth, and blessed be God Most High for handing over your enemies to you" (Gen. 14:20). To complete the ritual, "And Abram gave him a tithe of everything" (Gen. 14:20). We know nothing about these rites, the priest of the God Most High, nor any rules about tithes before Sinai. Again, it must be said, there was another theology utilizing priestly blessings, offering bread and wine and acceptance of tithes by the priests from the believers. These rites were pleasing to Yahweh for in the next chapter he tells Abram "your reward will be very great" (Gen. 15:1). There was another theology and we were kept in ignorance either by the priestly authors' design or omission.

7. "Among some Bronze Age (3000 B.C.) ruins found in Canaan in 1931 were pieces of pottery bearing the name of a Canaanite deity, YAH or YAHU" (4–310). When Moses and the sons of Israel sang a song in honor of Yahweh, one of the verses read, "YAH is my strength, my song, he is my salvation" (Ex. 15:2). When Moses inquired of God what he should tell the Hebrews in Egypt what God's name was, he received the response: "And God said to Moses, 'I AM WHO I AM' " (Ex. 3:14). The priestly writers who authored this definition of God's name had source material to draw from. "All the temples of Egypt had carved on their walls the words 'NUK PU NUK' (I AM WHAT I AM)" (20–156), and this many centuries before the time of Moses.

When Moses was receiving the Commandments from Yahweh on Mt. Sinai, and was absent from the Israelites for some time, they grew restless, cast an effigy of a golden calf and worshiped it: "Here is your God, Israel … who brought you out of the land of Egypt!" (Ex. 32:4–5) As a result of this transgression, Moses caused the massacre of 3000 of the calf worshippers at the command of Yahweh (Ex. 32:27); this is the first account in the Old Testament of the theme of religious intolerance which was to pervade the religious history of Israel. Ancient society knew very little of religious intolerance; polytheistic nations tolerated religious diversity and although polytheism was part of the Israelite religion prior to the Exile—there was no trace of monotheism—it was the priestly authors, these power-seeking priests, who for reasons of contrast invented a biblical history, which continuously blamed the conduct of the Jews for the punishment and disasters inflicted upon them by a "jealous" Yahweh for their "whoring" after other gods. Monotheism—in its more assertive form—bred intolerance and persecution, caused hatred of aliens, of non-believers and non-conformists. Monotheism—as defined in a prior chapter—means the belief in the existence of only one God and his exclusive worship; there are no other gods and there never were other gods. People worshipping other gods were worshipping false gods or mythical gods, or non-existent gods. The Second Isaiah, in one of his highly inspired moments, climbed the peak of rare thought and vision, stamped his definition of monotheism first and last, "I am Yahweh, unrivaled; there is no other God beside me, ... apart from me all is nothing." (Isaiah 45:5–6). Or Maimonides who spoke of the first cause, "He who brought all things into being ..." Or King Amenhotep IV (1380–1362 B.C.) of Egypt "who gave orders that the names of all gods but Aton should be erased; forbade artists to make images of Aton on the ground that the true god has no form" (4–205). He was far ahead of his time and his thoughts came into conflict with those of the wealthy and turf-protective Egyptian priesthood, who plotted against him as any other rapacious priesthood would if their livelihood and comforts were threatened, finally succeeded in snuffing out this true monotheistic spirit.

A few quotations from the Old Testament will suffice to illustrate that, at best, prior to Exile, the Israelites practiced polytheism, henotheism or monolatry and not monotheism: "You should bow down to no other gods, for Yahweh's name is a Jealous One; he is a jealous God" (Ex. 34:14–15). Jethro, a priest of Midian, father-in-law of Moses, heard of all that Yahweh had done for Israel, "Now I know that Yahweh is greater than all the gods ..." (Ex. 18:11); Moses and the sons of Israel sang a song in honor of Yahweh, "Who among the gods is your like, Yahweh?" (Ex. 15:11); "What god can compare with you: ..." (Micah 7:18); "... since they have abandoned me to offer incense to other gods ..." (Jer. 1:16); "For you have as many gods as you have towns, Judah, as many altars for Baal as Jerusalem has streets" (Jer. 2:28); "And I shall make an end—it is Yahweh who speaks—of any man in Moab who offers sacrifice and incense to his god on the high places" (Jer. 48:35). "The children collect the wood, the fathers light the fire, the women knead the dough, to make cakes for the Queen of Heaven; and, to spite me, they pour libations to alien gods ...—it is Yahweh who speaks—..." (Jer. 7:18–19).

"Yahweh had made a covenant with them and had given them this command: You are not to worship alien gods, ... and do not venerate alien gods.

Venerate Yahweh alone, your God, ... But they would not listen, and still followed their old rites" (2 Kings 17:35 ff).

"if you desert Yahweh to follow alien gods ... Then cast away the alien gods among you and give your hearts to Yahweh the God of Israel!" (Joshua 24:20 ff).

YAH or YAHU was the name of a Canaanite deity appropriated by the Hebrews as Yahweh; the interpretation of Yahweh's name "I AM WHO I AM" was appropriated from the Egyptians. Moses, at the behest of Yahweh, was the first to organize a massacre of religious non-conformists. The priestly doctrines corrupted the mind of Israel; the Covenant was responsible and laid the foundation for religious intolerance and persecution, which survives till today. The Israelites did not practice monotheism—except for the Second Isaiah they were unable to define the term—but polytheism and idolatry, and at the best henotheism and monolatry, which blended with the beliefs and practices of their neighbors. It was only the Second Isaiah who defined true monotheism, but it was not practiced till long after the return from Exile. That the true God had no image or form and therefore could not be represented by carved images, Moses learned from the Egyptian King Amenhotep IV (who described god Aton). The king rebelled against the practices and power of Egyptian priests, their concubines, their wealth, their corrupt and mercenary practices (so diligently absorbed by the Israelite priesthood) and dared to refer to their religion and animal sacrifices as crude idolatry. He declared that Aton symbolized peace and belonged to all nations, a most far-reaching advance. If only such a revolutionary had graced the horizon of the Israelites, what impact his thoughts would have exercised upon the religious obscurantism of the Mosaic priesthood; what influence he would have had upon the development of religious thought and on the history of the Israelites and the Jewish people. But the Israelites had no such revolutionary. When, now and then, during the period of ferment (200 B.C.–66 A.D.) a capable Jewish grass-roots leader appeared, the priestly establishment-turned-diplomat knew how to balance the scale and neutralize the effort by forming military accommodations in turn with the Ptolemies, Seleucids and Romans by means of a universal tool: the power of gold. None dared challenge the established priesthood; none but some lonely prophets challenged the priestly corruption and privilege—but they had no power to alter events or have a lasting effect. Priestly corruption, power-struggles and bad leadership shaped Israelite, Jewish religion and history, which mercifully ceased after the destruction of Jerusalem by Titus and the defeat of the Bar Kokhba revolt. It was priestly and rabbinic connivance which hatched, among others, the fatal and frivolous 66 A.D. uprising against Rome and the incendiary Bar Kokhba revolt in 132 A.D. The flames of mundane messianic aspirations, that cancer of Jewish rabbinic thinking, were extinguished by the flood of blood of the fallen in the Bar Kokhba rebellion. The priests who planted the tree of the "jealous" God, the exclusive covenant and Chosen People, a people superior, preferred and exclusive, which survived the destruction of the Temple and priesthood, the fruits of that tree have plagued the Jewish people for the past 2000 years.

Chapter 12

Anthropomorphism

1. Anthropomorphism in religion is the attribution of human traits to God; it is impossible for man to conceive of God except through human attributes. For an invisible, infinite, omnipresent deity cannot be defined in human language which uses finite terms; such a deity is indescribable, i.e., cannot be described in human language; his nature is not comprehensible whether the deity is transcendent or immanent. We must retreat into silence.

Man is not capable of worshipping a deity devoid of all human faculties. In later Judaism, anthropomorphisms were minimized in favor of allegorical and metaphorical interpretations. Mosaic Law prohibited any images of Yahweh (though only "carved" images were prohibited), however, Yahweh is described throughout in terms of human qualities; the God of the Old Testament must be read in human terms because it is a book written by men for men about God. The gods of ancient religions, whether idolatrous, polytheistic or henotheistic, were described in human terms, possessing human qualities, mostly war-like attributes of power bringing victory over neighboring hostile tribes or nations. This was common to all ancient cultures; there was nothing "civilizing" about reducing anthropomorphic attributes to gods; intellectual progress and ethical standards did not suffer because gods were described as full of anger, revenge, love and compassion.

No circumlocution or sophistry was necessary to explain away the common traits of gods and man, because it was instinctively known that man depicts himself in his gods. When the Jews desired to raise Judaism to the position of primacy among all the religions; when the claim was asserted that it was the first monotheistic religion and the first one which believed in an invisible God, superior and more theological; when anthropomorphic representations of God were looked upon as inferior—because common to all religions—than pure spiritual faith, it was then that the rabbis and other sages realized they faced a problem: The Torah—to which by the command of Yahweh nothing could be added or deleted—contained massive anthropomorphic attributes of Yahweh. If the Jewish God is invisible (and the religion therefore more monotheistic than if he were visible and had bodily parts), without form or image, then no anthropomorphic qualities can be attributed to him; the references to the deity in the Old Testament must be "explained." The rabbis and Jewish biblical scholars attempted the following explanations:

(a) Anthropomorphic expressions were used in order to focus more sharply on the meaning of the text. (Midrash)
(b) There were intermediate beings between God and man and the anthropomorphic expressions have reference to these beings. (Philo)
(c) Anthropomorphic expressions are to be understood in an allegorical manner only. (Maimonides)

2. "… it is accepted as a major axiom of Judaism, from the biblical period onward, that no material representation of the Deity is possible or permissible … it should be asked whether the expression is an actual, naively concrete personification of God … or an allegorical expression … (or) a method of … clothing spiritual contents in concrete imagery" (53–51 Vol. 3).

3. Judaism does not permit physical representations of God. Jewish tradition speaks of God who has no form or shape, cannot be seen, is eternal and without end. The Torah, God's direct revelation to Moses, does prohibit physical representation only if "carved" or made by human hands; it does not prohibit all physical or material representation. To say that God is eternal, infinite, has no form or shape, is to say that God remains unknowable, incomprehensible and forever beyond our understanding. Later Judaism had problems with God's physical and psychical personifications; every effort was made to attribute allegorical or non-literal meanings to direct physical and psychical references normally applicable to humans. Why were the rabbis and sages inventing this cover-up? Was a deity with "human" attributes inferior to an infinite and shapeless one? Did his invisibility elevate the religion above all others and ensured that the God of Israel was greater than other gods? Why did the rabbis and sages not admit

that since God has no form or shape, cannot be seen, is eternal and without end, that therefore finite man can never know the essence of God; that to define God is to limit him and that God cannot be described in human language? Did the rabbis and sages maintain that the Torah, God's sacred words, cannot be taken literally and must be colored with interpretations by profane human minds; that God's creation of the human mind was so inferior as to be unable to grasp God's word unless represented in allegorical form? This is blasphemy, pure and simple. They agonized over the irreconcilable gap between the simplistic, obscure, crude and unilluminated thought-processes of the priestly writers and redactors as against the intellectual, worldly, Greek-influenced thoughts of Jewish thinkers of the Diaspora. The rabbis and sages were prohibited by the Torah from adding to or deleting from the text. Were they violating God's holiness when they maintained that the Torah could not be taken literally? Did the rabbis and sages realize that by referring to the deity as "transcendental," they would limit the concept of God? They cannot have it both ways: That God has no form and is without end, i.e., infinite, and yet claim that he is transcendental; that the Torah is the word of God and yet add to and delete from the revealed text and thus corrupt it; that the sacred text of the Torah must not be taken literally and at the same time require Jews to adhere to the literal reading and obedience to the Law and Commandments.

4. God showed his "form" (Numb. 12:8) only to his servant Moses; spoke to him face to face, as a man spoke with his friend (Ex. 33:11), although Yahweh said to Moses in Ex. 33:21, "You cannot see my face ... for a man cannot see me and live." (This contradiction appears to be a later corruption of the text). God spoke to others not face to face but "in a vision," "in a dream," not plainly but in riddles (Ex. 12:6–8). It follows that of all the books in the Old Testament canon, the Torah has the only claim to be God's revelation, directly revealed to Moses, God's servant. The Torah must therefore be read literally and any allegorical or metaphorical interpretation would be blasphemous and undermine its sacredness. The Torah nowhere states that God is without body and without any form or figure. An intensely imaginative poet could spiritualize some of the physical references to the deity without doing injustice to the meaning. The Torah references that God went down a mountain; was determined to know; that his face was seen, that his face was gazed upon; that he wrote

with his finger; that his back could be seen; that beneath his feet was a sapphire pavement—such references could be "poetically" interpreted. However, most of the references which describe the "feelings" of God in human terms, such as hate, anger, revenge, regret, sadness, pity, jealousy, love, etc. must be taken literally so as not to destroy the meaning of the context in which they were applied—these are purely anthropomorphic. I shall cite a few excerpts from the Torah of anthropomorphic content; their exclusion from the text would not detract from the essence of the Torah message:

(a) "Yahweh regretted having made man on earth, and his **heart grieved**" (Gen. 6:7).
(b) "Yahweh **smelt**. the appeasing fragrance … (of burnt offerings)" (Gen. 8:21).
(c) "Now Yahweh **came down** to see the town and the tower that the sons of man had built" (Gen. 11:5).
(d) "I propose to **go down** and see whether or not they have done all that is alleged in the outcry against them … I am **determined to know**" (Gen. 18:21).
(e) "Yahweh gave me the two stone tablets **inscribed by the finger of God**, …" (Deut 9:10).

5. I shall cite some of the anthropomorphic references in the Torah about which there could be no doubt that the interpretation must be literal, so as to preserve the meaning of the text and the essence of the Torah message:

(1) "Let us **make** man in our own **image**" (Gen. 1:27).
(2) "The blood shall serve to mark the house you live in. When **I see** the blood I will pass over you …" (Ex. 12:13).
(3) "Yahweh will do the **fighting** for you; you only have to keep still" (Ex. 14:14).
(4) "I shall **wipe out** the memory of Amalek from under heaven" (Ex. 17:15).
(5) "For I, Yahweh your God, am a **jealous** God and **punish** the father's fault in the sons, … but I show **kindness** to thousands of those who love me …" (Ex. 20:5–6).
(6) "For in six days Yahweh made the heavens … but on the seventh day he **rested**; …" (Ex. 20:11).

(7)   "You must not be harsh with the widow, or with the orphan; ... my **anger** will flare and I shall **kill** you with the sword, ..." (Ex. 22:21 ff).

(8)   (Speaking of the Amorites, Hittites, etc.) "I shall **exterminate** these" (Ex. 23:24).

(9)   "I shall **spread** panic ahead of you; ..." (Ex. 23:27).

(10)   "So Yahweh **relented** and did not bring on his people the disaster he had **threatened**" (Ex. 32:14).

(11)   "I shall not go with you myself ... or I might **exterminate** you on the way" (Ex. 33:3–4).

(12)   "Yahweh would **speak** with Moses **face to face**, ..." (Ex. 33:11).

(13)   "This holocaust will be a burnt offering and the fragrance of it will **appease** Yahweh" (Lev. 1:9).

(14)   "I will **inflict** terror on you, ..." (Lev. 26:16).

(15)   "I myself have **chosen** the Levites from among the sons of Israel, ..." (Numb. 3:12).

(16)   "I will **strike** them with pestilence and **disown** them" (Numb. 14:12).

(17)   "... so that Yahweh may **turn from the ferocity of his anger** ..." (Deut. 13:17).

(18)   "Build me a sanctuary so that I (Yahweh) may **dwell** among them ... you must follow exactly the pattern I shall **show** you" (Ex. 25:8–9).

(19)   "God **heard** their groaning and **called to mind** his covenant with Abraham ..." (Ex. 2:24–25).

6. Works or ideas are inspired if they are the result of considerably above average and unique creativity and are considered by mankind as such. Shakespeare and Mozart were inspired creators. Revelation, on the other hand, is not the result of any human effort, but is solely caused by divine communication, which is direct and not third person (quoted). Man is but a recipient of such messages and cannot aspire to receive them on his own. A particular thought or work cannot be both revealed and inspired; it must be one or the other; revelation can give rise to inspiration but not the other way. When God told Moses that he was known to Abraham, Isaac and Jacob by the name "El Shaddai" (Ex. 6:2–3), that he was henceforth to be known as "Yahweh" (Ex. 6:4), and that it meant "I am who I am" (Ex. 3:14), these are examples of revelations; man could not generate such knowledge. God spoke directly to Moses, "face to face". (Numbers 12:8);

"plainly and not in riddles" (Num. 12:8); "Yahweh would speak with Moses face to face, as a man speaks with his friend" (Ex. 33:11). To others (Joshua, David, the prophets, etc.) God spoke not as to Moses but "in a vision," "in a dream" (Num. 12:6), not plainly but in riddles; it therefore follows that Moses was exclusively selected by God to be spoken to "face to face." So that, for example, when the Book of Joshua says (1:1) that "Yahweh spoke to Joshua ..." it was not face to face but in a dream or vision, not plainly and in riddles. And so with others.

However, when in Numbers 12:4–5, "Yahweh said to Moses and Aaron and Miriam 'Come, all three of you, to the Tent of Meeting,' ", did God only speak to Moses face to face, or to all three; or only to Moses face to face, and appeared to Aaron and Miriam in a vision; or did God appear in a vision to all three? Since all three promptly and simultaneously obeyed the command, God's message was the same to all three. God cannot be mistaken, but the author of the Torah must be; for either God spoke to others than Moses face to face (i.e. Aaron and Miriam) or God did not always speak to Moses face to face.

God is said to have spoken to others than Moses not plainly but in riddles, in a vision and in a dream. The recipient of the communication had to interpret the message in order to understand it. This was inspiration and required a higher form of intellect. God showed his "form" (Numb. 12:8) only to his servant Moses, spoke to him face to face, as a man spoke with his friend; it follows that the five books attributed to Moses, the Torah, are the only sacred Revelations; the books of the Old Testament canon attributed to others were, at best, inspired writings, i.e., of a lower standing as defined by God; inspired, not plainly but in riddles. From the above it follows that, as the Sadducees are known to have maintained, only the Torah carried divine authority because of its revealed message; that the other books of the Old Testament are inspired, at best, and carry no more divine authority than the inspired works of men, such as Shakespeare or Mozart. Similarly with the Talmud, etc., admittedly a purely human effort, however laboriously produced, carrying no divine authority and imprimatur. The Jewish religion, therefore, stands or falls on the divinity of the Torah, the revealed word of God to Moses.

Truth or facts need no revelation to be true or factual; revelation must be true or factual to be authentic. God's revelation, by definition, must be true and factual, for if not true and factual, cannot be attributed to God; such attribution would be blasphemous. Revelations cannot contain contradictory elements. If the study of the Torah reveals that it is full of contradictions, anachronisms, corruptions of text, mistranslations, the product of redactions by various authors, contains references to books now lost, and most importantly, calls into question the authorship of Moses, then it would follow that the Torah—far from being a product of revelation—is a fraudulent imposition. If Moses, to whom alone only God spoke "face to face," is not the author but the Torah was written by anonymous author/authors to whom God never spoke "face to face," then it is without divine authority.

7. To the extent that man can gain knowledge of God, he can do so only in human terms, i.e., only on a human scale; any other approach lies outside the competence of the human mind. The Torah says nothing about God's transcendence and infinity, nothing about his omnipresence, nothing about omnipotence, nothing about his omniscience: these terms cannot be understood by human intelligence and the gap between these and anthropomorphic terms is unbridgable; any attempt to pursue some reconciliation would lead to a chimera, to a reductio ad absurdum. Man should therefore accept the anthropomorphism of religious thoughts because that is the only approach to his understanding of religious beliefs. Any other way is a retreat into silence. Allegorical expressions and concrete imagery were common to all ancient polytheistic and henotheistic religions including the ancient Hebrew religion. It was the priestly desire for primacy of the Yahwistic faith, the exclusive Covenant with Yahweh's Chosen People, the superiority of its rituals, that they contrived the idea of the uniqueness of Yahweh (who was one of the many gods in the Pantheon of ancient gods), the exclusive God of Israel, which, as a consequence, also made the priesthood unique and superior. The priests condemned idolatry, alien gods, alien rituals, promoted customs in favor of Yahweh—which inured to their greater power over the Israelites and their own inevitable enrichment—who had no image, was jealous, tolerated the worship of no other gods, demanded sacrifice of only certain unblemished animals, all with the aim of making the Yahwistic religion the most superior of all. The later rabbis and sages, the Tannaim (whose opinions were collected in the Mishnah) and the Amoraim (whose opinions were collected in the Talmud) reinterpreted the script of the Torah; the Second Temple was destroyed and the influence of the priests

eliminated. It was up to the rabbis and sages to assert the uniqueness of the Torah, the monotheistic aspects of Judaism; the infinity of God or his transcendence; that he was formless and shapeless; that he was a personal God to whom man could pray to; who listened and cared about the people of Israel. Such attributes, however, contained too many contradictions which were ignored and glossed over, contradictions for which no solution was possible. It had to be one or the other. The rabbis and sages were determined that the scattered Jewish people survived the disaster of the uprisings against Rome, that Judaism as reshaped by them would inspire the Jewish people and give them cohesiveness. Survive they did, as a people separate and apart, observing a Judaism molded and reformed by the rabbis and sages, who reinterpreted the Torah in their light and wisdom. Living in the various lands of the Gentiles, the stage was set for interminable conflicts and opprobrium. The peculiarities of the special laws which made Judaism so distinct from other religions and the Jews so set apart from other peoples among whom they lived, that the rabbis achieved their aim:

(a) The Jews were not "polluted" by contact with non-Jews.
(b) Apostasy was limited to the bare minimum.
(c) Defection from the synagogue was practically impossible under the circumstances.

But the price paid was bitter: The life of Jews was one of almost continuous turbulence; life became unlivable but for the rabbinic inventions of divine reward and punishment in the hereafter which gave the Jewish people hope, none of which was vouchsafed to them in the Torah.

8. Anthropomorphism of the ancient Israelites was no different than that of the idolators who were their neighbors. Despite all the protestations about a transcendental and infinite (a contradiction in terms) God who had no form or shape, despite all the rabbinic reforms, Judaism remained anthropomorphic to an ever greater extent as a result of the need of a more personal God and also to some extent of the rising influence of the Christian religions. Any religion which involves prayer to a deity is anthropomorphic—the prayer is addressed to a personal God; it cannot be otherwise—any claim to the contrary is pure sophistry.

9. The writer/writers of the Torah made Yahweh utter statements about himself which were so blatantly anthropomorphic as to require no

further explanation or retreat into allegorical imagery. They are plain and to the point:

(a) "For I, Yahweh your God, am a jealous God ... I punish the father's fault in the sons, the grandsons, and the great-grandsons of those who hate me; but I show kindness to ... those who love me and keep my commandments" (Ex. 20:5–6).

(b) "I am Yahweh your God who brought you out of the land of Egypt, ... you shall have no gods except me" (Ex. 20:1–3).

(c) "For six days Yahweh made the heavens and the earth ... , but on the seventh day he rested" (Ex. 20:11).

(d) "I am Yahweh. To Abraham and Isaac and Jacob I appeared as El Shaddai; I did not make myself known to them by my name Yahweh" (Ex. 6:2–4).

(e) "You shall not make yourself a carved image... you shall not bow down to them or serve them ... I ... am a jealous God" (Ex. 20:4–5).

(f) "In every place I have my name remembered I shall come to you and bless you" (Ex. 21:25).

(g) "You shall bow down to no other god, for Yahweh's name is a Jealous One; ..." (Ex. 34:14).

(h) "Yahweh smelt the appeasing fragrance (of burnt offerings)..." (Gen. 8:21).

(i) "You cannot see my face, ... for man cannot see me and live" (Ex. 33:21).

(j) "... I forgive them as you ask. But—as I live, and as the glory of Yahweh fills all the earth ..." (Numb. 14:20–21).

(k) "This holocaust will be a burnt offering and the fragrance of it will appease Yahweh" (Lev. 1:9).

(1) "All the fat belongs to Yahweh. This is a perpetual law for all your descendants, ..." (Lev. 3:17).

Judaism, however transformed, cannot lay claim to a non-anthropomorphic deity; to an invisible God who has no image or form; the contradiction exists only on paper. The Jew who prays, addresses a personal God with all the human attributes and mental images; any other prayer would be unthinkable and a mockery of the language. It works, prayer does raise the level of piety, peace of mind; if it leads to good deeds and charity, it is to be respected and accepted. This is all religion is supposed to be about.

Chapter 13

The Exodus Explored

1. Of all the figures in Jewish history, by far the most outstanding in stature and importance was Moses, the law-giver, who liberated the Hebrews from slavery in Egypt, the person par excellence in Jewish history. In fact, his importance and influence was so overwhelming that great care has been exercised not to bestow a cult of personality on him and his activities, or even some part of divinity. So much so that a special point is made by. the rabbis that this greatest of all Jewish teachers, that intermediary between God and man, was still a fallible man with human faults; that the Jewish religion is the religion of God and that no individual, the greatness of Moses notwithstanding, would ever leave the field of humanity and be regarded with divine honors. Much is made of this feature as characteristic of Judaism that no particular reverence is accorded any personality, no special holidays are celebrated in his honor. It is even pointed out that Moses is not mentioned in the Passover Haggadah celebrating the Exodus of Jews from Egypt. It was pointed out that scant mention of Moses was made by the prophets—as noted in a previous chapter—that was, however, due to other reasons. There is a festival of lights, Hanukkah, celebrated by Jews honoring the deeds of a military hero, Judas Maccabeus, an incomparably lesser figure than Moses but unquestionably historical, which cannot be said about Moses; the latter could obtain audience with God at will—no other Jew was portrayed so close to God—and is inflexibly and unalterably tied to the Exodus of the Hebrews from Egypt, liberation from slavery and the Sinaitic Covenant. For if the Exodus story is not historical or did not occur as portrayed in the Torah, then Moses and his deeds become irrelevant; the nexus is broken between Abraham and the Covenant; the 400 year slavery of Abraham's descendants in a land not their own ("… where they will be slaves and oppressed for four hundred years" Gen. 15:13–14)

which was foretold by Yahweh to Abraham is fiction. Then the authors of the Torah erred: Yahweh did not foretell the slavery of Abraham's descendants for 400 years and their Exodus; the subsequent Sinaitic Covenant and Moses' divinely directed activities are a myth. For Yahweh spoke these words to the children of Israel assembled at Sinai, who had witnessed the miraculous liberation, "I am Yahweh your God who brought you out of the land of Egypt, out of the house of slavery" (Ex. 20:1–2).

2. Outside the Torah there is no independent verification of the Exodus. The Egyptian historians made no reference to it; nor do Egyptian records make any reference to a land called Goshen even though 2½ million Hebrews were confined to that small area—the Egyptian population numbered at that time between 5–6 million. We do not know the name of the Pharaoh at the time of the Exodus, nor the date, though it appears that the authors of the Torah made an effort to keep these facts from us. Redacted at least 700 years after the event, the Torah gives us the names of the two midwives (Ex. 1:16) who attended Hebrew women. Yahweh told Abraham that his descendants would be slaves and oppressed for 400 years in a land not their own; that "In the fourth generation they will come back here, ..." (Gen. 15:16);—it is difficult to equate four generations with 400 years—yet even the sojourn of 400 years as foretold to Abraham is in error, for in Ex. 12:40–41 it is stated, "The time that the sons of Israel had spent in Egypt was 430 years." In 1 Kings 6:1 we read that it was 480 years (even this calculation is wrong, it should be in excess of 600 years) after the Exodus and in the 4th year of King Solomon's reign that he began to build the Temple. This would place the Exodus in the 18th dynasty in Egypt, or about 1450 B.C. during the reign of Thutmose III (1479–1447 B.C.); the latter was an extremely powerful ruler and under his reign—it is the consensus of biblical scholars—Egypt was too strong for the Hebrews to revolt against her, or to conquer Canaan, which was firmly under Egyptian domain; likewise, maximum Egyptian control over Canaan by powerful Egyptian 14th century B.C. rulers would have made Exodus during that period impossible. Furthermore, the Torah states that the cities of Pithom and Rameses were built by the Hebrews for the Pharaoh (Ramses II 1301–1234 B.C. and named after him) so they still must have been in Egypt during that time. Most biblical scholars—the prior reference notwithstanding—find the 1290–1260 B.C. period for the Exodus most

acceptable. That time-frame presents two difficulties: (a) The Egyptian Merneptah stele (ca 1220 B.C.) enumerates peoples defeated in battle in Canaan, among them the people of Israel, which had to be well settled in Canaan by that date considering the frame of reference (b) Archaeological difficulties with the timing of the conquest (to be discussed later) make the last suggested date for the Exodus an impossibility. This leaves us with no suitable date.

3. In this and later chapters, internal conflict of facts will be pointed out between what Yahweh foretold and what is recorded as having happened; they both cannot be true, one must be false or they both are false. In such situations, it never will be suggested that Yahweh's statement was false but that the authors made a mistake, or that they made Yahweh make pronouncements which never occurred and which are their inventions.

4. Not all the Hebrews left for Egypt with Jacob, when his group consisted of 70 members. We do not know anything about the group of Hebrews which remained behind nor how they increased in numbers. They were not slaves and were free to multiply. The Jacob group grew to at least 2½ million people in 430 years or 4 generations (it must be one or the other, they cannot both be right). This figure is extrapolated from Ex. 12:37, "The sons of Israel left Rameses for Succoth about 600,000 strong … all men—not counting their families". It is related that in the second month of the second year after the Exodus there were a total of 603,550 men fit to bear arms (Numb. 1:46) and that total did not include the Levites. The circumstances were similar for the Hebrews left behind, so that they constituted a similarly substantial number. Since both groups in Egypt and Canaan were referred to as "Israel," this became a source of confusion. So when the Merneptah stele made reference to "the people of Israel is laid waste, their crops are not, …" around 1220 B.C., the crop producing people of Israel referred to was the one in Canaan and not the one still in Egypt who at that time was still called "Hebrews". The book of Joshua made no mention of encountering a people of Israel in Canaan; nor did it make any mention of an Egyptian military presence in relating the conquest.

5. The Hebrews resided in Egypt for 430 years, worshipping a calf or diminutive bull, as was the custom in Egypt without Yahweh or leaders, a

mighty force of about 2½ million people, or 35% of the population "groaning in their slavery, cried out for help ..." (Ex. 2:23), yet remained a cohesive people, the "sons of Israel" (Ex. 2:23). "God heard their groaning and he called to mind his covenant with Abraham, Isaac and Jacob" (Ex. 2:24–25). To state that God forgot his covenant is blasphemy; the priestly authors showed their folly. No one in his right mind could make such an assertion. This is anthropomorphism at its most absurd. Yet it is part of the Torah. Slavery was a painful experience for the Hebrews, something which would be etched in their mind for some time. Yahweh, as a severe punishment, was going to send the Israelites back to Egypt for a possible second slavery "by sea and by land" though he promised them "You will not see it again" (Deut. 28:68). It was a punishment "For not obeying the voice of Yahweh your God ..." (Deut. 28:63). After Yahweh overthrew the Egyptians and performed all the miracles which culminated in returning the sea waters and drowning Pharaoh's pursuing army "Israel witnessed the great act ... and the people venerated Yahweh; they put their faith in Yahweh and in Moses, his servant" (Ex. 14:31). Yahweh ordered the children of Israel "You must never go back that way (Egypt) again" (Deut.17:16–17). With the memory of Egypt and slavery still fresh in their mind, the escaping Israelites upbraided Moses "Were there no graves in Egypt that you must lead us out to die in the wilderness? What good have you done us, bringing us out of Egypt? ... we would rather work for the Egyptians! Better to work for the Egyptians than die in the wilderness!" (Ex. 14:11–13) It appears the Israelites were beginning to have second thoughts about the blessings of liberty, or was slavery not that bad after all? They had a home, their wives were not slaves, ate well, slept well, were fruitful and multiplied. When food became scarce and Yahweh was not prompt in providing, they grumbled to Moses already in the second month after Exodus: "Why did we not die at Yahweh's hand in the land of Egypt, when we were able to sit down to pans of meat and could eat bread to our heart's content!" (Ex. 16:3). If this is history, it is astonishing how much of an insight we can obtain from their complaints, an insight which would raise questions about the degree of oppression and exploitation suffered by them which resulted in their cry for help heard by Yahweh. The Israelites complained yet again to Moses: "Who will give us meat to eat? ... Think of the fish we used to eat free in Egypt, the cucumbers, melons, leeks, onions and garlic!" (Numb. 11:4–6). When the envoys came back with the report of the "powerful" inhabitants of the Promised Land, which indeed flowed with milk and honey, the whole community cried out, wailed all night and then grumbled against Moses and Aaron in a manner which again raises serious doubts about the severity of the Egyptian oppression: "Should we not do better to go back to Egypt? … Let us appoint a leader and go back to Egypt" (Numb. 14:3–4).

6. Modern biblical scholars are troubled with the historicity of events narrated in the Old Testament as factual; the doubts are based on contradictions and inconsistencies where there should be none or need be none. The story of Exodus, absolutely fundamental to Judaism, is predicated upon the slavery and liberation of Hebrews under Moses' leadership; then leading to the Law and Sinaitic Covenant, conquest of Canaan and the building of Solomon's Temple in Jerusalem. Taking the former paragraph as historical, the Israelites, most recently liberated from several hundred years of oppressive slavery in Egypt by the miraculous intervention of Yahweh, which they witnessed and "put their faith in Yahweh and Moses, his servant," shook with trepidation at the sight of Pharaoh's army, and wanted to return and "work" for the Egyptians. When food became scarce, they grumbled how well they could eat bread in Egypt to their heart's content. When they were faced with the prospect of eating the meager Manna, they complained to Moses again how well they ate meat and fish in Egypt and longed for those days. When they were faced with the prospect of fighting "powerful" men to claim the land of milk and honey—with the assistance of Yahweh—they wailed all night and decided it was time to appoint another leader and return back to Egypt! The miracles of Yahweh, the personal sacrifices and preaching of Moses notwithstanding—the Israelites contemplated life in Egypt with longing. It is time to critically review the whole reality of slavery of the Hebrews in Egypt, the need for liberation from oppression and abuse and the number of Hebrews involved. Non-biblical sources are silent on this matter.

7. Moses, whose name was Egyptian, was the great grandson of Levi, i.e., the fourth generation from Levi, no more than a lapse of about 150 years (and not 430 years). Whereas a growth from about 70 people to 2½ million within 430 years is rated as improbable, a growth of the same proportion within about 150 years is totally absurd. If the growth occurred within 150 years (which would more logically correspond to 4 generations), then all the

censuses in the Torah dealing with the Exodus and post-Exodus are pure fiction, the number of Israelite military manpower would have been too small to mount an invasion of Canaan, since even with the larger number, Yahweh decided not to drive out the Hivites, Canaanites and Hittites from before the Israelites in a single year because of their insufficient numbers, "Little by little I will drive them out before you until your numbers grow and you come into possession of the land" (Ex. 23:29–31).

8. Given the number of men who marched out (Ex. 12:37), it follows by extrapolation that the total involved about 2½ million people and additionally "People of various sorts joined them in great numbers; ..." (Ex. 12:38); we have no way of gauging how many were included in "great numbers." In addition; "there were flocks, too, and herds in immense droves" (Ex. 12:38); we have no way of gauging the size of "herds in immense droves." But we do know that all people, flocks and herds departed from Egypt on land in a single day (Ex. 12:17, 12:41–42). Apart from the insurmountable difficulty of organizing that many people and herds in immense droves into the direction of the wilderness—there could not have been many roads—at such short notice, it would have taken that many people (not counting the herds) marching continuously without rest and maintaining the same speed 24 hours per day, 36 miles per day, 6 people deep, a column about 365 miles long, marching about 10 days for all to exit Rameses. If marching in more than one column, but making the necessary stops—considering the aged, infirm and children—for eating and night-rest, it would have taken considerably more than 10 days. No miracle could have achieved it any faster; it could have given strength and endurance to all to walk continuously without rest or food. Leaving Rameses in the direction of Succoth, the front column would have reached the southern tip of the Sinai peninsula before the rear column departed from Rameses, ten days later.

This whole episode is badly written fiction by very naive or incompetent priestly authors—most likely around the 5th century B.C.—who were unfamiliar with the terrain and with plain elementary logistics.

9. "The sons of Israel did as Moses had told them and asked the Egyptians for silver ornaments and gold ..." (Ex. 12:35–36), and in the process "... they plundered the Egyptians" (Ex. 12:36). One and one-half million adult Hebrews in possession of gold and silver set out with their families for the

wilderness. Enough gold was gathered to cast an effigy of a golden calf without difficulty. Gold and silver were gathered later from the Israelites as a contribution to Yahweh for the Tabernacle and its furnishings, the ark, engraved plates of pure gold for the priests; tons and tons of it. The Israelites wandered with their riches for 40 years in a territory that should have swarmed with robbers, brigands and marauders. The news of all these riches should have spread to all corners; petty kings of all sorts looking for quick enrichment should have made their mark. The Torah is silent about any such attempts.

The Torah is very detailed in furnishing the many locations of encampment after leaving Rameses; from these they journeyed to Succoth, to Etham, to Migdol, to Marah, from there to Elim where they found 12 springs of water and 70 palm trees—so they encamped there: 2½ million people? This was considered adequate for their numbers? Several more subsequent sites are named but we have no idea where these were; archaeologists have not found any. Two and one-half million people and great herds of animals wandered through Sinai for 40 years, moving the Tabernacle as they went along; the priests dutifully performing the obligatory holocausts of bulls and sheep on a daily basis; at least 500,000 Israelites must have died a natural death and were buried with some material token of esteem placed in the grave; some pottery or artifacts left behind or buried; some dwellings or communal halls built and abandoned; yet archaeologists and other scientific explorers have been unable to find any trace, to this date, of material remains of human occupation. Can this be credible? A nation of 2½ million people left no trace after 40 years? And this from about the 13th century B. C., a relatively recent period? Nor is there a single mention from a neighboring nation (or any other non-biblical source) who, not being privy to Yahweh's plan, must have been astonished to see 2½ million people, rich in gold and silver treasures, wandering aimlessly for 40 years in the wilderness for no apparent reason?

On the other hand, in the period 2850–2650 B.C., Canaanite settlers in south-central Sinai produced copper from ore mines for transport to Canaan; they built more than 40 settlements and archaeologists can trace them. The Egyptians exploited copper and turquoise mines in the mountains of Sinai from about 3500–1200 B.C. and archaeological explorations found evidence of 2nd millennium B.C. settlements. It is only the 2½ million Israelites—or whatever the number—which left no trace, veiled in mystery.

10. Of all the biblical geographical locations, the most sacred by far is the mountain on which the God of Israel dwelt, on which the Law was given to Moses, where God first revealed himself to Moses in the burning bush, where Moses ascended the mountain to receive the Tablets of Law, where God gave Moses other laws and ordinances for the people of Israel, where God descended from the mountain and proclaimed the Ten Commandments: Namely, Mt. Sinai, also known as Mt. Horeb (Ex. 33:6). God told Moses, "After you have led the people out of Egypt, you are to offer worship to God on this mountain (Mt. Sinai)" (Ex. 3:12). Moses with Aaron, Nadab, Abihu and seventy of the elders of Israel went up Mt. Sinai, where they saw the God of Israel (Ex. 24:9–10). Moses led the people out of the camp "to meet God; and they stood at the bottom of the mountain. The mountain of Sinai was entirely wrapped in smoke, …" (Ex. .19:18). "Like smoke from a furnace the mountain went up, and the whole mountain shook violently" (Ex. 19:18–19). It was deemed by some to be a volcanic eruption. However, no volcanoes were active during biblical times in the Sinai peninsula; but then all theophanies in Ancient Near Eastern literature show such divine appearances during what are perceived to be volcanic eruptions.

The location of Mt. Sinai is not known; further its location is defined by reference to other place-names, which themselves are of unknown location. It defies comprehension how the location of Mt. Sinai escaped precise identification, given its extraordinary and unique importance to Judaism. The location of unimportant mountains, valleys and streams are known; but the location of the mountain where earth-shaking events are said to have taken place, where God dwelt and issued his Laws to Israel, was not recorded and the most diligent search by scientists proved fruitless. The following mountains, valleys and rivers, of third-rate importance, posed no difficulty of locating and identifying, just to name a few:

Elah (Valley of Terebinth), a valley in Judah	(1 Sam. 17:2)
Sorek, a valley	(Judg. 16:4)
Kishon, a river	(Judg. 5:21)
Mt. Gibbon, a mountain	(1 Sam. 31:2)
Mt. Tabor, a mountain	(Judg. 4:14)
Mt. Ebal, a mountain	(Deut. 27:4)

All these insignificant pieces of geography are duly recorded, identified and remembered. Mt. Sinai, despite its relative proximity to the hub of Israelite activity, the natural curiosity and pious remembrance it should have aroused, did no better than slide into oblivion. If the Exodus route were known, Mt. Sinai could be located, but the route location also slid into oblivion. The Torah tries to locate the site—area in the vicinity of Elim, Rephidim and Kibroth-Hattaavah—but these encampments cannot be located either. Everything is elusive.

11. The Egyptians have no record of Hebrew slaves, the land of Goshen and the Exodus. The Torah cannot name a single Pharaoh or point to a single date or reference of the Exodus, except that it occurred 480 years before the beginning of construction of Solomon's Temple; this figure is in error; it is low by at least 120 years which would bring the Exodus to sometime during 1700–1600 B.C.; this however, would place it during the Hyksos Arab domination (1800–1600 B.C.). They caused the physical ruin of the land and certainly did not need any slaves for construction purposes; store-cities of Pithom and Rameses were built for the Pharaoh, as stated in the Torah. The Arab Hyksos had no Pharaohs! They were not driven out till 1582 B.C. There is no non-biblical verification of the historicity of Moses. Yahweh has the Hebrews mark the homes they live in with blood, so that "when I see the blood I will pass over you and you shall escape the destroying plague" (Ex. 12:13–14), even though the Hebrews lived apart from the Egyptians in Goshen. The large number of Hebrews as cited in the Torah is not credible. The Torah cannot agree on the length of sojourn in Egypt: was it 400 years or 430 years or 4 generations? The escape routes from Egypt and the journey through Sinai are not known and no trace can be found. The location of Mt. Sinai—the dwelling place of God—is unknown and no trace can be found. Archaeologists cannot identify any location in the Sinai peninsula where the Israelites wandered for 40 years; no trace of any habitation attributable to the Israelites can be found although habitation of other peoples, some more ancient and their numbers infinitely smaller, can be identified.

The priestly authors supplied such ingenious particulars and nuances to the above referenced episodes to force credibility; but the many all too apparent contradictions, errors, and intentional omission of all names and dates except where it suited their purposes made their intentions apparent.

In the case of the Exodus, we absolutely have no suitable date particularly if anything even close to the number of Hebrews participating is claimed. Some biblical scholars advance the theory that no more than a few thousand people participated in some form of Exodus, many with Egyptian names: Such an Exodus cannot be dignified with the appellation and is a nullity. Could it then perhaps be, horribile dictu, that the Exodus as commonly known, is a total invention of the priestly authors who needed such an episode to couch the origin of Israel's history in clouds of epic drama? Give it uniqueness and exclusive care of Yahweh? A nation above all other nations, privileged and chosen for a special purpose? According to the Merneptah stele of about 1220 B.C., an accepted non-biblical source, Israel was already well settled in Canaan in sufficiently large numbers to merit mention as a military opponent of Egypt. We have to accept their presence as a fact and reconcile occupation with penetration from within.

The post-Exilic priestly authors and the exiled Jewish scribes and priests in Babylon were responsible for compiling and redacting the Torah in a form substantially as we have it today; they left us scavenging for bits of reality, so as to make some sense of the historical drama surrounding the biblical story; to buttress our convictions and give us the necessary sense of direction. All we find is a labyrinth of intentional misdirection which empty the concepts of their meaning. The priestly authors have, by design, obfuscated and befogged the story to make penetration and examination by future worshippers impossible. The rabbinic, talmudic and midrashic literature only adds to the problem; instead of arriving at simplified solutions they turned confusion and double-talk in all its splendor into an art. It must come as cold comfort that the truth of the Torah is taken as axiomatic, every passage, sentence, word analyzed by different scholars under cover of virtue with different results, spending endless time and pages in dissertations. But this is not some cross-word puzzle for misguided souls! Millions upon millions of Jews have died as martyrs for "Kiddush Ha-Shem" ("Sanctification of the Divine name") throughout history, choosing between dark and night, making the supreme sacrifice, fully convinced in the rightness of their cause. The face to face conversations between Yahweh and Moses, the covenant with Abraham, and the Sinaitic Covenant must be accepted on faith. But the date of the Exodus, the slavery of the Hebrews, the number of people in the Exodus, the Pharaohs involved, the length of sojourn in Egypt, the 40 years in the wilderness, the error in calculating 480 years from Exodus to the building of Solomon's Temple, the conquest of Canaan as narrated in the Book of Joshua, I say, these cannot be taken on faith and no solutions can be found to provide answers. All the so-called J,E,P,D versions, purported to have been redacted into the present version of the Torah, are intellectually barren and are overshadowed by the intentions of the Torah redactors, their alterations, their inventions, their falsifications, their copying errors, their cover-up and their destruction of contradictory or unassimilable documents. The rabbis and talmudic scholars contemplated the mysteries of the unfathomable divine plan, when in fact the writings bear the stamp of a plain conspiracy to shroud events in obscurity.

Chapter 14

The Torah

1. The Torah, also known as the Pentateuch or the Five Books of Moses, is the foundation of Judaism. Attributed—erroneously as will be shown—to the authorship of Moses, the greatest of Jewish prophets and leaders, the only person who spoke with God "face to face," directly and not in a dream, received the Torah as a divine revelation. The Torah, as handed down by Moses, is a unitary document wherein every verse, sentence and word is of divine origin, immutable and forever; by God's commandment nothing may be added to it and nothing may be taken from it and must be kept just like God laid it down to Moses; it is the only set of five books in the Jewish canon which can claim divine revelation. The rest of the books of the canon are admittedly by human hand and the authors were inspired in contemplation of the Divine Presence but did not receive revelation.

It is difficult enough to abide by this concept of the Torah with all the mistakes, contradictions, alterations, conflations, anachronisms, scribal errors and deliberate corruptions of the text which crept into this work; it appears, the Torah took its present final form around 300 B.C. But the rabbis and talmudic scholars, overwhelmed in contemplating the divine, their minds apparently unhinged by metaphysical speculation which burdened their thinking to the point of perversion, managed to reach such conclusions as that the Torah existed in heaven before the world was created; that God created the world by looking into the Torah; that God took counsel with the Torah before he created the world; that God created the world for the purpose of revealing the Torah; that man exists for the sake of the Torah and that the Torah was created before the creation of the world. These views were passed on to Jewish believers, some of whom were able to acclimate such views—and in their turn pass them on to the next generation—which have been held by certain religious segments of Jews up to the present time.

2. The peculiar commandments, laws and ordinances, in time, evolved a peculiar people set apart from other people; the Jewish nation is a peculiar nation as a result of peculiar laws mandated by the Torah. A study of the Torah will convince the reader that its primary aim was the arrogation of monopoly power by the priests for the benefit of priests; passage of priestly mandated laws to achieve and maintain such positions of prestige and preference that would establish absolute hierocracy; redacted in the Exilic and post-Exilic period, the priestly authors wrote a history of Israel from its origin up to their time (borrowing freely from the Babylonian and other libraries available) that was so arranged and so couched with divine sanctions as to accommodate their particular views while creating a national history, exclusive and divinely ordained territorial claims. The worship of Yahweh with its sacrificial cult was mandated in so far as it served the priestly aim. Civil laws, curses and laws of punishment served to create a framework conducive to orderly administration and had nothing to do with the salvation of the soul. The people were subjected to special religious laws and ordinances which were bound to instill in them views and outlooks at variance with their neighbors, and with the passage of time progressively widen the gap among them with telling consequences for the Jewish people throughout their history.

3. I shall attempt to demonstrate later in this chapter that Moses could not have been the author of the Torah. If he was not the author and the Torah was not therefore divinely revealed, his historical existence is irrelevant. The priestly sect appropriated freely from the Egyptian priesthood since the time of the monarchy and later also adopted from the Babylonian priesthood during the Exilic and post-Exilic periods some of the building blocks for its own elaborate and unique priestly order. It will be apparent that, in doing so, the aim of the priests was the establishment and preservation of a monopoly of power, privilege, prestige, preference and procurement of wealth; that the preservation of the highest attainable standard of living was the aim; that anything which was conducive to that end was the real aim of priestly laws and ordinances. The priests (Levites) placed themselves on center stage and everything was made to revolve around them; the welfare and happiness of Israel was secondary to their primary aim. The peculiar laws and ordinances imposed upon Israel made them a pecu-

liar people because the priests' practices were peculiar; they jealously guarded their privileges, condemned all apostasy because it was inimical to their interest and attempted to minimize all "whoring" after other gods by an avalanche of curses and punishments aimed as deterrent. The priests, who were not of worldly experience did not, and to a great extent could not, foresee the adverse sociological consequences their laws would have upon Israel and that the machinery once engaged assumed a life of its own. If the Jewish people displayed a ruthless attitude toward their neighbors, the fault was with their laws. It was the Torah which shaped the nature of Jews and the authors of the Torah who laid down those immutable laws and ordinances were so blinded by selfish motives that they did not grasp the extent of hatred aroused in the neighbors toward the Jews. The history of the Israelites and the Jewish people is replete with imputed reward and punishment for following or disobeying the laws of Yahweh respectively. The association of misfortune or bad crops with the wrath of Yahweh was immediate and the cause not hard to seek. The association of earthly calamities with the sins of people (and the reverse) was primitive idolatry; only priestly intervention and propitiation of the deity with the prescribed ritual sacrifice could make amends and thus make themselves indispensable. The priests demanded literal interpretation of the Torah; the people's response was prone to actions of predictable consequences: no misfortune if the commandments were obeyed, obstinacy the result.

4. The priestly privileges would be adversely affected under the rule of a foreign king or government, therefore, the priestly authors quoted Yahweh, "… you are not to give yourself a foreign king who is no brother of yours." (Deut. 17:15). Innumerable uprisings against foreign rule were the result of this commandment which was interpreted as opposition to any foreign rule; the Jewish people were decimated and almost exterminated in their unceasing effort, abetted by priests and later by rabbis, to shake off foreign rule against all odds. Below are some of Yahweh's commandments, laws and ordinances which are so slanted and partial toward priestly (Levitical) domination and preeminence that their sense is transparent:

"I myself have chosen the Levites from among the sons of Israel … the Levites therefore belong to me" (Num. 3:12–13). "Yahweh then set apart this tribe of Levi to carry the ark of Yahweh's covenant, …" (Deut. 10:8).

"If anyone presumes to disobey ... the priest who is there in the service of Yahweh your God, ... that man must die" (Deut. 17:12).

"The offering with which he has performed the rite of atonement is to revert to the priest" (Lev. 7:7–8).

"Do not neglect the Levite who lives in your towns, since he has no share or inheritance with you" (Deut. 14:27).

Yahweh speaking to the priests,

"The breast that was offered up and the thigh that was set aside ... when the fat was burnt, revert to you ... in virtue of a perpetual law as Yahweh has ordered" (Lev. 10:14–15).

"All the tithes of the land, levied on the produce of the earth or the fruits of trees, belong to Yahweh; they are consecrated to Yahweh. If a man wishes to redeem part of his tithe, he must add one-fifth to its value" (Lev. 27:30–31).

Yahweh speaking to Aaron,

"I myself have given you charge of all that is set aside for me. Everything that the sons of Israel consecrate I give to you as your portion, as well as to your sons, by perpetual ordinance" (Num. 18:8–9).

"See, to the sons of Levi I give as their inheritance all the tithes collected in Israel, in return for their services, ... The tithe that the sons of Israel set aside for Yahweh, I give the Levites for their inheritance" (Num. 18:21–24).

"When you receive the tithe from the sons of Israel which they must pay you and which I am giving you as your inheritance, ..." (Num. 18:26).

Israel is obligated to set aside the best of all produce for the Levites after which they (Israel) can freely consume the rest and not be concerned about committing any sin on this account,

"... once you have set aside the best; ... and you will not die" (Num. 18:32).

"The levitical priests, that is to say the whole of the tribe of Levi, ... they shall live on the foods offered to Yahweh and on his dues" (Deut. 18:1–2).

"These are the priests' dues from the people, from those who offer an ox or a sheep in sacrifice: the priest is to be given the shoulder, the cheeks and the stomach. You must give him the first-fruits of your corn, your wine, your oil as well as the first of your-sheep's shearing" (Deut. 18:3–5).

Moses said to Aaron,

"Take the oblation that is left over from Yahweh's burnt offering" (Lev. 10:12).

5. The priests interposed themselves between Yahweh and the people and had difficulty preserving the distinction. They presumptuously identified their interest with Yahweh's to soften the impact of their demands, had they been stated more openly. Further, proper homage to Yahweh was an essential attribute of priestly status; apostasy or deviation from commandments or ritual, sharing or usurpation of priestly prerogatives were rightly viewed as the beginning of decline of influence and combatted with ruthless punishment—totally out of proportion to the perceived offense—again many times blurring the distinction with the divine:

"… you are to make over to Yahweh all the first issues from the womb, and every first-born cast by your animals: these males belong to Yahweh" (Ex. 13:12–13).

"Anyone who sacrifices to other gods shall come under the ban" (Ex. 22:20).

This is a euphemism for the ultimate punishment and also evidence of the existence of henotheism.

"Everyone subject to the census must pay half a shekel, … this half-shekel shall be set aside for Yahweh (Ex. 30:13–14).

For the benefit of the sanctuary and the priests.

"You must bring the best of the first-fruits of your soil to the house of Yahweh your God" (Ex. 34:26).

"Do not have recourse to the spirits of the dead or to magicians; they will defile you. I am Yahweh your God" (Lev. 19:31).

"If you hear that in one of the towns which Yahweh your God has given you … there are men, scoundrels from your own stock … (who said)… 'Come, let us serve other gods'… then you must kill all the inhabitants of that town without giving any quarter; …" (Deut. 13:13–16).

"If any man of the House of Israel or stranger living among you who offers a holocaust or sacrifice without bringing it to the entrance to the Tent of Meeting to offer it to Yahweh shall be outlawed from his people" (Lev. 17:10–11).

6. To maintain their superior rank and to preserve their indispensability, the priests were made holy—just like Yahweh was holy—and consecrated to Yahweh. The people who supported the priests were polluted and profane; they could not offer sacrifices directly to Yahweh, but had to seek the priestly intermediary for such exclusive services. The priestly authors arrogated to themselves a vast number of propitiatory functions and provided themselves with impressive trappings of office—the most faint-hearted had to be impressed. The priests invaded almost every phase of human existence and made their influence felt. Speaking of priests and the chief priest, i.e., High Priest:

"They shall be consecrated to their God … For it is they who bring the burnt offerings to Yahweh, the food of their God; and they must be in a holy condition" (Lev. 21:6).

"The priest who is pre-eminent over his brother, on whose head the chrism (oil) is poured, and who, clothed with the sacred robes … He must not leave the holy place, so that he may not profane the sanctuary of his God; for he bears on himself the consecration of his God, …" (Lev. 21:10–12).

"No lay person may eat holy things: neither the guest of a priest, nor his hired servant … if someone does eat a holy thing by inadvertence, he shall restore it to the priest with one-fifth added" (Lev. 22:10–14).

So that the priests would inhabit a sanctuary in which to perform their soon to be defined duties—all in the wilderness of Sinai—Yahweh spoke to Moses,

"Tell the sons of Israel to set aside a contribution for me … You shall accept from them the following contributions: gold, silver and bronze; purple stuffs, of violet shade and red, crimson stuffs, fine linen, goats' hair … fine leather, acacia wood; oil for the lamps, … onyx stones and gems … Build me a sanctuary so that I may dwell among them. In making the tabernacle and its furnishings you must follow exactly the pattern I shall show you" (Ex. 25:1–9).

The Temple at Jerusalem became the exclusive sanctuary in which the priests officiated. Below are listed some of the spheres of work which became their concern, the legislation and administration of which became their exclusive domain and responsibility:

The Tabernacle and its furnishings. The Ark (Ex. 25:10 ff).
The altar of holocaust (Ex. 27:1 ff).
The daily holocaust, altar of incense (Ex. 29:38 ff, Ex. 30:1 ff).
The ritual of sacrifice (Lev. 1:1 ff).
The sacrifice for sin and other sin sacrifices, the sacrifice of reparation (Lev. 1:1 ff).
Rules concerning the clean and unclean (Lev. 11:1 ff).
Purification of a woman after childbirth (Lev. 12:1 ff) .
Sexual impurities of men (Lev. 15:1 ff).
Sexual impurities of women (Lev. 15:19 ff).
Day of Atonement (Lev. 16:1 ff).
The ritual for the annual feast (Lev. 23:1 ff).
Rules for redemption (Lev. 27:26 ff).
Nocturnal emissions (Deut. 23:11).
Ritual prescriptions: First-fruits, the third-year tithe (Deut. 26:1 ff).

7. Israel was assured that Yahweh favored them above all nations, set them apart, to be a people all his own; all that was required of them was to follow the voice of Yahweh, his commandments, laws and ordinances and to follow the priestly rituals. It was unnatural for a people to be so favored without apparent merit, promised to be made as numerous as the stars of heaven, promised to possess the land of other nations by slaughtering them, to best all their enemies. These had to affect their nature and their views adversely:

"I will shower blessings on you, I will make your descendants as many as the stars of heaven … Your descendants shall gain possession of the gates of their enemies" (Gen. 22:17–18).

"I will set up my dwelling among you, and I will not cast you off. I will live in your midst; I will be your God and you shall be my people" (Lev. 26:11–13).

"For us right living will mean this: to keep and observe all these commandments before Yahweh our God as has been directed us" (Deut. 6:25).

"And Yahweh commanded us to observe all these laws ... so as to be happy for ever and to live ..." (Deut. 6:24).

"... it is you that Yahweh our God has chosen to be his very own people out of all the peoples on the earth" (Deut. 7:6).

"If Yahweh set his heart on you and chose you ... It was for love of you and to keep the oath he swore to your fathers ..." (Deut. 7:7–8).

8. The priestly teaching of Yahweh's Laws apparently did not have much of an impact upon the Israelites; the benefits of compliance were not persuasive; the Israelites soon saw through the priestly scheme of things. The people who by Yahweh's command had to share their meals with the priests, who lived off the labor of the "polluted" people as parasites and leeches supported in a life of luxury. Scorned by the people, the priests reacted with the fury of a wounded tyrant raining curses upon them to cow them into submission with threats of outlandish punishments and terror. Brutal punishment would be inflicted on all of Israel for not keeping and observing "all the commandments and statutes" of Yahweh. This is addressed to God's Chosen People, favored above all nations, God's very own, a light unto all nations where, "All the nations of the earth shall bless themselves by your descendants as a reward for your (Abraham's) obedience" (Gen. 22:18–19). Is this fate to befall all of Israel because of the misdeeds or apostasy of a few? Would the same fate befall all the obedient keepers and observers of Yahweh's commandments and statutes? Is this fate to befall all of Israel if only some of the many of Yahweh's commandments and statutes were not kept? What is left of Abraham's reward if Israel did speedily perish and become the carrion for all the birds and beasts? What effect would the knowledge of such curses have on the mind of Israel? And on the mind of the Jewish people thousands of years later who regularly read the Torah? What of Yahweh's own commandments, "You must not bear hatred for your brother in your heart" (Lev. 19:17)? And "You must not exact vengeance, nor must you bear a grudge against children of your people. You must love your neighbor as yourself. I am Yahweh. You must keep my laws" (Lev. 19:18–19)? And "... you are to honor old age and fear your God. I am Yahweh" (Lev. 19:32)? One can only conclude that the priestly authors and redactors corrupted the Torah with inconsistent, contradictory, incomprehensible and implausible writings.

9. In previous paragraphs, I dealt with curses to befall Israel for not keeping Yahweh's commandments and statutes. In this paragraph I shall deal with the fate to befall Israel's enemies, real or imagined, in the implementation of Yahweh's plan for Israel and at Yahweh's sole direction, should they faithfully keep his commandments and statutes. Israel complied with and acquiesced to the – even for those times – brutal treatment of nations whose only fault was that they worshiped their own gods, lived in lands which were in the path to the Promised Land and lived in the land given by Yahweh to the descendants of Abraham. The same brutality was also demanded by the priests against worshippers of other gods and followers of "foreign" customs, not for the benefit of Israel but for the preservation of the priestly hegemony.

> "My angel will go before you and lead you to where the Amorites are and the Hittites, the Perizzites, and the Canaanites, the Hivites, the Jebusites; I shall exterminate these" (Ex. 23:23–24).

Yahweh speaking,

> "... I shall be enemy to your enemies, foe to your foes"(Ex. 23:23).
>
> "I shall deliver the inhabitants of the country into your hands, and you will drive them out ..." (Ex. 23:31).
>
> "You must make no pact with them or with their gods. They must not live in your country or they will make you sin against me; you would come to worship their gods, ..." (Ex. 23:33).
>
> "Take care you make no pact with the inhabitants of the land you are about to enter, or this will prove a pitfall at your very feet" (Ex. 34:12–13).
>
> "You are to tear down their altars, smash their standing-stones, cut down their sacred poles" (Ex. 34:13).
>
> "Moses was enraged with the commanders of the army, ...'Why have you spared the life of all the women? ... So kill all the male children. Kill also the women who have slept with a man. Spare the lives only of the young girls who have not slept with a man, and take them for yourselves' " (Num. 31:14–19).
>
> "Then we captured all his cities and laid whole towns under ban, men, women, children; we spared nothing but the livestock which we took as our spoil, ..." (Deut. 2:34–36).
>
> "Devour, then, all these peoples whom Yahweh your God delivers over to you, show them no pity, ..." (Deut. 7:16).

"When Yahweh your God has annihilated the nations whose land
Yahweh your God gives you, ..." (Deut. 19:1).
In a captured town if it opened its gates to the Israelites, "all the people to be found in it shall do forced labor for you and be subject to
you. But if it refuses peace and offers resistance ... you are to put all
its men folk to the sword. But the women, the children, the livestock
... you may take for yourselves as booty" (Deut. 20:11–14).

That is how the Israelites were to deal with far-distant towns not belonging to the nations near them.

But as regards towns which the Israelites received as inheritance from
Yahweh, "... you must not spare the life of any living thing" (Deut.
20:16). Yahweh promised Abraham's descendants the land between the
wadi of Egypt and the river Euphrates; the land from Canaan to Lebanon
as far as the river Euphrates. That promise was false, Israel never possessed the whole of the land described; the priestly authors were mistak-
en. We cannot compare the mores of those times with our present views;
times were brutal by our standards and survival demanded that no quarter
be given! This applied to ordinary nations! But what about a people chosen by God as his very own, a light unto nations? The priestly authors
described Yahweh in chauvinistic terms not suited to a universal God; it is
obvious that the priestly authors had no conception of a universal God, an
idea not raised till the Second Isaiah, "I am Yahweh, unrivaled; there is no
other God beside me ... apart from me, all is nothing" (Isaiah 45:5–6). It
was not the divinely revealed Torah but the Second Isaiah who gave the
world the idea of a universal God, a God to all nations. The priestly
authors quote Yahweh as counseling wholesale killing of men, women and
children, which must have included widows, orphans, the infirm and the
aged. There is no explanation offered how this squared with the commandments, "You shall not kill" (Ex. 20:13) and "You must not be harsh
with the widow, or with the orphan; if you are harsh with them ... my
anger will flare and I shall kill you with the sword ..." (Ex. 22:21–24).
Israel was continually reminded by Yahweh that they were strangers in the
land of Egypt; strangers after 430 years? Yet Israelites were not strangers
in a land which they were to inhabit at some future date! The non-Israelite,
formerly a native in Canaan, became a stranger in his own land.
Nevertheless, in some of the sublime passages of the Torah we read, "You

must not molest the stranger or oppress him, ..." (Ex. 22:20); "You must not oppress the stranger; you know how a stranger feels, for you lived as strangers in the land of Egypt" (Ex. 23:9); "If a stranger lives with you in your land, do not molest him. You must count him as one of your own countrymen and love him as yourself—for you were once strangers yourselves in Egypt. I am Yahweh your God" (Lev. 19:33). Yahweh is described as "never partial, never to be bribed. It is he who ... loves the stranger and gives him food and clothing. Love the stranger then, for you were strangers in the land of Egypt" (Deut. 10:18–20). In light of the just quoted divine commandments, is it credible that the merciless killing of the non-Israelite strangers, the prohibition against showing any pity to them, prohibition against sparing the life of any living "thing" and the prohibition against their being allowed to live "in your country" would also be divine commandments? It is not credible and the priestly authors were mistaken. "Strangers" by definition were non-Israelites and the Torah does not distinguish between strangers to be loved and not molested and strangers—who committed no offense—to be extirpated.

The ever present priestly hand is seen when commandments were issued to make no pact with the nations to be expelled, nor worship their gods, nor marry their women, to dutifully tear down their altars, smash their standing stones and cut down their sacred poles. Did the latter, symbols of rank idolatry, constitute such a threat in the minds of priests to the enduring faith of Israel despite all the divine manifestations? As mentioned in Exodus, when the Israelites left Egypt, about 600,000 on the march—all men—not counting their families (Ex. 12:37–38), the total including their families would amount to 2½ million. We are told in Deuteronomy 7, that the land the Israelites were entering contained "seven nations greater and stronger than yourselves," which would make it a population in excess of 17½ million people! Historical chronicles do not show a single record of the grim pre-Canaan battles and conquests; kings mentioned are outside of history and lack authenticity. But, if not historical, why were these pre-Canaan battles and brutalities mentioned in the Torah? One can only conjecture. After the return from Babylon, when the Jews in Judah were weak, divided, poor, and intermarried with non-Jews, and without much hope for the future, Ezra, by introducing them to the Torah (for the first time), boosted their morale and solidified their national consciousness by acquainting them with their ancient glorious "history" and their many past military conquests. They were described in the only primitive manner then known.

10. Moses received the Torah from God at Sinai and presented it to the Israelites "This is the law which Moses put before the sons of Israel" (Deut. 4:44) and commanded the children of Israel the Torah as an inheritance of the assembly of Jacob (Deut. 33:4). It was the written Torah which the Israelites were commanded to follow; by God's commandment nothing could be added to it or taken from it. This language is as clear as could be. The whole Torah was handed down by Moses and is divine revelation from beginning to end. It is everlasting and unchangeable; anyone who denies the divine authority of even one verse or one word, denies the whole Torah, as stated by Maimonides.

The Torah contains contradictions, obscure passages and verses which are either susceptible to various interpretations or are not intelligible; the many scribal transcriptions or interpolations no doubt added to the confusion; many words or sentences were changed or left out altogether by the scribes, either by intent or error, so that some of the meaning is lost to us forever. This would be understandable and amends could have been made by the sages to supplement the meaning by admittedly human effort, however intelligent, if so indicated by scholia appended or noted in documents so identified. Judaism would not have suffered any ill-effects on this account. But it is a totally different matter to claim that the Torah, the Written Law, could not be properly understood without the benefit of the Oral Law, which the rabbis and sages claimed existed from the moment of the Written Law and were both given together to Moses at Sinai; that it was impossible for the Torah to exist without the Oral Law; that the Torah was given on the basis that it would be explained by the Oral Law; that the Oral Law was handed to the sages and rabbis from generation to generation who later memorialized it in the Mishnah (completed around 200 A.D.) which later became part of the Talmud (finalized around 400 A.D.—the Jerusalem Talmud; around 500 A.D.—the Babylonian Talmud). The talmudic sages and rabbis went so far as to proclaim that in certain cases the Oral Law could circumvent the Torah; that the whole of the Oral Law was given to Moses at Sinai and that the Oral Law was mutable and therefore retained its vitality with the passage of time.

The Oral Law is not the Torah, has no divine sanction, is the invention of the Pharisees, rabbis and sages; written down in the Mishnah (which later formed the basis of elaborations embraced in the Talmud) by the Tannaim, sages from Hillel to the final redaction of the Mishnah around 200 A.D.; the verses in the Torah (Deut. 17:8–11) which served as the justification for the belief in the Oral Law were based on pure sophistry. What the Tannaim asserted simply comes to this:

(a) The Torah was given to Moses as the Written Law, which by its very nature could not be totally comprehended.
(b) The Torah—the Written Law—needed an Oral Law, given to Moses concurrently, to properly interpret and understand the Torah and to complement it.
(c) The Oral Law was handed down from generations of sages to generations of sages unchanged in one continuous unbroken process.
(d) The Oral Law was finally written down in the Mishnah (around the 1st and 2nd centuries A.D.) and carried in certain cases more authority than the Torah.

The extension of the above analysis would involve hair-splitting casuistry; the primacy of the Torah is fundamental to Judaism and must remain undisputed. Among the books included in the canon, the Torah is the only one attributable to divine revelation; the rest of the books may be inspired but contain no divine imprimatur. The Mishnah is admittedly a purely human literary work. The Sadducees, a sect within Judaism (opposed to the Pharisees) accepted only the Torah as binding, accepted its literal interpretation and totally denied the validity of the Oral Law. They denied also resurrection of the dead, the doctrine of immortality and belief in angels as not validated by the Torah (For these same denials the young Spinoza was denounced to the Amsterdam synagogue authorities). Another sect, the Karaites, who came into being around the 8th century A.D., rejected the Talmud as an invention of the rabbis, rejected all talmudic and rabbinical tradition, rejected the Oral Law and urged their followers to strict adherence to the Torah.

11. Moses is described by the Jews as the author of the Torah; we do not know when and by whom he was depicted as the author, but in time he was universally acknowledged as such. There is no evidence that Moses was

the author; there is no extrabiblical evidence attesting to the historicity of Moses as all the evidence stems from the Torah. Despite extensive efforts made to-date by archaeologists they failed to come up with any clues attesting to the existence of Moses, like in so many other biblical events we have to rely solely on the Bible for authenticity. In a prior chapter reference was made to the many prophets who never mentioned Moses or his activities, certainly a most curious matter. King Josiah (640–609 B.C.) was the first king who heard of Moses from Hilkiah, his High Priest, through the discovery in the Temple of a Book of Law (assumed to be part of Deuteronomy) which would be, by accepted dating, about 600 years after the time of Moses.

My inquiry is not directed to finding out who wrote the Torah but only whether Moses was the author. Moses, the only man who spoke with Yahweh face to face, directly like to a friend and not in a vision or dream, was handed the Law directly by Yahweh on Mt. Sinai. This makes the Torah holy and revealed, the only book in the Old Testament about which such a claim can be asserted. The other books are admittedly man-written, inferior and not fundamental to Judaism. The Torah is the essence of Judaism and Moses had to be the author for it to retain its divinely revealed character. For if the Torah was not authored by Moses, it was therefore not a divine revelation—for a third person could not recite the colloquy between Yahweh and Moses and a second-hand disclosure is not revelation—then all the Jewish claims of preference, such as being selected by God as a people above all others as his own, favored above all other nations, destined to be a light unto nations, with whom God made a special and unique Covenant—such claims are spurious and no more than literary inventions. The moral maxims of the Torah, the ethical ordinances, the sublime social directives stand on their own merits regardless of who the author of the Torah was because of their ageless and universal applicability; only the particularism of the special election of the Jews would be subject to dispute. Over 1000 years before the Torah, the Egyptians had a code of moral, civil and criminal laws and a code of elaborate priestly laws. "The Mosaic code, though written down at least 1500 years later, shows no advance, in criminal legislation upon the code of Hammurabi; in legal organization it shows an archaic retrogression to primitive ecclesiastical control" (4–338). The Jewish historian, Abram Leon Sachar, speaking of Moses, "Yet of his life, of his very existence, we have no conclusive proof. Not a contemporaneous document, not a stele, not a shred of evidence has been found to authenticate his historicity ... the most influential personality in Jewish history may be merely the product of Jewish imagination" (5–16).

12. (a) Genesis contains the history of the Hebrews prior to the time of Moses; Moses is not mentioned and we are not told how or from where Moses received the information. "This is the story of Isaac son of Abraham" (Gen. 25:19); "This is the story of Joseph" (Gen. 37:2); we are not told from what source the story is derived and differs from the other books of the Torah where Yahweh, Moses or some other attribution is mentioned.

(b) "Here are the kings who ruled in the land of Edom before an Israelite king ruled" (Gen. 36:31–32).
A contemporary author could not know of events which occurred about 200 years later.

(c) "You will bring them and plant them on a mountain ... the place you have made your dwelling, Yahweh, the sanctuary ..." (Ex. 15:17).
Soon after Exodus, Moses made reference to Yahweh's Temple in Jerusalem. A contemporary author could not know of an event which occurred over 250 years later.

(d) "Abram passed through the land ... At that time the Canaanites were in the land" (Gen. 12:6–7).
A contemporary author could not know that the Canaanites had been driven out from Canaan after the death of Moses.

(e) "When Abram heard that his kinsman had been taken captive, he mustered his supporters, ... and led them in pursuit as far as Dan" (Gen. 14:14–15).
A contemporary author could not know that the city "Dan" was not so named till long after the death of Joshua (Judges 18:29).

(f) "Then Yahweh said to Moses, 'How much longer will you refuse to keep my commandments ...?' " (Ex. 16:28)
A contemporary author had to know that up to that point in time no commandments had been given by Yahweh to the Israelites.

(g) "The priests, the men who do approach Yahweh, ..." (Ex. 19:22).
A contemporary author had to know that up to that point in time the priestly order had not been established by Yahweh.

(h) "The sons of Israel ate manna for 40 years, up to the time they reached ... the frontier of the land of Canaan" (Ex. 16:35–36).
If Moses was the author, he could not have known that after the Israelites pitched their camp at Gilgal and kept the Passover there, "From that time ... the manna stopped falling" (Joshua 5:12). Moses died before that time.

(i) "These are the words spoken beyond the Jordan to the whole of Israel ... Moses spoke to the sons of Israel as Yahweh had ordered" (Deut. 1:1–3).
If Moses was the author, he could not have spoken beyond the Jordan since he never crossed the Jordan.

(j) "Now Moses was the most humble of men, the humblest man on earth" (Num. 12:3).
If Moses was the author, he could not have spoken these words about himself.

(k) "There in the land of Moab, Moses the servant of Yahweh died as Yahweh decreed; ..." (Deut. 34:5–6).
If Moses was the author he could not have spoken these words about himself.

(1) "... but to this day no one has ever found his grave" (Deut. 34:7).
A contemporary author could not have spoken these words "to this day" which would refer to a time far removed, and Moses certainly could not have written these words.

(m) "The sons of Israel wept for Moses in the plains of Moab for 30 days" (Deut. 34:8).
If Moses was the author, he could not have written these words.

(n) "Since then, never has there been such a prophet in Israel as Moses, the man Yahweh knew face to face" (Deut. 34:10–11).
A contemporary author could not have spoken such words. It had to be written after many of the prophets were known, at least 600 years after the death of Moses.

(o) "And taking the Book of Covenant he read it to the listening people, ..." (Ex. 24:7); "Moses committed this Law to writing and gave it to the priests, ..." (Deut. 31:9). "When Moses had finished writing in a book the words of this Law to the very end ..." (Deut. 31:24–25); "Moses put all the commands of Yahweh into writing, and early next morning ..." (Ex. 24:4).

Certain conclusions can be drawn from the four quotations cited. If the author was Moses, he chose to refer to himself in the third person (which style was used almost throughout the Torah) even though he was writing a book within a book, an event more suited for description in the first person; that the book (Book of Covenant or Book of Law) was short enough that it could be read in one sitting, "Call the people together for them to hear it ... ," (Deut. 31:12); that book is now lost to us. After Moses wrote all the commands of Yahweh, "and early next morning" would imply that the writing took one day or less. In subsequent history, no reference is made to its existence until possibly the High Priest Hilkiah found the "Book of Law" in the Temple between 640-609 B.C. which could have been the same book of Moses; if so, it certainly could not have been the book of Deuteronomy on account of its shortness.

13. A divinely revealed book cannot contain contradictory versions of events. This would indicate the author was confused or there was more than one author and they did not conform their story. In either case the writing could not have been divinely revealed.

(a) The Torah contains two accounts of the sequence in creation. The first account in Gen. 1:1 and 2:4—reference is made to vegetation and living creatures only—the sequence was: Plants, Animals, Man and Woman. The second account in Gen. 2:5–25 the sequence was: Man, Plants, Animals, Woman. The creation stories are so primitive that they are beneath criticism, but the sequences in both versions are so different that they must have been written by more than one author.

(b) In commanding the Israelites to remember the Sabbath day and keep it holy, Yahweh informed them that for six days he made heaven, earth and all that these held, "but on the seventh day he rested" (Ex. 20:11), and that was the reason why he blessed the Sabbath day. The second version mentioned nothing about creation or Yahweh resting on the seventh day. Instead, the Israelites were commanded to observe the Sabbath day and keep it holy because they were servants in the land of Egypt and Yahweh their God brought them out of there with a mighty hand. "... because of this, Yahweh your God has commanded you to keep the sabbath day" (Deut. 5:15). Both versions are so contrary that the pen of more than one author was at work.

14. Writing the Torah long after the events described occurred enabled the author to focus on prophecies which came true. The final redaction of the Torah occurred about 450 B.C. to 300 B.C., long after the events described in the Torah, but apparently not long enough for certain key prophecies to be proven false by the test of subsequent time. A divinely revealed book cannot contain false prophecies of any kind, let alone events which go to fundamental issues.

(a) "Yahweh spoke to Moses and said, 'Phinehas the priest ... has turned my wrath away from the sons of Israel because he was the only one among them to have the same zeal as I have; ...To him I now grant my covenant of peace. For him and for his descendants after him, this covenant shall ensure the priesthood for ever" ' (Num. 25:11–13).
That prophecy is false. The priesthood endured up to the destruction of the Second Temple in 70 A.D.

(b) Yahweh made a Covenant with Abraham,
"To your descendants I give this land, from the wadi of Egypt to the Great River, the river Euphrates, ..." (Gen. 15:18–19) and Moses quoting Yahweh to have said at Mt. Horeb "... go to the land of Canaan and to Lebanon as far as the great river Euphrates. This is the land I have made over to your fathers, Abraham, Isaac and Jacob, and to their descendants after them" (Deut. 1:7–8).
This prophecy is false. Israel never occupied the extent of the land described.

(c) Yahweh spoke to Abraham,
"I will shower blessings on you, I will make your descendants as many as the stars of heaven and the grains of sand on the seashore. Your descendants shall gain possession of the gates of their enemies. All nations of the earth shall bless themselves by your descendants, as a reward for your obedience" (Gen. 22:17–18).

Not only are all four prophecies false, but the author displayed a total ignorance of astronomy and geography.

15. Beginning with the 18th century, modern biblical scholars began to see, in time, as many as four different (or more) major sources of the Torah based on topical, stylistic and linguistic distinctions and different variations of the same story; they referred to them as J (Yahweh source), E (Elohim source), P (Priestly source) and D (Deuteronomy source). These were all combined in order not to challenge their authenticity if presented separately and pacify different factions. These studies are very plausible. For my purposes suffice it to say their studies do not point to Moses as the author of the Torah.

16. The Torah was written by authors who lived long after the events described, i.e., long after Moses; it was written for cities and not for the desert (Deut. 14:27); the laws and ordinances applied to people who were well settled and engaged in agriculture and not nomads living in the desert.

The priests were the only ones who had the learning and intelligence to be the authors of such a book; they were the interested party; the commandments, laws and ordinances primarily benefited them, both as to achieving monopoly power and wealth; it was written with a view of maintaining control over Israel against encroachment of all alien "poachers" from without and from within. The Torah could not be divinely revealed because its priestly laws made Israel a nation apart, different from the Gentiles, admonished not to have contact with foreigners or alien religions, not to eat with them or intermarry or show them any favors, which would assuredly pollute them and preclude them from being a holy nation. They were taught that their religion could not be practiced in foreign lands because their God did not dwell there; all with the result that these peculiar priests caused Israel to become a peculiar people with a peculiar mind and nature, set on a collision course with far more numerous and powerful neighbors who reciprocated the hatred: the rest is history. These bad laws could not be attributed to an omniscient God, who cared for Israel and the stranger, i.e., for all the people in the world.

The Torah shaped the nature of Jews, since most assimilated its teachings regardless of whether its origin was divinely revealed or not; they believed in it and guided their lives accordingly. Not long after the Torah was redacted (between 450 B.C. and 300 B.C.) and about 500 years later after the destruction of the Second Temple in 70 A.D., the priests and their descendants which were to endure "for ever" mercifully disappeared from history. The Jews, who by then embraced their bequeathed particularism, peculiarity and exclusivity, faced the Diaspora with damning consequences. It was the enmity of non-Jews which, by irony of fate, helped preserve the Jews and Judaism; the seeds of enmity were planted long before the onset of the Catholic Church which multiplied the burden of the Jews a thousandfold, whose priesthood learned the lessons well from the Mosaic priests concerning the need to destroy alien religions ruthlessly—Judaism in particular—eliminate all opposition and achieve monopoly power.

17. After the destruction of the Second Temple and with the disappearance of the priesthood, the rabbis and later also the geonim (originally title of heads of Jewish academies in Sura and Pumbedita in Babylonia, later on title of respect for rabbis of great learning of the Torah) took over the spiritual leadership of the Jewish people who were by that time scattered over many countries. This new leadership became, in time, the new aristocracy of privilege, well remembering the position of wealth and power of the bygone priesthood, jealously guarding against opposing claimants and playing the same political strategy of self-preservation. All this is understandable. But they inherited the Torah precepts which they meticulously enforced (with some exceptions, mainly that of animal sacrifices, which were tied to the Temple) even though the Jews lived mostly outside Palestine, viewing their attachment to the most minor details as piety. Guilty of the same mistakes as perpetrated by the bygone priests, including the fomenting of hopeless and frivolous uprisings against powerful rulers and always ending up on the losing side, the rabbis were, in time, reconciled to the status of Jews as "strangers" and minority in foreign lands (with all the disabilities this imposed) making the best of things until the advent of the Messiah (as the rabbis assured would happen in time), only to encounter head-on a much more powerful and much more resourceful opponent: Christianity. The rabbis were unable to grasp the damage some of the peculiar priestly writings inflicted on the nature and mind of the Jewish people; their views aided, abetted and consoled by the writings of talmudic scholars; refusing to recognize the changing conditions in which they lived; endorsed and subscribed to such mind-perverting command-

ments, laws and ordinances which emanated from the divinely revealed Torah, citing just a few:

Death to witches.

Death to apostates.

Death to those who insult or disobey the priest.

Death to heretics and blasphemers of Yahweh.

Death to the profaner of the Sabbath.

Death to anyone who curses his father or mother.

Death by stoning of a stubborn son who will not listen to his father's voice.

Death by stoning of a young wife who cannot show evidence of her virginity.

Jews are the Chosen People of God as his own, over and above all other nations.

Given in perpetual heritage by God the land between the wadi of Egypt and the river Euphrates.

Instructed by God not to associate in any way with their neighbors, a people confined to its own. Moral and ethical behavior is mandated as between Jews; as to non-Jews, there is no restriction as to behavior.

Some foods were prohibited and not to be eaten by Jews; this differentiated them even more from non-Jews.

They were not to eat with non-Jews at one table.

They were not to bear non-Jews any friendly feeling.

Jews had an exclusive Covenant with God.

For the deed of one man or a few, a nation shall suffer. The misdeed of father shall pass on to son, grandson, great-grandson.

Choice of one tribe (the Levites) as perpetually advantaged over the other tribes, hereditary and decreed by God.

God punishes a whole people, regardless of children, aged, sick or infirm.

God is invisible, no images can be made, yet he is portrayed in a most anthropomorphic form.

Non-Jews are mercilessly extirpated (whole nations) on God's command for no other reason than that they were placed in the wrong spot by God.

God shall be the enemy of the enemies of Jews.

God shall exterminate the nations of the Amorites, Hittites, Perizzites, Canaanites, Hivites, Jebusites, to make room for the Jews in the Promised Land.

When a woman has slept with a man they will be both unclean until the evening.

Jews were to devour all those peoples whom Yahweh delivered over to them, show them no pity.

Jews must not eat any animal that has died a natural death. They may give it for food to an alien or sell it to a foreigner.

A woman becomes unclean at childbirth and more so if the child is a daughter.

If a man or woman violates Yahweh's covenant, he or she must be stoned to death.

Jews are not to give themselves a foreign king who is no brother of theirs.

If a prophet presumes to speak in the name of Yahweh, a thing which he has not commanded, that prophet shall die.

A Jew must not lend on interest to another Jew, but he may demand interest on a loan to a foreigner.

When two men are fighting and the wife of one intervenes by putting her hand on the other's private parts, the husband shall cut off her hand and show no pity.

If the Jews do not obey the voice of Yahweh, they will become a thing of horror for all the kingdoms of the earth, they will be accursed, they will never be anything but exploited and plundered continually, no one will come to their help, Yahweh will scatter them among all peoples from one end of the earth to the other, there will be no repose among nations.

18. Put plainly and in simple terms, the elders and sages of Israel always associated defeat or disaster with disobeying the voice of Yahweh. Judaism was so structured that the consequences of following the voice of Yahweh and obedience of his laws always resulted in Israel receiving blessings and all the good life, prosperity and advantages so frequently promised in the Torah. So that if Israel suffered defeat, bad harvest, drought or any other disaster, the soul searching followed inevitably and the blame targeted with telling regularity: Israel caused the anger of Yahweh to blaze by violating some of his laws. Yahwism provided for no other solution. The priests, in

order to keep Israel under control, desired to teach in the Torah that the land of Yahweh corresponded with his worshippers, that Yahweh could not be worshiped outside his land (where the priests centralized the worship in the Jerusalem Temple and where in the land they exercised monopoly of power), that the land of foreigners was unclean and profane. Israel could only worship in the land where Yahweh dwelt, i.e., where his Temple stood. This concept applied limitations to Yahweh since outside of his land other gods had to be worshiped.

The Jews faced the threat of exile with horror since that would deprive them of worshipping Yahweh and bring all the disastrous curses upon their heads. Yet this was not so. Yahweh's laws had to be kept as long as Israel lived in the land of milk and honey, in the Promised Land. In Deut. 12:1 we find: "… these are the laws and customs that you must keep and observe, in the land that Yahweh the God of your fathers had granted you to possess, as long as you live in that land." The meaning should be clear: These laws and customs were not required to be kept and observed in a land other than the one mentioned in Deut. 12:1. For in Deut. 28:63 ff, it is stated that for not obeying the voice of Yahweh, he would take delight in bringing Israel to ruin and destruction and foretold that Israel would be torn from the land destined to be their own and would be scattered among all peoples, from one end of the earth to the other and **"there you will serve other gods of wood and stone** … Among these nations there will be no repose for you, …" (Deut. 28:64–65). The Jews, who left for the foreign lands (Alexandria, Rome, Cyprus, Cyrenaica, etc.) prior to the destruction of the Second Temple, did so voluntarily and kept their bonds with Jerusalem: They felt bound to practice the religion of their fathers. Yahweh continued to favor them with good fortune. With the destruction of the Second Temple and their country, the Jews had to conclude that Yahweh's hatred blazed against them because they disobeyed his voice. The expulsion to many foreign lands would relieve them from obedience to Yahweh's laws and customs. If the message was not clear, it certainly came through like a thunder with the disastrous defeat of the Bar Kokhba revolt some 60 years later. The decimation, enslavement and expulsion of Jews was so overwhelming that the message came through loud and clear: Yahweh took delight in bringing them ruin and destruction, placing on Israel "an iron yoke on your neck until you perish" (Deut. 28:48).

The rabbis, distraught and in search of meaning could find none. In their view Jews were more just and faithful, were less deserving of punishment than their enemies and neighbors. They concluded that Yahweh withdrew from all intervention in the affairs of Jews and simply abandoned them. Listed among his last instructions, Moses admonished Israel to stay faithful to Yahweh; that he taught them all his laws and customs; that when they would come to know the benefits of all these teachings they would all exclaim: "No other people is as wise and prudent as this great nation" (Deut. 4:7).

But Moses was mistaken! The authors were mistaken!

Chapter 15

The Book of Joshua
and the Conquest

1. The Book of Joshua relates the story of the conquest of Canaan by the children of Israel. Unlike the Covenant with Abraham in which Yahweh "gave" to his descendants the land from the wadi of Egypt to the river Euphrates, the land of Canaan was inherited by military force, it had to be conquered. Further, in Joshua 1:4–5 the definition of the land is changed by adding "… to the great river Euphrates" an additional definition "… and to the Great Sea westwards , …" Israel never occupied the land to the river Euphrates and only a small strip to the Great Sea westwards; that prophecy was false and the author was mistaken.

It is claimed that Joshua wrote the book; that Yahweh directed all the military campaigns which led to the conquest of Canaan; that there were ongoing dialogues between Yahweh and Joshua and that Joshua obediently carried out Yahweh's instructions. It is apparent that Joshua could not have been the author, that the book was written long after Joshua's death (probably six centuries), that the content of the book presents serious difficulties about the historical aspects of the Conquest, and that the actual author, not privy to the frequent colloquies with Yahweh, is not to be trusted.

2. When Joshua requested of Yahweh for the sun to stand still over Gibeon (apart from the absurdity of this request and the transfer of the author's ignorance to Yahweh, Yahweh could not respond since he would have to order the earth to stand still and not the sun, which already stood still) it is stated in Josh. 10:13, "Is this not written in the Book of the Just? …" Not only did the "Book of the Just" disappear from history (it left no trace) but it must be of later dating than Joshua for we read in 2 Sam. 1:17–18, "Then David made this lament over Saul and his son Jonathan. It

165

is written in the Book of the Just ...", an event that occurred about 200 years later than the date of Joshua. Other indications that Joshua could not be the author:

(a) "It was then that the place was given the name the Vale of Achor, which it is still called now" (Josh. 7:26).
The author recalled what happened long after the time of writing the book.

(b) "Then Joshua burned Ai, making it a ruin for evermore, a desolate place even today" (Josh. 8:28–29).
The author recalled what happened long after the time of writing the book.

(c) "... a great cairn was reared over it; and that is still there today" (Josh. 8:29).
The author recalled what happened long after the time of writing the book.

(d) "... Joshua made them wood-cutters and water-carriers for the community, and bound them, down to the present day, to wait on Yahweh's altar ..." (Josh. 9:27).
Speaking of the Gibeonites, the author recalled what happened long after the time of writing the book.

(e) "Great stones were laid at the mouth of the cave, and these are still there today" (Josh. 10:27).
Speaking of the five kings who were thrown into the cave of Makkedah after their hanging, the author recalled an event long after the time of writing down the story.

(f) "But the sons of Judah could not drive out the Jebusites who lived in Jerusalem; the Jebusites lived in Jerusalem side by side with the sons of Judah, as they still do today" (Josh. 15:63).
The author recalled what happened long after the time of writing the book.

(g) "Israel served Yahweh throughout the lifetime of Joshua and the lifetime of those elders who outlived Joshua and had known all the deeds that Yahweh had done for the sake of Israel" (Josh. 24:31).
Joshua could not be the author of this verse.

(h) "There was never a day like that before or since, when Yahweh obeyed the voice of a man, ..." (Josh. 10:14).

The author recalled what happened many generations after the time of writing the book.

3. Again, in a time-barren vacuum, hanging in the air, filled with gaseous verbiage, unrecorded by history, unverifiable by any independent source except the Old Testament, a story is told in a manner that was meant to be unverifiable, obfuscating and full of mind-poisoning bigotry. Joshua—of whom no non-Biblical reference exists—and his army doing strictly Yahweh's bidding, slaughtered every human being in militarily conquered towns which offered resistance, without mercy or compunction and called it piety. The story goes on that Yahweh hardened the heart of enemies of Israel, so they would not surrender without bloodshed and thus be slaughtered in battle by the Israelites whom Yahweh wished to be victorious; as if the Israelites could not, in light of their conduct, slaughter them without the pretext of resistance. Did the Israelites not suffer any casualties on account of Yahweh's strategy? But then the author let his imagination run wild, as with the five Amorite kings who joined forces to take the town of Gibeon and Yahweh hurled hailstones from heaven on them, "More of them died under the hailstones than at the edge of Israel's sword" (Josh. 10:11–12).

4. It is generally accepted by biblical scholars that the Conquest (and therefore the Exodus) occurred in the time frame between 1475 B.C. and 1220 B.C. Various reasons are given for views which hold a period closer to 1475 B.C. or closer to 1220 B.C. Suffice it to say that no non-Biblical texts refer to the Israelite conquest of Canaan and that continuously updated archaeological evidence challenges scientific opinions concerned with a firmer dating. In any event, there do remain serious differences of opinion on the subject. The resolution of the problem will have to weigh the following:

(a) The Conquest (if there was one, for there is no assurance of its historicity) had to take place between 1500 B.C. and 1150 B.C.; there is no other time-frame within which to place it. The Hyksos ruled Egypt from about 1650 B. C. to about 1550 B. C. and the Exodus and Conquest could not be earlier than 1500 B.C. By consensus of biblical scholars, the period of Jephthah (Judges) has to be dated no later than 1100 B. C., the accession of Saul to about 1050 B.C. to 1040

B.C., so that the latest date for the Conquest could not be after 1150 B.C.; even that date would be too late anyway for it would not leave any room for the period of Judges, which must have been well in excess of 200 years.

(b) We read (1 Kings 6:1) that the Exodus occurred 480 years before the 4th year of Solomon's reign (967 B.C.) which would date it 1447 B.C.; the Conquest would be dated 40 years later, or about 1407 B.C. The calculation in 1 Kings 6:1 is in error for, following strictly biblical data, the figure would be in excess of 600 years, which would approximate the upper limit of 1500 B.C.

(c) The stele of Pharaoh Merneptah (1233–1220 B.C.) made reference, circa 1220 B.C., to the people of Israel as defeated in battle in Canaan by Egyptian forces. Israel must have been well settled by that time to be mentioned as an opponent of a powerful Egyptian ruler and to merit mention on a stele.

(d) From 1500 B.C. until the reign of Rameses III, Canaan was occupied and ruled by strong Egyptian rulers who stationed military garrisons throughout Canaan which would make the Conquest practically impossible. It was not until Rameses III (1182 B.C.–1151 B.C.) that Egypt abandoned occupation of Canaan.

(e) No mention was made in the Book of Joshua of Egyptian garrisons which we know occupied many forts throughout Canaan between the 15th and the beginning of the 12th centuries B.C. .

(f) No single city besieged by the Israelites sought help from the Egyptian garrisons despite facing complete annihilation; they paid tribute to Egypt and the Egyptians would most certainly have come to their aid if for no other reason than to secure the flow of tribute to Egypt. This was the purpose of their occupation of Canaan.

What conclusions can be drawn from the above?

(a) We have the parameters for the Conquest dating between 1500 B.C. and 1150 B.C. No biblical scholar ever suggested an earlier or later date for the Exodus or Conquest.

(b) There is no non-biblical mention of the Conquest.

(c) The Book of Joshua did not mention Egyptian military garrisons which would have certainly interfered with the military activity of the Israelites.

(d) Towns which were said to have been attacked made no call for help to the Egyptian garrisons stationed throughout Canaan.

The el-Amarna texts made no reference to any calls for help.

(e) The Book of Joshua made no mention of encountering any Israelites who, by 1220 B.C., were settled in Canaan according to the Merneptah stele.

(f) If the Book of Joshua is history, the Conquest had to take place before 1300 B.C.

(g) Canaan was occupied by strong Egyptian military garrisons between the early 15th and the beginning of the 12th century B.C. to secure the steady flow of tribute; Egyptian rulers would have reacted swiftly to any Israelite interference or military presence. Nothing on the subject was mentioned in the Book of Joshua. If the Israelites had 600,000 men of military age equipped for war and a people numbering 2½ million in total, the silence in the el-Amarna tablets is inexplicable.

(h) It therefore appears that the military Conquest cannot be placed within the time-frame between the late 15th and beginning of the 12th century B.C. The position of many biblical scholars is moving away from military conquest of Canaan to a concept of peaceful infiltration (or even to the merging of native tribes without outside infiltration); this would nullify the Book of Joshua.

4. But there are much more serious reasons for questioning the historicity of the Conquest as described in the Book of Joshua, some of the military conquests as described in the Book of Numbers and the sojourn in Sinai as described in the Book of Deuteronomy. Archaeological evidence indicates some of the cities (towns) were already destroyed within the period from the 15th to the 13th century B.C. Similarly, for towns or locations mentioned in Numbers and Deuteronomy. But certain key cities (towns) mentioned and claimed to have been destroyed by Joshua were not destroyed by Joshua and his army for the simple reason that there were no such cities to destroy; they simply did not exist or were without habitation between the 15th and 13th century B.C. Similarly for towns or locations mentioned in Numbers and Deuteronomy.

Jericho   Joshua 6 relates the destruction of the city by the Israelites. City destroyed by fire before 1450 B.C.; no remains or evidence of population in 1250 B.C. or occupation. If so, the story in Joshua 6:1 ff is fiction from beginning to end.

Ai   Joshua 8 relates the destruction of the city by the Israelites. There is no evidence of occupation between 2400 B.C. and 1200 B.C. If so, the story in Joshua 8:1 is fiction from beginning to end.

Gibeon   Joshua 9:3 describes the ruse of the Gibeonites. There is no evidence of settlement between 15th and 13th century B.C., none has been found. If so, the story in Joshua 9:3 ff is fiction from beginning to end.

Hebron   Joshua 10:36–37 describes the destruction of the city by the Israelites. The city was destroyed before 1450 B.C.; populated again around 1200 B.C. If so, the story in Joshua is fiction.

Arad   Numbers 21:1–3 describes the destruction of the town by the Israelites. The site was abandoned from 2000 B.C. to 1200 B.C. If so, the story in Numbers 21:1–3 is fiction.

Hormah   Numbers 21:1–3 describes the destruction of the town by the Israelites. The town was fortified from 1900 B.C. to 1550 B.C., about which time the town was destroyed. It was resettled in the 12th century B.C. There was no intervening occupation. If so, the story in Numbers 21:1–3 is fiction.

Dibon   Numbers 21:30 mentions the destruction of the town by the Israelites. No town existed between 2300 B.C. and 1200 B.C. If so, reference in Numbers 21:30 is fiction.

Kadesh-Barnea   According to Deut. 1:19 ff, the Israelites spent most of their 40 years in Sinai around Kadesh-Barnea. There is no evidence of occupation at any of the possible sites for Kadesh-Barnea between 1500 B.C. and 1200 B.C. If so, there are serious problems with the story of the Sinai wanderings of the Israelites.

I have chosen four cities (towns) from the Book of Joshua and four towns (locations) from the Books of Numbers and Deuteronomy because the events of Exodus and Conquest are closely linked and dependent on each other for historical evidence and also because the dating of one affects the dating of the other. Although scientific deductions from archaeological explorations may arrive at varying results in the future, there appears to be no doubt about the dating of the 8 locations cited above: The biblical author was mistaken and his manipulative endeavor transparent. It must come as cold comfort to the student of the Bible to face the realization that, for example, the biblical story of the conquest of Jericho, the lengthy and elaborate story of the conquest of Ai, the treaty with the Gibeonites, Joshua's call to Yahweh for the sun to delay setting for a whole day till the people had vengeance on their enemies, and all the reported colloquy between Yahweh and Joshua in connection with the events connected with these three cities, were inventions of the author and fiction from beginning to end.

5. But the problems go further.

Jabin, King of Hazor was captured by Joshua and put to the sword; the Israelites put every living creature in Hazor to the sword, not a soul was left and thereafter burned the city of Hazor (Josh. 11:10 ff). However, in Judges 4:2 ff, we read that the Israelite army led by Barak killed Jabin, the King of Canaan, who reigned at Hazor.

Joshua built an altar of undressed stones to Yahweh on Mt. Ebal. "There Joshua wrote on the stones a copy of the Law which Moses had written for the Israelites" (Josh. 8:32–33), all Israel with their elders, scribes and judges took their places, half of them in front of Mt. Gerizim, and half of them in front of Mt. Ebal. Joshua read all the words of the Law exactly as written in the Book of the Law by Moses and read it in the presence of the full assembly of Israel, including women, children and strangers living among the people. Nothing written down by Moses was left unread. (Josh. 8:33 ff). This story is relevant for two reasons:

(a) That the whole Law of Moses, i.e., the Torah, was written down on the stones of an altar by Joshua leaving nothing out; that the Law was read by Joshua to the whole assembly of Israel. The Law therefore was not of the length of the Torah as we understand it today but an infinitely smaller version of it. The contradiction cannot be resolved.

(b) The full assembly of Israel, half in front of Mt. Gerizim and half in front of Mt. Ebal; the size of the people within the earshot of Joshua could not possibly number 2½ million. Therefore the 603,550 men over 20 years old fit to bear arms (Num. 1:46 ff) and their families could not anywhere approach the number assembled by Joshua. The contradiction cannot be resolved.

The Reubenites, the Gadites and half-tribe of Manasseh left Shiloh in the land of Canaan to build an altar beside the Jordan, beyond the territory of the Israelites. The Israelites sent the priest Phinehas and the ten leading men to upbraid them for their treachery committed against the God of Israel by building an altar, an act of rebellion against Yahweh himself as a result of which Yahweh's anger would be roused against the whole community of Israel (Josh. 22:9 ff). Behind the story, or the moral of the story, lurks the hand of the priest whose authority and prerogatives were invaded by this act of "treachery" and "rebellion". Suffice it to say that despite all the miracles of the Exodus, Moses, Yahweh's leadership in the Sinai, the miracle of assistance in Joshua's conquest of Canaan, the oaths and acceptance of Yahweh's Commandments, the freshness of it all in the minds of the Reubenites, Gadites and half-tribe of Manasseh, the defection from Yahweh and the apostasy and backsliding continued. The rest of the Israelites were ready to march against the "rebels" and make war on them. The reason for the "treachery" given by the three tribes gets a bit garbled (no doubt rewritten many times by the priestly author till the original story or message was emptied of its meaning), but the priest Phinehas set them straight and restored their fidelity, to everybody's relief.

6. The priestly author is skulking behind the scene and his hand is visible directing the drama. The priests are involved in the battles; they lead the ark into combat; saw to it that all battle plans originate with Yahweh; prescribed that in the case of Jericho, all gold, silver, things of bronze and iron were consecrated to "God's treasury," i.e., priests' treasury in the sanctuary. In order to prevent any backsliding and "whoring" after other gods on the part of the Israelites, which would diminish the function and power of priests, it served their purpose that all inhabitants of the captured cities were to be totally eradicated. Those were cruel times for losers in most battles; for the sake of survival, the quality of mercy and forgiveness were not virtues. But the Conquest consisted of unprovoked aggression, as in "Joshua and all of Israelites with him ... turned aside to Debir and attacked it" (Josh. 10:38) and the result invariably was that after defeating their opponent, the Israelites put all the men, women and children to the sword,

slaughtering them all and left none alive; and just in case a spark of remorse or pity caused damage to the mind, the priests reminded one and all that all this was "... as Yahweh the God of Israel had commanded" (Josh. 10:40), that every single soul should be delivered over to the ban, i.e., slaughtered. All this to place a Chosen People in "a land where milk and honey flow." But not all people were slaughtered; the priestly efforts to protect their flock from "whoring after other gods" resulted in issuing already familiar warnings: Keep all that is written in the Book of Law of Moses, never turn aside from it, never mingle with the people who are still "left", do not utter the names of their gods, do not serve them, be loyal to Yahweh your God. "But if you prove faithless, if you make friends with the remnant of those peoples who are still left beside you, if you form kinships with them and intermarry ..." (Josh. 23:12–13) then the people of Israel must certainly expect that Yahweh would no longer protect them; they would vanish from the good land that Yahweh gave them and he would fulfill all his threats of evil. Yet, despite all this, some Israelites have gone astray, for Joshua warned them, "If you desert Yahweh to follow alien gods ..." (Josh. 24:20) and cautioned them, "Then cast away the alien gods among you and give your hearts to Yahweh the God of Israel!" (Josh. 24:23–24). The people answered Joshua, "It is Yahweh our God we choose to serve; ..." (Josh. 24:24). This has a familiar ring to it, see Ex. 23:32–33 and Ex. 24:3 ff.

7. Such is the story of Joshua and the Conquest. Why would the author invent so much? Why would the author invent the conquest of Jericho, Ai, and Hebron and the total annihilation of their populations? Was it his purpose to boost national pride in founding a heroic history of the nation? It certainly would serve his priestly purpose to make the Israelites aware of the gratitude owed the benevolence of Yahweh, their God, for the acquisition of the "... land where milk and honey flow." Yet despite all such dark propaganda, all he left was a baleful legacy.

8. The Book of Joshua is in the canon; it is set in concrete. It has been read, studied, debated, argued, critically examined throughout Jewish history. What effect did all the savagery—the slaughter of innocent men, women and children on order of and with full blessing of Yahweh, which would make it "just" by definition, whose only crime was defending their homes and families—have on the Jewish mind, regardless whether it is history or

fiction? Jews have faced merciless and pitiless extermination many times in their history and were likewise guiltless. The Crusades, the Catholic Inquisitions, forced conversions, blood-libels, the Holocaust, to name a few. In contemplating the magnitude of the disasters which struck the Jewish people throughout history, the enormity of which deprived reason of its foothold, did any of the rabbis, geonim and sages feel the slightest twinge of remorse or contrition in reviewing the barbarities described in the Book of Joshua? Did it remotely remind them of anything? There is no answer! To have done so would be regarded as rank blasphemy and the confessor treated as an outcast. The priestly devised codes and the priestly authored history of the Israelites, as written in the Torah and the Book of Joshua, could not help but leave deep imprints on the mind of Jews who consider these books sacrosanct; they read and reread them with awe and religious punctilio.

To the extent that, and if as a result of this, they chose a lesser "good" or worse "bad" in their struggle for self-preservation and survival and which efforts were vitiated on that account, then to that extent it can be said their conduct was affected by mind-perverting influences. To the extent that, and if as a result of this, their conduct and relationship with their non-Jewish neighbors throughout history was adversely affected, causing hostility and animosity which turned ugly, then to that extent their conduct was affected by mind-perverting influences.

These influences will come to the fore in the subject matter of the next and later chapters.

Chapter 16

Uprisings, Priests and Rabbis

1. So that the reader can better visualize the connection and sequence between biblical narration and actual history as it evolved to more certain footing, I shall furnish the briefest of outlines of events of the Israelites and Jews from Moses to the Bar Kokhba revolt against Rome to serve the intended purpose. When no dates are furnished it is because none that are certain exist. Where only approximations are furnished it is because that is what is available.

Moses, followed by Joshua, the period of "Judges" (about 200–300 years of recurring defections from and reaffirmation of Yahweh, including such figures as Deborah, Barak, Gideon, Jephthah, Samson), Samuel (decision to install monarchical government), Saul, David (ca 1010 B.C.–970 B.C.), Solomon (ca 970 B.C.–922 B.C.), division of kingdom into Judah and Israel after Solomon's death and the rule of the Kingdom of Judah under his son Rehoboam (ca 922 B.C.–915 B.C.) and the Kingdom of Israel under Jeroboam (ca 922–901 B.C.), leader of the rebellion against Solomon and Rehoboam; the Kingdom of Israel after the rule of 19 kings was defeated and led into captivity by the Assyrians in 722 B.C. and disappeared from history; the Kingdom of Judah, after the rule of 19 kings and one queen, was led into Babylonian Exile in two stages by the Babylonians and finally defeated by them 587 B.C. (who also destroyed the Temple); allowed to return from the Exile to Jerusalem ca 537 B.C. under the Persian ruler Cyrus (Persia during the Exile of Jews conquered Babylonia). Under Cyrus' successor Darius I, the Second Temple was built in Jerusalem and dedicated ca 515 B.C.; ca 458 B.C. Ezra dedicated the Torah to the Jerusalem Jews; Nehemiah was appointed governor of Judea by Persian ruler Artaxerxes I ca 445 B.C. and ruled as governor for about

12 years; Malachi (the last Prophet) was active between ca 464 B.C.–424 B.C.; Persian domination ended 333 B.C.; Judea was subject to the Egyptian Ptolemies 312 B.C.–198 B.C.; in 198 B.C. Antiochus III defeated Ptolemy V and made Judea part of the Seleucid empire; Maccabean revolt against the Seleucids between 168 B.C.–142 B.C.; political independence under Hasmonean rulers 142 B.C.–63 B.C.; Roman General Pompey conquered Judea 63 B.C.; reign of Herod the Great 37 B.C.–4 B.C.; his son Herod Archelaus succeeded him after his death and ruled 4 B.C.–6 A.D.; Roman Procurators governed from 6 A.D.–41 A.D.; Herod Agrippa I was King of Judea 41 A.D.–44 A.D.; Roman Procurators ruled again 44 A.D.–66 A.D.; Jewish revolt against Rome 66 A.D.–70 A.D. ending with defeat of the Jews, the destruction of the Second Temple and the dissolution of the Jewish State; the function and power of the Temple priesthood ceased; Jewish revolt against Rome under Bar Kokhba 132 A.D.–135 A.D. (who established a Jewish State which existed for over 3 years) ending with total defeat and expulsion of Jews from Jerusalem.

The above brief outline does not include many other Jewish revolts which will be mentioned later in this chapter; suffice it to say here that the Jewish blood which flowed from the time of the Maccabean revolt till the Bar-Kokhba final defeat is mind-boggling. No estimates are available but it is safe to say that the Jewish losses exceeded by far 1,500,000 lives, including the flower of Jewish youth and manhood. After so many frivolous and ill-advised revolts, the major ones fomented and instigated by the priests and rabbis, which never really brought the desired results, the Jews were resigned to abandon the quest for freedom and for their own State by force of arms; instead, they faced the long dark Diaspora strengthened by their writings and the new teachings of the rabbis, the successor of priests, that God would not abandon them in their suffering and that in their darkest hour would intervene by sending them a Redeemer, a Messiah, to restore their glory. But the rabbis were mistaken: The Messiah never came.

2. What was the legacy of the Torah and the priestly laws? How did they prepare the Jewish people for statehood and the essential comity among nations on which their survival as a State and nation depended? How did they prepare the Jewish people for the life among Gentiles in foreign lands? The land of Canaan is called Yahweh's house, it is his land, it is clean, it is holy; all foreign lands are unclean, polluted and profane;

Yahweh cannot be worshiped in foreign lands. If Israel did not keep Yahweh's Law, he would no longer protect them and they would be expelled from the land of milk and honey. Jews must not mingle with foreigners because they are polluted and unclean and thus would become polluted and unclean, be made unworthy of Yahweh; they would cause them to turn to the worship of other gods. All the curses would be hurled at them and make their lives unbearable. The Jews must not serve foreigners, nor show them any kindness or friendship, must not mingle with them, share the same table nor let their sons and daughters marry the foreigners' sons and daughters. All these tenets, in time, became part of their culture and nature, caused them to be a people apart. "I, Yahweh your God have set you apart from the peoples" (Lev. 20:25) and "Make no pact with the inhabitants of the land ..." (Ex. 34:15). This was bound to lead to a deeply implanted hatred of non-Jews which hatred was fully reciprocated; it isolated them from all other peoples. The most destructive command was the one which dealt with the appointment of a king to rule over them, "... it must be a king of Yahweh's (i.e., priestly) choosing who you appoint over you, it must be one from among your brothers that is appointed king over you, ..." (Deut. 17:15). The Jews could not long remain under foreign kings, i.e., rulers—which could be loosely defined and made to conform to any given situation as required—without fear that Yahweh's anger could blaze out against them and wipe them from the face of the earth (Deut. 6:15–16).

The many revolts, ill-advised, were the result of this indoctrination and were the undoing of the Jewish State. Prior to the Babylonian Exile, i.e., prior to the introduction of the Torah, the Kingdoms of Judah and Israel were undone because of purely political intrigues rampant in those times among kingdoms and nations; the Israelites did not behave differently than the idol-worshippers. But after the return from Exile when the introduction of the Torah made its imprints on the minds and conduct of Jews; incited by priests and later by rabbis; intoxicated with their own perceived importance and divine backing; unmindful of their smallness of numbers and vulnerability, they threw caution to the wind and abandoned all prudence, their minds perverted by priestly corrupted commands: Not to permit to be ruled by a foreign ruler, nor serve him, nor pay him homage as was the custom, for fear of committing idolatry and thus violate the divine commands.

The innate instinct of self-preservation was obscured. The self-centered priestly tree was bearing its corroding fruit.

> "You must follow my customs and keep my laws; by them you must lead your life" (Lev. 18:4).

There were no exceptions; there were no social forces in play.

The many civil wars and fratricidal conflicts resulting from misreading some of the commandments pushed into obscurity and isolation one of the truly divine commands:

> "You must not bear hatred for your brother in your heart" (Lev. 19:17).

No attention was paid. Drowned were the majestic universal commands:

> "You must not molest a stranger or oppress him, ..." (Ex. 22:20) and "Love the stranger then, ..." (Deut. 10:19).

No attention was paid to these truly social forces. These were not priestly inspired commands.

3. Over 200 years after the return from the Babylonian Exile, the misdeeds of a few—theologically speaking—were no longer chargeable to the whole nation; Ezekiel's contribution that each person received his or her just dues in this world, although an advance from assigning guilt or merit to the whole nation, was nevertheless in conflict with reality: Many of the wicked were flourishing and many of the pious were suffering. No one expressed it more beautifully than Habakkuk: "... the wicked man gets the better of the upright, and so justice is seen to be distorted" (Hab. 1:4), and again, speaking to Yahweh, he asks: "Why do you look on while men are treacherous, and stay silent while evil man swallows a better man than he?" (Hab. 1:13). Since it was taken as axiomatic that Yahweh was a just God, something was amiss. Similarly with the nation of Israel; Yahweh's chosen, his holy nation, fulfilling the burdens of his Law, preferred above all other nations, yet suffering the pangs of oppression, privation and humiliation for which the Jews had no rational explanation. The Torah no longer could supply the answers and answers had to be furnished: The doctrine of immortality, reward and punishment after death supplied the first answer; the doctrine of the Messiah supplied the second answer. Neither doctrine had any divine sanction and was the invention of convenience of Israel's

holy men and sages; they were accepted as valid explanations and, in time, absorbed as the credo of Judaism. The Pharisees (precursors of the rabbis), the rabbis, the talmudic sages applying the rankest of mysticism and duplicity supplied the two answers. The concept of "Messiah" will be analyzed since it contributed to the many uprisings and revolts of Jews in their refusal to accept reality as conforming to God's will; their interpretation of God's commands imposed on them the perceived sacred duty to place no limits on actions, however violent and reckless, to help bring about and expedite the desired goal. As a result of total failure to achieve their goals by use of force, the Jews abandoned use of violent means as a method of achieving their freedom and liberation from oppression, and, to this day, it is considered blasphemous by the ultra-orthodox Jews to force God's hand, but are instead admonished by their leaders to passively wait for the coming of the Messiah, whom God will send in the time of his choosing.

4. The word "Messiah," in Hebrew "Mashiah," in Greek "Christos," means "anointed"; the Kings of Israel and Judah, and priests were anointed with oil to make them sacred, "Samuel took a phial of oil and poured it on Saul's head; ..." (1 Sam. 10:1 ff), telling him that he was the man who must rule Yahweh's people; it was part of a ritual of confirmation to office. Also the Tent of Meeting, the ark, all its furnishings were anointed by Yahweh's command (Ex. 30:26 ff), i.e., consecrated, made holy. Anointment brought the spirit of Yahweh upon that person. Samuel, looking for replacement of King Saul as ordered by Yahweh, noticed David when looking over Jesse's sons, heard the voice of Yahweh, "Come, anoint him, for this is the one" (1 Sam. 16:13). Thereafter "... the spirit of Yahweh seized on David and stayed with him from that day on" (1 Sam. 16:13). The Scripture reinforces the selection of David, "I will give you fame as great as the fame of the greatest on earth" (2 Sam. 7:9–10); "I will preserve the offspring of your body after you and make his sovereignty secure ... I will be a father to him and he a son to me ... Your House and your sovereignty will always stand secure before me and your throne established for ever" (2 Sam. 7:12–16). Ezekiel prophesied that Israel and Judah would again become one kingdom and spoke the words of Yahweh addressed to him, "My servant David will reign over them ... David my servant is to be their prince for ever" (Ezek. 37:24–26). All these prophecies proved to be totally false. Zerubbabel, a descendant of David, governor of Judah during

the post-Exilic period, greeted by the prophet Haggai with messianic titles as the representative of the restored dynasty of David, appeared briefly on the scene only to disappear, never to be heard from again, nor of any descendant of David. During the Herodian and Roman period of government of Judea, all possible Davidic claimants were hunted down and executed; none survived. So much for the preservation of "for ever" and the throne of David's descendants "secure for ever." This is all there is to the myth of a Redeemer, a Messiah or Messiahs, who were always to be human beings, ruling on earth, setting things right, bringing justice and glory to the Jewish people in the hour of need; all apocalyptic or eschatological later additions are pure inventions. The concept of two Messiahs, a royal and priestly, ruling side by side are later fabrications to embellish a tale of hope. It is to the credit of the Temple priests—who supplied their own share of fabrications—that they opposed the idea of 'Messiah" even if for purely selfish reasons and not reasons of doctrine—as did the Sadducees—for being without divine warrant and pure invention. The danger to the Jews in later times was that they engaged in endless speculations about the coming of the Messiah, aided and abetted by the enduring Kabbalah mystics—who gave apocalyptic esotericism a bad name—to relieve their suffering rather than doing something creative and constructive about their situation. The talmudic and rabbinic fabrications so perverted their minds that they were easy prey to every scoundrel and lunatic who claimed to be the Messiah—who managed to secure some following—and only increased their suffering by losing hope after the pretender's fraudulent credentials were exposed.

Before Bar-Kokhba's defeat, many rabble-rousers, capable of gathering a following, cloaked themselves with messianic pretensions and hoped to achieve their goal by violent action which always seemed to end in failure, execution of the leaders and many of their followers. To rebel against the power of Rome with the help of a few thousand followers, hoping for God's intervention on their behalf, and to do so on many successive occasions when prior attempts ended in disastrous failures, showed the influence of the religious teachings of the day and the resultant mind-perversion.

5. I shall say a few words about the messianic pretenders who appeared in Europe between the 13th and 17th centuries. I selected four of them, the

most notorious scoundrels of them all, whose chief claim was that they managed to capture in the hysteria they created otherwise hard-nosed and down-to-earth businessmen and some rabbis, among many others who, in expectation of imminent departure to the Holy Land, sold all their possessions and were totally impoverished when sanity was restored. Abraham Abulafia, a 13th century Kabbalah dabbler, obsessed with the efficacy of word and number permutations, proclaimed himself the long-expected Messiah, admired and ridiculed until his death. Among his notorious exploits was his effort to convert Pope Nicholas III to Judaism in Rome in 1281. Needless to say he was unsuccessful. David Reubeni and Solomon Molcho, two 16th century brain-damaged fanatics, each in time proclaimed Messiah respectively, the former died in Spanish prison in obscurity, the latter, a relapsed Christian, was burned at the stake by the Spanish Inquisition. They both, on separate occasions, made a great impression on Pope Clement VII, who, incredibly, was sympathetic to their aims, which did not speak well of the latter's intellect. Zabbatai Zevi, the most notorious of them all, was a 17th century impostor and self-proclaimed Messiah, who appeared at the time of the disastrous Chmielnicki massacres of Jews in Poland and the Ukraine. The longing for a miracle by the persecuted Jews was understandable; one would have expected more from the relatively free and prosperous English and Dutch Jews, particularly the latter, many of whom sold their possessions in preparation for the long-sought journey to Jerusalem. All of them were devastated and humiliated when the Messiah-impostor, given the choice between conversion to Islam or death, chose the former. The craving for a miracle, a Messiah, a Redeemer, who would sweep away the persecution and humiliation suffered by Jews in Christian Europe during those times, was promoted by the rabbis who had no other explanation to offer to their people except that all the suffering was a test imposed by God upon the Jews, expiation of sins of present and past generations and that the redemption would come soon; that the just and pious would receive their due reward after death. Life would have been otherwise unbearable in those days without such hopes and dreams. These cravings were distorted by the Kabbalah mystics, who thought that by a proper combination of letters, words and numbers they could set off an apocalyptic chain reaction which would bring about the long-awaited redemption of Jews. Such were the messianic visions in Christian Europe. There were frivolous revolts or armed conflicts, causing suffering and casualties without any possibility of alleviating the plight of Jews; the cause of their plight lay elsewhere: God's hand could not be forced. By contrast, the messianic dreams of the Jewish people during the Seleucid and Roman periods—unaffected as they were by any Kabbalah mystics (for they were over a thousand years away) or rabbinic inventions of immortality of soul and reward and punishment after death—were vitiated by corrupt Temple priests and priestly aristocracy; obedience to Yahweh's commands permitted no compromises, accommodations or negotiated settlements; permitted no thoughts of admission of weakness of their position (for fear of being accused of not trusting in God) nor the imposing strength of opponents, since it was hoped the scale would be set right by Yahweh's intervention if only Jews showed determination, courage, full faith in Yahweh and assured the continuation of Temple rituals and daily sacrifices. The Jews, buttressed by their religious beliefs, became a most contentious people; it did not take any major provocation to set them off to rebellion and bloodshed. The extremists were not only following the commands aimed against foreign kings or rulers, but some of the new Jewish sects wanted no king or ruler except God; they wished for a Kingdom of God and would accept nothing less. The Hasmoneans, at first hailed as liberators, soon created discontent among Jews by usurping the office of High-Priesthood and by founding a family dynasty of rulers; by causing civil wars of succession between brother-claimants to the throne, one of whom fatally appealed to Pompey (a Roman general) for help—who was only too willing to oblige. Judea became a Roman client-State in 63 B.C.; the road from there led gradually but predictably to the great revolt against Rome and the destruction of the Second Temple and Judea. It will be clearly shown in this chapter that Jews, their minds affected by priestly, rabbinic and scriptural obfuscations, when faced with difficult life-sustaining choices, managed, in most cases, to make the wrong one. The messianic dreams led to military revolts against at first foreign but later all authority, Jewish as well. It took massive defeats and catastrophic losses of life and punishment to convince the Jews to abandon use of force as a means of achieving the long-sought freedom and alleviating their plight; the cause of their plight lay elsewhere. God's hand could not be forced.

6. In speaking of the Jewish proclivity for frivolous and reckless revolts against authority without realistic hope of success, I must digress and tra-

verse 2000 years beyond Roman times to note a major exception and pay highest tribute to the Warsaw Ghetto armed uprising against the Germans (and there was other armed resistance by Jews of lesser magnitude to the Germans of World War II) and honor the memory of these heroes, these martyrs, these proud and brave Jewish men and women. Only about 1200 (out of the remaining 40,000 Jews in the Ghetto), with full knowledge of facing certain death by gassing in extermination camps, chose to die instead with whatever dignity was left them, ill armed (2 submachine guns, 17 rifles, 500 pistols—of no use in street fighting—, several thousand grenades and Molotov bombs), undernourished, ill-trained, without medical facilities, they rose in revolt on April 19, 1943 when about 2100 German army and S/S troops entered the Ghetto to deport its remaining Jews to extermination camps. They managed to battle fully equipped enemy troops (they had howitzers and other artillery pieces) house to house, door to door, bunker to bunker for over 3 weeks and inflicted many enemy casualties. They faced certain death and defeat, could not affect the course of anything, their only choice the manner of death; they left a powerful message to the Jews who survived. They expected no Messiah, no miracles, no divine intervention.

7. Many Jews emigrated from Judea and established settlements in foreign countries before the 5th century B.C., long before any forced expulsion. In due time they became prominent in cities like Rome, Cyrene, Alexandria, Babylon, Antioch, Tarsus, the island of Cyprus and along the many coastline cities of the Mediterranean. At first, they chose cities with close proximity to Judea; there was a large and prosperous Jewish community in Alexandria already by the 3rd century B.C., once counted as 40% of the population; 2 of the 5 districts of Alexandria were almost exclusively Jewish; they concentrated together for religious reasons, to ease compliance with dietary laws and proximity to their Houses of Worship. Later they did so for another reason: To ward off hostility towards them of the predominantly Greek population. Alexandria was a true mirror of the earliest major commingling of Jews and non-Jews outside Palestine; the influence of the Torah and Jewish customs upon the social intercourse with the Gentiles in time aroused deep mutual hostility, for in Alexandria the Jews experienced in flesh and spirit the first tinge of hatred, of anti-Semitism (in the common usage of the term), anti-Jewish riots and

pogroms. That mirror reflected the shape of things to come in the Diaspora long before the onset of deceitful Christian promoted anti-Semitism and its false accusations. For the hatred of Jews was only intensified by Christian propaganda in the struggle for the primacy of their faith. They did not have to invent it, for the social and economic hatred of the Jews was established long before then by the impact of their conduct and attitudes exercised upon the Gentiles; these, in turn, were consequences of the Torah and priestly laws and commands Jews were obliged to observe. But the Jews did not have to observe anything; outside of Palestine they were free to modify their religious outlooks, however firmly they became part of their nature. For whereas Jews were given no choice when confronted with Christian persecution except conversion to Christianity or continuance of their suffering, which was a choice between dark and night—they did have a choice when confronted by pre-Christian anti-Semitism and modify some of their uncompromising conduct and assertion of superiority: They chose not to change because it suited their interest not to change and thus brought upon themselves the opprobrium of Gentiles. This sequence of events was not confined to Alexandria, but was typical of other Gentile pre-Christian communities where Jews played a significant part.

What typified the conduct of Jews? What cultural legacy have their fathers bequeathed them? What was their inheritance they took with them to foreign lands? Jews were intolerant because their religion was intolerant. They were a people quick to take offense; taught to be unfriendly to non-Jews; known for their boastfulness and exclusiveness; preaching their superiority over paganism; continuously demanded privileges not accorded others; permitted to live according to their traditional laws, rituals and ordinances; regularly sent the Temple tax to Jerusalem; followed the decisions of the Sanhedrin in Jerusalem; won exemption from service in the army for fear of violating the Sabbath and dietary laws; were exempt from even giving only lip-service to the formalities of State worship—a sign of disloyalty; did not have to perform any work or service on the Sabbath; were allowed their own courts of law so they could be tried under Torah laws and not under the laws of the State they lived in; received exemption from taxes in some cases so they could pay tithes to the Temple; made usurious loans to non-Jews; claimed to be a separate nation chosen by God above all other nations; forbidden to eat with strangers at one table or bear them any friendly feelings; claimed special sanitary regulations; looked upon non-Jews as polluted and ritually unclean; did not socialize with them; did not permit intermarriage with them; kept themselves apart; displayed hate and enmity towards other people; made regular pilgrimages to Jerusalem and the close connections with Jerusalem brought upon them the accusation that they were a separate nation, foreigners who lived in their midst for their own benefits and were without patriotism. When the Jews of Jerusalem rebelled against Rome (66 A.D.), the Gentiles pillaged the Jews of Alexandria (and Jews in other cities) to show their solidarity with Rome. Claudius, one of the few enlightened Roman Emperors (41 A.D.–54 A.D.),friendly toward the Jews and close friend of Herod Agrippa II, warned the Alexandrian Jews that they had to be more reasonable toward other people's religions and that "if they prove intolerant, he will treat them as a people who spread a general plague throughout the world" (6–136). What a legacy! What an inheritance! A religion without any semblance or pretense of being a social force, destined to travel on the road to disaster with morbid recklessness. Not one sage, not one pained soul, not one pragmatist, not one social thinker spoke out against the sheer madness of such conduct, the impropriety of abusing the hospitality extended to Jews in neighboring countries, and the absolute certainty that such conduct could only lead to disaster; so blinded were the Jews by their religion and their leaders. The sage Hillel (at about the end of the 1st century B.C.) asked by a pagan to be taught the Torah while standing on one foot, is said to have replied, "What is hateful to you, do not unto your neighbor; this is the entire Torah. All the rest is commentary …" That was a beautiful statement by a humanitarian, but it was false. That it was not the message of the Torah was only too well demonstrated by the history of Jews, something Hillel could not have visualized; or could he? It is incredible that it did not occur to a single Jewish soul to question, horribile dictu, whether possibly their unusual conduct and peculiar views, not even remotely shared by any other people and nation throughout the world, could be the cause of arousing hatred for Jews among Gentiles.

8. Commencing with the Maccabean revolt and continuing till the appearance of the Zealots and the Sicarii, the mood of discontent among Jews grew ever more intense and apocalyptic in their struggle for freedom and compliance with God's command not to be ruled by a foreign king; in

time, it was deemed sacrilegious to violate this specific command. As frustration grew, caused mainly by constant failures and disappointments with their exertion to rid themselves of foreign rule, they grew bolder and more reckless, the vision came more and more into focus that no efforts be spared to hasten the onset of the messianic age by any means, however violent. The Jews, however, were divided on this issue mainly as far as the means to be used were concerned; one segment, the well-to-do and conservative element, had a stake in the status quo and perceived rebellion against Rome as sheer madness, with no possibility of success. For the clarion call across Judea sounded increasingly more strident, "No king but God"; "Rid the sacred land of foreign pollution" and "No tax but to the Temple". Applying unrelenting pressure and terrorism to the point of savagery against Jewish non-conformists, most of them gradually came to share the view of the Zealots, like it or not, or simply had no choice but to go along for their own safety.

Judea became a veritable cauldron seething with unrest and discontent which only reinforced the convictions that these trials were the "pangs of the birth of Messiah"; a fever of martyrdom swept the land. The Procurators (including one Jewish apostate from Egypt, Tiberius Alexander, 46 A.D.–48 A.D., a nephew of Philo), most of them without any experience in governance—given to rapacity as their special reward—confronted with these turmoils responded with such severity in suppressing the disorders that they bordered on the barbarous; such conduct only inflamed the Jews more and persuaded the sane-thinking moderates that perhaps rebellion might be the only way out.

The Hasidim, the pious ones, had been the supporters of the Hasmonean revolt, became disenchanted with the monarchy when it assumed prosaic habits, wished for foreign intervention to dispense with the monarchy. So with the Pharisees, the spiritual descendants of the Hasidim, interpreters of the Torah and Oral Law, of non-priestly descent; precursors of the rabbis who opposed monarchical imperialism. As a result of their opposition to the Hasmonean King Alexander Jannaeus, a civil war raged for 6 years causing large casualties and climaxed with Jannaeus crucifying 800 Pharisees in an act of vengeance. Whereas the Hasidim and Pharisees vigorously opposed impious Jewish monarchs and at first preferred foreign rulers to restore order, they learned from bitter experience the error of their views—foreign monarchs once settled as occupiers never left on their own accord—and were gradually swept by the tide of opposition to foreign rule of any kind. The Pharisees, in time, came to despise all aliens, tore down the royal eagle of the Romans from the Temple placed there by Herod as a provocation; the culprits were burnt alive by Herod. The conditions were ripe for views that the end of the world and the coming of the Messiah were at hand. The Torah, its literal interpreters, its scrupulous observers, its Oral Law modifiers and its learned and pious men, could not deflect the inevitable coming of the Day of Judgment.

9. Before proceeding to catalogue key documented uprisings and disturbances from the Maccabeans on to the final disasters hundreds of years later, it is important to note that there were some sane and cool heads who, despite accusations of collaboration with Rome and unpatriotic leanings by future Jewish historians, warned the Jews what was in store for them if they persisted in rebelling against Rome. Josephus reported the speech of Herod Agrippa II (War of the Jews, Book II, Chapter 16) in 66 A.D. just as the revolt commenced but was still reversible. The speech was given to an assembly of Jews in a square in Jerusalem before the Hasmonean Palace. Agrippa, his father was grandson of Herod the Great, was educated in Rome at the court of Emperor Claudius; named King of Chalcis in southern Lebanon in 50 A.D. and later also of parts of Galilee and Perea; he later sided with the Romans and in 70 A.D. (when the cause was lost) aided Titus in the final conquest of Jerusalem. His speech was full of sound REALPOLITIK, showed a grasp for historical events that would do credit to Machiavelli; it must have been a bitter pill for his listeners to swallow, given their highly charged emotional and reckless state of mind. I shall quote in parts:

> "... some are earnest to go to war because they are young, and without experience of the miseries it brings, and because some are for it out of an unreasonable expectation of regaining their liberty, ... But as for war, if it be once begun, it is not easily laid down again, ... as to your desire of recovering your liberty, it is unseasonable to indulge it so late ... you ought to have labored earnestly in old time that you might never have lost it; ... that you might never have admitted the Romans (into your city), when Pompey came first into the country

... you, who have accustomed yourself to obedience from one generation to another, and who are so much inferior to those who first submitted, ... will venture to oppose the entire empire of the Romans. While those Athenians, ... pursued Xerxes, that proud prince ... are yet at this time servants of the Romans; ... ten thousand other nations there are who had greater reason than we to claim their entire liberty, and yet do submit. You are the only people who think it a disgrace to be servants to those to whom the whole world has submitted. What sort of an army do you rely on? What are the arms you depend on? Where is your fleet, that may seize upon the Roman seas? and where are those treasures which may be sufficient for your undertaking? ... Will you not estimate your own weakness? Has not your army been often beaten even by your neighboring nations, while the power of the Romans is invincible in all parts of the habitable earth? ... Are you richer than the Gauls, stronger than the Germans, wiser than the Greeks, more numerous than all men upon the habitable earth? ... Do you also, who depend on the walls of Jerusalem, consider what a wall the Britons had; for the Romans sailed away to them, and subdued them ... What remains therefore is this, that you have recourse to Divine assistance; but this is already on the side of the Romans; for it is impossible that so vast an empire should be settled without God's providence ... and how can you then most of all hope for God's assistance, when, by being forced to transgress his law, you will make him turn his face from you? and if you do observe the custom of the sabbath days, and will not be prevailed on to do anything thereon, you will easily be taken, as were your forefathers by Pompey, ... and how will you call upon God to assist you, when you are voluntarily transgressing against his religion? ... But certainly no one can imagine ... when the Romans have got you under their power, they will use you with moderation, or will not rather, for an example to other nations, burn your holy city, and utterly destroy your whole nation ... the danger concerns not those Jews that dwell here only, but those of them which dwell in other cities also; ... whom your enemies will slay, in case you go to war ... so in every city which has Jews in it will be filled with slaughter for the sake of a few men ... Have pity, therefore, ... spare the temple and preserve the holy house, ..."

Matters have gone too far for a speech of this kind to have any effect. The power of Rome did not remain invincible forever; it came to an end less than 400 years later. The Jews took on Rome when it was at its zenith; when Rome was finally destroyed it was too late for the Jews.

10. I shall now catalogue the key documented uprisings and disturbances.

(1) **166 B.C.**   The Maccabean uprising against the Seleucids (Subject will be treated later in Chapter 17).

(2) **109 B.C.**   John Hyrcanus (Hasmonean king and High-Priest 134 B.C.–104 B.C.) created a mercenary army; was spreading the Jewish faith by forced conversions at the point of the sword (Edomites, Idumeans); destroyed the Samaritan Temple to Yahweh (129 B.C.).which was built on Mt. Gerizim, and ravaged the territory of the Samaritans—they were Jews centered in Shechem—destroyed Shechem in 109 B.C. The cause of all this bad blood was religious and the existence of a competing Temple. They created their own canon which included only the Torah. This caused great tensions between the two communities and weakened the Judean Jews later in the revolt against Rome.

(3) **63 B.C.**   Civil war raged between two Hasmonean brothers, Aristobulus II and Hyrcanus II; the Roman General Pompey, requested by the Pharisees—who desired to end the dynastic quarrel of the two Hasmoneans—to restore order, declared war on Aristobulus and conquered Jerusalem (and Judea) on a Sabbath when Jews refused to fight. Nearly 12,000 Jews perished in the war. The strategy of the Pharisees was ill-conceived and foolhardy because after restoring order Pompey did not leave just because he was asked by the Pharisees to do so.

(4) **57 B.C.**   Alexander, son of Aristobulus II, recruited a considerable force and rebelled against Gabinius, proconsul of Syria. Gabinius and his aide Mark Antony defeated the insurgents in a battle near Jerusalem.

(5) **56 B.C.**   Aristobulus II, who escaped from captivity in Rome with his son Antigonus, were defeated in battle against Romans near Macherus. The former Hasmonean military leader Pitolaus and a group of Jewish warriors fought on the side of Aristobulus II.

(6) **55 B.C.**   Alexander (who organized a rebellion in 57 B.C.) organized a war of liberation against Rome. His forces were crushed by Gabinius near Mt. Tabor.

(7) **53 B.C.**   Hasmonean General Pitolaus rose in revolt against Rome because Crassus—who replaced Gabinius as proconsul to Syria—robbed gold from the Jerusalem Temple treasury. Pitolaus was defeated near Lake Kinneret by the Roman Cassius—who replaced the fallen Crassus—and 30,000 Jewish captives were sold as slaves. Pitolaus was killed on the order of Antipater (father of Herod the Great).

(8) **40 B.C.**   Parthians invaded Palestine, established a kingdom in Jerusalem with the Hasmonean Antigonus (son of Aristobulus II) as king and High-Priest, who reigned from 40 B.C. to 37 B.C. Herod the Great with the help of the Roman army defeated him an 37 B.C.; Antigonus and 45 members of the Sanhedrin were executed. The Hasmonean dynasty in Judea was terminated with the death of Antigonus.

(9) **4 B.C.**   Because of the violent death of some Pharisees murdered by Herod the Great prior to his death, a revolutionary crowd gathered in Jerusalem demanding, among other, the replacement of the High-Priest with one of their choice. Archelaus, son of Herod and successor to his throne, using his entire army subdued the revolutionaries, killing about 3000 of them on the Temple grounds.

(10) **4 B.C.**   Judah, son of Hezekiah executed by Herod the Great, rebelled against Sabinius, the Procurator, became leader of Galilean insurgents, attacked the Romans in Galilee and generally created havoc wherever he appeared with his followers.

(11) **4 B.C.** Simon, a former servant of Herod the Great, rebelled with a group of followers in Transjordania, proclaimed "King" by his followers, defeated an entire army unit of the Romans near Emmaus; rebellion was put down by Varus, the Roman vice-regent in Syria, who after total victory had about 2000 of the rebels crucified. Simon was captured in battle and beheaded.

(12) **4–2 B.C.** Athronges, a shepherd, aspired to kingship, was designated "King" by his followers, overrun the country, pressed hard in the slaughter of both Roman and Herodian troops, feared no bloodshed and engaged in guerilla warfare. Finally defeated by the Roman Gratus and Herod Archelaus.

(13) **6 A.D.** Judas of Galilee, led a revolutionary movement during the Roman census, rebelled against Romans in protest of direct rule imposed by the Romans. He founded the movement of Zealots (Sicarii). He taught that Jewish society was a theocracy acknowledging the rule by none other than God. He urged his countrymen to resistance, urged them not to submit to taxation by Romans, not to submit to any human master after serving God alone; Jewish society was to live directly under the rule of God. Preached that a Herodian ruler was to be opposed as any Roman Procurator; in his opinion the rule of man was a sacrilege. He was killed in battle and his followers scattered.

(14) **35 A.D.** A Samaritan protest procession in Jerusalem led by a religious messianic prophet was attacked by Pontius Pilate, the Procurator. Their protest to Rome caused the recall of Pontius Pilate.

(15) **38 A.D.** Pogroms against Jews in Alexandria, Egypt. (Subject will be treated later in Chapter 18)

(16) **44 A.D.** Theudas, during the reign of Procurator Fadus (44–46 A.D.), rebelled against Rome in protest against their direct rule and taxation; considered a Messiah, he promised to imitate the miracles of Moses. Fadus slew many of his

followers and beheaded Theudas. His severed head was paraded in Jerusalem as a warning to any Jew who might share his views of liberation from Roman rule.

(17) **46–48 A.D.** The revolt of Jacob and Simon, sons of Judas the Galilean, was short-lived. Both were defeated and crucified by Procurator Tiberius Alexander (46–48 A.D.), a Jewish apostate and nephew of Philo.

(18) **48–52 A.D.** A conflict between Galileans and Samaritans, which led to the death of one Galilean, created a great tumult and disorder in Jerusalem. Eleazar ben Dinai—during the reign of Procurator Cumanus—who led a group of Zealots, devastated a number of villages in Samaria; Cumanus sided with the Samaritans and sent an army against the Zealots. Many were killed and taken prisoner. The Jewish leaders of Jerusalem persuaded the Zealots not to cause an insurrection and so many deaths on account of one Galilean killed; they had some success in persuading the Zealots to disperse. Such was the turbulent and unsettled mood of the populace.

(19) **52 A.D.** While on guard at the Temple during the Passover celebration, a Roman soldier was guilty of insulting behavior. This act led the Jews to riot and assumed the proportions of an armed revolt; it was put down only after great loss of Jewish lives.

(20) **52–60 A.D.** During the reign of Procurator Felix Antonius, a Jewish prophet from Egypt gathered around him thousands of Jews and camped with them on Mt. Olives near Jerusalem. He induced his followers—who then numbered about 4000—to invade Jerusalem and capture a Roman garrison; he assured them that the ramparts and walls would crumble at their approach like the walls of Jericho did when their forefathers laid siege to that city. Felix's army dispersed them and many Jews paid with their lives.

(21) **66 A.D.**	Menahem, son of Judas the Galilean, was leader of a group which captured the fortress Masada. He was killed by rivals in his own camp when on his way to Jerusalem to be crowned "King of the Jews."
(22) **66 A.D.–70 A.D.**	The first great Jewish revolt against Rome. (Subject will be treated later in Chapter 19)
(23) **73 A.D.**	Zealots, remnants of a defeated army who fled from Judea, while in Egypt and Cyrenaica, aroused revolutionary activity against Rome.
(24) **115 A.D.–117 A.D.**	Jewish rebellion in Egypt, Cyrene and Cyprus all but destroyed Jewry in those countries. (Subject will be treated later in Chapter 20)
(25) **132 A.D.–135 A.D.**	Bar-Kokhba rebellion, the second great Jewish revolt against Rome. (Subject will be treated later in Chapter 21)
(26) **161 A.D.**	A revolt against the Romans took place in the last year of the reign of Emperor Antoninus Pius. The revolt was connected with the expectation that the Parthians—who were preparing for war against Rome—would aid the Jews in their struggle for freedom. The revolt was badly organized, based on false hopes and soon suppressed. The Parthian assistance never came, and new persecutions organized against Jews.
(27) **202 A.D.**	Septimius Severus, Roman Emperor 193–211 A.D., suppressed a revolt in Judea. The Roman Senate accorded him a "Jewish Triumph."
(28) **351 A.D.**	The Jews of Sepphoris, Tiberius and Lydda revolted against the Roman army of Ursicinus, who wreaked vengeance against them. The largest Jewish cities in Palestine were destroyed.

Chapter 17

The Maccabean Uprising

Part A

When a peace Treaty was finally concluded between the feuding Seleucids and Ptolemies (ca 240 B.C.), Judea remained under Egyptian control. The king of the Seleucids, Antiochus Callinicos, incited the Judeans to revolt (most likely making promises of lower taxes), as a result Onias II, High-Priest (and son of the High-Priest Simon the Just), sided with him and refused to pay the annual tax of 20 Talents to Ptolemy. This refusal gave sufficient offense to the Egyptians so that Joseph, son of Tobiah (brother-in-law of Onias II) was sent on a mission to Alexandria to calm matters with Ptolemy Euergetes, the Egyptian king. Joseph must have been a resourceful schemer since he managed to get himself appointed head tax gatherer of all the Palestine districts and the king gave him an army of 2000 soldiers so he could fulfill his duties more efficiently. He performed the same services for the king's successor Ptolemy IV Philopator (222–206 B.C.). The Jews of Alexandria had been living under the Greeks for over 100 years and were sufficiently acculturated to be referred to as Hellenized Jews; they became prosperous and adopted Greek commercial customs in their business dealings. Alexandria was a busy port engaged in far-flung international shipping, commerce and banking. The Jews of Alexandria brought their Hellenizing influence to bear upon their brethren in Judea, especially among the well-to-do and those engaged in commercial activities, who soon adopted Greek customs. Joseph upon his return to Judea introduced the Dionysian festivals, which were popular among the Alexandrian Jews (the teachings of Epicurus were well received). Hellenized Judeans began to question whether the teaching of Judaism demanded denial of self-gratification and whether the strict interpretation of Judaism (at that time not yet benefitting from the Mishnah) placed too great a restraint on their commercial activities to place them at a competitive disadvantage. Joseph, whose tax gathering business was extremely profitable, died a wealthy man in 208 B.C.; during his life-time he had a major share in contributing to the well-being of Judea, which could not help but find the Hellenizing process profitable, given the former state of poverty of the country. Joseph, who had seven sons by his first marriage, was succeeded by his youngest and ablest son (a son by his second wife) Hyrcanus, to the great chagrin and jealousy of his brothers, who were pro-Seleucid; Hyrcanus had to flee the city. Philopator died in 206 B.C.; Antiochus of Syria and Philip of Macedonia battled for the crown of Egypt; Joseph's other seven sons, called Tobiades, sided with Antiochus against Egypt; they formed a Seulecidean party, assisted the Syrian king openly and Judea came under Seulecid domination in 198 B.C. after some intervening wars with the Egyptians, which destroyed a large part of Jerusalem and damaged the Temple. The Syrian king gave orders to rebuild the city and repair the Temple. The Judeans were allowed to govern themselves according to their own laws and were not to be hindered in the practice of their own religion.

What are the conclusions from Part A?

That Hellenization of the Judeans was primarily introduced by Alexandrian Jews (who numbered around 200,000 at that time), mostly prosperous, who conducted commercial visits to Jerusalem and received visitors from Jerusalem. The wealthy Judeans involved in commerce were in the forefront of the Hellenizing process; to them it represented progress; it was not forcibly imposed upon them by sinister pagans, but introduced by Jews in an atmosphere ripe for it. Perhaps, in their view, the strictures of the Torah were an unnecessary restraint upon their commercial and related activities.

That the Hasidim (the pious ones), fearful that the strong bonds of Judaism would loosen the grip on the Judeans, were vehemently opposed to all aspects of Hellenization and in constant conflict with it that it so divided the Jews as to be easy prey for unscrupulous scoundrels, be they priests or High-Priests, business men, farmers or rabble rousers. In their scheme of things there was no room for compromise or difference of opinions (which fact was to exact a terrible price later on), everyone had to toe the same fundamentalist line and Hellenization was looked upon as pagan, destructive and an abomination (mercifully the ultra-orthodox and liberal Jews nowadays tolerate each other and life somehow goes on).

That the mostly wealthy priestly families, leaders and governors of the community and recognized as such by foreign potentates, engaged in cold-blooded political intrigues devoid of any spiritual connection with the Torah; this will become only too evident later on.

THAT the Judeans had all the religious freedom under the rule of the Egyptians and yet they chose to abandon them for the Seleucids; they had all the religious freedom under the rule of the Seleucids, but fate was unkind to the Jews: Antiochus, King of Syria, declared war on Rome!

Part B

Antiochus was totally defeated by the Romans (190 B.C.), obliged to pay a war indemnity of 15,000 Talents per year for 12 years, and send his son Antiochus Epiphanes to Rome as hostage. Antiochus was therefore for sometime in great need of money. The temple treasuries of various nations seemed to him a proper target. The money problem was shared by his son Antiochus Epiphanes and the history which evolved could have been written by a good dramatist, so obvious were the consequences. The office of High-Priest was closely tied to the Temple treasury, which was a repository of great wealth; gold and silver sent as gifts from Jews in the Diaspora, deposits from wealthy individuals, also widows and orphans, the steady stream of obligatory one-half shekels from Jews of the land and Diaspora. It was a lucrative office, worth bidding for and sold to the highest bidder.

The Hellenist party—it must be restated that it consisted of Jews and Jews only—requested Antiochus Epiphanes' interference in the internal affairs of Judea: There were too many discords. The Hellenists apparently had the upper hand, they had the wealth, requested that Epiphanes remove Onias III from High-Priesthood and name his brother Joshua, who was a Hellenized Jew using the name Jason, as High-Priest, for which act they promised him a large sum of money. The office was for sale to the highest bidder. Jason's followers denied the truth of Judaism. Yet because Jason was still partial to Judaism, the Hellenists were intriguing against him and set their sights upon one, Menelaus, of a prominent but not priestly family, who offered Epiphanes 300 Talents more than Jason and bought the office of High-Priest. Menelaus was opposed to Judaism! Unable to deliver fully on the payment he was summoned by Epiphanes for an explanation, leaving his brother Lysimachus in charge to loot the Temple of its valuables and by that means make good on his obligation to the king. The populace threatened the two violators of the Temple with death. Lysimachus armed his followers and was killed in the ensuing tumult. Menelaus brought an accusation against the rebels, convinced the king of Jewish guilt, that his enemies favored Egypt, but most importantly, persuaded the king that the Torah, the law of Moses, was full of hatred of humanity, that specifically it forbade Jews to share meals with non-Jews or to show any kindness to a non-Jew.

Antiochus embarked on his long hoped for adventure: war with Egypt (170 B.C.). This was closely watched in Jerusalem, for if the Egyptians were victorious, then the Menelaus era was over. A false report spread that Antiochus Epiphanes had fallen. The deposed High-Priest Jason hurried back to Jerusalem accompanied by 1000 men; Menelaus barricaded the gates of Jerusalem. A civil war (a former High-Priest against an incumbent High-Priest!) ensued and Jason succeeded in entering Jerusalem. Menelaus took refuge within the fortress of Acra. Antiochus Epiphanes left Egypt in 169. B.C., informed of events in Jerusalem he attacked the city, massacred the inhabitants, forced his way into the Temple, removed the golden altar, the candlestick and all the treasures which still remained. Menelaus dutifully assisted him in the plunder.

Antiochus Epiphanes ventured to conquer Egypt the second time (168 B.C.) but was foiled by order of the Romans. Told that the Judeans celebrated his degradation and that Israel's God had humbled him, Epiphanes vented his frustration upon the Judeans; one of his aides entered Jerusalem with troops and on a Sabbath, when Jews did not resist, attacked them killing all men they got their hands on and sending women and children to the slave markets. Epiphanes issued a decree, after Menelaus determined that Judaism was to be **abolished**, commanding the Judeans to renounce the laws of their God and offer sacrifices only to the gods of the Greeks; that only swine should be used at sacrifices and proscribed, under penalty of death, the practice of circumcision, the festivals and dietary laws. He appointed officials to supervise compliance and punish violators; the Temple was dedicated to Jupiter, the Torah was burnt and the statue of Jupiter placed on the altar. Resistance, particularly in the countryside, was encouraged by the Hasidim whose secret hiding places in caves were betrayed to the Syrians by Hellenist Jews, and since they did not defend themselves on the Sabbath, fell victims to the Syrians in great numbers. When all seemed finally lost, an aged father, a priest, and five of his sons appeared on the scene to start a rebellion, the Maccabean rebellion.

What are the conclusions of Part B?

That the Syrian king was greatly in need of money to pay his debts to the Romans. It was the corruptible office of the High-Priesthood which was available to the highest bidder regardless of qualification for office. It made a mockery of holy and anointed men.

That the constant discords among the various factions of Jews, the Hellenists and Hasidim in particular, brought Epiphanes into the internal affairs of Judea, because he was requested to do so by Hellenist Jews. Once such interference was established, it became a matter of right.

That an aspirant to High-Priesthood known to be opposed to Judaism managed to buy the High-Priesthood with considerable backing; that it was not an accident but a carefully laid-out plan that this Jew schemed to destroy Judaism from within and convinced Epiphanes that it was in his interest to aspire likewise.

That it was the Temple treasures which attracted aspirants to the High-Priesthood more so than learning or religious convictions.

That the populace of Judea, unmindful that power was with the Syrian king, nevertheless threatened his Jewish appointee with death, willing to risk the inevitable consequences. Speaks for very ill-advised leadership and perverted minds.

That the population of Judea, unmindful of its weakness, unmindful of the enmity of Epiphanes, managed to recklessly and frivolously insult him publicly (twice) and bring death and destruction upon themselves. Speaks of incompetent leadership and totally perverted minds.

That the Hasidim, the then sole remaining rock of Judaism, foolishly refused to defend themselves on the Sabbath and in the process let their wives and children be butchered without raising a finger. It was a faulty interpretation of the Sabbath rules even for those days and manifested irresponsible leadership. The Maccabees and later Jewish sages reached a different conclusion.

That it was a Jewish High-Priest who encouraged and assisted Epiphanes in his decrees to abolish Judaism, prohibit its practice and decree the worship of Jupiter; who convinced Epiphanes that it was in his interest to do so in order to insure tranquility in his realm; who convinced Epiphanes that Jews had religious laws which made blending together with non-Jews impossible, as the Romans concluded in 135 A.D. when they tried to stamp out what they regarded as the cause of recurrent rebellions.

That it was the Maccabees, the father and his five sons, who saved Judaism from extinction.

That perhaps Jewish youths of the day disdained the Law of Moses, animal sacrifices and dietary laws, a religion of a small people confined to an area of 20 square miles around Jerusalem, a religion no one else recognized or heard of, as opposed to a new world-wide culture breaking on the horizon, letting the spirit of men soar free in thought, architecture and arts. That perhaps the Jewish youths rebelled against the cultural strictures of Judaism in which they were badly or improperly instructed. Jewish young men must have felt strongly enough for the Greek gymnasium and Olympic contests to have undergone painful surgery to hide their circumcision and conceal that they were Jews.

That the efficient cause of Jewish persecutions of those days should be laid at the doorstep of Jews, High-Priests no less.

That the Jews were misguided and mind-perverted enough to have risked civil war over whether one or the other scoundrel—neither qualified—should be High-Priest.

Part C

In the village of Modin, north of Jerusalem, a Syrian overseer placed a heathen altar in the square. When a Hellenist Jew came forward with a burnt offering, Mattathias, an aged priest, killed him on the spot. With his five sons and followers they killed the overseer and destroyed the altar; thus began the Maccabean uprising against the Seleucids in 167 B.C.—the first religious war ever fought. The rebels fled to the hills to organize and train their followers militarily, whose numbers were increasing daily, into a cohesive unit fit to stand up to the Syrians. They moved about the land killing Syrians and Hellenized Jews without noting the distinction and made the decision to defend themselves on the Sabbath. The aged Mattathias died (166 B.C.) and Judas Maccabeus was placed in command. As confidence increased, Judas confronted the Syrian army led by Apollonius and defeated them; Apollonius was killed. This victory increased the confidence of Judas. A Syrian army under Heron, guided by some Hellenists, met Judas' army at Beth-Horon and were totally defeated (166 B.C.). Epiphanes, distracted by a revolt in Parthia, convinced that Hellenization of Jews was a failure, decided to eliminate them. He put Lysias in charge of a large army equipped with elephants to destroy Judea and its people, who, upon learning of his intentions, unified their efforts in the face of such danger. Lysias appointed his General Gorgias to lead an army of 40,000 (augmented by the antagonized Samaritans) to march against the Maccabean army, who with about 6000 warriors met the enemy at Emmaus, completely outwitted Gorgias and defeated his army the following year (165 B.C.). Judas, with an army which increased to 10,000 warriors, defeated the army led by Lysias. Lysias escaped to fight another day. Judas marched into Jerusalem, entered the Temple, destroyed all statues of Jupiter, the altar, and cleansed the Temple thoroughly, built a new altar and in 165 B.C. the Temple was consecrated with sacrifices and thanks-giving. Anticipating further battles with the Syrians, he fortified the town of Beth-Zur. News reached the Judeans that Antiochus Epiphanes had died (164 B.C.) from an illness contracted in the Parthian campaign. Judas took advantage of the ensuing lull to improve conditions in Jerusalem. He decided to lay siege to the Syrian fortress Acra, occupied by Hellenists who continued to attack the fortifications of the Temple. Some of the trapped Hellenists made their way to Antioch and convinced the young King Antiochus V not to let Acra fall into the hands of the Maccabeans. Lysias in 163 B.C. at the head of a large army with elephants marched on Judea. The garrison at Beth-Zur was forced to surrender for lack of provisions. Lysias then marched on Jerusalem. Judas decided to meet him in battle at Beth-Zachariah, was defeated and forced to retreat to Jerusalem where he and his army occupied the Temple fortress. Lysias laid siege to the fortress, which was about to fall, when he had to hasten to Antioch to defend the city against his rival. Lysias concluded a peace treaty with the Jews, promised to abrogate all laws against Judaism; Syria would not interfere in the conflict between Hellenists and Hasidim; he had Menelaus removed from office and executed; Jews were to recognize the supremacy of the Seleucids and the latter were to retain the right to appoint the High-Priest. Lysias appointed Alcimus, of the House of Aaron, as High-Priest. The governing council controlled by the Hasidim accepted the peace terms against the advice of Judas. In 162 B. C. there was a change in Syrian rulers; in a coup, Demetrius claimed the royal title. Alcimus lodged a complaint with the new king against the Maccabees, accusing them of causing the country's instability and that there would be no peace as long as Judas Maccabeus lived. Judas retreated from the city with his followers; he fought two more victorious battles against superior Syrian forces led by Nicanor at Caphar-Salama and Adarsa (160 B.C.). Judas entered Jerusalem again as victor. Alcimus withdrew to safety. Informed of the disaster which Nicanor suffered, Demetrius sent Bacchides with a large army to Judea. Judas left Jerusalem but only 3000 warriors followed him. Facing the formidable army of Bacchides, all but 800 warriors deserted Judas; in the ensuing battle Judas Maccabeus fell at Eleasa (160 B.C.), his army was defeated and dispersed. Alcimus returned to Jerusalem and resumed the office of High-Priest. Demetrius left undisturbed Lysias' peace terms concerning religious freedom. The Jews had learned, after spilling oceans of blood, that religious freedom was a blessing that sufficed and that political independence was out of reach for the moment. They made the annual tribute payment to Syria and had peace.

Bacchides succeeded (160–159 B.C.) in eliminating all armed opposition to Syrian rule. After the death of Alcimus, the Temple had no High-Priest for seven years. Jonathan, brother of Judas, successor to leadership of the Maccabees after Judas, was involved in a side-war with Bacchides in which he gained the upper hand and demanded a truce, which was granted. Fortune had smiled again: Alexander Balas and Demetrius were involved in a power struggle and competed for Jonathan's alliance. Balas appointed Jonathan High-Priest (152 B.C.), declared him friend of the Syrian monarch. He was the first Hasmonean to attain this office. The disintegration of Syria helped in the rebirth of Judea.

There were still three brothers of Judas Maccabeus left: Jonathan, Simon and Johanan. These Hasmoneans and their descendants became the future leaders of Israel. Johanan was killed in a skirmish, Jonathan was assassinated in 143 B.C., and Simon was murdered with his two sons by his son-in-law in 134 B.C. Simon's third son, John Hyrcanus (134–104 B.C.) declared king and High-Priest; he accepted as divine command that the whole of Palestine was the inheritance of the Jewish people, that it was his duty to bring this about; hired foreign mercenaries; conquered territories of the Galileans and Idumeans and forcibly converted them to Judaism by the sword (the latter's conversion came to haunt the Jews in the form of the Herodian brood); plundered the tomb of King David (3000 Talents of silver) to finance his wars; showed intolerance and utter contempt for the faith of others. His son Aristobulus (104–103 B.C.) succeeded him by seizing the throne and High-Priesthood after murdering his mother, a brother and imprisoning his other brothers. After the rule of one year he was succeeded by his brother Alexander Jannaeus (103–76 B.C.), king and HighPriest, who gave "cruelty" a bad name, passing most of the 27 years of his reign in foreign or civil wars (battling Pharisees at home) employing foreign mercenaries. One civil war lasted 6 years and cost the lives of an estimated 50,000 Jews. He was succeeded by his wife Salome Alexandra (76–67 B.C.) who was the most capable of all the Hasmonean rulers; she was succeeded by her sons who rendered more of the same, till at last, the people tired of all the dissensions, quarrels of succession and abuse of High-Priesthood, asked (the Pharisees especially) the Roman General Pompey in 63 B.C. to restore order. With that the lights of political independence (142 B.C.–63 B.C.) and Hasmonean rule went out again in Judea.

What are the conclusions from Part C?

That according to the records available, Judas Maccabeus fought eight major battles against the Seleucids; won the first four, lost the fifth, won the next two, lost the final eighth in which he was killed.

That Judas fought for Judaism (as a son of a priest understood it) and not for religious freedom. The peace treaty offered by Lysias in 163 B.C. (accepted by the Jerusalem's governing council) called for, among others, the abrogation of all Syrian laws against Judaism, i.e., restoration of religious freedom except the right to appoint the High-Priest. This was not acceptable to Judas (who was saved from total defeat by Lysias by the peace treaty) who thought that the peace treaty would restore to power aristocratic Jews whose greed caused all the problems in the first place. Someone should have told him that these were the facts of life.

That all talks of religious reforms, however well intentioned, were treated by the Hasmoneans as treasonable.

That the Maccabeans killed enemy soldiers and Hellenist Jews as enemies of the same kind.

That the statues of Jupiter, which Judas destroyed in the Temple in Jerusalem, were placed there by the High-Priest and Hellenist Jews.

That the Maccabeans never had the support of all the Jews in Judea.

That Judas Maccabeus was not popular, was abandoned before his last battle (which was a ritual suicide), rejected as a trouble maker and as politically too ambitious.

That the High-Priesthood was treated by the Hasmoneans as a political power base (During the 2nd Temple period, the priesthood became the aristocracy and the High-Priest the political leader of the people) without any indication that it had any religious effect upon them.

That John Hyrcanus treated the whole of Palestine as the inheritance of the Jewish people by divine command because it suited his political ambitions.

That the Hasmoneans were totally ignorant of the harmful effect forcible conversions of pagans would have upon the unity and solidarity of the Jewish people.

That commencing with the rule of John Hyrcanus, the Hasmonean rulers resembled oriental despots in their conduct, full of rapacity, revenge, greed, cruelty and lust; their religious affiliation is not recognizable even though many were High-Priests. They suffered from corruption of power.

That last but not least, the Judeans were offered the same terms of religious freedom by Antiochus in 198 B.C. as Demetrius offered them in 160 B.C., after Judas Maccabeus was killed in battle. The Jews accepted both offers! Neither terms offered them political independence.

Chapter 18

Pogroms Against Jews in Alexandria, Egypt

1. When the Jews first settled in Alexandria around 300 B.C., they brought with them the customs and commands of the Torah compatible with life outside of Judea, i.e., most of the commands except those affecting the Temple and animal sacrifices, which by Torah ordinances could only be carried out in Jerusalem. It was therefore necessary to obtain from the rulers certain privileges and special rights which would enable them to fulfill these obligations under the Torah commandments and ordinances, as if they lived in Judea. These privileges and special rights were peculiar to Jews only and not available to members of any other faith. It was mandatory for residents of any particular country to worship according to the customs and religious laws of that country; this was regarded as a sign of patriotism and gratitude to the rulers of the host country of residence. Privileges and special rights not available to other citizens or residents create inequality by their very nature; if prosperity, wealth and position are viewed, rightly or not, as attributable to them, then envy, jealousy and ultimately hatred by the rest of the population are inevitably the result. Although this was the fate of Jews in various foreign cities and countries of their settlement, it was nowhere more evident in antiquity than in Alexandria, where the resentment against Jews boiled over into anti-Semitism and murderous pogroms. There were other factors which contributed to the resentment: The great number of Jews as a percentage of the population, reaching in time 40% in the case of Alexandria and the proximity of Alexandria to Judea, which exacerbated the view that Jews were disloyal foreigners. The Jews must have had something to offer either in industry, wealth or other abilities that the rulers, by granting such privileges, in fact limited their power over them; powerful emperors such as Caesar and Augustus would not lightly have done so unless they derived

substantial benefits. On the negative side, the possession of such privileges enjoyed by Jews—who were invariably a minority—often resulted in over-reaching and abuse; it was only natural in a hostile environment. This, however, gave them a false sense of security since a privilege granted could be withdrawn for cause, or a privilege granted by one ruler could be denied by his successor without any cause. The pogroms in Alexandria, it must be remembered, occurred long before the onset of Christianity, which for reasons of its own not only embraced the anti-Semitism of the day (in particular that of the Greeks) but fused it with a more virulent anti-Semitism based on theology.

2. What were the privileges and special rights that the Alexandrian Jews obtained? Similar privileges were obtained by Jews in the lands of the Roman Empire wherever they established settlements. The time-frame is restricted to the Roman period, since the documentation is more reliable:

(a) Jews formed an autonomous community, headed by a council of 71 elders.

(b) They had full freedom of worship and the right to observe the custom of their ancestors.

(c) They had the right to live according to their own laws and statutes and were not required to observe local or imperial religious edicts.

(d) They had their own Courts to which even Jewish-Roman citizens could appeal.

(e) They were exempt from military service in the Roman legion because it would conflict with the Sabbath observance and dietary laws.

(f) They were authorized to collect special levies for community and religious purposes.

(g) They were not to be summoned to Court on the Sabbath or a holiday, nor required to perform any civil service which entailed work on the Sabbath.

(h) They were allowed to send (export) gold and silver to the Jerusalem Temple.

(i) They had a right to social and spiritual autonomy.

(j) Money which was sequestered and designated to be sent to the Jerusalem Temple was to be considered "holy money" and was to remain untouchable by non-Jews.

(k) They had a right to have a synagogue in any part of the city.

(1) They had the right to maintain dual citizenships.

(m) Many of them had the right to become Roman citizens.

(n) There were no restrictions in the occupations they could engage in. They were not challenged when they considered themselves publicly friends and allies of Rome; they regarded the Romans as their protectors.

3. The Alexandrian Greeks envied the privileges and special rights granted to Jews by the Romans; the privileges and special rights were massive, the Jewish community practically constituted a State within a State and such a relationship was confirmed and made secure by no lesser giants of the Roman Empire than Julius Caesar and Augustus who called the Jews their "allies and friends". Despite, or because of, the privileges and special rights, Alexandrian Jews refused to associate with non-Jews and kept themselves apart. I refer the reader to Chapter 16, Paragraph 7, detailing the anti-social conduct of Jews. They sided with the Judeans in the resolution of disputes, so much so that in 66 A.D. when the Judeans rose in armed rebellion against Rome—and before the Alexandrian Greeks attacked the Alexandrian Jews as a show of solidarity with Rome—the Jews of Alexandria rebelled against Rome (their benefactor) in sympathy with the Judeans. Their revolt was crushed, ironically, by Tiberius Julius Alexander (an Alexandrian Jewish apostate, nephew of Philo) and 50,000 Jews were killed.

4. Herod Agrippa I (b. 10 B.C. – d. 44 A.D.) one-half Hasmonean and one-half Herodian, long-time friend of Caligula in Rome, was heir to Herod Antipas' province of Galilee and Perea when Caligula banished Herod Antipas. On account of his friendship with Caligula, the latter showed favors to Agrippa and Judea, much to the dislike of Alexandrian Greeks who were envious. Because of all the privileges extended the Jews in Alexandria (and other parts of the Roman Empire), the feeling of envy turned into hatred and reached its peak during Agrippa's sojourn in Alexandria. They looked with envy at the wealth and success achieved by Jews thinking it due to the favoritism extended them by Caligula and prior Roman emperors. Several writers of the era spread hatred of Jews in their writings, which could not help but further incite frictions with Jews. The author Apion excelled in provoking the people to the peak of animosity toward Jews; according to him, the tenets of Judaism obliged the Jews to hate non-Jews. Certainly, acquaintance with certain Torah commands (by

then translated into Greek and available in the Alexandrian library) would lead a reader to such conclusions and only add fuel to an anti-Semitic propagandist in Alexandria bent on provoking the Greek and native populations. The Greeks envied the economic gain achieved by Jews; the Greek merchants. disliked their Jewish competitors. The hostility toward Jews was contained during the reign of Augustus (27 B.C.–14 A.D.) and Tiberius. (14–37 A.D.). When Caligula became emperor (38 A.D.), Alexandrians knew their governor Flaccus, a friend of Tiberius, was compromised and would be careful not to interfere with their anti-Jewish schemes. Caligula's appointment of Agrippa as king of Upper Galilee overjoyed the Alexandrian Jews but motivated the anti-Jewish forces to action. The two Alexandrian leaders of that faction, Isidorus and Lampo, managed to exercise influence over Flaccus and became the leaders of the mob. Caligula, more so than his predecessor emperors, not satisfied with deification after death, sought recognition as "god" during his lifetime and demanded due reverence accorded such a "deity," such as placing the statue of his likeness in the temples and offering prayers and sacrifices. Caligula also made such demands upon Jews. In 39 A.D., pagan inhabitants of the city of Jamnia, Judea, set up an altar to Caligula which was destroyed by Jews. Caligula, upon learning of this episode, ordered that his statue be placed in the Jerusalem Temple through governor Flaccus. The Jews refused to comply, asserting that the privilege guaranteeing them full religious freedom, in fact, exempted them from compliance.

When Agrippa passed through Alexandria from Rome on his way to Judea (July 38 A.D.), the Jews understandably used this occasion for major celebrations. This and Agrippa's presence inflamed the mob to violence. After some trivial mocking and farce, the mob rushed into the synagogues the next day and placed in them the statues of Caligula; they further induced governor Flaccus to withdraw from Jews of Alexandria the right of citizenship and national privileges, which he did, calling them foreigners and strangers. He had publicly flogged many members of the supreme Jewish council. The Jews were driven out of the principal parts of Alexandria and confined to the harbor quarter of the town, since, according to Flaccus, Jews had illegally settled in other quarters of the city instead of the one part they were given the right to settle (Delta-the harbor quarter). The most greedy for spoils fell upon the deserted homes of the wealthier Jews, pillaged and burned 400 of them, and in the process threw some of the Jews into the burning homes; many Jews were murdered, synagogues defiled and closed. The fury was not spent. The mob surrounded the Delta quarter and laid siege to it in the hope of starving the Jews. When some ventured out driven by hunger, they were tortured, burnt alive or crucified. This pogrom lasted till the middle of September 38 A.D., when Flaccus was recalled for an unrelated reason. The new governor insisted that the Jews should accord divine honors to the images of Caligula; when they refused, he forbade their observance of the Sabbath. Some Jews abandoned Judaism out of fear for their lives, including Tiberius Julius Alexander, nephew of Philo, who later gained high honors in the Roman Empire. The Alexandrian Jews decided to send a delegation headed by Philo to Rome to plead their case before Caligula. The Greek Alexandrians did the same, their delegation included Apion and Isidorus, both rabid anti-Semites. Caligula's first words to the Jewish delegation set the tone: "So you are the despisers of God, who will not recognize me as the deity, but who prefer worshipping a nameless one, whilst all my other subjects have accepted me as their god." He continued: "And how is it that you do not eat pig's flesh, and upon what grounds do you hold your right of equality with the Alexandrians?" He did not wait for an answer; it was apparent the Greek delegation got to him first. As mentioned previously, Caligula issued commands for his statue to be placed in the Jerusalem Temple; to enforce this order, he commanded Petronius, the governor of Syria, to enter Judea with his legions and carry out his command by force of arms, if necessary. Seeing that this would certainly provoke bitter resistance, Petronius sent a letter to Caligula reviewing the situation and detailing the difficulty in carrying out this order without causing great bloodshed. Caligula received the letter and demanded immediate compliance; before this letter reached Petronius, Caligula was assassinated, Jan. 41 A.D. His successor, Emperor Claudius (on friendly terms with Herod Agrippa II), emperor 41–54 A.D., fully restored by an edict the rights and privileges of Alexandrian Jews, restored to them complete religious freedom and placed them in a position of equality with the Greek inhabitants of Egypt. That such restoration was necessary would indicate to what extent and with what rapidity (within 2 years) the privileges of Jews were revoked. Claudius freed the Alabarch Alexander (the head of the Alexandrian Jewish community) from prison; he resumed his position of leadership. The lawful government was re-established and order was restored.

5. After these disturbances and those which followed in 66 A.D. and 115 A.D., the Alexandrian Jewish community steadily declined. It was a bitter lesson from which the elders of this once flourishing community should have drawn wisdom and passed on their findings to future generations; nothing was passed on. A minority can never be secure no matter how much ink was used. A minority should not recklessly indulge in provocations which it cannot control. A minority should not needlessly invite conflict just because it may seem the shortest distance between two points. But most importantly, a minority's approach, view or solution may be mistaken or faulty and there is nothing sacrosanct about willfully maintaining its position without even conceding the possibility that others could be right.

Chapter 19

The First Great Jewish Revolt Against Rome

1. The first great uprising against Rome cannot be explained in strictly conventional terms as a revolt planned from the beginning to rid the Jews of foreign rule and install the rule by one of their own; a revolt by revolutionaries who weighed the risks and consequences of their actions even though they may have been too optimistic of success, as revolutionaries always are. But then the revolt against Rome was no ordinary revolution. It was not fought by a people united in a common cause; it was not fought by a people who had any idea of war strategy and tactics; a people who were willing to bury their differences at least until victory was achieved; organizing their limited resources in a rational manner against the mightiest power possessing the mightiest army then existing; making discreet alliances with their neighbors or other nations similarly minded; biding time until all preparations were completed; bribing enemy officials, where necessary and feasible; providing for the safety of non-combatants, such as the elderly, infirm, women and children, who would be a hindrance in the war effort and consume limited resources.

2. Instead, the rebels conducted themselves as if victory was not the main aim; they fought each other in several bloody civil wars until the Roman General Titus approached the city in April 70 A.D.(Jerusalem and the whole country except for three fortresses including Masada were defeated in September 70 A.D.),but by then it was too late; they were totally irresponsible in destroying food supplies (grain reserves); they were split into many hostile factions such as priests, aristocrats, the wealthy, Zealots and Sicarii, with power and advantage shifting to this or to the other faction; they were totally unmindful of the losses in human lives inflicted by them upon their own population; provoking hostile actions by

Roman Procurators and Governors (who were for the most part scoundrels and criminals) with no tangible benefits to gain; frivolously picking fights with the hostile Greek population living in Palestine; showing great sensitivity in reacting to insults, more befitting a world power than a subjugated people planning a fight for freedom; when all hope of victory was lost, refusing to accept any compromises; refusing several offers of surrender where the Romans might have shown some leniency in order to avoid total destruction of Jerusalem and the slaughter of its population (Josephus, Tiberius Alexander, Agrippa II and Berenice—Titus' paramour—were in Titus' military camp); last but not least, executed any of their brethren who counselled moderation or against continuance of a hopeless war. All this at a time when the population of Jerusalem suffered from critical starvation with no possibility of replenishing supplies. All these factors combined to lead to a disastrous tragedy for the Jews and hastened the Jewish State to its ruin. The Jews blundered in expecting effective support from Diaspora Jews. There was class hatred between the aristocratic and wealthy Jews (largely Hellenized) and their impoverished brethren and the early moderate government—before the radicals took over—gave no hint of even acknowledging the problem. This attracted the impoverished to radical causes out of sheer despair; they joined the ever increasing groups of bandits who swarmed all over the country robbing, pillaging and murdering the wealthy and setting villages on fire. There were violent actions within the ruling class intent on keeping their dominance among Jews; between zealous radicals; within the High-Priestly families all out to seek their own gain; not taking the war with Rome too seriously in the firm conviction that Providence would never let them suffer defeat in the struggle for the fulfillment of divine commands.

3. But none of the above cited causes or combination with others would help explain the disastrous course of events, and how a people could so recklessly travel down the road to national suicide. There were two additional causes:

(a) **Misperception of Roman political conditions.**

Jewish political and military leaders could not help but notice, despite a show of force by the Procurators, that civil strife, disorders and civil war seemingly weakened the power of Rome. Nero (54–68 A.D.), who was 17 years old when he became emperor and 29 years old when Jews rose up in armed rebellion against Rome, commanded no respect and leadership, was a sexual pervert, a degenerate, a profligate who spent his time in Olympic contests instead of attending to affairs of State; incapable of governing and finally committed suicide after the Roman Senate declared him public enemy. Succeeded by the senile Galba—who previously joined in the insurrection against Nero—had his head cut-off in 69 A.D. His successor Otho committed suicide after 95 days of reign. Succeeded by Vittelius who was slain within 90 days of reign in Dec. 69 A.D. The last three emperors were either assassinated or committed suicide within a span of one year. A superficial observer of this turmoil and disruption of political power could not help but come to the conclusion between 66 A.D. and 69 A.D. that the Roman Empire was in decline; its government disorganized; its aristocratic leadership demoralized so that a rebellion in the Near East would not rank uppermost in their mind, nor could they marshal the necessary resources or power to subdue a distant rebellion of Jews. The Roman treasury was empty. This was apparently the impression gained, albeit erroneous, by the Jewish political and military leaders whose reaction to provocations by Procurators and the Greek population in Palestine before the rebellion was so impulsive and impetuous as to lead to the conclusion that they thought the time ripe for revolution against Rome and throwing off the yoke; Rome assuredly had more pressing problems than little far off Judea could pose. But fate fooled the Jews, they were influenced by superficial views and completely misread the situation. Rome was only seemingly disorganized; powerful and highly efficient rulers appeared on the scene on a collision course with Jewish freedom aspirations and thwarted their armed rebellions three times: Vespasian, 69–79 A.D. (the 66–70 A.D. rebellion); Trajan, 98–117 A.D. (the 115–117 A.D. rebellion) and Hadrian, 117–138 A.D. (the Bar Kokhba 132–135 A.D. rebellion).

(b) The effect of certain Torah Laws and prophecies of Scripture.

If the perception of the Jews that Rome was in decline was faulty, the perception of Jews that the turbulent times after Herod Agrippa I (44 A.D.) were the precursor of the apocalyptic period fulfilling the prophecies of the sacred writings—that God was putting the Jewish people to the final test and would raise up a liberator king of the Jewish people and establish the rule of God on this earth—that perception was catastrophic, based on mind-perverted reasoning which could only lead to national suicide: The destruction of the Jewish State and Temple, the dispersion of Jews throughout the world. The majority of Jews were caught up and sucked into the maelstrom, and the resultant disaster forever changed the direction of Jewish theological thinking. From the radical offshoot of the Pharisees, successor of the former Hasidic (also called Hasidean) party, a fanatic religious fundamentalist Zealot party grew up, joined by the radical Sicarii after 50 A.D., committed to the use of violence in achieving their purpose. From the teaching of fundamentalist Pharisees, from apocryphal writings, Wisdom and Apocalyptic literature, incited by the doctrine of the Zealot party (The Fourth Philosophy, as described by Josephus) a religio-political outlook took hold that God would not abandon the Jews in their suffering, would send a Messiah to restore their glory, a kingdom forever as promised to David and that God would not permit his House to be ruled by polluted foreigners. All Jews were expected to participate in this struggle and those standing aside, opposing this outlook or friendly towards the Romans, were treated as traitors to the cause who deserved the same fate as enemies of God. Their battle-cry was "No king but God" and "No tax but to the Temple," advocating a rebellion not only against foreign rulers but against any human rulers, i.e., total anarchy. They plundered wealthy Jews, particularly those who sided with the Romans whom they, for that reason, did not recognize as Jews and therefore considered it no crime to destroy them. The High-Priests and High-Priestly families felt free to practice lawlessness and violence against poor priests robbing them of their legal tithes, among other misdeeds, and thus contributing to dissension and disunity. The people fragmented into many opposing factions, ruled by radical leaders fighting each other in bloody civil wars; a population of about one million bottled up in Jerusalem in an area of only a few square miles; unable to escape that boiling cauldron (only a few managed it). All attempts to escape were considered by the radicals as treason and punishable by execution. All awaited the onslaught of the might of the Roman Empire. What sacred writings motivated the religious fundamentalists, the Zealots and Sicarii, to plunge the nation into armed revolt against Rome? What perverted their minds so as to disregard all instincts of self-preservation?

Quoting from Scripture:

> "This is the land I have made over to you; … the land that Yahweh swore to give to your fathers, … and to their descendants after them" (Deut. 1:8).
>
> "All the peoples of the earth will see that you bear the name of Yahweh and will go in fear of you" (Deut. 28:10–11).
>
> "I, Yahweh your God, have set you apart from these peoples" (Lev. 20:25).
>
> "Make no pact with the inhabitants of the land …" (Ex. 34:15).
>
> "You shall bow down to no other god, …" (Ex. 34:14).
>
> "If you appoint a king to rule over you … it must be one from among your brothers … you are not to give yourself a foreign king who is no brother of yours" (Deut. 17:15).
>
> "I will provide a place for my people Israel; I will plant them there and they shall dwell in that place and never be disturbed again; nor shall the wicked continue to oppress them …" (2 Sam. 7:10–11).

Speaking of David's descendants,

> "I will preserve the offspring of your body after you and make his sovereignty secure … and I will make his royal throne secure for ever" (2 Samuel 7:12–13).
>
> "David my servant is to be their prince for ever" (Ezekiel 37:26).

Why were the Jews so apoplectic when the Jerusalem Temple treasury was tampered with? Portions of the treasury were sacred funds, they belonged to Yahweh according to the Torah! "When you receive the tithe from the sons of Israel … out of these you are to set aside a portion for Yahweh, … Out of all the gifts you receive you will set aside a portion for Yahweh. From the best of all things you will set aside the sacred portion" (Num. 18:26–29).

A people following such commands and ordinances with a passion bordering on exhilaration and accepting the clear message of the prophecies, would not tolerate the constant abuse, provocations, oppression, and terror of a foreign occupying power whose Procurators (Governors), for the most part, were totally unqualified for their position and thought nothing of compensating for their incompetence with brutal force. On the other hand, a people following such commands and ordinances could not help but consider it the divinely ordained duty to challenge, test, obstruct and provoke at every opportunity the "enemies" of God without regard to the consequences and to treat it as sacred duty to assist in the realization of what was believed to be God's purpose and plan.

4. There was another consequence of the uprising fiasco: the destruction of the Jewish State, Temple and failure of prophecies. In the primitive and pragmatic way, the conviction spread among many Jews and most pagans (the latter making a great fuss about it), that Yahweh had abandoned the Jews and that they no longer were his favored people. The Jewish-Christian movement, starting however so humbly, received its strongest impetus from the perception that Yahweh's Covenant with Israel had been abrogated and that a "New Covenant" had replaced it, a Covenant no longer based on Mosaic Law and priestly ordinances. From the oceans of Jewish blood needlessly and recklessly spilled sprung the foundation of a new and, in time, much more powerful religious movement which almost succeeded where mighty Rome failed: The destruction of the Jewish people and of the Jewish religion.

5. After 44 A.D., the radical party of Zealots came on the scene in earnest, dedicated to the abolition of foreign rule by use of violence and terror. Later, the Sicarii joined them, a party using the dagger as the tool of murder of Jewish and pagan opponents. To their thinking, the end of time and advent of the Davidic Messiah was near. They formed the nucleus of the revolutionary party (war party) and radically opposed the peace party, to which belonged the Hillel (moderate) wing of the Pharisees, the wealthy, the aristocrats and some wealthy priestly families who, in order to safeguard their wealth, preferred the status quo under Rome and feared the anarchy of the rebels. The turmoil in Jerusalem (for in the rest of Judea the Jews were not actively promoting armed rebellion against Rome) was exacerbated by three events in themselves not connected except for the reaction of Jews whose thinking cannot be defined as anything but convoluted and mind-perverting.

(a) In Caesarea, founded by Herod, the seat of Roman Procurators of Judea, the majority of the population was Greek and anti-Semitic. There were frequent disturbances and clashes between Greeks and

Jews, the latter seeking equal rights with the Greeks. On a Sabbath, a Greek sacrificed a bird (chicken?) in front of the synagogue in an effort to insult the Jews. In indignant response (on a Sabbath!) some of the Jews armed themselves and a bloody riot followed, suppressed by Procurator Florus—who sided against the Jews—with heavy Jewish losses.

(b) When the news reached Jerusalem it caused a commotion since it was known that Florus was the recipient of large bribes for protecting Jews from Greeks in Caesarea. But Florus, as was his style, outraged the Jews further by demanding payment to him of 17 Talents from the Temple treasury. Some horrified Jews (since this involved sacred funds and was therefore viewed as sacrilege) mocked the Roman Procurator by soliciting alms for the "needy" Florus. Learning of this obvious slight, Florus came to Jerusalem and demanded that the High-Priest hand over to him the culprits who mocked him; the High-Priest refused. Florus responded by letting his troops plunder the upper city (inhabited by the wealthy) and in the process killed more than 3600 Jews, causing substantial property damage; the prisoners taken were crucified.

(c) Incredibly, Florus demanded that the people welcome the incoming two Roman cohorts and in this manner demonstrate their goodwill toward Rome. The Jews did so (urged by the High-Priest) but the troops did not respond. So what? End of story? No! In a matter of total unimportance and of no possible consequence they chose instead, inexplicably, to heap abuse upon the Roman Procurator which drew a quick response from the troops. The soldiers with drawn swords attacked the Jews, who suffered many dead and wounded. But the die was cast. The people rushed to occupy the Temple area (to save it from further plunder) and demolished the porticoes between the Temple and fortress Antonia (occupied by Roman soldiers, who kept watch over the Temple for signs of any tumult). For his safety, Florus decided to leave Jerusalem for Caesarea and withdrew the greater number of troops. Eleazar ben Ananias, leader of the Zealots and son of a High-Priest, ordered the daily Temple sacrifices for the emperor halted; the payment of taxes (tribute) to Rome was halted; the revolutionaries burned the archives where records of debts were kept (thereby attracting the poor to their cause); homes of the wealthy Jews and aristocrats

were burned and those who did not flee were killed; Menachem ben
Judas with the Sicarii conquered the fortress Masada and executed the
Roman garrison; the Zealots conquered the fortress Antonia killing all
the Roman soldiers; they stormed Herod's palace where Roman soldiers offered to surrender and leave the country, which the rebels granted, if the Romans laid down their. arms. Upon doing so, the rebels
slaughtered all the unarmed soldiers. The revolutionaries were now
masters of Jerusalem. By August 66 A.D. there was no turning back:
The armed uprising against Rome had begun; the break with Rome
was complete and nothing short of complete victory was acceptable to
the rebels.

6. When news of Jerusalem events reached Caesarea, the Greeks started
a pogrom against Jewish inhabitants of that city, in which over 20,000 were
killed and any who survived were sold as slaves; after the pogrom no Jews
were left in the city. When news of the massacre (and others, such as in
Bethshean and Alexandria) reached Jerusalem, most of the people
embraced the cause of the Zealots. Cestius Gallus, Roman Governor of
Syria, realized the dangerous situation in Judea and with an army of 30,000
soldiers and many auxiliaries, among which were 3000 foot soldiers and
2000 horsemen loaned to the Roman army by none other than Agrippa II,
marched from Antioch to Jerusalem. Wealthy and aristocratic Jews of the
ruling class who feared the power of the Zealots, attempted, but failed, to
open the city gates to the Roman army. For six months Gallus besieged the
city achieving only minor successes, but in the end retreated to fight another day. It was during his retreat that the Zealots fell upon his army, attacked
his rear and flanks and completely routed them. The Romans left 6000
dead and the Zealots captured a great quantity of arms, implements of war
and money chests, which were all brought to Jerusalem as trophies of their
victory.

7. The population of Jerusalem was ecstatic and the peace party lost all
influence. No one dared speak of submission to Rome or suggest peace
negotiations with Rome. Total independence was the goal and the Zealots
were convinced that it was within their grasp; the whole of Judea and
Galilee were cleared of Romans. The ruling power vested in the Great
Synhedrion, a provisional government comprising members of aristocrats,
priests and Pharisees, headed by Simon ben Gamaliel, of the House of

Hillel. The country was divided into various administrative districts and each district was assigned a military commander. Joseph ben Gorion, an aristocrat and Anan, son of a former High-Priest, were appointed to the district of Jerusalem and defense of the fortresses. Joseph ben Mattathias, later to be known as Josephus, was appointed commander of Galilee; he was opposed by the Galilean Zealots, led by John of Gischala, who suspected his resolve to the revolt. After the defeat of Cestius Gallus, the Jewish leadership knew it was only a matter of time before Rome would send a large enough army under an able commander to subdue the Jews. In Jerusalem, preparations for war began in earnest, the city was fortified, the walls strengthened, weapons produced, men trained and disciplined for warfare; likewise in the districts outside of Jerusalem. But the people of Jerusalem were not unified. The Synhedrion was not unified, some of its wealthy and priestly members secretly sided with Rome and were guilty of duplicity; the whole body was replaced after two years as totally ineffective and the Zealots, who by then constituted the most powerful force, took over the government.

8. The Emperor Nero appointed Vespasian commander of an army with orders to crush the Jewish rebellion. In the winter of 66–67 A.D., commanding three experienced Roman legions (5th, 10th, 15th), he gathered additional auxiliaries in Antioch, Alexandria and also several thousand troops from Agrippa II. In the spring of 67 A.D., Vespasian with over 60,000 seasoned and well equipped troops commenced his campaign in Galilee. Methodically and ruthlessly he subdued Galilee, an area containing a population of about 3 million; the resisting population was either put to the sword or sold into slavery. Many cities offered no or little resistance and some communities were openly friendly to the Romans. By July 67 A.D., Jotapata, Josephus' fortress, was taken partly due to treachery after a siege of over 40 days, more than 40,000 men lost their lives, the women were sold into slavery and Josephus surrendered to Vespasian who treated him with courtesy. Considering that several hundred thousand Judean fighters and civilians lost their lives in Galilee resisting the Romans, Josephus' conduct (as revealed also later) and manner of surrender was high treason. When news of his conduct reached Jerusalem, the Zealots executed those members of government who had appointed him military commander of Galilee. The first stage of the war—the conquest of

Galilee—was over toward the end of 67 A.D. and Vespasian moved his troops to winter quarters near Caesarea in the winter of 67–68 A.D. The Galilean fighter, John of Gischala, escaped from Galilee to Jerusalem with his troops and many followers.

9. The Zealot John of Gischala, after his return to Jerusalem, declared the moderate government "friends of the Romans"; occupied the Temple Hill and elected Phineas High-Priest. The authority of the High-Priest Hanan was challenged as was that of the whole priestly aristocracy; a civil war broke out, the Zealots were outnumbered and called on the Idumeans for help; with the latter's help the Zealots became the ruling power in Jerusalem and took their revenge by initiating a ruthless purge of moderates and of those suspected of negotiating with the Romans; they killed Joseph ben Gorion, commander of the Jerusalem defense. A leader of another group of Zealots and experienced warrior, Simon bar Giora, was admitted to Jerusalem secretly by opponents of John of Gischala (who by then was sole ruler of Jerusalem and the people, by then, apparently had enough of him) and another bloody civil war broke out. The Zealots led by John of Gischala retired to the Temple area and Simon bar Giora became ruler of the rest of the city in the spring of 69 A.D. While Vespasian and his troops were preparing for the siege of Jerusalem, the streets of the city ran with blood due to constant civil strife among Zealot factions who fought each other for greater influence, power and glory. The three Zealot leaders involved were (1) John of Gischala, (2) Eleazar ben Simon, (3) Simon bar Giora. While Vespasian procrastinated (for reasons related in the next paragraph), the Jerusalem defenders were killing each other, destroying the property of the wealthy, fighting for booty, even burning down the grain storage and, in general, conducting themselves as the real traitors of Jewish freedom aspirations. Unable to unite until it was too late, they dissipated the manpower and assets of war, not making provisions for a protracted siege; ignoring the needs of civilians who were bound to suffer from food shortages and generally behaving as if the war had already been won, or that the Romans gave up on the siege due to political conditions in Rome. The armed defenders of Jerusalem disposed of no more than 25,000 fighting men out of a population of nearly one million; this should have been an indication of the extent of their concern; but they considered themselves invincible.

10. Vespasian knew that a large percentage of the Jerusalem population, the wealthy in particular, were ready to capitulate. He also knew that the military defenders were engaged in bloody civil wars; he saw advantage in delay and let the strife weaken all. Vespasian concentrated instead in subduing all the distant parts of Judea and by the spring of 68 A.D. all of the country within a wide radius of Jerusalem was in his hands. As he began preparations for the siege of Jerusalem, news reached him that Emperor Nero had committed suicide (June 68 A.D.). All further military preparations were halted; Vespasian waited for new orders. After the next three emperors (Galba, Otho, Vitellius) were assassinated or committed suicide all within one year (the last one in Dec. 69 A.D.), Vespasian was elected by the armies of the East as their candidate for emperor, which title was confirmed in Dec. 69 A.D. and Vespasian became emperor. He assigned the task of conquering the Jews to his 29 year old son Titus, who appeared before Jerusalem in Feb. 70 A.D. to commence the assault. The two years between spring of 68 A.D. and spring of 70 A.D. were wasted by the Jerusalem Zealots, Sicarii and Idumeans in strife, street fighting and depleting their supplies and forces. It was only when they realized that Titus commenced the assault upon Jerusalem in earnest that they ceased fighting among themselves and united their forces; but it was too late. Titus with an army of over 80,000 soldiers (four legions, the 5th, 10th, 12th, 15th) and vast numbers of siege equipment, resolved to starve the city into submission; he surrounded the city with a stone wall to tighten the noose and interdict any food supplies from reaching the besieged city. The siege lasted from April to September 70 A.D. Various requests for voluntary surrender and thus spare the civilians were summarily rejected by the Zealots, even though famine raged in Jerusalem and was beginning to take a heavy toll. The Romans breached the walls and after vicious close-range fighting (too brutal to describe) all resistance came to an end September 70 A.D. Jerusalem and the Temple were in flames and destroyed, the population decimated from starvation and by the sword of the Romans, who were authorized by Titus to plunder the city. Only a few managed to flee, mainly priestly families and the sage Johanan ben Zakkai who was smuggled out in a coffin, for the Zealots would have executed him. The remaining strongholds in Hurdium, Macherus and Masada were captured by 73 A.D. The war was over; the Jews totally defeated; the Temple and country destroyed and plundered; the surviving population impoverished and desolate.

11. When Titus first asked the Jerusalem Jews to surrender, he demanded only acknowledgment of the Roman rule and the payment of taxes to Rome; these were lenient terms indeed, considering the hopeless military situation of the defenders. These were most unusual terms for a victorious Roman commander to offer, but the presence in his camp of Josephus, Tiberius Alexander and Agrippa II must have had something to do with it. More than one million Jewish lives were lost; about 900,000 were taken captive during the war, of which many were crucified, died of hunger, sent as slaves to mines; youths under 16 and most females were sold into slavery. The Jewish communities in the Roman Empire, particularly those in Asia Minor, Rome and Alexandria, suffered the hatred of the pagans who desired nothing less than the annihilation of all of the Jews. No more than 25,000 rebels (of whom 5000 were Idumeans), most of whom started as bandits who robbed their own countrymen, cleverly exploited the mood of the times—the religious expectations. The resistance to the Roman Procurators' brutality and thievery; the malcontent of the peasants and farmers with their grinding poverty; the perceived disorder and paralysis of Rome's political leadership; the hostility and open anti-Semitism of the Greek population living in Palestine and, last but not least, the priestly and Pharisaic interpretation of Scripture calling for God's intervention in their struggle against foreign rulers, succeeded by force of their weapons and readiness to use them, without a master-plan, but through butchery of all opponents and ad-hoc reactions to situations as they arose, to suck the Judeans gradually into the whirlpool of rebellion—the majority against their will—and act of sheer madness and national suicide.

12. The man who was destined to restore the humiliated nation of Israel to its former spiritual strength after the destruction of Jerusalem, who counseled the Zealots to submit to the Romans when all seemed lost, and who initially in 66 A.D. opposed the revolt against Rome, Johanan ben Zakkai, maintained that Judaism must be freed from the corruption of the Jewish State. When Titus, through Josephus, offered lenient surrender terms to the rebels, history might have taken a different course had a referendum been conducted of the Jerusalem inhabitants; a choice freely made by a free people. But then the freedom fighters, who sought independence for Jews to conduct their affairs freely, rejected the surrender terms out of hand without consulting with the population. A handful of

freedom fighters took it upon themselves to decide the fate of a million Jews. How ironic! This was the highest of treasons.

13. We owe our detailed knowledge of the revolt against Rome to the accounts of Josephus, a contemporary observer and reliable historian. I have intentionally omitted certain passages of his historical narrative—though uncontradicted—because of a possible bias.

Chapter 20

The Jewish Rebellion Against Rome 115–117 A.D.

1. We do not have adequate documentation of the massive Jewish uprisings against the Romans during 115–117 A.D., in Emperor Trajan's reign (98–117 A.D.). Josephus, the Jewish historian who gave us detailed accounts of the prior Jewish revolts (see Chapters 18, 19) was dead; he died around 100 A.D. We have to rely on the most meagre accounts of the Roman historian Dio Cassius (ca 115–ca 230 A.D.) and the Christian Church historian Eusebius (ca 260–ca 340 A.D.).

2. After the catastrophe of 66–70 A.D., the Romans still recognized the Jewish religion as "religio licita" (the lawful, permissible religion). The Temple, priesthood and sacrifices were gone, but most of the Jewish privileges were recognized. The Jews of Palestine and all the Jews living in the Roman Empire outside of Palestine (i.e., including those not involved in the revolt) had to send the same annual tax to support the rebuilding of the Temple of Jupiter in Rome which they previously sent to support the Temple in Jerusalem. This was the first blanket discrimination against all Jews and was also meant to hinder the proselytizing of pagans; conversions to Judaism became rare. Some of the Jews who interpreted the recent events as proof that God, as already spelled out by some prophets a long time before then, did not care for animal sacrifices and remembered a quotation from Jeremiah how the Law had "been falsified by the lying pen of the scribes" (Jer. 8:8), did not view the destruction of the Temple as an end of Judaism; they were greatly influenced by the preaching of certain Jewish sects, among them the Jewish-Christians. The latter were recognized as a sect of Judaism by the Romans for some time.

3. Many of the Zealots found their way (after the destruction of Jerusalem) to Alexandria, Egypt, Cyrenaica, Cyprus and Mesopotamia;

they and the next generations continued to stir up the Jewish populations against the Romans, waiting only for an opportune moment—namely Roman weakness—to strike a blow against Rome in the mystic hope that God would send the long awaited Messiah to fulfill the prophecies, as then preached by the rabbis. The Jewish State would be reborn, the Temple rebuilt and God would again favor the Jewish people, as promised in the Torah. For the restoration of this glory and for the obedience to God's commands as they understood them, the Jews were willing to risk all, their relatively prosperous circumstances, their lives and the lives of their families. The Jews suffered greatly from their Greek and Gentile tormentors who lost little time stirring them up with disparaging statements, such as, that God had abandoned them, Judaism was a false religion, Jews no longer enjoyed God's special protection and that the Roman gods were stronger than the God of the Jews. They must have considered these as blasphemous statements and were waiting for scores to be settled.

4. Not long after the fall of Masada, a rebellion broke out among Egyptian Jews (other than in Alexandria) which was quickly suppressed and in retaliation the almost 300 years old Temple of Onias in Heliontopolis was closed by the Romans. Emperor Trajan, striving to emulate the glory of Alexander the Great, invaded Parthia in 115 A.D.—there appeared to be a dispute for royal succession where a great number of Jews lived with full freedom and the privilege of self-government. The Jews and native population rose up against the Roman invaders, who kept advancing, victory after victory, towards India and created great military difficulties for them in the rear conquered areas. Trajan was forced to abandon further advances and turn back to deal with the uprising. Parthia was always a difficult antagonist for the Romans and Trajan, in preparation for this contingency, withdrew many of the troops stationed in other strategic places of the Roman Empire in order to enlarge his invading army.

In 115 A.D. a rebellion broke out in Judea (not much is known about it), a rebellion also broke out in Cyrenaica as a result of racial riots against Jews, soon to be joined by a rebellion of Jews in Egypt and Cyprus. The Jews all made common cause as if guided by an invisible hand and took advantage of the depletion of Roman forces which were deployed in Parthia. Trajan sent his General Martius Turbo to deal with the Jewish uprising in Cyrenaica, Egypt and Cyprus, after the Jewish rebel forces defeated the local Roman General Lupus (this was a full scale war) and after allegedly killing 220,000 Greeks and Romans in Cyrenaica and 240,000 Greeks in Cyprus (according to Dio Cassius). Trajan also sent his favored General Lucius Quietus to Palestine as Governor of that land with orders to crush the Jewish revolt there. This same general destroyed many thousands of Jewish fighters in subduing the rebellion in Mesopotamia. The Jewish losses in lives were staggering. Most of the Alexandrian Jews were annihilated and the ancient Alexandrian synagogue destroyed; the Jewish community—once the most flourishing and cultured—soon disappeared. All the Jews on the island of Cyprus were killed; no Jew was allowed, under penalty of death, to set foot on Cyprus. All the uprisings were totally crushed in 117 A.D. The revolts of 115–117 A.D. achieved nothing for the Jews, only setbacks; the enormous losses of Jewish lives were completely wasted: Rome prevailed again.

5. What conclusions can be drawn from this historic debacle?

(a) The almost simultaneous uprisings in Egypt, Cyrenaica, Cyprus, Judea, Lybia and Mesopotamia (considering the distances and primitive communication methods available in those times) lead one to the conclusion that the uprisings were planned well in advance; almost years in advance (except possibly the reaction to the Roman invasion of Parthia/Mesopotamia—even the planning of that invasion was known for some time). So with the arming and military training of Jewish rebels, provision for logistical supplies—all had to be prepared well ahead to confuse the Romans and obscure the rebels' intentions; for although the rebels were defeated in the various battles, they did fight major military encounters.

(b) There is no evidence that the Diaspora Jews aided or attempted to aid the Judean and Galilean Jews in the 66–70 A.D. uprising. Did the horrors of that human disaster, the destruction of cities and the Temple, massive crucifixions, enslavement of civilians and Diaspora dispersions weigh heavily upon the conscience of Diaspora Jews? Were they about two generations later spurred on by accounts as narrated by Zealots who managed to flee? About the superhuman courage shown by the Jewish fighters? How did the drama impact upon the mind of prospering Diaspora Jews, enjoying the relative freedom of worship and privileges who contemplated the annihilation of their brethren?

(c) Did the rabbis, successors to the Pharisees, still preach the coming of the Messiah from the House of David?; did they prophesy the early rebuilding of the Jerusalem Temple, as it is alleged they had done (54, II, 394) as the focus of Jewish revival and reconstruction of the Jewish State? Did the rabbis and Zealots spread the notion that as long as there were willing Jewish rebels the cause was not lost and that God would not abandon all the Jews?

(d) Did the Diaspora Jews suffer from a sense of guilt for violating the Torah Laws and commandments, such as not to be ruled by a foreign "king," paying their sacred tithes for the support of idolatry (Temple of Jupiter), living permanently in foreign and polluted lands where no Temple of God could be built and no sacrifices offered?

6. The above subparagraphs (a), (b), (c), (d), could offer an explanation (as if there had to be one) for the Diaspora Jews risking all in one more concentrated attempt to remove the Roman yoke and restore the Jewish State. However, the bloody attempt of 115–117 A.D. failed tragically and Roman might prevailed. The influence of the Torah and the rabbis (the priestly order was gone) again perverted the mind of Jews, made them forsake the natural laws of self-preservation, causing them to choose options which did not serve their true interest and, as the Christian historian Eusebius aptly stated (History of the Church – Book IV, 2), referring to the 115 A.D. uprising: "... the Jewish tragedy was moving through a series of disasters towards its climax."

7. There is no other explanation. The one offered by other modern Jewish historians (Graetz, Dubnov, Sachar, Grayzel and others) that the revolt was a reaction to provocations, a war of revenge against hostile Romans, Greeks and Gentiles who relished harassing and insulting the Jews—just is not credible. Trajan was no Caligula. He did not harm the Jews. And if the Jews risked all—to achieve what? Revenge? Their advisors and leaders would have had to be stark mad! The cruelty and violence was staggering on both sides. Nothing was learned from previous uprisings and the same mistakes repeated. The stage was set for the last major uprising, which failed just as miserably and incurred much larger Jewish losses: The Bar Kokhba rebellion against Rome, just a bare 15 years later.

Chapter 21

The Bar Kokhba Rebellion

1. The Roman Empire at the time of Hadrian's rule (117–138 A.D.) contained a population in excess of 60 million people, extended from Britain south to Mauretania (North Africa), from Britain east along the Danube to all the sides of the Black Sea, from there south-east to Mesopotamia, from there south-west to Syria, Palestine and Egypt, from there due west along North Africa back to Mauretania. The Mediterranean was a "Mare Internum", a Roman sea, completely surrounded by its possessions. It resembled the form of a parallelogram, 3600 miles by 1800 miles. Rome had at its disposal a standing army of over 30 legions, plus vast numbers of auxiliaries (foot-soldiers and cavalry). This vast Empire was acquired by conquest and harbored hostile nations and peoples who aspired to freedom, but for the visible presence of Roman might and the certainty of brutal punishment. It was the genius of the Roman ruling class that they managed to govern such a vast Empire successfully, consisting of so many diverse nations and maintain the Pax Romana for several hundred years; for a troop disposition of 3 to 4 legions with auxiliaries (about 60,000 to 80,000 men) was a vast and costly undertaking, which depleted the forces from various provinces. A rebellious nation had the advantage of time and distance; moving of troops within this vast expanse was a slow process; if guided by proper military intelligence, could wreak havoc to an Empire supported by plunder, tribute and taxes from its subdued peoples—for the military forces at its disposal were limited and spread thin over a large area, considering the vastness to be protected and seldom matched the rebellious local forces at the moment of explosion.

2. Bar Kokhba, the Jewish rebel leader, was a man of superior military ability and possessed a firmness of character required of a successful

national revolutionary leader. The military situation in 132–134 A.D., the first years of the rebellion appeared to be:

(a) Bar Kokhba had a unified military command with loyal and properly trained subordinate officers.

(b) His army consisted—according to Dio Cassius—of 580,000 trained warriors, fully equipped.

(c) Bar Kokhba, from the letters discovered in 1952–1961, exercised absolute control over logistical supplies and was prepared to mete out harsh punishment for disobedience.

(d) The Romans had about 2 legions and auxiliaries (ca 40,000 men) at their disposal in the region.

(e) Hadrian, after an extended visit to Egypt, Palestine and Syria during 129–131 A.D., left Syria for Greece in the summer of 131 A.D. Bar Kokhba waited for that moment.

(f) All military preparations of Bar Kokhba were undetected, despite an abundance of Roman spies and some local traitors.

(g) Bar Kokhba fully utilized the advantage of time and distance which factors initially favored the rebels.

(h) When Hadrian became aware that Roman local forces and auxiliaries he sent could not control the local uprising—which should have sufficed under usually predictable circumstances—he confirmed the seriousness of the situation by summoning his best general, Julius Severus, from Britain and gave him command of 12 experienced Roman legions and auxiliaries with orders to crush the revolt.

(i) The Roman forces in various provinces were depleted as a result of assembling 12 legions.

3. The main sources of history of the Bar Kokhba rebellion are the Roman historian Dio Cassius and the Christian historian Eusebius. According to Cassius, one of Hadrian's projects was building a new city on the ruins of Jerusalem on a Roman model and constructing a temple to Jupiter on Temple Mount. Hadrian must have been aware that the Jews, informed of his intentions, historically prone to rebellion over religious issues and disposing of a large number of men of military age, would be highly motivated to revolt. This is the same Hadrian who after Trajan's death withdrew Roman legions from Parthia because, in his pragmatic view, the gains could not be defended and Hadrian desired peace. As related, the

sequence of events lacks credibility. What kind of man was Hadrian? As described by Will Durant (The Story of Civilization, III, P 415 ff):

> "...(Hadrian for)... twenty years governed with wisdom, justice and peace ... He read and admired the Stoic Epictetus, ... he visited the sick, helped the unfortunate, extended existing charities to orphans and widow, and was a generous patron to artists, writers and philosophers ... under his care, ... the Empire was probably better governed than ever before or afterward ...(he) earned the reputation of a fair and learned judge ... He issued ... decrees, usually in favor of the weak against the strong ... he was at heart a scholar and philosopher ... The Roman army was never in better condition than in his reign ... Never before ...(the Roman Empire) had it been so prosperous ... And no man had so beneficently ruled it as Hadrian ..."

Is it credible that this same Hadrian would have promised the Jews, for example, the restoration of their Temple in Jerusalem and then arbitrarily changed his mind? Is it credible that Joshua ben Hananiah, head of the Synhedrion and known for his desire for peace, would have gone to Egypt in an attempt to dissuade Hadrian from carrying out his plan (to build a temple to Jupiter) and then be ridiculed by him for his effort? It is not credible that Hadrian could be guilty of such conduct in view of his personality profile.

4. Trajan sent his favored general, the ruthless Lucius Quietus, to Palestine as Governor. Hadrian recalled him later and had him executed for conspiracy with other generals. But was the revolt of 115–117 A.D. in Judea fully suppressed or did it end in a stand-off? During the early years of Hadrian's reign, the Jews on several occasions advanced the idea of rebuilding the Temple. If the Judean revolt had been crushed in the typical Roman manner, no army of 580,000 Jews could have been raised 15 years later. Furthermore, Hadrian announced during his visit to Palestine, Egypt and Syria (129–131 A.D.), that he intended to rebuild Jerusalem as a Roman pagan city with circuses and theaters. Construction of the temple to Jupiter on the Temple Mount was commenced—if at all—but not finalized during his last visit. This being so ,the time span between the commencement of the revolt (132 A.D.) and the date of Hadrian's announcement (130 A.D.) was not sufficient to conscript, train and equip an army of 580,000 men and provide all the logistical support in so secretive a manner as to

fool the Roman spies. It is strongly maintained by modern Jewish historians that Hadrian's announcement of his intentions was the principal cause
of the revolt.

Furthermore, during the liberation of Palestine by Bar Kokhba and during his reign when Jews had time to mint several issues of coins, nothing
is known about using that opportunity to expunge from the Holy City all of
Hadrian's abominations and pagan vestiges, the existence of which was
alleged as the cause of the revolt. It is therefore apparent that no construction was commenced at all before the revolt. It is also alleged that a prohibition against circumcision caused the Jews to revolt in 132 A.D.; it was
part of the law against mutilation and castration enacted by Emperor
Domitian (81–96 A.D.), brother of Titus, several times modified and
remodified; it was still law when Hadrian became emperor. Therefore, any
negative impact could not be attributed to Hadrian. The following conclusions can be drawn: The arming, recruiting, training, construction of under-
ground storage facilities for arms and food provisions, military logistics of
a major army of 580,000 warriors under Bar Kokhba, which was so well
organized and disciplined for revolt in 132 A.D. against mighty Rome,
could not have been accomplished between 130–132 A.D. but was an effort
lasting many more years, particularly since they managed to keep it secret
from Roman spies. (They could not proceed openly but preparations had to
be carried out in secret, gradually and by degrees). Powerful and rich Rome
having at its disposal all facilities required for gathering and arming their
30 legions did so at great expense and effort. The 580,000 Jewish warriors
exceeded in number the 30 Roman legions and auxiliaries. Rome also
maintained a vast spy information system throughout the Empire to report
early on local disturbances and preparations for armed moves. The alleged
causes for the 132 A.D. revolt, i.e., Hadrian's plans for a Roman pagan city
and a temple to Jupiter in Jerusalem (according to Cassius the decision by
Hadrian predated the revolt by about 2 years) and the prohibition against
circumcision which had been law for over 30 years prior to the revolt
(which laws the Jews managed to circumvent)—could not be the real causes of the uprising but were only the pretext. The real causes of the revolt
were elsewhere.

5. The aspirations of Jewish freedom fighters were not extinguished in
Judea after 117 A.D. The belief in the inevitable divine intervention which

followed from all the articles of faith of the Torah, promises to David and prophetic teachings, were only strengthened by the horrors of destruction inflicted on Judean and Diaspora Jews.. They were interpreted by the rabbis and sages as the necessary prelude to the coming of a Redeemer, an earthly king-Messiah. He would restore the Jewish people to the glory promised by God and the prophets. The restoration of the Jewish State to full freedom, the rebuilding of Jerusalem as the Holy City and the Temple as the House of God, the reinstitution of the obligatory sacrifices, the rededication of the children of Israel to the Torah Law and Commandments—these were the aspirations kept alive by the rabbis and preached to the Judeans. Most rabbis exhorted the people to rebellion against Rome, keeping alive the flame which was only dimmed in 117 A.D.; preaching the need for unity, better organization and better timing than in previous uprisings and avoiding past mistakes. These would have been sufficient reasons to energize the Jews for rebellion in due time. The aged and highly respected spiritual leader, Rabbi Akiba, came upon a military leader, convinced that he was the king-Messiah, the Redeemer. The man named Simeon bar Kosevah was proclaimed the long awaited and promised Messiah by Akiba; his name was later changed to Bar Kokhba, and became known to history by that name. His greatest protagonist, Rabbi Akiba—despite some misgivings expressed by a few rabbis—travelled throughout Judea preaching that the Messiah had come who would lead a new military rebellion against Rome and accomplish the dream of the Jews for an independent Jewish State with all the features restored. The people believed Akiba, for Bar Kokhba managed to achieve a unity of purpose among Jews never recorded before or since.

6. The rumors of an Aelia Capitolina, a Roman pagan city built on the site of Jerusalem, and a temple to Jupiter built on the site of the Temple Mount, were just that prior to the revolt—rumors. They were not the cause of the 132 A.D. revolt nor was the alleged sudden prohibition against circumcision. The spiritual and fomenting activities of Rabbi Akiba, his proclamation of Bar Kokhba as the long promised king-Messiah which understandably aroused the deep-seated aspirations of the Jewish people to risk all in a final supreme effort to follow the divine Messiah in crushing their alien tormentors and God's enemies—these were the real causes of the 132 A.D. revolt and the culmination of the 115–117 A.D. rebellion in

Judea which Quietus did not crush. The preparation for this massive military effort and rebellion must have commenced soon after 117 A.D. and was therefore many years in the making. The cited conduct of Hadrian and his Procurator Rufus were a convenient sideshow. The revolt, so long in preparation, would have exploded even had Hadrian and Rufus been above reproach. Bar Kokhba and his followers were preparing to revolt, no matter what Rome did or did not do. So much for the effect of divine inspiration. The Jews saw no risk in the undertaking and were certain of complete victory since the proclaimed Redeemer was their leader. The might of Rome was put out of their mind.

7. Rabbi Akiba (Akiba ben Joseph) was recognized as the spiritual and chief leader of the Judeans after the death of Joshua ben Hananiah. His beginnings were very modest. In his early life he was employed as a shepherd, was not literate and disliked all forms of scholarship. In later life (it is said through his wife's influence) he acquired great learning, attended one of the great academies at Lydda and later the academy at Jabneh. Joshua ben Hananiah was one of his early teachers; he became one of the foremost Jewish religious scholars of his time and an outstanding teacher. To his credit, he played a role in the formulation of the Mishnah. He played a major non-military part before and during the revolt by inspiring and exhorting his people to ready themselves for a final blow to be rid of the foreign rule of Romans. His greatest contribution to the revolt was his proclamation that Simeon bar Kosevah was the long expected Messiah, the divinely appointed military leader of Israel, and herald the news among the people. Considering the source, his proclamation carried maximum credibility. He was born ca 50 A.D. and was executed by the victorious Romans after the collapse of the revolt in 135 A.D. He was modest and humble; he died a martyr's death.

8. Bar Kokhba (translated from Hebrew: the son of a star) as he was later known, the chief hero of the 132 A.D. revolt against Rome, was referred to in letters written during the revolt to him or for him (discovered during the years 1952–1961) as Simeon bar Kosevah. The name Bar Kokhba given to him by Rabbi Akiba was a symbolic messianic name, a reference to messianic expectations (Num. 24:17): "There shall step forth a star out of Jacob" or "… a star from Jacob takes the leadership, a scepter arises from Israel." Several sets of coins were minted to honor the liberation, some

make reference to Bar Kokhba as "Simeon Nasi of Israel" (Simeon Prince of Israel) which had a messianic connotation. Considering the preparation for and conduct of the rebellion, Bar Kokhba was an extremely able administrator and military commander, who ruled with an iron hand as required by the exigencies of the times. Nothing is known about his background. He initially defeated the forces of Rufus, the Palestine Procurator, the forces of Marcellus, the Syrian Governor and the various auxiliary forces sent by Hadrian, all in open battle. His ultimate aim of meeting the forces of Julius Severus in open battle was denied him—where his superiority in numbers would have carried the day, by the tactics of a general who had no intention of doing so since better options were available to him: Subduing Bar Kokhba's forces piecemeal in their fortified positions and starving them into surrender by interdicting food and water supplies, options which were anathema to the opposing commander. Bar Kokhba was simply outmaneuvered and out-foxed by a more experienced tactician and better general, who starved his forces into submission. The outcome was never in doubt.

9. After Hadrian departed from the East, the Jews of Judea, led by Bar Kokhba, rose in open military rebellion against Rome in 132 A.D.; with an army estimated between 400,000 and 580,000 men he was ready to take on the Romans. The local Roman Procurator Rufus tried to suppress the revolt, but had to retreat from Judea before the superior forces of Bar Kokhba. Marcellus, the Syrian Governor came with his legions to Rufus' aid, but he too was defeated. Bar Kokhba's forces then occupied the whole of Judea, Galilee and Samaria, which were cleared of enemy forces. Jerusalem was liberated, Israel was liberated and Bar Kokhba became the ruler of the country. Eleazar, the High-Priest, rededicated the altar and the ritual of sacrificial offerings was reinstituted. There was no time to consider rebuilding the Temple nor the walls around Jerusalem. But time was found to mint several issues of coins. The years on the coins were numbered sequentially, beginning with "Year 1" and the following year "Year 2," and were meant to reflect the start of a new era; the coins had various inscriptions, "Jerusalem." "For the freedom of Jerusalem." "Year one of the redemption of Israel," "Simeon Prince of Israel," "Year two of the freedom of Israel," "the priest Eleazar (Eliezer Hakohen)." Letters dating from the revolutionary period were found by archaeologists in the years 1952–1961; they reflect the involvement of Bar Kokhba in administrative

details, leasing and sales of properties, resupply operations, setting the quota of grain to be produced, confiscation of agricultural land of those who failed to cultivate them, preventing concentration of property in the hands of a few, etc. Hadrian kept sending auxiliary forces to Judea but all were defeated. Finally, he decided to recall his best General Julius Severus from Britain, assigned 12 Roman legions to him and substantial auxiliary troops, with orders to crush the Judean revolt. Severus did not plan to meet Bar Kokhba in open battle, but decided to encircle the enemies' bases and hiding places (making use of information of traitors) and starve them into surrender. Time was on his side. He reduced one fort after another in this manner and intentionally prolonged the war since starvation, a sure winner, was a slow process. The Jews suffered heavy losses and the Romans executed all prisoners. Finally, reduced to the last fortress Bethar where Bar Kokhba made his final stand, about 80,000 of his warriors put up a valiant struggle. Severus was forced to impose a regular siege to Bethar, which was finally conquered due to starvation of its defenders and lack of water. All rebels in the fortress were killed, including Bar Kokhba; the date was August 135 A.D. The land was devastated, all towns and villages were destroyed. Once again, the population was decimated; the rebels lost over 580,000 killed in battle; women and children were taken to slave markets. The final Jewish rebellion against Rome ended with disastrous consequences for the Jewish people.

10. Hadrian wasted no time in rebuilding Jerusalem as a Roman/Greek pagan city and named it Colonia Aelia Capitolina. This time he was resolved to break the Jewish spirit. He built a temple to Jupiter Capitoline on Temple Mount, several statues to himself, other pagan shrines and deities including statues of other Roman and Greek gods. He forbade circumcision, the observance of Sabbath, Jewish festivals, study of the Torah or maintenance of Jewish study schools; the Council of Jabneh was dissolved and outlawed. Violations of these prohibitions were punishable by death. His Procurator Rufus returned to enforce compliance of these decrees with the help of many spies. He imposed on all Diaspora Jews a much heavier temple tax for Jupiter's temple in Rome than the one imposed by Vespasian. The Jews were forbidden to set foot in Jerusalem on pain of death except once a year, on the anniversary of the destruction of the Temple, when they could pay for the privilege of visiting the old Temple site.

11. All the pain, efforts and sacrifices of the Bar Kokhba rebellion were in vain. The Jews, however well intentioned, sacrificed their lives and those of their kin for nothing. Nothing was achieved except a substantial deterioration in the relationship with their foreign ruler and Gentile neighbors; total loss of credibility; abrogation of religious freedom; impoverishment; decimation of their people and most importantly, total disparagement of the messianic concept that an independent Jewish State can be won by military means and force God's hand. Hadrian had it right: The Jews will be a rebellious people, set apart from others, unable to blend and intermarry with their neighbors, a proud people above all others, claiming privileges on account of their perceived superiority and hating their neighbors as long as the religious traditions of the Torah had a hold on them. In Hadrian's Roman simplistic, legalistic thinking the solution seemed obvious: Separate the Jews from the Torah and the Jews will become like any other people. He passed laws in an attempt to bring this about, but failed just as all others like him failed: The Jews simply did not wish to be separated from the Torah; that was the only possession they could claim exclusively.

12. The Bar Kokhba rebellion was ill conceived, faulted from the start and bound to fail. Thus ended the mightiest Jewish effort made to-date to throw off the yoke of foreign oppression. But it illustrated one more time the flawed connection between the Torah—as a guide for conduct and the life-style of a small people thrust among a multiplicity of nations—and the perverting influence it exercised on the mind of Jews through its Laws and Commandments at a time and conditions totally unsuited for them. These were authored by priests, for the benefit and support of priests, priestly government and for the priestly domination of the children of Israel. The rabbis, successors to the priests, took over the functions of priesthood—enlarged upon it substantially in due time—benefitted from the product without accepting the burden of its authorship. The age of priestly tyranny was ended; the age of the influence of rabbis commenced.

13. This revolt clearly showed the effects of the Torah and messianic ideas, fomented by rabbis and Orthodox Jews (as the term is understood nowadays), who incited the deep-seated yearning of oppressed Jews for divine intervention and the coming of a Redeemer in the form of a king-Messiah. With such backing, victory seemed assured; all caution was thrown to the

wind; precedents and warnings were ignored and the power of Rome became another challenge to be overcome. No Jew dared stand aside. For many centuries the Jews did not recover from the effects of the Bar Kokhba catastrophe. The rabbis were mistaken; the Jewish religious Zealots were mistaken: The Messiah did not come and God did not intervene.

Chapter 22

Judaism as a Social Force

1. A social force is a confluence and convergence of causes which bring about a harmonizing, composing and beneficial effect in the condition of or relationship between two or more entities. Religion can be termed a social force if it influences its believer to be in harmony with his fellowman; to compose the differences with his fellowman; to have a beneficial effect upon the relationship with his fellowman. It is a matter of degrees and shades. The negative can be stated more forcefully. A religion can be termed not to be a social force if it disrupts, damages, vitiates the relationship between its believer and fellowman; causes acrimony, hatred, violence, destruction, persecution and murder between the believer and his fellowman. The same holds for a group of people and nations. Human relationships are affected by many factors, with religion only one of them; the many factors may outweigh the social force effect of religion, in which case it would only augment or diminish the effect of the other factors. This is my understanding of the social force of religion. A religion which is not a social force in the context of the above definition would have difficulties justifying its divine origin, for it must be taken as axiomatic that harmony is more divine than conflict; peaceful solutions to disputes more divine than violence and compromise more divine than spilling of blood. If one were asked to define the purpose of religion and do so while standing on one foot (to borrow Hillel's famous figure of speech), one could say without remorse: To be a social force to man and mankind—the rest of the dogma, creeds, rituals, ordinances and commandments are "commentary." If religion is not to be a means of propagating social forces, then what is its purpose? Is it to foster piety and blessedness? These are social forces. Is it to foster the study of the Bible? Is it to ensure the salvation of man's soul? These could evoke social

forces. Is it to encourage man to love God and the practice of morality and ethics? These are social forces. In the Torah and Prophets there are to be found eloquent illustrations of the concept of social forces, for example:

"Honor your father and your mother ..." (Ex. 20:12).

"You must not oppress the stranger; ..." (Ex.23:9).

"You must love your neighbor as yourself" (Lev 19:18).

"Cease to do evil. Learn to do good, search for justice, help the oppressed, be just to the orphan, plead for the widow" (Isaiah 1:16–17).

"... this is what Yahweh asks of you: only this, to act justly, to love tenderly, and to walk humbly with your God" (Micah 6:8).

2. When, however, the religion of the Jews contained in its foundation a special Covenant with God that was eternal, could not be abrogated and peculiar as to them only; when they were selected exclusively as God's Chosen People; preferred above all other people; given the Torah through Moses which taught the rituals of animal sacrifice, laws of purity and pollution, slavish obedience to priestly ordinances, hatred of neighbors (idolators); making Jews a people separate and apart; given to exclusivity and superiority; debasing religions of other people and ordered to exterminate them; given by their God a Promised Land whose acquisition required the merciless total slaughter of several indigenous nations, whose only blame was that they were in the way; commanded not to be ruled by a foreigner despite their small size and the many powerful neighbors—that religion could only lead to disaster and could not be defined as a social force; it perverted the mind of its believers. The divinely (priestly) commanded hatred of Gentiles and pagans was more than reciprocated. As if to bring this point home to the future generations of Jews, the priestly redactors of the Old Testament recounted wars, battles, horrors of exterminations, merciless slaughters of men, women and children, destruction of towns and communities—all allegedly committed by Israelites at the command of their God. But these were for the most part downright fictions, pure inventions of the priestly redactors, inserted to glorify the power of the God of Israel, completely oblivious to the lasting perverting effects of such storytelling upon the mind and soul of future generations of Jews who believed these narrations as sacred text.

3. Scattered among nations, seeking privileges in order to comply with the religion of their ancestors, any outside interference with the doctrines of their belief provoked them to rebellion which only increased the friction with neighbors. The reckless uprisings against Rome—without any prospect of success—fomented, guided and misguided by priests, religious fanatics and rabbis who added frivolity to tragedy by inventing apocalyptic messianic false expectations, resulted in the destruction of the Jewish State, the Jerusalem Temple, decimation, impoverishment and enslavement of most of the Jewish inhabitants. Jerusalem became the pagan Aelia Capitolina and the site on the Temple Mount became the location of the pagan temple to Jupiter Capitoline. Severely restrictive laws were passed prohibiting the practice of Judaism, reserving the death penalty for violators. The priestly tree bore its fruit of poison: The religion they created proceeded to its logical conclusion, its social forces were irrelevant. But this was only the first stage. Much more serious disasters were to plague the Jewish people in the time to come. The rabbis assumed the leadership of the Jews. The age of rabbinic influence commenced. Was rabbinic Judaism ready to become a new religious social force? The social force of priestly Judaism collapsed.

4. After 135 A.D., with all the history of disasters visited upon the Jewish people to contemplate, what did the rabbis—the new spiritual leaders—do in their attempt to influence the conduct of Jews after the period of failed rebellions? By that time anti-Jewish feelings among Gentiles and pagans were exerting ever greater influence based on the outward conduct of Jews. Did the rabbis admit their failed advice and participation in the uprisings? There is no record of it. Did it ever occur to the rabbis—as it did to Claudius, Vespasian, Trajan, Hadrian and Marcus Aurelius—that there were certain roots in priestly Judaism that so affected the mind of the Jewish people as to incline them to revolt and to difficulty of living in amity with their non-Jewish neighbors? Did it ever occur to them that the commandments and ordinances of the Torah so affected the conduct of Jews as to invoke enmity and hatred with non-Jews? That such conduct— endemic to Jews—could only lead to misfortune? That anti-Jewish feelings were not always due to the "evil nature" of non-Jews? The rabbis did not even have an inkling that there was a problem and proceeded to institutionalize rabbinic Judaism, which in time became the dominant form of

Judaism—in complete oblivion of the non-Jewish world. They showed no awareness of Hosea's indictment of priests: "… it is you, priests, that I denounce … you are the ruin of your people …" (4:4–5).

5. The rabbis did come to some conclusions which were based on the reality of then recent history. A Jewish State of the type of the Second Commonwealth was no longer necessary for the survival of Judaism or the Jewish people; the use of military force was not to be any longer the means of achieving an independent Jewish State; that the hand of God must not be forced—later declared blasphemy—but that God would establish an independent Jewish State at a time of his choosing and by means of a messianic leader of his choosing.

6. The rabbis did come to some other conclusions: The reduction to writing of the Oral Law—the Mishnah. The priests used the obligatory sacrificial rituals to maintain dominance over the children of Israel. The rabbis used the stranglehold of the Mishnah, supplemented later by the Talmud, to maintain dominance over the Jewish people. The Mishnah, the first dogmatic code of Judaism, which was declared the authoritative interpretation of the Torah, the Written Law, was a redaction around 200 A.D. by the Tannaim (rabbis) of the Oral Law given—according to them—to the first Rabbi, i.e., Moses, and passed on orally to Joshua. From him it was passed on orally to the Elders, then to the Prophets, then to the sages in each subsequent generation, word for word without any changes, until it was communicated to the rabbis. The Mishnah was supplemented later by the Talmud (Palestinian and Babylonian, completed ca 500 A.D.), a collection of various commentaries and opinions on the Law by the Amoraim (rabbis). Both the Mishnah and Talmud are, generally speaking, interpretations and commentaries on the Torah; they are not of divine origin but are products of human hands—the rabbis. It was the invention partly of the Pharisees (precursors of rabbis) but mostly of the rabbis, that the Oral Law was communicated to Moses by God and that the Torah could not exist without the Oral Law. It suited the purpose of the rabbis to hold forth such opinions which gave a divine foundation to their undertaking and a future commanding position among Jews. The Torah was immutable and could not be changed; the Mishnah was mutable, evolving and adaptable to changed conditions. Rabbinic Judaism emerged about 70 A.D. and lasted until about 500 A.D.

7. The biblical canon, as applied to the Old Testament, the Jewish Bible, is a closed list of authoritative books accepted as divinely revealed; it did not comprise all the body of literature of Jewish writers who wrote on biblical and sacred themes between 200 B.C. and 200 A.D., which are referred to as Apocrypha (unknown author) and Pseudepigrapha (false author ascription); these writings were not included in the canon. The list of writings included in the canon was compiled by the rabbis of the synod of Jabneh (in Palestine) around 100 A.D. The list was closed and no further additions were made to the biblical canon. The rabbis included certain works and excluded others; we do not know the basis of the selection process used. We do know that the selection process showed no consistency, since the rabbis included among sacred books accepted as divinely revealed works whose authors claimed no revelation or divine inspiration, such as Joshua, Kings and most of the Writings (such as Proverbs, Job, Ezra, Nehemiah, etc.). There are 24 books in the biblical canon (or 39, if the minor prophets, the second books of Samuel, Kings and Chronicles are listed separately) which is divided into three sections: Torah, Prophets and Writings. The Torah—consisting of the five books of Moses—is the only work which can lay claim to divine revelation and yet its present form was not settled till some time around the fourth century B.C., a full 1000 years after the supposed time of its author. What is astonishing is that the rabbis, in their wisdom, included in the canon works like Esther, Ruth and Song of Songs—works of highly dubious value and omitted works like the Wisdom of Ben Sira, Enoch and The Testaments of the Twelve Patriarchs, works whose teachings were of inestimable value as social forces—they were elevating to the mind and soul and inspired ethical conduct. The rabbis spent considerable time debating the mishnic treatment of the Sabbath law and ordinances, ritual purity and diets; they misjudged the worth of the Wisdom of Ben Sira (which directs man to the love of wisdom and promotes ethical conduct); Enoch ("Woe unto you who rejoice in the suffering of the righteous ones ... Woe unto you who engage in oppression and give aid to injustice") and the Testaments of the Twelve Patriarchs (which deals with the value of integrity, piety, uprightness, honesty, generosity, compassion and self-control).

8. What was the response of the rabbis to the increasingly anti-Semitic (anti-Jewish and anti-Judaism attitudes) feelings of their non-Jewish

neighbors? Did they consider the conduct of Jews sacrosanct and that of non-Jews full of iniquity and abomination? How did they face the certainty of a prolonged Diaspora, away from the Promised Land and life among hostile Gentiles and pagans? Did they consider that God could not be worshiped outside his own land (1 Sam. 26:19)? That foreign countries were unclean and unfit for a sanctuary (Amos 7:17, Joshua 22:19)? That God ruled with kindness, justice and integrity on earth and that it would please him if his nation would do likewise (Jer. 9:24)? The answer of the rabbis was:

(a) To impose upon the Jewish people their casuistic writings of the Mishnah, Talmud, Gemara, Midrash, Tosefta and Baraita; to lead the Jewish people to total immersion in these works and total absorption of their mind and energies in understanding the complex teachings, rules and ordinances of these writings; to convince them that the pursuit of these studies was a religious duty. These studies sharpened their mind; erected a wall of defense against the demeaning and intimidating effects of anti-Semitism; discouraged apostasy and heresy; raised the communal defensive spirit so necessary during an era of almost continuous persecutions. But it also made them slaves to a system of thought, built on a man-made system of thought which was static and stagnant from generation to generation and of mind-perverting influence due to the self-imposed isolation from the outside world. The rabbis, in order to preserve their dominant standing in the community and thus perpetuate their power, permitted their flock no freedom of thought or criticism or pursuit of secular studies, branding such endeavors—in their own inimitable way—as impious and leading to sacrilege or worse. They displayed the greatest intolerance toward non-conformists. For example, when certain sectarians promoted the view that God's love was the characteristic feature of Judaism, the Mishnah cautioned its readers against this opinion and ordered silence to be imposed on one who desired to express this view in prayer (54, Book II, 471). When a Jewish historian, Azariah dei Rossi, wrote a book of Jewish history in 1573 A.D. and subjected the writings of rabbis and sages to rational analysis pointing out where the wise men had erred, his "... work aroused intense resentment among Orthodox learned Jews (rabbis). The great codifier Joseph Caro, the most influential Jewish scholar of his time, died just before he could sign a decree ordering the book to be burned ... The Rabbi Judah Loew ... the dominant figure in the next generation ... thought that Rossi's sceptical investigations into talmudic legends and Jewish history would undermine authority and destroy belief ... (Rossi's book) was banned to Jewish students without special rabbinical permission ..." (6–288). The Karaites, a Jewish sect founded by Anan ben David in the 8th century A.D. in Baghdad, rejected the Talmud as the invention of rabbis and urged the return to the pure Torah. The geonim (rabbis of the Babylonian community between the 6th and 11th centuries A.D.) denounced him to the Caliph (head of State) and Anan fled to Palestine to escape execution.

(b) That the reward of full observance of the precepts of the Law would be a share in the world to come; they taught the doctrine of resurrection, of reward and punishment after death; that life on this earth was only a preparation for the hereafter. But these were pure rabbinic inventions, for they also authored the doctrine that those who maintained that resurrection was a myth would have no participation in it.

(c) The belief that God would not let the Jewish people suffer forever but would intervene by sending a Redeemer, a Messiah, to free them from the clutches of their oppressors and restore them to glory.

These were the responses of the rabbis. They were unable to foresee the consequences of their creations any more than the priests, scribes and redactors of the Torah could years before. Although the dogma of the Catholic Church was still in a stage of development by 500 A.D., the trend was unmistakable and should have put the rabbis on notice. By that time Christianity was rapidly gaining political ascendancy and power; their unalterable and irrevocable hostility to Jews and Judaism had to be known to the rabbis as well as the fulminations of Saint Chrysostom (4th century A.D.), whose anti-Semitic sermons already reached a level of stridency and virulence remarkable for those early days of Christianity. But the rabbis did not pay attention; they were insulated by their own creations and isolated by their perverted mind to the rising danger.

Chapter 23

Jewish Martyrs

1. After the last major rebellion against Rome (132 A.D.–135 A.D.) ended in disaster for the Jewish people, the Romans issued laws against the practice and teaching of Judaism in an attempt to do away with what was for them a festering problem; Jews caught violating the prohibition paid the supreme penalty. The rabbis and their followers had varied views on the risks of discovery and practiced their faith and its teaching mostly in secret; but some did so openly in bitter defiance of the Romans and suffered the harsh penalties willingly. The number of Jews was greatly reduced by past military disasters and it became an issue of great importance for the survival of Jews as a nation, whether to sacrifice one's life recklessly in open spiritual rebellion against the oppressor or bide time in the hope that a successor to Emperor Hadrian would mitigate or even abrogate the prohibitions. The Jews had more than their share of martyrs in the last two centuries and the question challenged the rabbis whether Jews should remain faithful to their beliefs at the cost of life or submit to the exigencies of the times. When an individual joins a military force and takes the oath of loyalty, desertion could affect the morale of the whole unit, cause its defeat and possible death to all combatants. The violation of some Torah laws or commandments does not fall into that category. The violation may be voluntary, in which case the offender would be the recipient of divinely prescribed punishment; or the violation was meant to affirm his apostasy, in which case the offender abandoned his faith and beliefs and would face his Maker in due time; in either case the Jewish community would have no involvement. What act of desertion is the Jewish violator guilty of? Does not the Torah provide for his punishment? How is the Jewish community affected by his violation? Is their faith so frail as to be endangered by his act? Did the rabbis fear that unless additional severe deterrents were

placed upon the violator, the oppressors of the Jewish people would carry the day and adversely affect the influence and dominance of the rabbis? Did the rabbis think that obligatory martyrdom would restrain potential violators and serve as a powerful demonstration of the Jewish people's commitment to God and Torah? Were no options given to compliance or death?; is the Jewish people's faith in God and Torah diminished in any manner by the violator's forced choice? The rabbis must have agonized over the answers to these problems, but answers had to be found.

2. If the violation is coerced and the violator's choice is suicide, of what possible benefit would his death be to the Jewish community? If the choice is submission which could not be evaded and suicide the only way out, of what possible benefit would his suicide be to the Jewish community, the loss of a martyr of strong enough convictions to give up his life rather than violate his perceived duty to God? The preservation of such a potential martyr within the community could be of immense benefit, particularly when it is realized that whole communities and hundreds upon hundreds of thousands of Jews chose martyrdom rather than submission; they were forever lost to the Jewish people; as apostates they could perform some useful service to the Jewish cause. Most importantly, in view of the continuously changing conditions, a return to the Jewish fold in the future of some or many remained a distinct possibility. Many of the famous rabbis and sages of the thriving 17th century Jewish community of Amsterdam were Spanish and Portuguese marranos (insincere converts), who abandoned the Catholic faith upon emigrating to Amsterdam and returned to the faith of their ancestors. But to allege that martyrs, by their deeds and sacrifice, created a "fund of goodwill" for future generations—when such martyrs murdered (and it was murder in its ugliest form) their children— are utterances by totally perverted minds and unworthy of Jews who claim a sacred bond with God. The life of every Jew must be deemed sacred and there is nothing in the Torah which commands suicide for transgressions of the Law: Whether the transgression is voluntary or involuntary, not obeying the commandments of Yahweh will bring all the curses upon him (Deut. 28:15). The killing of one's children to prevent them from falling into non-Jewish hands and be brought up as non-Jews, is rank premeditated murder and a violation of the 6th Commandment: "You shall not murder." The death of children ends any possibility of rescue or recovery; the mur-

derer made a judgment with finality; he made no claim to prophetic inspiration. Any martyr who fulfilled his religious duty as he saw fit in expectation of collecting the divine reward in after-life is guilty of barter; his religious compliance is tarnished.

3. In the 2nd century A.D., the foremost rabbis assembled in Lydda (Palestine) to contemplate the problem facing the Jews of the day: Martyrdom. Some rabbis advocated the choice of a martyr's death rather than suffer guilt for the transgression of the Law; others advocated saving one's life if the transgression of the Law occurred under compulsion. The issue was put to a vote and the majority voted that under threat of death a Jew may violate all laws and commandments except for those prohibiting: Murder, idolatry and fornication (including incest, adultery, unchastity). It violates all notions of reason to place the prohibition of murder on equal footing with adultery or unchastity. As far as idolatry was concerned, no distinction was made between outside exhibition or inner convictions. If murder is defined as premeditated killing of a human being, it is difficult to conceive of murder committed under compulsion.

The rabbis came up with two new terms: Kiddush Ha-Shem (sanctification of the divine Name) and Hillul Ha-Shem (defamation of the divine Name); the former implied glorification of God; the latter denigration of God. According to the rules of Halacha (The whole legal system of Judaism the study of which—as declared by the rabbis—is the supreme religious duty of Jews; some are of Sinaitic and others of rabbinical origin), another work and collection of rules and regulations compiled and redacted by rabbis, a Jew who suffered martyrdom rather than violate the above mentioned three specific exemptions (murder, idolatry, fornication) earned all the divine rewards of "Kiddush Ha-Shem"; failure to do so would earn him all the divine curses of "Hillul Ha-Shem." From the time of the Lydda rabbinical decisions, anyone suffering death for the "sanctification of the divine Name" was recognized as suffering a martyr's death. The rabbis of Lydda never had any doubts about the wisdom of their decision in ruling on martyrdom. They could not—any more than the priests and scribes could 500 years earlier—foresee the effects their decisions would have on future generations of Jews. They could not conceive of the virulence of future Christian anti-Semitism bent on converting the Jews or exterminating them. They could not conceive of the corrupting effects of misinterpretation by future Jewish sages of their Lydda decisions. They certainly could not have had any premonitions of what influence the misconstrued decisions would exert upon the mass-suicides and wholesale martyrdom of the Jewish people during the Middle Ages. The rabbis were involved in many halachic decisions which affected this or that ritual, prayer or dietary proscriptions; their decisions were interpretative and of an admittedly human hand. Their Lydda decisions regarding martyrdom dealt with suicides and the choice of life and death under prescribed circumstances; in failing to consider all the possible consequences which could flow from their decisions, they committed grievous error and caused incalculable damage and suffering to the Jewish people. These decisions were pure inventions of the rabbis, totally without any divine sanction, nor revelation, nor inspiration, nor any sacred signs. The rabbis left a baleful legacy of confused verbiage and mental tyranny which drastically affected the Jewish people for many centuries to come. Their rules and regulations regarding martyrdom—and the many talmudic discussions they generated—considered sacred by the Jews, while totally irresponsible, guided parents to murder their children and each other in the ill-conceived and ill-perceived act of Kiddush Ha-Shem in the full expectation of divine reward after death. They carried the burden and full responsibility for flawed decisions made by very imperfect Jews—what does it make the rabbis of Lydda and their successors?

4. The legacy of martyrdom, that mental tyranny invented by the rabbis of Lydda which haunted the future generations of Jews, can be exemplified by the murderous acts of the Crusaders, these "warriors of Christ," who were bent on plundering the earthly possessions of Jews and in the process either forcibly baptize or exterminate them. "The spring of 1096 turned out to be fatal for the Jewish communities on the Rhine ... (in the) city of Speyer ... the crusaders with the aid of local Christians attacked the Jews of the city and killed 11; they had refused to yield to baptism ... the Jews of Worms ... only a few escaped death through feigned conversion; the others died for their faith—or committed suicide. Mothers killed their children, who could not stand up against forced conversion ... those Jews who hid in the castle of the bishop of Worms (who offered them protection)... urged them to accept baptism in order to save their lives ... They had preferred suicide ... and the survivors were either killed or subjected to forced

conversion ... The few Jews of Mainz who yielded to baptism under threat of death ... committed ... suicide" (46 Vol. 2–672 ff). A contemporary chronicler gave the following account of the martyrdom in Mainz,

> "... They said to one another, 'Let us be strong, in order to endure what the holy faith imposes upon us ... Soon enemies will kill us ... our souls will survive for the eternal bright paradise. Blessed is the one who perishes in behalf of the One and Eternal ... Whoever has a knife ... let him cut our throats in the Name of the Eternal One—and let him cut his own throat, or stick it into his belly ...'...(the) women summoned courage, and killed their sons and daughters, and then themselves. Men killed their wives and children ... A father sacrificed his son, a brother his sister, a mother her daughter, a neighbor another, a bridegroom his bride. Everyone brought a sacrifice, and himself turned into a sacrifice. And thus the blood of parents mixed with that of their children; ... All of them immolated themselves in behalf of the great and awesome Name ..." (46 Vol. 2–675).

The horror continues, "Everywhere, the Jews evinced an unusual steadfastness, and died for their faith unflinchingly and courageously. The number of suicides was considerable. Entire families threw themselves into the Rhine, with the cry 'Hear, 0 Israel!' and were drowned" (46 Vol. 2–676). This is just a small historical excerpt of the forced conversions and martyrdoms suffered by Jews in Catholic Europe, especially in Germany, Spain, Portugal and France. What an indictment of the oppressors. What a revelation of the workings of the mind of Jews and the influence of rabbinical spiritual tyranny.

5. The dictum of the rabbinical council in Lydda that under threat of death a Jew could violate all laws and commandments except for three became twisted and corrupted by subsequent rabbis and sages and what emerged, under the exigencies of the times, was a declaration that Jews must remain loyal to the faith of their fathers, choose martyrdom if confronted with any forced conversion and that divine reward was in store for those who fulfilled this religious duty; nowhere was there any expectation or requirement that the martyr kill his children, or anyone else. It was the influence of the Talmud, that collection of cogitations gone berserk, that declared the sacrifice of one's life to be the duty of every

Jew—and thereby sanctify the divine Name—rather than convert to another religion and abandon Judaism. The fundamental basis for the directive was another invention of the rabbis: That life on earth was a test; that all was ordained by God; that a martyr's death was the gate which led to the bliss of paradise where the faithful would enjoy eternal life. It can be said that but for the promise of reward in after-life, few martyrdoms would have taken place. If Jews were freely to consent to baptism—and keep reducing their numbers—as soon as pressure was applied, it would set an example for easy imitation. This could not sit well with rabbinical community leaders, for if a Jew was lost to their flock anyway by baptism or death—it was preferable to impede abandonment of faith upon experiencing the least coercion and surround the deed with bloody horror and torment.

6. The rabbis built new inventions upon old inventions, new myths upon old myths, all man-made, fallible, contradictory and without any thought given to the long-term effects and yet they exercised a fated spell over the Jewish people. Most of the Jews, particularly in Spain and Portugal, where the majority of them lived prior to forced conversion, sought to fulfill their religious duty and earn their reward by submitting to baptism under duress; they continued to live the life of crypto-Jews, "New Christians," marranos, anusim (forced ones) in the hope that the storm would pass after some time—as it always did in the past—and they could return once again to the Jewish faith. It was thought to be a divinely planned test; they would be strong and endure the torment. It worked for those who managed to emigrate soon after baptism and return to Judaism in a tolerant surrounding. For those who were forced to stay behind, their simulation and Judaizing brought paroxysms of hate from "old" Christians and horror to the Catholic clergy who were determined to thwart the "New Christians". Members of the religious order of Dominicans, co-sponsored by Pope Gregory IX, advocated institution of the Inquisition and achieve by fear, terror and brutal force what persuasion could not accomplish: Extirpation of any vestige of Judaizing and heresy. The crimes of the Inquisition will be treated in a later chapter. Suffice it to say for now that despite the burning of "New Christian" Judaizers and "heretics"; secret denouncements; confiscation of property; long imprisonment in dungeons; humiliating acts of penance; children denouncing their parents secretly to the Inquisitors—the converts

still maintained clandestine contacts with Jews and were encouraged by them in their secret practice of Jewish ceremonials. The result was that Jews were given the peremptory option: Baptism or expulsion from Spain. Most accepted baptism; the hardy ones—about 50,000—boarded ships only to be robbed and abused by the ship-captains; many thousands died on the journeys and many thousands were forcibly converted at the destinations. In the final analysis, about 20,000 Jews made it as Jews to Genoa, Naples, Corfu and the Ottoman Empire, where they resumed the open and unfettered practice of their faith. Portugal, which in 1492 admitted about 100,000 Jewish fugitives from Spain, in time, forcibly baptized all the Jews and only a few thousand succeeded in emigrating to North Africa and the Ottoman Empire. By 1492 in Spain and 1497 in Portugal there were no more Jews left. At the peak there were about 800,000 Jews in Spain and 200,000 Jews in Portugal; only about 25,000 were successful in reaching their destination as Jews and practice the tradition of their fathers in their new homelands.

7. The Jews of Spain and Portugal, by far more populous than in any other country, first settled there about 1500 years before in the days of the Roman Empire—suffered the most severe kind of persecution and harassment at the instigation of the Catholic Church. The ordinances of the rabbinical council in Lydda and their redirection by the talmudic declarations about obligatory martyrdom in cases of forced conversion, lost their efficacy and persuasion; Jews were confronted by a much more powerful, organized and dedicated force than available to the Romans: The Catholic Church. The Jews were too disorganized to update a new application of Kiddush Ha-Shem; the old one was useless in the 14th and 15th centuries of Catholic Europe; the rabbis were overwhelmed and spiritually paralyzed. When confronted with no escape from forced baptism or death, almost all Jews chose survival; for the gradually more intolerable conditions they lived under had to have, so they reasoned, the sanction of Providence. Self-preservation and that of their family became their first duty, as should have always been the case.

8. Pre-Christian anti-Semitism and its prevalence was outlined in prior chapters. That hatred was "quasi-civilized" in that it could be mitigated by Jews in abandoning certain objectionable conduct and customs. With the onset of the Christian religion and the formulation of the teaching of the

Catholic Church all this changed. The primitive hatred of Jews was augmented by one of implacable animosity. The charge of deicide—that Jews conspired and were culpable in the death and crucifixion of Christ—was the most virulent and spawned a multitude of other destructive theological accusations levelled against Jews and Judaism. The power of the Church permitted no defense; the rabbis and the Talmud offered no cover. The Church tolerated no mitigation of the charges which were pressed with confidence in their veracity.

In the next chapters, I shall examine the historical and theological foundation of these charges and accusations.

Chapter 24

The Jesus Movement and After

1. According to the Gospels, Jesus was born a Jew, lived and died a Jew. He made no effort to found a new religion, his followers were sectarian Jews but Jews nevertheless. His movement was not a revolutionary effort to overthrow the yoke of the Roman Empire, liberate the Jews and establish a Davidic kingdom. His effort—his Gospel—was the proclamation of the imminence of the Kingdom of God in his lifetime (the present age was to come to an end soon), symbolized by the coming of the Messiah, the Christ, Son of David, King of Israel, defining who will enter the kingdom of heaven; teaching the golden rule; performing miracles of curing the sick; prophesying his death at the hands of the Jewish elders, chief priests and scribes and to be raised up on the third day. He accepted the Old Testament as he found it; he did not come to abolish the Law or the Prophets but to complete them; "not one dot, not one little stroke, shall disappear from the Law ... the man who infringes even one of the least of these commandments ... will be considered least in the kingdom of heaven; ..." (Matt. 5:18–19). His movement had the aura of a social revolution, teaching that the poor, weak, children and lame were better thought of than the rich and powerful. He preached the fatherhood of God and the brotherhood of man; associated the poor with meekness and humility; ownership of wealth made virtue hard to achieve. Quoting Jesus: "I tell you solemnly, it will be hard for a rich man to enter the kingdom of heaven" (Matt. 19:23–24); "How hard it is for those who have riches to enter the kingdom of God" (Mk. 10:23–24); "Go and sell everything you own and give the money to the poor, and you will have treasure in heaven; ..." (Mk. 10:21). The gap between rich and poor kept widening; the social classes were in turmoil; the poor oppressed by the rich; the peasant—the mainstay of the economy—exploited by the rich moneylenders forced to either abandon his farm or become a tenant-farmer. This

state of affairs had nothing to do with Roman oppression. The poor felt they had nothing to gain from a political Messiah, removal of Roman oppression and independence of Judea. The Christian New Testament writers have overrated the value of an anointed Messiah to the majority of Jews in Judea who would claim the title King of Israel. In fact, there was no general expectation of the Messiah until after the destruction of Jerusalem, when Jewish literature picked up on the subject of a Davidic Redeemer. The Gospel writers did not know Jesus personally and wrote after the destruction of Jerusalem; they were unfamiliar with the mood of the Jews (two or more generations before they wrote) and were guilty of an anachronism by depicting the times in which they lived as applicable to the times of Jesus. The New Testament writers were totally unaware (or ignorant) of the cruelty, rapacity and illegal conduct of the Roman Prefects/ Procurators and their provocations. From the time of Herod to Jesus, there were three known political Messiahs (Judas of Galilee, Simon and Athrongas), all had a minor following and none evoked much interest, though the times were turbulent and full of agitation. The claim that Jesus was crucified for being a political Messiah is a myth. The appeal of Jesus—if he was historical—was to the poorer element of the population and the slaves to whom he promised salvation and entry into the kingdom of heaven.

It was a peculiar Jewish custom of the times to keep their distance from non-Jews so as not to become polluted. Jesus, the Jew, was the product of this environment. A pagan woman approached him to cast the devil (a gross insanity of the times) out of her daughter, to which Jesus responded: "The children should be fed first, because it is not fair to take the children's food and throw it to the house-dogs" (Mk. 7:27–28); the meaning was that Jewish children had his preference. When Jesus sent his twelve apostles (all Jews) on certain missionary work, he instructed them: "Do not turn your steps to pagan territory, and do not enter any Samaritan town; go rather to the lost sheep of the House of Israel" (Matt. 10:5–6). To the Jews of the time the Samaritans were a heretical group, though they worshiped the God of Israel; an ancient hostility based on jealousy prevented any contact. In the last quoted verse Jesus, not opposing this unjust and baseless view, was the product of his times.

The significance of the last two verses is that Jesus considered himself a loyal Jew throughout.

2. From these humble beginnings, a religious movement evolved which drew its validity from the fulfillment of the Old Testament prophecies; quotation after quotation are cited from the Old Testament; that they applied to Jesus, the Messiah, the Christ (Greek for Messiah, the anointed); that the Old Testament was not fulfilled but replaced by a "New Testament"; that the Old Testament was not fulfilled because the Jews lost favor with God whom they had abandoned; that the old Covenant was no longer valid and was replaced with a "new" Covenant. Judaism no longer fulfilled the divinely ordained mission of Israel and a new religion, Christianity, based on the life and teaching of Jesus Christ, the only begotten Son of God, sent by his Father to redeem the Jews and pagans, rejected by the Jews, crucified by them, sacrificed his blood on the Cross for the remission of man's sins, his salvation and redemption; was resurrected and ascended to heaven to take his place at the right side of his Father; to return to earth (Second Coming) at the appointed time to establish the Kingdom of God.

Jesus did not create a new religion or Church. The Church that followed was the consequence of the failure of Jesus' prophecy about the coming of the Kingdom of God in his lifetime. "I tell you solemnly, there are some of these standing here who will not taste death before they see the Son of Man coming with his kingdom" (Matt. 16:28). Jesus proclaimed the Good News in Galilee: "The time has come and the kingdom of God is close at hand. Repent, and believe the Good News" (Mk. 1:15). Jesus' prophecies were mistaken; the "Second Coming" had to be invented and the Church had to create dogmas and doctrines to fill in the gaps. It created the doctrine of "Parousia" (the Second Coming of Christ) which is an eschatological (final times) concept, when Jesus would return in glory, the crowning triumph of Jesus Christ, as Savior, and confront all humanity in final judgment. The Church that followed is the best example that Jesus' prophecy about the coming of the Kingdom of God in his lifetime was a failure.

3. Christianity, like many religions before it, at first sought its converts peacefully, converting Jews and pagans alike; modifying its conversion requirements to suit the circumstances; pursuing its mission peacefully by example of conduct and persuasion. The Jews knew nothing of a dying Messiah, firstly, because the Hebrew Scripture contained no such concept; secondly, because a dying Messiah was a contradiction in terms, since a Messiah was associated by them with life on this earth and not

with a transcendent figure. Furthermore, the Christian theologians took the Old Testament reference of son of God literally. It was to be understood in a figurative sense since every Jew is the "son of God". Yahweh never revealed to Moses that he had a son who sat at his right side. For these reasons Christianity had a difficult time gaining Jewish converts; Judaism is based on Law, Christianity on the divine Jesus, who died on the cross for our Sins and replaced the significance of the Law. The mind of the Jew was not trained to grasp this Christian concept. There existed a small pre-Christian sect of Jewish followers of Jesus called Nazarenes (also Nazoreans) which was ascetic in character, and Ebionites (the poor) who regarded Jesus as a mere man who died on the cross and would be resurrected. But this happened before Paul's dogmatism changed the nature of Jesus. The Nazarenes and Ebionites lost their significance after the destruction of Jerusalem. The Nazarenes were excluded from Judaism by 85 A.D. and the small sect of Ebionites were later persecuted out of existence by the Catholic Church.

It was Jesus of the Synoptic Gospels (especially Mark), one of the messianic figures preaching the judgment of God in his generation who influenced some Jews; it was Paul's Christ Jesus, with all the shedding of blood and human sacrifice implications (which made the Law of Moses superfluous) that became the dogma of a new religion, Christianity, and made rapprochement with Jews impossible.

4. When it became apparent that the "Second Coming" would be delayed indefinitely, a whole new theology surrounded the formation of the Roman Church, an organized body of ecclesiastical officials headed by Bishops, and later by a Pope (Papa is Latin for Father), the Vicar of Christ, i.e., Christ's earthly representative with full theological and secular power over Christians. The Church, Popes and Bishops claimed their legitimacy and rights to office by establishing the doctrine of apostolic succession of Bishops, successors to the apostle Peter (the foundation of papal authority), based on a very questionable set of facts; it resembled more the survival of the fittest in the power struggle between the various sects and power bases of the early Christian Fathers and ecclesiastics. The Bishops needed financial support, so they sought power and power corrupted; factions of Bishops developed, love of neighbor was set aside, and a commonplace secular power struggle took place among the various factions, to

the end that the fittest survived and others were eliminated or banished. The history of Popes, particularly from the 9th to the 11th century, gave Christianity the blackest eye possible by engaging in conduct so criminal that it defies description. The struggle for Church supremacy was not unlike a thousand other secular power struggles which were known since recorded history. The Church became catholic, i.e., universal, and was referred to as the Catholic Church. When the Church acquired the right to own land—a right wisely withheld from Israelite priests—its theology mixed with secular power; they raised armies like any other State, fought wars, hired mercenaries and all the time invoked the blessings of God.

Like all monotheisms, Christianity became intolerant and brutal in its struggle for primacy—the jealous Yahweh incarnate—continuously in search of converts by any means, however corrupt or violent, and jealously guarded its flock against inroads by proselytizers, protecting the faithful from unbelief. In the canonical Gospels, Epistles and the writings of the Church Fathers, we find a radical anti-Judaism tone pervading which, in time, acquired a virulence without historical precedent. The Old Testament was the only Bible the Christians had in the 1st and part of the 2nd century; They cannibalized the Hebrew Scripture by appropriating from it, at will, passages they found useful for their new religion; they were influenced by the Gnostics—precursors of Christianity—who regarded the world as so evil that God could not have created it; that it was created by an evil power (Demiurge-Creator) identified with God of the Jews; that the Jews were evil and the people of the Devil; that Marcion, a Greek convert ca 120 A.D., found the Septuagint (Greek translation of the Old Testament) so monstrous a document that he rejected it in a complete breach with Judaism. What the early Christians could not swallow was the lack of success they experienced in converting the Jews, the majority of whom totally rejected the Gospel of Christ, the doctrine of salvation through Jesus' death and Resurrection. Early Christianity, which was on shaky theological grounds to begin with, saw in Judaism and the Jews the greatest threat to its existence; gave up on conversion by persuasion and resorted to forcible conversions by making the life of Jews a hell on earth. For the Church preached to its adherents that until the Jews became Christians, until they accepted Jesus Christ as their Savior, there could be no "Second Coming" of Christ; that the Jews must suffer as an eternal reminder of their error in their refusal to recognize Jesus as the long awaited Messiah, prophesied by their own prophets; that until they recognize their error they deserved the punishment of exile, wandering throughout the world never to find peace, a people accursed and persecuted. The Catholic Church showed violence also to the schismatics—whom it termed heretics—who differed from them on doctrinal interpretation or anyone, although a Christian and believer in Jesus as Savior, who dared question the authority of the Church. An institution was created, founded on the life and teaching of Jesus, which, in time, turned into an absolutist imperium, brooked no opposition to its powers and proceeded to eliminate all interference and opposition with utmost ruthlessness. In its formation, developing and maturing years the Catholic Church displayed rapacity, greed, venality and Machiavellian plottings typical of a secular State, light-years away from the spirit of simplicity and brotherhood of the Jerusalem Congregation of James, or the Nazarenes, the first sect of Jewish-Christians. The Popes and Curia engaged in political intrigue that has darkened its history. I shall document their foul deeds and high crimes; the assassinations, murders, sexual depravity and false imprisonment; the sale of ecclesiastical preferments and bishoprics; the sale of the papacy itself; the forgeries, such as the "Donation of Constantine"; the anti-Popes; the horrors of the Crusades and the Inquisitions; the enrichment of Church purses through confiscation of properties of innocent victims forced to confess heresies and Luther's indictment of the papacy.

5. By the 4th century, the persecuted Church turned persecutor after Christianity became the official religion of the Roman Empire and did so with vengeance. By the end of the 4th century, the power of the Church and Bishops increased to such a degree that St. Ambrose, Bishop of Milan, was able to declare that the Roman Emperor was subject to their authority. The Pope, Bishops and priests learned well from their predecessor counterparts, namely, the Jewish High-Priests, priests and scribes, all the means of controlling the people, to manipulate events to their advantage and to convince the people that all the rituals, ceremonies, the institution of the priesthood itself were sacred and handed down from divine authority. The preservation of the Church was the most important function of the papal, episcopal and priestly order.

Chapter 25

The Mystery of Jesus' Crucifixion

1. Christianity, the Roman Catholic Church in particular, claimed to be in possession of the "Truth," the true religion, to the exclusion of all other religions; it claimed sole possession of the key to salvation. Wherever it set foot it persecuted those who refused to convert and accept its views; it hounded its own believers for the slightest infraction, deviation or disobedience, using not persuasion but the torture chambers of the Inquisition and the fiery stake. It cleverly hid behind the secular arm of the State for the execution of punishment. It trampled on the rights of believers and non-believers; terrorized them into submission; opposed all freedom movements; condemned free speech and thought it the work of the devil; opposed any scientific advance that conflicted with its dogma; for a time forbade the laity possession of the Bible under penalty of death for fear that Bible reading led to heresy; disposed of opponents by declaring them to be heretics and excommunicated others—killing these was not considered murder, by order of the Church. It forbade any assertion that—despite the great number of errors in the Bible—the sacred writers erred. In the 14th century during a papal schism, two Popes were elected (one in Rome, the other in Avignon), who were both deposed for heresy and a third Pope elected, so that for a time there were three Popes each claiming to represent Christ on earth. Many Councils were convoked throughout the history of the Church to rule on dogma; settle and rule on theological disputes and, in particular, clarify matters for the benefit of the clergy. The Council of Chalcedon (451 A.D.) was called to clarify one of the issues that confused the clergy about the nature of Christ: "The Council defined one Christ, perfect God and man, consubstantial with the Father and consubstantial with man, one sole being in two natures, without division or separation and without confusion or change. The union does not suppress the

difference in natures; however, their properties remain untouched and they are joined together in one Person, ..." (57–425 ff). This definition does not require any comment as to its "clarity."

I shall list a few more Council decisions: "The Fifth Ecumenical Council in 553 A.D., made heretics (anyone who denied Christian dogma) subject to savage punishment including death ... at the Council of Macon in 585 A.D., one issue debated was whether or not women are human ... In 680 A.D., the Council of Constantinople declared an earlier pope ... a heretic for his ... belief that Christ had only one will. It also decreed that a man rather than the traditional lamb should be portrayed on the cross ... at the second Nicaean Council in 787 A.D., the worship of angelic beings was approved ... the Council of Tours ... in 1163 condemned the Albigenses, who wished to read the Bible for themselves and who refused to worship images, saints, angels and the Virgin. They also ... denied the miraculous power of bells, crosses and sacred. bones ... By 1215 the Lateran Council had forbidden physicians to undertake medical treatment without ecclesiastical assistance, ..." (49–54 ff).

2. Many who doubted could not speak out for fear for their lives; those who spoke out, courageous and pious men, such as John Hus, de Molay, Savonarola and Arnold of Brescia, paid the supreme penalty. Wars fought by Christians over dissenting theological ideologies cost millions of Christian lives; over 200 million died in Christian wars since the dawn of Christianity. Gibbons, the historian, declared that the Church of Rome defended by violence what it had acquired by fraud. The Church fiercely opposed by force of arms and any other violent method at its disposal the Christian sects which held differing beliefs from the orthodoxy. Among those against whom the venom of the Church was directed were: Arians, Gnostics, Huguenots, Albigenses, Manicheans, Jansenists, Cathari, Waldenses, Bogomiles, Nestorians, Valentinians, Ebionites, and many others. The Church forces destroyed them not by invoking the doctrine of apostolic primacy of St. Peter, but by the exercise of brute force: Extermination. Might was right.

3. If Jesus was the Son of God, Judaism is false. If Jesus was not divine, Christianity is false. Judaism and Christianity are irreconcilable; it is a fallacy to assert that they are two aspects of the same thought. They cannot

both be true but they can both be false; each faith is a threat to the other. The Church had always persecuted the Jews as a danger to its theological existence; the Jews were weak, scattered, without a country, an easy target for abuse because they could not strike back (The Christians could not mistreat the followers of Islam for fear of retaliation). The opposition to Judaism of the Christian faith can never be removed, it is endemic; the proof of Christian truth involves Jewish failing; the success of Christianity involves the defeat of Judaism. A faith that claims the monopoly of truth, the sole key to salvation and has the power on its side will revile all other faiths. It will be demonstrated in a future chapter that the Jesus of the Gospels is different from the Christ of Paul. Paul put all his cards on the death and Resurrection of Jesus; there is no fall-back position, no hedging but a declarative statement: Without the death and Resurrection of Jesus there could be no Christianity. "If there is no resurrection of the dead, Christ himself cannot have been raised, and if Christ has not been raised our preaching is useless and your believing it is useless; ... For if the dead are not raised, Christ has not been raised, and if Christ has not been raised, you are still in your sins. And what is more serious, all who have died in Christ have perished" (Paul 1 Cor. 15:13–19). "Resurrection" is the key phrase in Paul; the verse represents twisted and tortured reasoning, a faulty syllogism from which no conclusion can be drawn and it equates Christ with man. If Christ was divine, he cannot be judged as a "man." This is the sort of circular reasoning: "How do we know that the Gospel story is true? Because it confirms the prophecies of the Old Testament. But how do we know the Old Testament prophecies are true? Because they are confirmed by the Gospel story" (15–135). Jesus was not a Christian, nor the founder of Christianity or the Church; nor did he reject the Mosaic Law (which he mistakenly thought to have been written by Moses); nor did he reject slavery, despite all his concern for the poor and downtrodden; he did not teach the doctrine of the Trinity nor the doctrine of the Resurrection; agreed with the concept of Genesis as written in the Pentateuch; he did not object to the oppression of women; mistakenly believed that the world would end during his lifetime; never mentioned his virgin birth; mistakenly thought that circumcision goes back to the Hebrew Patriarchs only; mistakenly told a Palestinian audience that a wife should not seek a divorce (wives could not, only husbands could); he believed in evil spirits causing sickness; he did not originate the Sermon on the Mount which is a compilation of Old Testament quotations; believed in sorcery and the efficacy of witchcraft; add to this the contradictions of the Gospels, Acts and Paul: Jesus taught non-resistance (Matt. 5:39); taught resistance (Luke 22:36); Jesus commanded baptism (Matt. 28:19); did not command baptism (1 Cor. 1:17). Christ is equal with God (John 10:30); not equal with God (John 14:28); Christ's mission was peace (Luke 2:13–14); not peace (Matt. 10:34); unforgivable sin (Mark 3:29); forgivable sin (Acts 13:39). Add to this that in the epistles of Paul, Jesus lived an obscure life on earth; that evil spirits were responsible for his crucifixion in an unknown past and is completely silent about most of the recorded events in the Gospels (his epistles predate the Gospels and he was dead when the Gospels were written).

Some Roman emperors were declared divine and ascended to heaven after their death. The idea of a slain and resurrected god is pre-Christian. There are close pagan parallels of the virgin birth, the sacrificial death and resurrection that recalls some of the savior cults of pre-Christian times, e.g., Adonis, Attis, Mithras, Osiris; so were the Virgin Mother and her Dying Son. Confusion reigned supreme and invention was paramount.

4. The death of Jesus was essential for Christianity as there was a divine plan for Jesus to die; Jesus, the divine Christ, knew in advance what particular events would happen, a plan that would inevitably lead to the cross. A cosmic divine plan was unfolding, devised by God to send his only begotten Son, Jesus Christ, into this world to suffer and through his death on the cross redeem the sins of mankind and that everyone who believes in him may find eternal life; that anyone who refuses to believe in the Son will never see life. Jesus said, "I am the Way, the Truth and the Life. No one can come to the Father except through me ... To have seen me is to have seen the Father, ... Do you not believe that I am in the Father and the Father is in me?" (John 14:6–10). If Jesus was divine and therefore omniscient, why is his wisdom amazing? Why are his prophecies, miracles, suffering, foreknowledge amazing? Why is his resurrection amazing? Why is the New Testament so unforgiving in blaming the Jews for making his plan possible, for helping unwittingly to bring about the chain of events for which they earned his cursing and vilification: "The devil is your father, and you prefer to do what your father wants. He was a murderer from the start; he was never grounded in the truth; there is no truth in him at all: ... because he is a liar, and the father of lies" (John 8:44). John's Gnostic

affinity is obvious. What an invitation for Jew-baiting! What room for misunderstanding! Did not the divine Jesus foresee all that? Did it fulfill prophecies phrased 700 years ago by prophets applicable in their lifetime or shortly thereafter? It took a council of 300 Bishops (Council of Nicea) assembled in 325 A.D., nearly 300 years after the Resurrection of Jesus, to confirm Jesus' divinity.

5. The Gospels accuse the Jews of deicide, the killing of God with a capital "G," the God of the universe, that incredibly vast expanse going well beyond the "four corners" of the Bible, the "firmament" and the "water below," as described in Genesis. How are we to understand this? A group of Jews got together about 2000 years ago and decided to kill God? And they had a choice? Is there anything more absurd in the brain-damaged thinking of the accusers? Did Jesus, Christ, Son of God, one of the three members of the Trinity yet identical with the other two, co-equal and consubstantial with God, his Father, consent to his execution? The Jews certainly could not execute him against his will. If he did consent, what was his plan? Whatever it was, he must have approved of it. He had foreknowledge of events that were shaping his destiny. It is Jesus speaking: "… that he was destined to go to Jerusalem and suffer grievously at the hands of the elders and chief priests and scribes, to be put to death and to be raised up on the third day" (Matt. 16:21); "The Son of Man is going to be handed over into the power of men; they will put him to death, and on the third day he will be raised to life again" (Matt. 17:22–23); "… and the Son of Man is about to be handed over to the chief priests and scribes. They will condemn him to death and will hand him over to the pagans to be mocked and scourged and crucified; and on the third day he will rise again" (Matt. 20:18–19); "… the Son of Man was destined to suffer grievously, to be rejected by the elders and the chief priests and the scribes, and to be put to death. …" (Mark 8:31–32); "The Son of Man will be delivered into the hands of men; they will put him to death; …" (Mark 9:31); "Now we are going up to Jerusalem, and everything that is written by the prophets about the Son of Man is to come true. For he will be handed over to the pagans and will be mocked, maltreated and spat on, and when they have scourged him they will put him to death;…" (Luke 18:31–34). All the above quotations from the Gospels speak in the future tense, of events described to happen, of events "destined" to happen and that which was written by the

prophets 700 years ago "is to come true". All that happened was part of his plan; if it was not his plan, how could the Jews frustrate the will of God? If it was part of his plan, the Jews acted as his conduits and were the vehicles in the fulfillment of his foreordained plan; this means the Jews had no choice. Yet he knew they would be accused of murder, of deicide, and that vengeance would be exacted by future generations of Christians against Jews. Whether this is true history or not, the charge of deicide against the Jews is history; the Jews were vilified, cursed and branded as Christ-killers, their religion was defiled and blackened on account of this charge. From the Church pulpits the venom was hurled against them which could not fail but make an indelible impression upon the adherents who, seized by an avenging spirit, determined to set the matters right: They demonstrated their loyalty to Christ by killing Jews. And so it was throughout the history of the Middle Ages. When the Church lost its power and it was no longer fashionable to kill Jews, the charge of deicide—that most odious of all charges—brought out hostile feelings of Christians against Jews: in short, anti-Semitism as a religious duty.

6. But on what religious certainty does the accusation of deicide rest, a charge that was leveled against every generation of Jews on the doctrine of collective culpability? The Church did not look for "certainties" in professing its animosity toward Jews; it developed such "certainties" as the accusations of ritual murder, image desecration, desecration of the consecrated host, sorcery and magic (to name a few); charges which were all fabrications and falsifications and acknowledged as such today by most Christians; but the charge of "deicide," that accusation of all accusations, stood firm despite the modern criticism of the New Testament. "If a prophet or dreamer of dreams arises among you and offers to do a sign or a wonder for you, and the sign or wonder comes about; ... (and he preaches apostasy) ... That prophet or that dreamer of dreams must be put to death, for he has preached apostasy from Yahweh your God ..." (Deut. 13:2–6). If Jesus preached a doctrine that Jewish authorities regarded as heretical, they were obliged to put Jesus to death. If the Christians accepted the Old Testament as the sacred word of God, they could not blame the Jews for obeying God's commandment. If the Pentateuch is the revealed word of God, religious persecution is a commandment; the penalty for heresy is death.

In the Gospel of John, after Jesus raised Lazarus from the dead, some of the Jews who witnessed this miracle went to tell the Pharisees what Jesus had done: "Then the chief priests and Pharisees called a meeting. 'Here is this man working all these signs ... and what action are we taking? If we let him go in this way everybody will believe in him, and the Romans will come and destroy the Holy Place and our nation ... it is better for one man to die for the people, than for the whole nation to be destroyed'... Jesus was to die for the nation ... From that day they were determined to kill him" (John 11:47–53). According to John, the raising of Lazarus was the last straw for the priests and Pharisees: Jesus had to die. Did the Romans care about some Jew "working all these signs"? The Romans would destroy the nation of Israel because "everybody" would believe in one Jew? Can anyone believe that priests and Pharisees could be capable of such absurd talk? John was the last of four Gospel writers; yet the story of this miracle, the raising of Lazarus, to which John attaches so much importance in linking it to the decision to kill Jesus—is nowhere mentioned in the other Gospels: not one word. Many Christian theologians have solved this riddle by interpreting John's account of Lazarus' raising as purely symbolic and non-historical. There is a curious similarity between the burial and resurrection of Lazarus and that of Jesus, a story related later. But the charge of "deicide" stands!

Paul, the self-declared apostle of Jesus, was his contemporary but they never met; wrote his Epistles at least a generation before Mark's Gospel, the first of the Gospel writers; his story of Jesus should therefore be the most untarnished. But Paul believed that Jesus was crucified "at the instigation of evil supernatural powers ... he does not give it a historical setting—because he was convinced that Jesus lived an obscure life on earth; ..." (27–97); "Paul does not know who Jesus' human enemies were and how they had him crucified" (27–97). Paul's Epistles "give no indication of the time or place of his earthly existence" (26–22). The Jesus of Paul's letters is incompatible with the Jesus of the Gospels, yet Paul was the founder of Christianity as a separate religion. We read in 1 Th. 1:14–15, "... in suffering the same treatment from your own countrymen as they have suffered from the Jews, the people who put the Lord Jesus to death, and the prophets too." This verse is deemed by most biblical scholars to be an interpolation. Paul was greatly influenced by the Wisdom literature of the Jews.

7. There are only three categories of reasons why Jesus was condemned to death; they are not exclusive and could overlap:

(1) He was guilty of blasphemy and/or heresy.
(2) He was politically a danger to Rome.
(3) He died so that the Scripture would be fulfilled—the prophets in particular.

The political Messiah, in order to arouse the Romans, had to perform some military/political act, such as an act of rebellion against Rome, civil disturbance, killing Roman soldiers, disparaging the emperor, refusal to pay taxes to Rome, siding with the enemies of Rome. What acts did Jesus perform? He preached the end of times; the need to keep the Law of Moses; cured the sick and ailing; performed signs and miracles such as the feeding of many; converted water to wine; taught in parables the moral laws; encouraged the poor and weak; sent his disciples to preach his mission; preached sermons and spoke about the Kingdom of God; the latter in mystifying language. Nowhere did he issue any command that even remotely resembled a military order; his disciples were untrained and not clever; he was alone without any staff that could be described as military; preaching meekness and love of neighbor and enemy. To describe him as the Davidic Messiah is to be hallucinating. Jesus never publicly claimed to be the Messiah; he held his twelve disciples to strict secrecy about it, never to mention it to anybody; the idea of a secret which had to remain a secret until his "resurrection" would indicate that nothing was known of a messianic claim of Jesus. It is true that the title of "Messiah', the anointed, signified a Jewish king who was anointed. So were the priests; the Dead Sea Scrolls have revealed that a priestly (not Davidic) Messiah of Aaron's line was expected. The Messiah expected by the Jewish people was a politico/military leader who would restore the Kingdom of Israel in this world and had to be of Davidic descent. Jesus was not and never claimed to be of Davidic descent. There were many self-proclaimed Messiahs before the time of Jesus, whose following was insignificant, who overtly displayed their military zeal by violent acts and were crucified by the Romans; they were not preachers or moralists; did not seek meekness and love of enemies but military leaders, with an army of followers (however small) equipped with weapons to sustain their insurrection. Their acts were open and notorious, there was no secrecy about them nor was the High-Priest or

Sanhedrin involved in taking any countermeasures. The only overt rebellious acts attributed to Jesus were the cleansing of the Temple and the "Messianic entry" into Jerusalem.

8. The overturning of the tables in the Temple and chasing out the money-changers was an openly rebellious act. But was it historical? Just before Passover, Jesus went up to Jerusalem "and in the Temple he found people selling cattle and sheep and pigeons, and the money changers sitting at their counters there. Making a whip out of some cord, he drove them all out of the Temple, cattle and sheep as well, scattered the money changers' coins, knocked their tables over and said to the pigeon-sellers, 'Take all this out of here and stop turning my Father's house into a market'" (John 2:13–17). (Again, so that Psalm 69:8 should be fulfilled "... zeal for your house devours me, ...", a total non-sequitur). A similar narrative is mentioned in the other Gospels. The whole episode is preposterous, written by people who had never seen the Temple, its design, had no idea of its dimensions and no idea of what activities were carried on typically in the outer Temple courts. The selling and buying of sacrificial animals was a typical activity and required the services of money-changers. It was all carried out in the outer Temple courts in an area reserved for them which was not near the Temple proper. The Gospel writers knew nothing of the 20,000 or so administrators, priests and other personnel permanently stationed at the Temple, the sizeable Temple police forces, the Roman guards (army) stationed in the adjacent tower overlooking the Temple area, eagerly watching the activities in the Temple courts for any tumult or signs of disturbance, particularly during the time preceding the Passover festivities. It certainly would not compliment Jesus' military talents had he, with a few followers, picked a fight; his indignation was absurd (a construct of the Evangelists when sacrifices were history) and the total story is bogus. The Temple police did not obstruct Jesus, nor did the Roman army; and the cattle dealers and money-changers did not just fold and flee at the sight of Jesus' whip. Jesus with the aid of his twelve disciples could have accomplished nothing. "So they reached Jerusalem and he went into the Temple and began driving out those who were buying and selling there; ..." (Mark 11:15). The "they" refers to Jesus and the twelve disciples (Mark 11:12). Jesus had no force with him when he cleansed the Temple, only his twelve disciples. He could not have faced the overwhelming forces confronting

him. What did Jesus do after this momentous event? "And when evening came he went out of the city" (Mark 11:19). The story, as written, is an invention of the Evangelists; it was inserted to show the Jews as desecrating their own Temple; the House of God, and treating the holy place as nothing but a "robbers' den" (Jer. 7:11).

9. The other potential politico/military act was his entry into Jerusalem riding on a colt (to fulfill a prophecy of Zech. 9:9); was greeted by "many people" (Mark 11:8); and then nothing, the story ends. He produced no miracle to astound the crowd which accorded him such honors. Jesus did nothing except "... entered Jerusalem and went into the Temple. He looked all around him, but as it was now late, he went out to Bethany with the Twelve" (Mark 11:11). And that is all! A gathering of people might have aroused the suspicion of the Romans or the High-Priest, but nothing else happened except the people greeting Jesus: "Hosanna in the highest heavens!" (Mark 11:10–11). This greeting is nonsense since the Jewish crowd (quoted by the Gospels) is alleged to have misunderstood "Hosanna" as "blessing" instead of its true meaning "Save us," in which case the greeting made no sense. "Hosanna to the Son of David" (Matt. 21:9); the person who misunderstood the Hebrew word was the Evangelist, or his source, who invented the whole episode. The people did nothing except greet Jesus. Besides Mark, it was Matthew and John who use the greeting "Hosanna," with the same mistaken meaning when describing Jesus' entry into Jerusalem (they copied from Mark). In addition, the Evangelists quoted the following statements of the greeting crowds: "Blessings on the coming Kingdom of our father David" (Mark 11:10); "Hosanna to the Son of David! Blessings on him who comes in the name of the Lord!" (Matt. 21:9); 'Blessings on the King who comes, in the name of the Lord!" (Luke 19:38); "Hosanna! Blessings on the King of Israel, who comes in the name of the Lord" (John 12:13–14). These greetings were fraught with danger. The entry into Jerusalem was described by the Evangelists as the "Messianic Entry." How did the crowd which gathered to welcome Jesus know he was the Messiah? The "secret" was known only to the Twelve (Jesus forbade his disciples to make known his Messiahship).

Was it that news of his miracles of curing the blind or raising Lazarus reached the crowd? A miracle which they had not witnessed? But the role of the Old Testament Messiah was not performing miracles or conversely, miracle workers (of whom there were many) were not regarded as "Messiah." In Matt. 21:10–11 it is stated: "And when he entered Jerusalem, the whole city was in turmoil 'Who is this?' people asked, and the crowds answered, 'This is the prophet Jesus from Nazareth in Galilee.' " In this version Jesus is referred to as "Prophet" and not "Messiah" even though the greetings referred to "Son of David." In Mark, the greeting refers to "the coming kingdom of our father David", no reference to "Messiah." In Luke, the greetings refer to "King," which could mean "Messiah." In John, the greetings refer to "King of Israel," definitely a reference to "Messiah." Apart from each quotation being different in a material way (only one version could be true, but all versions could be false) they were politically highly provocative (most so John's) to the Roman ear and to the spies of the High-Priest, considering the charged atmosphere in which they were pronounced by a large multitude. The mention of "our father David," "Son of David," "King" and "King of Israel" at the time of approaching Passover festival would have given the Romans and the High-Priest apoplectic fits; they would have reacted swiftly and forcefully to the provocation. But nothing happened; the authorities paid no attention and noticed nothing unusual. Those who accept the triumphal entry as historical cannot explain why the Romans and High-Priest remained silent; this could not be the case if the story was in fact true. Instead, the event is alleged to have taken place so that the prophecies of the Old Testament could be fulfilled, taking Psalm 118:26 "Blessings on him who comes in the name of Yahweh!" (completely out of context since this verse is part of the "Procedural hymn for the feast of Tabernacles") and totally misunderstanding Zechariah 9:9–10 "See now, your king comes to you; he is victorious, he is triumphant, humble and riding on a donkey, … He will banish chariots from Ephraim and horses from Jerusalem; the bow of war will be banished." No such prophecies applied to the Messianic Entry into Jerusalem by Jesus. The Messianic Entry was not mentioned at Jesus' trial before the Sanhedrin nor before Pilate; and the crowd greeting Jesus so passionately with all kinds of titles of honor and forbidden meanings so that the whole city was in turmoil, only a few days later demanded at Jesus' trial before Pilate: "Let him be crucified!" (Matt. 27:23); "Crucify him" (Mark 15:14); "Crucify him, crucify him!" (Luke 22:22); "Take him away, take him away! … Crucify him!" (John 19:15). Not one voice of dissent was heard! Not one voice defending Jesus!

10. Apart from the two episodes described in Paragraph 8 and 9 above, there was not a single act of Jesus that would have aroused the Romans or the High-Priest to the exploits of Jesus. Nothing that Jesus was quoted as saying in the Synoptic Gospels was anti-Roman or blasphemous (the Gospel of John will be treated later); Jesus' claim—implied or overt—to be the Messiah was not blasphemous, carried no meaning of divinity and did not reach the attention of the Romans by some overt act; his parables, his many arguments and disputations with the Pharisees and Sadducees; his reference to himself as the "Son of Man," if he used that title (Jesus spoke Aramaic and in that language that title did not exist; besides "Son of Man" merely denotes "Man"); his prophecy of the Passion; the miracles and healing of the sick; his walking on water; his dealings with John the Baptist—none of these would stir enough ripples to draw attention to himself of the Jewish authorities or Romans, for "the chief priests and scribes to look for a way to arrest Jesus by some trick and have him put to death" (Mark 14:1–2). The Jews were described by the four Evangelists as always plotting to put Jesus to death; they schemed to put the Jews in the worst possible light, particularly John, in whose Gospel the term "the Jews" was used over sixty times to describe the enemies of Jesus. Was it because of any messianic claim Jesus put forward? There were many others who claimed to be the Messiah who were not disturbed by the High-Priest; he made no such overt claim except in response to a question at his trial (except in the Gospel of John), a trial which was not witnessed by anyone who could preserve the record for history. The whole story of the trial proceedings is so incongruous as to be suspect of literary invention.

The Synoptic Gospels are unanimous in referring to Jesus' accusation at his trial before the High Priest and the Sanhedrin:

Matthew has the High Priest Caiaphas pronounce the charge against Jesus, "He has blasphemed ... you have just heard the blasphemy" (26:65–66) and "He deserves to die." (26:66).

Mark has the chief priest pronounce the charge against Jesus, "You have heard the blasphemy" (14:64). Members of the Sanhedrin responded, "he deserves to die." (14:64).

Luke has Jesus respond to the question asked by one of the chief priests, "If you are the Christ, tell us" (22:67): "But from now on, the Son of Man will be seated at the right hand of the Power of God." (22:69–70). This was rank blasphemy! The chief priest and scribes said, "What need of witnesses have we now?" (22:71). The whole assembly brought Jesus before Pilate.

John has the high priest question Jesus about his disciples and his teaching. "Then Annas sent him (Jesus) still bound to Caiaphas the high priest." (18:24) (This is John's whole report of the trial proceedings.)

Summary

In all four Gospels (specifically in the Synoptic) Jesus was accused of "blasphemy" and no other charge (Suffice it to say there were no witnesses to record the proceedings of any of the trials so that the Gospel stories are pure speculation). But the Sanhedrin did not have to bring Jesus before Pilate for accusation and sentencing. Under the Roman rule, the Sanhedrin had full authority to carry out the death sentence by stoning in cases of blasphemy, which they did, e.g., in the case of Stephen and James, according to the New Testament. Had Jesus' accusation been of a political nature, the Sanhedrin had no authority to judge him, but would refer the matter to Pontius Pilate for examination, trial and sentencing. If Jesus was accused of blasphemy, the Sanhedrin retained exclusive jurisdiction to determine his guilt and, if found guilty, to mete out the appropriate punishment.

After Jesus' death, the Jerusalem Congregation was quite openly preaching that Jesus was the Messiah without being harmed by the Temple authorities. But the stories about "the Jews plotting the death of Jesus" fit neatly into the authors' "Passion and Resurrection" drama, essential to the foundation of Christianity. Jesus, however, did nothing to stand out above the other miracle workers and healers, so numerous in those days, to mark him for special attention; he was a practicing and loyal Jew; had a minor following (Jesus' period of missionary activity can be compressed into three weeks, except for his forty days sojourn in the wilderness) constituting a Jewish sect, one sect among many others. Palestine had a population of 2 million (at least) and Jerusalem 1 million (at least); the Essenes merited mention by Josephus though their following was no more than 4000. The Jesus sect merited no mention by Josephus.

The Gospel of John, the last of the four Gospels to be written and included in the canon, contradicts the Synoptic Gospels on numerous points; it is based on the Wisdom literature and Gnosticism. It begins with: "In the beginning was the Word, and the Word was with God and the Word was God" (John 1:1). It picks up from the pagan mystery cult, quoting Jesus: "I tell you most solemnly, if you do not eat the flesh of the Son of Man and drink his blood, you will not have life in you" (John 6:53). This reason-perverting language, these contradictions and religious hallucinations flood his Gospel; and throughout his Gospel is his thinly-veiled pathological hatred of the Jews. He differs from the other Gospels in that he made Jesus claim to be Messiah. "The woman said to him, 'I know that Messiah—that is, Christ—is coming; and when he comes he will tell us everything!' (To which Jesus responded) 'I am speaking to you', said Jesus, 'I am he' " (John 4:25–26). He differs from the other Gospels in that, after differentiating between God and Jesus, he identifies God with Jesus in making Jesus claim to be God himself. "what the Father has taught me is what I preach; …" (John 8:28); "my glory is conferred by the Father" (John 8:54); "for the Father is greater than I" (John 14:28); "The Father and I are one" (John 10:30); " To have seen me is to have seen the Father … I am in the Father and the Father is in me" (John 14:9–11). The first three cited verses teach the Fatherhood of God; the last two verses quoted are rank blasphemy; the Jews fetched stones to stone him for blasphemy, saying to Jesus: "You are only a man and you claim to be God" (John 10:33). This claim to be God is only made in the Gospel of John who engages in tortured lines of reasoning. It is not credible that Jesus could have made such statements that he knew were blasphemous; and he knew the penalty for blasphemy!

John had Jesus respond to the charge of blasphemy: "Is it not written in your Law: I said you are gods? … and scripture cannot be rejected" (John 10:34–35), and further, still in response to the charge: "Yet you say to someone 'You are blaspheming' because he says, 'I am the Son of God' " (John 10:36). The author of this colloquy wrote utter nonsense. In the first place, such a verse "I said you are gods" does not exist in the Hebrew Scripture, and in the second place, in the offending verse Jesus claimed not to be "God" but the "Son of God," the latter term is not blasphemous.

"This is what Yahweh says: Israel is my first-born son" (Ex. 4:22); speaking of the people of Israel: "You are sons of Yahweh your God" (Deut. 14:1); Yahweh speaking of Israel: "I reared sons … I brought them up, …" (Isaiah 1:2); Yahweh speaking: "Bring back my sons from far away, ..." (Isaiah 43:6); Yahweh speaking: "Is Ephraim, then, so dear a son to me, ..." (Jer. 31:20); "For I am a father to Israel, ..." (Jer. 31:9); "When Israel was a child I loved him, and called my son out of Egypt" (Hos. 11:1); Yahweh speaking of David: "I will be a father to him and he a son to me" (2 Sam. 7:14). Every Jew was the son of God. Jesus was a Jew and could claim to be a son of God. If Jesus claimed to be God, a rank blasphemy, (which verse must be a later interpolation) then the Jews had a religious obligation to stone him to death according to Scripture; these are God's commands:

"The one who blasphemes the name of Yahweh must die; the whole community must stone him. Stranger or native, if he blasphemes the name, he dies" (Lev. 24:16). In Luke 4:12: "You must not put the Lord your God to the test," Jesus, answered the devil who tempted Jesus to worship him. In Matthew 4:10: "Then Jesus replied, 'Be off, Satan! For scripture says: You must worship the Lord your God, and serve him alone.' "

Jesus was speaking to religious Jews only and no Jew could have grasped or understood the meaning of his claim to be "God." These verses are later interpolations, reflecting later times when such claims were made with the doctrine of Trinity, that does not appear in any of the Gospels. (The Doctrine of Trinity developed gradually over several centuries, and finalized in the 4th century. The New Testament makes no reference to it.). The other Gospels keep the separation between Jesus and God: "This is my beloved son, in whom I am well pleased" (Matt. 3:17); " 'Abba (Father)!' he said 'Everything is possible for you. Take this cup away from me' " (Mark 14:36). Jesus speaking: "I bless you, Father, Lord of heaven and of earth, for hiding these things from the learned and the clever ..." (Luke 10:21). John is at least a generation apart from Mark, the first Gospel author. The claims to be Messiah, Son of Man, Son of God, are not blasphemous; Messiah is a leader, Son of Man is a "Man," and all Israel was the Son of God.

The obsession with the term "Son of God," and the total misunderstanding and misinterpretation of its application in the Hebrew Scripture caused the Synoptic Gospel writers to have the Sanhedrin (or High-Priest) condemn Jesus on meaningless, baseless and trivial charges. The interrogators even inquired of Jesus whether he was the "Christ," and therefore the "Son of God," as if there existed any connection between those two terms. The Pharisees, who knew their Bible, could not have had their religious feelings offended by the charge "Son of God"; they would have considered the charge of blasphemy ludicrous; it was a term well understood and well known by Jews and nothing metaphysical. In the Gospel of John, we vainly search the verses dealing with the interrogation of Jesus for any charge whatsoever brought against him by Annas, the father-in-law of Caiaphas, "who was high priest in that year" (John 18:14).

The Sanhedrin, composed of Sadducees and Pharisees, all above average in intelligence and education, conversant with the Mosaic Law and Scripture, could not judge the terms "Son of Man," "Christ" (Messiah) and "Son of God" to be blasphemous. It is the Gospel authors who mistakenly picked the wrong charge with which to convict Jesus; the trial was therefore a sham. They erred in putting across their design. The trial before the Sanhedrin was a literary invention that fulfilled the purpose for which it was designed, i.e., to condemn the Jews for conspiring in the death of Jesus. If Jesus was crucified, it was for conduct not mentioned in the Gospels. Was it to fulfill prophecy? This subject will be treated in the next chapter.

The death plotting stories were meant to have another effect: Anti-Jewish feelings and anti-Semitism. In this the Gospel writers succeeded. For all four canonical Gospels bring out the concentrated hostility against Jews which subsequent generations of Christians built upon, lie after lie, fabrication after fabrication, till a crescendo of anti-Semitism was achieved that well served the purposes of Christians, the Catholic Church in particular. Jesus was not guilty of blasphemy or heresy; he was not a political danger to Rome and he did not die fulfilling any prophetic messages.

Chapter 26

So That Prophets, Psalms, Scripture May Be Fulfilled

1. God makes his will known to chosen individuals. The prophet is selected by God to deliver his message to the people of Israel. The Hebrew term for prophet is "NAVI." i.e., speaker or interpreter, a spokesman; he is God's mouthpiece. "Yahweh said to Moses, 'See, I make you an oracle to Pharaoh, and your brother Aaron shall be your spokesman (navi)' " (Ex. 7:1). God did not speak to the prophets directly or clearly (like he spoke to Moses only) but made himself known to them in a vision and spoke to them in a dream (Numb. 12:6), not plainly but in riddles (Numb. 12:7). "If any man among you is a prophet I make myself known to him in a vision, I speak to him in a dream" (Numb. 12:6). "I will raise up a prophet ... I will put my words into his mouth and he shall tell them all I command him. The man who does not listen to my words that he speaks in my name, shall be answerable to me for it ... 'How are we to know what word was not spoken by Yahweh?' When a prophet speaks in the name of Yahweh and the thing does not happen and the word is not fulfilled, then it has not been spoken by Yahweh. The prophet has spoken with presumption. You have nothing to fear from him" (Deut. 18:17–22). It was not so with Moses, of whom Yahweh says: "... I speak with him face to face, plainly and not in riddles, ..." (Numb. 12:8). Therefore the prophets (other than Moses) only received the word of God by the aid of their imagination through the medium of dreams or visions. The prophets transmitted the divine messages mostly in allegories and parables; used obscure language which was subject to various interpretations and meanings to give sense to their creative imagination; for they were men of vivid imagination. The nexus between prophecy and dreams is direct in Scripture: "If a prophet or a dreamer of dreams arises among you and offers to do a sign or wonder for you, ..." (Deut. 13:2–3). Prophets had to offer a "sign" to warrant the truth of the prophecy or that they received

the message as true prophets. Such a "sign" consisted mostly of predicting some future event, which had a certain immediacy about it, for the future event predicted had to be tested by the confirmation of the event predicted during the lifetime of the hearers—certainly during the lifetime of the prophet. The prophets always addressed their prophecy to a contemporary situation. An example of the immediate application of prophecy:

> "Yahweh says this: stand in the court of the Temple of Yahweh. To all the people of the towns of Judah who came to worship in the Temple of Yahweh you must speak all the words I have commanded you to tell them, … Perhaps they will listen and each turn from his evil way: if so, I shall relent and not bring the disaster on them which I intended for their misdeeds" (Jer. 26:2–4).

For the test of a true prophet was the veracity of his predictions, which if extended too far into the future would frustrate the test. The predictions were based upon the interpretation of past and current events, and the more the prophet was gifted the greater his capacity and imagination in interpreting God's message revealed to him in dreams and visions. Since the messages proceeded directly from divine visions and dreams, i.e., not clearly, we can understand why prophets held conflicting opinions due to their varying capacities to absorb the messages, which, we are told, depended on certain outside stimuli. Ecstatic dances, seizures or fits, and other similar experiences affected their prophecy; a pleasant and cheerful disposition was conducive to optimistic prophecies, just as a melancholy and sullen disposition led to pessimistic prophecies. There was also jealousy among prophets who accused each other of being false prophets and impostors:

> (The word of Yahweh was addressed to me as follows), "Son of man, prophesy against the prophets of Israel; prophesy, and say to those who make up prophecies out of their heads, 'Hear the word of Yahweh. The Lord Yahweh says this: woe to the foolish prophets who follow their own spirit, without seeing anything! …'" (Ezk. 13:1–4).
>
> "They have empty visions and give lying prophecies and say: It is Yahweh who speaks, although Yahweh has not sent them; and they are still waiting for their words to come true" (Ezk. 13:6–7).

"Yahweh says this against the prophets who lead my people astray: So long as they have something to eat they cry 'Peace.' But on anyone who puts nothing into their mouths they declare war" (Mic. 3:5).

" ... her priests take a fee for their rulings, her prophets make divinations for money" (Mic. 3:11).

"Priests and prophets are reeling from strong drink, ... they totter when they are having visions, they stumble when they are giving judgment" (Isaiah 28:7).

"The prophets are prophesying lies in my name; I have not sent them, I gave them no orders, I never spoke to them. Delusive visions, hollow predictions, daydreaming of their own, that is what they prophesy to you" (Jer. 14:14–15).

"Yes, even prophet and priest are godless, I have found their wickedness even in my own House—it is Yahweh who speaks" (Jer. 23:11).

"the prophets prophesy falsely, the priests teach whatever they please" (Jer. 5:31).

The prophets could not please everyone and their activities led to conflict, animosity, bitterness and a life of loneliness. Isaiah, Jeremiah, Micah, Ezekiel, Hosea and Amos led a life of anguish, rejection and ridicule. Their activities reached their peak during the rise and fall of empires which involved Israel and Judah; it was their destiny to become the messengers and prophets of ruin and destruction which were to befall Israel and Judah. Their lot was not a happy one and this mood is reflected in their writings, so painfully summed up in Jeremiah: "A curse on the day when I was born, ... (20:14); Isaiah: "Turn your eyes away from me, let me weep bitterly; do not try to comfort me ..." (22:14). But the prophets (the greatest among them) did not always preach the message of Yahweh. From their visions and dreams, from their ecstasies and trances, there came forth a concept of universalism far ahead of their time, detached from the particularism and parochialism of priests and Temple; a rejection of cultic sacrifices which undermined the teachings of the Torah; a purified vision of Yahweh set apart from wars, conquests and merciless punishments. They cried out against the oppression of the poor by the rich, against corruption in the moral and ethical field, against greed, exploitation, luxury, lust for power: in short, they were radically opposed to the Mosaic priesthood. It is for their moral and ethical criticism and not for their localized predictions that prophets became true interpreters of social forces.

> "What are your endless sacrifices to me? says Yahweh. I am sick of holocausts of rams and the fat of calves … Bring me your worthless offerings no more … Take your wrong-doing out of my sight. Cease to do evil. Learn to do good, search for justice, help the oppressed, be just to the orphan, plead for the widow" (Isaiah 1:11–17).
>
> "Your holocausts are not acceptable, your sacrifices do not please me" (Jer. 6:20).
>
> "For I am Yahweh, I rule with kindness, justice and integrity on earth; yes, these are what pleases me—it is Yahweh who speaks" (Jer. 9:24).

2. The Hebrew prophets (The designation of "Hebrew," as opposed to "Israelite," is used here to conform with convention) therefore were not a reliable source of information; many of their predictions only addressed contemporary situations, were false and they were, by definition, false prophets. None of their predictions addressed messianic agitations 600–700 years into the future. The Torah, the only revealed Scripture, speaks volumes of false and lying prophets without naming them: As of the present time, we do not know which prophets were false and which were true. We do not know whether a prophet is a false prophet if he stumbled only once: Does that color his other prophecies? We do not know which prophets were prophesying lies in God's name, whether he ever spoke to them in a vision or dream, whether he gave them orders to reveal messages to the people; we do not know whether a prophet who spoke about justice and righteousness was acceptable to God: we are not the recipients of any divine revelation. As to the unknown prophets, those who gave pseudepigraphic ascriptions to works, they are, by definition, unreliable; we cannot know the full extent of their other prophecies written under another name or pseudonym, which could disqualify their acceptance as true prophets. The ritual of sacrifices and holocausts is detailed in Leviticus, a revelation to Moses by Yahweh; these were to be perpetual laws and ordinances from generation to generation. What are we to think of prophets, who did not speak face to face with Yahweh, who boldly contradicted the laws of Leviticus treating some of God's own laws as worthless, who declared, claiming to speak with the voice of Yahweh, "Bring me your worthless offerings no more" (Isaiah) and

"... your sacrifices do not please me" (Jeremiah)? Were these prophets false or did God only test the people? We do not know. The writings of certain prophets were included in the Hebrew canon, others, like Enoch, were excluded. Who were the experts who made the decision to include some and exclude others? Fallible men who summoned councils, consisting of Pharisees and Rabbis. Did they know that there were at least three different "Isaiah" authors? That the first wrote chapters 1–23 and 27–35; chapters 36–39 were written by an unknown author; chapters 40–55 written by the unknown "second" Isaiah; chapters 56–66 written by the "third" unknown Isaiah and chapters 24–26 were written after 200 B.C., i.e., by an unknown author? Knowledge of these facts should have certainly excluded the Book of Isaiah from the sacred canon. That Jeremiah could not be the author of the whole book ascribed to him? That the Books of Ezra and Nehemiah were not written by them? That the Book of Daniel was written after 200 B.C. and therefore Daniel could not be the author? The Book of Daniel (commonly believed to have been authored in the 6th century B.C.) was written by an unknown author or authors during the Maccabean uprising in the second century B.C. Jesus mistakenly attributed it to the prophet Daniel (Matt. 24:15). The author or authors had no problem "predicting" spurious future events with great accuracy—events which occurred several hundred years before and were historical. That the other prophetic books are only fragments of the original and other parts have been lost? That some of the prophetic writers whose names appear as authors were in fact spurious? Who were these unknown writers? We do not know. Yet these books, corrupted by writings of unknown authors, were included in the Old Testament canon and treated by Christians as sacred and authoritative and to be relied upon as God's word, "so that the prophets may be fulfilled"! These two stalwart prophets, Jeremiah and Isaiah, were also guilty of false prophecies, which were addressed to contemporary times. Jeremiah: King Zedekiah **did not** die in peace; Isaiah: King Ahaz **was** defeated.

> "... I will raise a virtuous Branch for David, who will reign as true king and be wise, practising honesty and integrity in the land. In his days Judah will be saved and Israel dwell in confidence" (Jer. 23:5–6). This prophecy is false!
>
> "My servant David will reign over them, ... David my servant is to be prince for ever" (Ezek 37:24–26). This prophecy is false!

"If anyone still wants to prophesy, his father and the mother who gave him birth shall say to him, 'You have no right to live, since you utter lies in the name of Yahweh' … When that day comes, every prophet shall be ashamed of his prophetic vision; …" (Zechariah 13:3–4). So much for the art of prophesying.

3. The Gospel writers made a concerted effort to prove that Jesus was the long awaited Messiah as prophesied in the Hebrew Scripture; they searched the prophetic books and Psalms for material they could use as proof that Jesus' messianic personage was foretold; that he was the fulfillment of the messianic prophecies; that events occurred in Jesus' life which were spoken of by the prophets; that they applied to Jesus and him alone; that even though the prophecies were spoken many centuries before the life of Jesus and commented on situations of their own day, they were nevertheless applied to particular episodes in the life of Jesus several hundred years removed. The Gospel writers were fitting the facts to the biblical text to fulfill the Hebrew Scripture; to bring the story in line with the prophecy where needed. The Gospel writers claimed that certain details, no matter how trivial, were foretold by the prophets. They regarded the prophecies as unimpeachable testimony, sacred, divinely revealed, to be relied upon as fulfillment and proof that the messianic prophecies applied to Jesus. But the Gospel writers were mistaken for I have shown that the Hebrew prophets were not a reliable source of information; many of their prophecies were false; that some of them were lying prophets; that to some Yahweh gave no orders, never spoke to any of them; that they were prophesying lies in his name and, last but not least, that their prophecies applied to the period in which they were made. Since the time of the last Hebrew prophet Malachi (ca 464–424 B.C.), we received no divine revelation as to which prophets were acceptable to Yahweh and which were not. We cannot, therefore, say with any sense of certitude that all the prophets included in the Hebrew Scripture were true prophets, or for that matter, that any one of them was. Therefore, lacking that information, the Gospel writers (for that matter all the New Testament writers) erred in using the Hebrew prophets as proof-texts for their stories about Jesus. Considering that the New Testament contains about 250 citations from the Old Testament (of which the majority were from the prophetic books and Psalms) and about 900 references to the citations, we can understand Justin the Martyr's (100?–165 A.D.?, one of

the Fathers of the Church) statement that but for the fulfillment of the messianic prophecies he would have placed no belief in Jesus (56–125). Origen (185?–254 A.D.?, one of the Fathers of the Church) testified that the fulfillment of the Old Testament prophecies was the strongest proof for the Christians of the truth of their teachings (56–124).

4. Nameless prophets, lying prophets and prophets to whom God had not spoken, could nevertheless be the authors who spoke of high morals and social justice of universal dimensions:

> "… since what I want is love, not sacrifice; knowledge of God, not holocausts" (Hosea 6:6).
> "I hate and despise your feasts, I take no pleasure in your solemn festivals … I reject your oblations, and refuse to look at your sacrifices of fattened cattle … But let justice flow like water, and integrity like an unfailing stream" (Amos 5:20–25).
> "… this is what Yahweh asks of you: only this, to act justly, to love tenderly and to walk humbly with your God" (Mic. 6:8).
> "… but the upright man will live by his faithfulness" (Habbakuk 2:4).

The prophets were, nevertheless, totally unsuited for predicting the coming of a Messiah 600–700 years in the future, his virgin birth, suffering, arrest, crucifixion and his being raised up to heaven. True and God approved prophets would be necessary who clearly spoke of events to happen not in the near future, as was the custom, but in a time several centuries removed; who did not speak in riddles; whose language was not ambivalent; whose message was not divided into bits and pieces that had to be sewn together to make any sense. For it would be a truly momentous prophecy made by Hebrew prophets, who were Hebrews throughout, not about a Messiah described in the Scripture who would establish a kingdom of David and the political liberation of Jews as promised by God in the Torah, but instead about a Messiah whose kingdom was not of this world, whose stated mission they would not have comprehended, who would be rejected by the Jews and die on the cross. We do not know whether there were such prophets and who they were. The Gospel writers were mistaken in using the Hebrew prophets as proof-text for their narratives about Jesus.

5. It is the height of cynicism for New Testament writers to extract fitting passages from the Hebrew prophets and thus sanctimoniously treat the work

as sacred, while denying the efficacy of the Law, the only revealed work in the Old Testament meriting this description; they picked verses that suited their purpose without making sufficient effort to test their authenticity or comprehend their true meaning. They tore the prophetic writings to shreds by reading meanings into them that were not there and which never entered the mind of the authors. All this to prop up the historical evidence of Jesus where no other evidence existed and thus establish a historical personage because "it was written in the prophets." As I explained in this chapter, this reliance was misplaced, unwarranted and without assurance. The prophetic writings were not sacred or revealed and therefore could not be used as proof-texts to establish the historicity of Jesus. For example, a reading of Chapters 42 to 59 of Isaiah (commencing with the "First song of the servant of Yahweh"),will demonstrate that "a thing despised and rejected by men," i.e., the "suffering servant" verses do not refer to Jesus but to the people of Israel. I shall quote some of the verses:

> "You are my servant (Israel) in whom I shall be glorified; …" (Isaiah 49:3).
> "And now Yahweh has spoken, he who formed me in the womb to be his servant, to bring Jacob back to him, to gather Israel to him: 'It is not enough for you to be my servant, to restore the tribes of Jacob and bring back the survivors of Israel; …" ' (Isaiah 49:5–6).
> "I put my words in your mouth, I hid you in the shadow of my hand, when I spread out the heavens and laid the earth's foundations and said to Zion, 'You are my people' " (Isaiah 51:16).
> "For my part, this is my covenant with them, says Yahweh. My spirit with which I endowed you, and my words that I have put in your mouth, will not disappear from the mouths of your children, nor from the mouths of your children's children for ever and ever, says Yahweh" (Isaiah 59:21).

6. The same criticism applies to the Book of Psalms whose author is reputed to be David. This ascription is false; it was written by various unknown authors, compiled during and after the Babylonian Exile. They are a collection of 150 Psalms, divided into hymns, entreaties and thanks-givings addressed to special situations faced by the authors of those times: National catastrophes, defeats, national emergencies, prayers for deliver-ance, successful harvests, deliverance from sickness, etc. The Psalms were

written in poetic form, set to musical accompaniment. The Gospel writers considered some of the Psalms to contain prophetic elements, to be of messianic significance, foretelling the messianic age with special applicability to Jesus, in particular Psalms 22, 31, 69, 110. The language is sufficiently broad to read many meanings into it. The authors were not inspired, did not claim that Yahweh spoke to them in a dream or in a vision and cannot be classified as prophets. They did not pronounce oracles; simply weaved stories of hope, dreams and aspirations, which were broad enough to assimilate the desired passages. No reliance can be placed on quotations excerpted from Psalms by New Testament writers; certainly none that affected Jesus of the Gospels.

7. If I were to be inconsistent and use quotations from the unknown "Isaiah"—that skulking author who masqueraded as the "second" secret Isaiah, a writer of no scriptural validity or authority—verses which were ignored or overlooked by the New Testament writers for understandable reasons, because they conflicted with the dogma that Jesus Christ was the Savior par excellence, it would be an "Isaiah" at his literary and spiritual best affirming the absolute supremacy of Yahweh, the God of Israel for eternity, the only Savior, whose actions are not reversible, who is without rival and supreme. This left no room for Jesus Christ, the divine Savior.

> "I, I am Yahweh, there is no other savior but me. It is I who have spoken, have saved, … I am your God. I am he from eternity. No one can deliver from my hand, I act and no one can reverse it" (Isaiah 43:11–13).
> "I am the first and last; there is no other God besides me" (Isaiah 44:6).
> "I am Yahweh, unrivaled; there is no other God besides me … apart from me, all is nothing" (Isaiah 45:5–6).

8. The reader possessing more than a superficial knowledge of the Gospels should be astounded at the below selected quotations from the Old Testament books of Prophets, Psalms, Lamentations and Wisdom utilized by the Gospel authors, and will be more than confounded by the suggestive content of the first quoted excerpt from the Book of Wisdom (2:10–20), written in Greek by a Hellenized Jew in the 1st century B.C., i.e., before Paul's Epistles, Mark, Matthew, Luke and John were written: "As for the

virtuous man who is poor, let us oppress him; … let our strength be the yardstick of virtue, … let us lie in wait for the virtuous man, since he annoys us and opposes our way of life, reproaches us for our breaches of the law … he claims to have knowledge of God and calls himself son of the Lord … the very sight of him weighs our spirits down; his way of life is not like other men's, … in his opinion we are counterfeit; he holds aloof from our doings as though from filth; … and boasts of having God for his father, let us see if what he says is true, let us observe what kind of end he himself will have. If the virtuous man is God's son, God will take his part and rescue him from the clutches of his enemies. Let us test him with cruelty and with torture, … and put his endurance to the proof. Let us condemn him to a shameful death since he will be looked after—we have his word for it."

"My God, my God, what have you deserted me?" (Ps. 22:1).

"into your hands I commit my spirit," (Ps. 31:5).

"when I was thirsty they gave me vinegar to drink." (Ps. 69:21).

"a thing despised and rejected by men, a man of sorrow and familiar with suffering … he was despised and we took no account of him." (Is. 53:3).

"Hear and hear again, but do not understand; see and see again, but do not perceive." (Is. 6:9).

"And I saw, coming on the clouds of heaven, one like a son of man … On him was conferred sovereignty, glory and Kingship, and men of all people's nations … became his servants." (Dan. 7:13–14).

"after a day or two he will bring us back to life, on the third day he will raise us and we should live in his presence." (Hos. 6:2–3).

"… I am going to send my messenger to prepare a way before me" (Mal. 3:1).

"Blessing on him who comes in the name of Yahweh" (Ps. 118:26).

"… for my house will be called a house of prayer for all the peoples." (Is. 56:7).

"Do you take this Temple that bears my name for a robbers' den?" (Jer. 7:11).

"Yahweh's oracle to you, my Lord, 'Sit at my right hand and I will make your enemies a footstool for you.'" (Ps. 110:1).

"… they divide my garments among them and cast lots for my clothes." (Ps. 22:18).

"... the maiden is with child and will give birth to a son whom she will call Immanuel" (Is. 7:14).

"But you Bethlehem, the least of the clans of Judah, out of you will be born for me the one who is to rule over Israel; ..." (Mi. 5:1).

"... I called my son out of Egypt." (Hos.11:1).

"A voice cries 'Prepare in the wilderness a way for Yahweh. Make a straight highway for our God across the desert." ' (Is. 40:3).

"... but the humble shall have the land for their own ..." (Ps. 37:11).

"... to offer his cheek to the striker, to be overwhelmed with insults." (Lam. 3:30).

"... what I want is love, not sacrifices;" (Hos. 6:6).

"I am going to speak to you in parable and expound the mysteries of our past." (Ps. 78:2).

"Say to the daughter of Zion, look, your savior comes, ..." (Is. 62:12).

"Shout with gladness, daughter of Jerusalem! See now, your king comes to you; he is victorious, he is triumphant, humble and riding on a donkey, on a colt, the foal of a donkey." (Zee. 9:9).

"Blessing on him who comes in the name of Yahweh." (Ps. 118:26).

"And they weighed out my wages: thirty shekels of silver ... this princely sum at which they have valued me." (Zee. 11:12–13).

"I offered my back to those who struck me, ... I did not cover my face against insult and spittle." (Is. 50:6).

"He relied on Yahweh, let Yahweh save him!" (Ps. 22:7–8, Ws. 2:18–20).

"See, I am Yahweh ... , is anything impossible to me?" (Jer. 32:27).

"Away from me all you evil men!" (Ps. 6:8).

"It was the stone rejected by the builders that proved to be the key-stone; ..." (Ps. 118:22).

"... and letting himself be taken for a sinner, ..." (Is. 53:12).

"... into your hands I commit my spirit ..." (Ps. 31:5).

"... zeal for your house devours me, ..." (Ps. 69:9).

"... do not let those who hate me for no reason exchange sly glances." (Ps. 35:19).

"... taking care of every bone, Yahweh will not let one be broken." (Ps. 34:20).

"They will look on the one whom they have pierced." (Zec 12:10).

9. It is without historical precedent that a group of Evangelists, bent upon breaking away from Judaism and setting up a new religious creed opposed to Judaism, would seek the latter's writings for clues to its own justification. The Evangelists searched the Old Testament writings for suitable verses to lend credence to their story, namely, that it was clearly foretold—in their judgment—in ancient times. That is what they needed: a seemingly reliable source from which to lay the foundation that could withstand the test of time and forcefully favored their conclusions. What they needed was support from an ancient established religion, to give it an aura of permanence so as to generate greater acceptance among converts. The Evangelists felt that they succeeded. With the many verses taken from the Hebrew Scripture they laid the foundation of a new faith. Christianity started and matured with no original doctrine (it borrowed from other religions).

However, the prophets did predict an event to happen not in their life-time, but at some unknown future date, transmitting the divine message in clear language as spoken by Yahweh, about the ingathering of his scattered people to the Promised Land, led by an anointed King, a Messiah of his own choosing.

It is Yahweh speaking:

"... if you return to Yahweh your God, ... Yahweh your God will bring back your captives ... and gather you once again out of all the peoples where Yahweh your God has scattered you ... and bring you back to the land your fathers possessed ..." (Deut. 30:2–5).

The prophets speaking:

"he will gather you from every nation wherever you have been scat-tered." (Th. 13:5).

"I will restore your fortunes and gather you from all the nations and all the places where I have dispersed you—it is Yahweh who speaks. I will bring you back to the place from which I exiled you." (Jer. 29:14).

"I will gather you together from the peoples, I will bring you all back from the countries where you have been scattered and I will give you the land of Israel." (Ezk. 11:17).

"I mean to restore the fortunes of my people of Israel; they will rebuild the ruined cities and live in them, ..." (Am. 9:14).

"... I will gather the remnants of Israel, bring them together like sheep in the fold; ... their King will go in front of them, Yahweh at their head." (Mi. 2:12).

"Now I am going to save my people from the countries of the East and from the countries of the West. I will bring them back to live inside Jerusalem. They shall be my people and I will be their God ... (Zech. 8:7–8).

"I will bring your offspring from the east, and gather you from the west ... Bring back my sons from far away, my daughters from the end of the earth, all those who bear my name ... (Is. 43:5–7).

The meaning is unmistakable: The chosen Old Testament Messiah would lead the scattered people of Israel back to the Holy Land. During the time Jesus of the Gospels is said to have lived, the people of Israel were not scattered and therefore did not need a Messiah to lead them back to the land of their fathers.

Nor did God foretell the coming of a Messiah, whose function would be to define who would enter the kingdom of heaven, or sacrifice his blood on the Cross for the remission of man's sins, the salvation and redemption of mankind so that those who believed in him would gain everlasting life and who would assume the title of Savior to confront humanity in final judgment. Such a Messiah is the pure invention of New Testament writers, who desecrated, debased, distorted and perverted the word of Yahweh, the God of Israel, whose chosen Messiah would gather the scattered people of Israel, bring them back to the land of their fathers and establish a Kingdom of God on earth to rule over them. This was foretold by Israel's prophets. Therefore, the Christian concept of a Messiah is not the fulfillment of the Old Testament.

The great reliance Christianity placed upon quotations from the Hebrew Scripture for its authentic foundation was of no help to it, for it was shown that the Scripture was not the result of divine revelation, but written by profane hands and carried no imprimatur of divinity. On the contrary, it is evident that in its efforts to establish the historicity of Jesus of the Gospels by borrowing episodes from the Old Testament to buttress the foundation of the New Testament, it was mistaken and created fiction.

Chapter 27

Christology: The Problem

1. The story of Paul (Saul) claimed that he was a contemporary of Jesus but never met him. Born in Tarsus (present day Turkey) between the period 5–15 A.D., he belonged to the sect of Pharisees; was a tent-maker by trade and in Jerusalem claimed to have studied under Rabbi Gamaliel. Paul was in the employ of the High-Priest, arresting followers of Jesus and sending them to prison; his activities on behalf of the High-Priest also took him to Damascus. On the road to Damascus in the year 36 A.D., a miracle occurred to Paul—Jesus appeared to him—he was blinded by the appearance, was led to Damascus where he was cured and baptized by a certain Ananias; he was converted to Jesus and determined to devote his life to the preaching of Christ, first to the Jews, later exclusively to the Gentiles. He died a martyr's death ca 67 A.D.

The first problem that crops up is his "persecution" of Jesus followers in Jerusalem. What were these people guilty of? The period was between 30 A.D. and 36 A.D.; what could they have believed at that stage that warranted their harassment and imprisonment? We have it only from Paul's writing. Paul's Epistles were not yet written; the Gospels were not yet written; only Jesus' preaching, miracle-work, healing and belief in his Resurrection were known to the Jesus followers of that time. There was no offense in this and Paul is not believable. His story about being sent to Damascus to arrest followers of Jesus and bring them to Jerusalem is not believable. The police authority of the High-Priest did not extend beyond Judea (if that), but certainly not as far as Damascus which was not then under Roman rule. The other problem is his claim of being born a Jew. The Ebionites, a community of Jewish Christians, who were Paul's contemporaries, stated that Paul was not a Jew by birth or a Pharisee. Another problem is the fierceness with which he allegedly pursued the Jesus followers, claiming that it was indicative of his Pharisaic zeal. This is wrong. The Pharisees (vehemently opposed to the Sadducees) were not opposed to the early Jerusalem sectarian movements.

Jesus of the New Testament was not the founder of Christianity; Paul of Tarsus was. During all his reputed Pharisaic activity Paul did not know that Jesus, who died about 30 A.D.–33 A.D., whose followers Paul arrested, was his contemporary and died during his lifetime. How could this square with the story of Jesus related in the Gospels?

2. Paul—converted to Jesus in about 36 A.D.—persecuted Jesus followers in Jerusalem within a few years of the crucifixion of Jesus (30–33 A.D.). The persecution took place after Jesus' death (30 A.D. at the earliest) and before Paul's conversion (38 A.D. at the latest). There is a span of some 8 years, at the maximum, during which he could have been involved in police work for the High-Priest. He attended the stoning of Stephen (36 A.D.), so we know for sure he was active as a persecutor in that year. At the trial of Stephen, Paul heard Stephen's speech, which toward the end contained the following: "In the past they (the Jews) killed those who foretold the coming of the Just One (Jesus), and now you have become his betrayers, his murderers" (Acts 7:52–53). He was clearly accusing the Jews of Jesus' murder; this was a clear statement that the Jews murdered Jesus "now," in recent times. How could Paul have had a complete lapse of memory when referring to Jesus' death that evil spirits were responsible for this crucifixion, that his crucifixion was not traceable to history, that he lived in obscurity on earth? How could he have been silent that Jesus lived on earth in recent past? How could he have been ignorant of what he heard from Stephen if it had really occurred and is historical?

1 Thessalonians, widely accepted as Paul's earliest letter, dated about 50 A.D., "... as they have suffered from the Jews, the people who put the Lord Jesus to death, and the prophets too" (1 Th. 2:15) is accepted by biblical scholars to be a later interpolation, placed there for obvious reasons. Paul's silence is incomprehensible. Paul's statements that Jesus lived in obscurity on earth is incomprehensible in light of the knowledge about Jesus he must have gained from the Jesus followers he persecuted. His ignorance of the facts about Jesus raises serious troubling problems for

Christians and about placing Jesus in the first third of the 1st century A.D. It must then be concluded there were no facts to find out, that Paul was not a contemporary of Jesus and that his views regarding Jesus' death occurring in remote times is valid. A redating of the crucifixion would create havoc with the Christian doctrine.

3. Paul is said to be the author of 14 Epistles, of which only 5, possibly 7 are authentic. The authentic are: Romans, 1 Corinthians, 2 Corinthians, Galatians, 1 Thessalonians, possibly also Colossians and Philippians. The rest are forgeries. Even the authentic Epistles were corrupted by interpolations to conform the text to later Christian dogma, since the interpolators were pained and embarrassed by what they read. Paul wrote his Epistles between 50–60 A.D., before any canon Gospels were written. The Jesus Christ of his early Epistles was a remote figure thought to have been crucified but not traceable in history. Jesus' life on earth was lived in obscurity and suffering, no time and place of his earthly existence was mentioned; the image of the invisible God, the first born of creation and that evil spirits were responsible for his crucifixion. Nothing was said of the miracles, signs or wonders performed by Jesus, nor his trial before Roman officials; Paul appropriates the ethical teachings of Jesus as his own; in short, he does not credit Jesus for anything he may have done in his lifetime. In Paul's view, he existed as a supernatural personage before God "sent" him into this world (parallels Wisdom literature). Jesus assumed human flesh, later adding, a Jew born according to the flesh. He called himself an apostle of Jesus Christ; some of the more known excerpts from his Epistles:

"... the Son of God ... was a descendant of David ... it is about Jesus Christ our Lord ..." (Rm. 1:3–4).

"... by being redeemed in Jesus Christ who was appointed by God to sacrifice his life so as to win reconciliation through faith" (Rm. 3:24–25).

"Since God did not spare his own Son, but gave him up to benefit us all, ..." (Rm. 8:32).

"But now the Law has come to end with Christ, and everyone who has faith maybe justified" (Rm. 10:4).

"It is a wisdom that none of our masters of this age have ever known, or they would not have crucified the Lord of Glory; ..." (1 Co. 2:8–9).

"... Christ died for our sins, in accordance with scriptures; that he was buried; and that he was raised to life on the third day, in accordance with the scriptures; ..." (1 Co. 15:4–5).

"... if Christ has not been raised then our preaching is useless ... For if the dead are not raised, Christ has not been raised, ..." (1 Co. 15:14–17).

"... that I had been commissioned to preach the Good News to the uncircumcised ..." (Ga. 2:7)".

"Christ redeemed us from the curse of the Law by being cursed for our sake, ..." (Ga. 3:13).

"It is I, Paul, who told you this: if you allow yourselves to be circumcised, Christ will be of no benefit to you at all" (Ga. 5:2–3).

"We believe that Jesus died and rose again, and that it will be the same for those who have died in Jesus ..." (1 Th. 4:14–15).

The above quoted verses represent the basic Christology of Paul. He first deified Jesus and then claimed revelation from him to help establish the doctrines of Christianity as a separate religion from Judaism. His difficulties with the Jerusalem Nazarenes was his insistence (1) To convert Gentiles (2) Not to insist on circumcision (3) Not to insist on acceptance of the Law. Minor requirements were imposed, but from that period on Paul was going his own way, spreading Christianity among the Gentiles and establishing his place through his writing as the true founder of Christianity.

4. Paul believed that Jesus was crucified one or two centuries before his time. He knew nothing of Pontius Pilate; the place of execution; the burial in Jerusalem; of the virgin birth; his ministry; John the Baptist; his miracles; his betrayal by Judas. Paul wrote before any canonical Gospel was written. The earliest of Mark was written about 80–90 A.D.; the other three between 100–120 A.D. The Gospel writers (the Evangelists) weaved a complex life-story of Jesus, relating incidents in his life, some in common and others not. The authors were anonymous and Bishop Papias (Hierapolis in Asia Minor), 2nd century A.D., was the first to mention the Gospels of Matthew and Mark. None of the authors knew Jesus nor his disciples, nor anyone who knew Jesus in person; Mark was the original of the four Gospels, he may have drawn from a more ancient source; Matthew and Luke copied from him extensively. John copied less extensively and made use of Wisdom literature.

Had the Evangelists read Paul's Epistles, they could not have written as they did; had Paul been acquainted with the Jesus story as later related in the Gospels, he could not have written his Epistles as he did.

"…while the Jews demand miracles … here we are preaching a crucified Christ; …" (1 Co. 1:23–24). Had Paul known, would he not have stated that Jesus worked miracles? Would Matthew and Luke have related the virgin birth story had they read in Paul, Ga. 4:5: "God sent his son, born of a woman, …" i.e., normal birth?

"Bless those who persecute you, never curse them …" (Rm. 12:14). Would Paul have taken that statement as his own had he known that Jesus said: "… love your enemies and pray for those who persecute you; …" (Matt. 5:44–45).

Paul, after relating his Hebrew background that he was a loyal Pharisee, goes on to say: "But because of Christ, I have come to consider all those advantages that I had as disadvantages" (Ph. 3:7–8). But Christ would disagree with him. Paul certainly had not known that Jesus taught: "Therefore, the man who infringes even one of the least of these commandments and teaches others to do the same will be considered the least in the kingdom of heaven; …" (Matt. 5:19). The Pauline Epistles show a total ignorance of what was later taught in the Gospels about Jesus. Their tone is incompatible with that of the Gospels. Paul calls himself an apostle to the Gentiles (Rm. 11:13). Would he have maintained it had he known that Jesus charged his twelve disciples not to convert the Gentiles? (Matt. 10:5–6). The discrepancies between Paul and the Gospels are unbridgable. This is total chaos, the differences cannot be reconciled so soon after the death of Jesus. Is Paul speaking from ignorance? Post-Pauline but pre-90 A.D. other epistles display the same ignorance; they could not all be equally tendentious. Post 90 A.D. epistles refer to Jesus more like in the manner of the Gospels. There appears a cut-off point for the epistles: Pre-Gospel and post-Gospel. Pre-Gospel reflect Paul's views; post-Gospel epistles reflect views analogous to the Gospels. So the problem is historical; around 90 A.D. a new Christology emerged, one with which we are familiar from the Gospels, one that was newly put together and one that was not known before. The author or authors tried to place Jesus in a historical perspective; write his biography as vividly as they could; color his life with events; give drama to his Passion story. The new pagan Christian converts needed that personal contact with Jesus—as they had previously with their gods—by knowing something about him and the Gospels supplied it. But was it authentic history? The Gospels were not eyewitness documents; derived from a single-source of older tradition now lost to us; reduced to writing two to three generations removed from Jesus' time and his disciples; no witnesses then alive to corroborate or contradict the account and after the destruction of Jerusalem (70 A.D.) when most of the underlying records were destroyed or scattered. The Gospel writers were safe in weaving their story; safe from fear of contradiction for no one was alive to dispute their account and the Church Fathers saw to it that harmful documents, wherever found, were destroyed. Of the many Gospel accounts written (about 40) the number was reduced to four canonical Gospels and they have credibility problems of their own.

5. Not only do the Gospels seriously differ from the pre-90 epistles but they differ from each other in many fundamental respects and what kind of person Jesus was. Neither Jesus nor his disciples left any written documents; some of the areas where they differed:

(a) Only Matthew and Luke trace the ancestry of Jesus. Matthew traces his ancestry back to Abraham and forward to Joseph. Luke from Adam to Joseph. Only two names, David and Joseph, are common to both lists. How is such a genealogical fiasco possible? Was the urge to prove Jesus' Davidic ancestry so strong as to risk ridicule? Joseph is named Jesus' father on both lists, to fit into the ancestry cited he had to be his natural father. How does this square with Christian theology that Jesus did not have a natural father, but he had to have one to claim ancestry from David? Matthew and Luke should have left this one alone—as did the other two Gospel writers—because it tarnished their credibility. The Gospels were never meant to be read together.

(b) Jesus' birth is only reported in Matthew and Luke.

(c) Trial and Crucifixion occurred on the day before Passover (John), the first day of Passover (Mark, Matthew, Luke).

(d) The Resurrected Jesus appeared in Galilee (Matthew); in Emmaus (Luke); none named (Mark); Sea of Tiberias (John).

(e) Jesus' cry on the cross: "My God, my God, why have you deserted me?" (Mark, Matthew); not mentioned by Luke and John.

(f) Jesus' death sentence carried out by Jews (Luke, John); by Romans (Mark, Matthew).

(g) Ascension not mentioned (Matthew and John).

(h) Do not refer to virgin birth (Mark, John).

(i) Jesus born in Bethlehem (Matthew, Luke); Nazareth (Mark); not mentioned (John).

(j) Raising of Lazarus reported (John); not mentioned (Mark, Matthew, Luke).

(k) Raising of daughter of Jairus reported (Mark, Matthew, Luke); not mentioned (John).

(l) Lord's Prayer and Sermon on the Mount reported (Matthew).

(m) Killing of innocent children by Herod reported (Matthew).

6. Other Gospel observations about Jesus.

Jesus baptized no one in his lifetime and did not instruct his converts to be baptized.

Jesus thought Moses was the author of the Pentateuch. He was mistaken. He thought that the prophets named were in every case the authors of the work attributed to them. He was mistaken.

Jesus performed healing miracles to prove he is the Messiah, yet forbade his miracles to be made known even when notoriety made the secrecy impossible. Why? Was it to conceal his Messiahship? Was it the wish of Jesus or the authors for if they were secret they could not be controverted? Jesus did not profess to be the Messiah.

When the disciples in Mark 8:28 report the opinions of the people concerning Jesus, they cannot mention anyone who held him to be the Messiah. Jesus' cry on the cross: "My God, my God, why have you deserted me?" shows it had not been his purpose to die.

John reports Jesus teaching in Jerusalem on several occasions. The Synoptics do not mention it; they represent his going to Jerusalem for the Passover (Messianic Entry) for the first and only time. Jesus did not possess the Davidic descent required of a Jewish Messiah; that would have excluded him from consideration by most Jews, including (by Gospel characterization) the "dimwitted" High Priest and the Sanhedrin.

Pontius Pilate was willing to release Jesus even though he referred to him as "the king of the Jews" (Mark), or "crucify your King" (John). Both authors were hallucinating; it showed their distant removal in time and geography from the scene not to have grasped the political implication of his statement which could have gotten Pontius Pilate into dangerous trouble with Rome. Or did the Gospel writers also consider him "dimwitted"?

If Jesus was so well known as the Messiah—despite the enforced secrecy, viz., the Messianic entry into Jerusalem—why did Judas have to betray him and point him out to the Jewish authorities? What were the Temple police and spies doing; were they also "dimwitted"? Why was Jesus alone arrested and his disciples left untouched at the time of his arrest and after his execution? If Jesus was guilty, why were his closest associates not harmed?

Jesus performed many miracles to prove that he was the Messiah, yet no one from the public recognized him as such.

In the time of Jesus there was no general expectation of a Messiah, let alone of a divine Messiah. Only after the destruction of Jerusalem did such expectation arise; the Gospels were written after the destruction. In Mark 4:12, Jesus declared that the purpose of his parables was to obscure his teaching: "… so that they may see and see again, but not perceive; may hear and hear again, but not understand; …"; what could possibly be his purpose? Was it again that the prophecy (Isaiah 6:9–10) be fulfilled?

The miracles Jesus performed had nothing to do with proof of his Messiahship—in the Jewish sense. Miracles have no messianic significance. In Mark there is no suggestion that miracles have messianic significance. Mark 13:32 has Jesus speaking when the kingdom of God would come, yet Jesus displays ignorance of the time despite it being the essence of his message: "But as for that day or hour, nobody knows it, neither the angels of heaven, nor the Son; no one but the Father."

Jesus speaking to his twelve disciples about the imminent coming of the Son of Man (certainly within their lifetime): "I tell you solemnly, you will not have gone the round of the towns of Israel before the Son of Man comes" (Matt. 10:23). Jesus was wrong, the Son of Man did not come.

Jesus believed that evil spirits inhabited the bodies of sick people and that he could cure them by forcing the spirits out. A peculiar notion of the time. Christian theology rejected the Law of Moses despite Jesus' repeated affirmation of it.

Jesus prayed to God to remove the suffering (prior to his arrest) from him: "Abba (Father)! Everything is possible for you. Take this cup away from me" (Mark 14:36).

The doctrine of Trinity is not mentioned in the Gospels. The Sanhedrin trial in John does not describe any charges brought against Jesus.

There was no Jewish custom to have a convicted criminal released to them at their request during the Passover festival or at any other festival. The Gospel writers were wrong when they stated that the Sanhedrin could not execute prisoners.

Only the unclean spirits, the demons he cast out, recognized Jesus' divine status and wherever they saw him they would fall down before him and shout, "You are the Son of God! But he (Jesus) warned them strongly not to make him known" (Mark 3:12).

When Jesus foretold the treachery of Judas: "... one of you is about to betray me, ... one who is dipping into the same dish with me" (Mark 14:18–21), the culprit was identified yet the other eleven did nothing to restrain Judas. Jesus never said a word to his twelve disciples about his dying and be raised again; they would not then have been amazed at his "resurrection."

The Gospels are worthless as biographies of Jesus. Matthew 2:1 places the birth of Jesus before the death of Herod in 4 B.C. That would make Jesus about 35 years old at the time of his crucifixion. In Luke 2:1 his birth is placed at the time of the first Census while Quirinius was Governor of Syria—he became Governor of Syria in 6 A.D. In the first place, in 6 A.D. the Census did not apply to Galilee (which was ruled by Herod Antipas) so that Joseph and Mary were not affected. In the second place, in 6 A.D. the birth of Jesus would be 10 years later than commonly assumed, so that when Jesus was crucified (30 A.D.–33 A.D.) he would be between 24 and 27 years old. Because Jesus settled in Nazareth, Matthew has this as the fulfillment of a prophecy: "He will be called a Nazarene" (2:23). There is no such prophecy, he simply invented one. In the Gospels (John in particular) there is the undercurrent about Jesus' divinity, being co-equal with God and even God who took human form. But Jesus distinctly refers to God as his "Father" (as separate and superior to him) and God refers to him as his "son" (as separate and inferior to him).

"This is my Son, the Beloved; ..." (Matt. 3:17).
"... when he comes in his own glory and in the glory of his Father ..." (Luke 9:26).
"This is my Son, the Chosen One" (Luke 9:36).

"... I will disown in the presence of my Father in heaven" (Matt. 10:33).

"My Father, if this cup cannot pass ..." (Matt. 26:42).

"... Any plant my heavenly Father has not planted ..." (Matt. 15:1314).

"... it was not flesh and blood that revealed this to you but my Father in heaven" (Matt. 16:17–18).

"... so that your Father in heaven may forgive your failings too" (Mark 11:25).

"Yes it is my Father's will that whoever sees the Son and believes in him shall have eternal life, ..." (John 6:40).

7. The worship of Jesus Christ is the life of Christianity. On the bright side shine the many claimed attributes which made him loved and adored by so many admiring followers (over a billion of them), namely, the teaching of love (of neighbor), compassion, forgiveness, mercy, meekness, humility, all the blessings of morality and fellowship; he is the Prince of Peace, in short: a social force of greatest magnitude. This is quite apart from the teaching of theology, as exemplified in Gospel verses—even though many were borrowed from the Old Testament:

"I give you a new commandment: love one another; ..." (John 13:34); (Lev. 19:18).

"You must love your neighbor as yourself' (Matt. 22:39–40); (Lev. 19:18).

"So always treat others as you would like them to treat you; ..." (Matt. 7:12); (Tobit 4:15).

"Honor your father and mother" (Mark 10:20); (Dt. 24:14).

"Be compassionate as your Father is compassionate" (Luke 6:36); (Ex. 34:6–7).

In light of the above, the less charitable side of Jesus (or words the Gospel authors made him say) is astounding. Nowhere does the chimerical character of Jesus come to the fore as in his ethical, moral and social teaching. The Gospel writers have outdone themselves in who could come up with a more inconsistent, contradictory, nonsensical and discordant Jesus in whose mouth they put their expression of character. For it is one thing to create historical fiction about this or that episode without fear of contradiction and leaning on prophetic fulfillments. It is another thing to make Jesus express views on conduct, where the authors stood naked and unsupported and hid their views behind claimed divine wisdom. That is most baffling. This is Jesus speaking:

> "Do not suppose that I have come to bring peace to the earth: it is not peace I have come to bring, but a sword. For I have come to set a man against his father, a daughter against her mother ..." (Matt. 10:34–35).
>
> "He who is not with me is against me ..." (Matt. 12:30).
>
> "I tell you solemnly, it will be hard for a rich man to enter the kingdom of heaven" (Matt. 19:23–24).
>
> "... offer a wicked man no resistance ... if anyone hits you on the right cheek, offer him the other as well ... if anyone wants to borrow, do not turn away" (Matt. 5:39–42).
>
> "... everything you ask and pray for, believe that you have it already, and it will be yours" (Mark 11:24–25).
>
> "That is why I am telling you not worry ... what you are to eat, nor about your body how to clothe it ... So do not worry about tomorrow: tomorrow will take care of itself' (Matt. 6:34).
>
> "Do not judge, and you will not be judged; ... (Matt. 7:1).
>
> "So I tell you this, that for every unfounded word men utter they will answer on Judgement day, ..." (Matt. 12:36–37).
>
> "... love your enemies and pray for those who persecute you ... you must therefore be perfect as your heavenly Father is perfect" (Matt. 5:44–48).
>
> "Alas for you, scribes and Pharisees, you hypocrites! ... alas for you, blind guides! ... Blind Pharisee ... You are the sons of those who murdered the prophets ... Serpents, brood of vipers, how can you escape being condemned to hell? ... I am sending you prophets and wise men and scribes: some you will slaughter and crucify, some you will scourge in your synagogues ... and so you will draw down on yourself the blood of every holy man that has been shed on earth ..." (Matt. 23:13–35).
>
> "You must call no one on earth your father, since you have only one Father, and he is in heaven" (Matt. 23:9–10).
>
> "Go and sell everything you own and give the money to the poor and you will have treasures in heaven; then come, follow me" (Mark 10:21).

"Love your enemies, do good to those who hate you, bless those who curse you, pray for those who treat you badly" (Luke 6:27–28).

"I have come to bring fire to the earth, and how I wish it were blazing already!" (Luke 12:49).

"Do you suppose that I am here to bring peace on earth? No, I tell you, but rather division. For from now on a household of five will be divided: three against two and two against three; the father divided against the son, son against father, ..." (Luke 12:51–53).

"If any man comes to me without hating his father, mother, wife, children, brothers, sisters, yes and his own life too, he cannot be my disciple" (Luke 14:26–27).

"No one who believes in him will be condemned, but whoever refuses to believe is condemned already, ..." (John 3:18).

"... but anyone who refuses to believe in the Son will never see life: the anger of God stays on him" (John 3:36).

8. How does one reconcile the commandment to love one another with setting father against son and hating one's father and mother? How does one reconcile the command to love one's neighbor with the venom spewed at the Pharisees? To honor one's father with the son hating his father? To treat others as you would like them to treat you and instantly punish those who are against you? These thoughts are contradictory and could not be preached by the same voice, divine or other. The Gospel writers erred in making Jesus pronounce these, there is no speaking in parables intended, no scheme of confusing people. It is one thing to preach no resistance to the wicked man, to love one's enemies, to do good to those who hate you and make no provisions for tomorrow—another to apply such dicta in life on an ongoing basis and survive; the God-created forces of nature, human nature, would devour such persons. It cannot be done and has not been done by Christians or non-Christians. As shown in future chapters, the opposite morality prevailed throughout the evolution and maturation of Christianity.

Does anyone think it possible to associate such venom and moral nonsense with Jesus? Downright hatred and malevolence towards family members? Such dislike of riches, such execration of non-conformists? Such quick resort to punishment and condemnation to hell? Such inane advice to take no foresight for one's needs; to love one's enemies; pray for those who persecute you; to give all your possessions to the poor (so as to become one of the poor) and offer no resistance to the wicked man? Such blanket condemnation of Pharisees calling them murderers of prophets? The latter is obviously a later Christian interpolation spoken from the safety of time and distance and not in the turbulent time of the Palestine scene where the dagger of the Sicarii, or revenge of the Zealots, would not have missed the accuser. Yet all these vituperations are in the Gospels, in the New Testament, to be sermonized and are there as divine testimony. It is not possible to maintain that the same person preached the former and latter verses. Could such shallow reasoning be divine? With all the tampering the Gospel text was exposed to, the falsification and distortions the writings have suffered at the hands of the early Church Fathers determined to rewrite history, each adding or deleting some verses. Is it any wonder that the texts command little credibility? They stand, however, as sacred documents, treated as divinely inspired, canonical and of unquestioned authenticity, breathing the dark side of hatred, enmity and intolerance. It was the Gospel authors (and their crude interpolators) who were intellectually barren.

9. Exposed on moral and theological aspects of the Gospels, the early Christian Church Fathers sought cover in mysterious Christology which would silence and confound. For it was with great difficulty that one was able to keep the deeds of Jesus the man separate from the deeds of Jesus the Christ, the Son of God, the co-equal with the Father, namely God. If the latter is represented in the Gospels, the narrative of his ministry, suffering and death, but most importantly, his message is lost in the blurred image of the divine drama, played out on an artificial stage debilitated with foreknowledge of events to come. To which "Father" is Jesus praying? To which "Father" is he appealing? What does he mean when he says "no one but the Father" knows? His false prophecies are inexplicable; his false prediction of the imminent coming of the kingdom of heaven proved a theological disaster which did not fit into any pattern of his plan. But, if on the other hand, we assume the Gospel story to be about Jesus, the man born of a woman, who grew in the sight of God and in whom God was well pleased, "my favor rests on you", the whole drama becomes understandable and of human proportions; his disputes, aggravations and disappointments become vivid and real; his suffering and cry on the cross become the bitter conclusion of his aspirations. Between these two concepts of Jesus,

the Gospels, in constant state of vacillation, have no answer or solution. Instead, we are confronted by a quasi-this and quasi-that personage; forced to read between the lines; forced to resolve glaring contradictions and forced to state and repeat the incomprehensible: Christ was simultaneously fully divine and fully human; that he was pre-existent, unbegotten and the head of creation; the visible form of the divine Logos, the pre-existent cosmic principle of God's wisdom and power; the absolutely real presence of God in the world; part of the Trinity of Father, Son and Holy Spirit—the fundamental mystery of Christianity—that the Son is God of one substance with the Father. The canonical Gospels contain no such Christology; there is only one description that befits these definitions: Incomprehensible mysteries, to stay forever incomprehensible.

10. The conclusion is inescapable: The Jesus (Yeshua) of Paul, the mythical remote figure, the slain and resurrected Deity, is incompatible with the Palestinian Jesus of the Gospels, the teacher and miracle-worker. They created a preaching Jesus who had no resemblance to the Jesus of Paul of Tarsus, who was raised among mystery religions featuring dying and resurrected Saviors, whose Jesus existed in an unknown past as a supernatural personage before God sent him into this world to redeem it by shedding his blood on the cross, so that those who believed in him would have salvation and eternal life. The content of his authentic Epistles is pre-Christian Gnostic. Paul claimed that his mission was to reveal this secret hidden for long ages and many generations: "... when God made me responsible for delivering God's message to you, the message which was a mystery hidden for generations and centuries and has now been revealed to his saints. It was God's purpose to reveal it to them and to show all the rich glory of this mystery to pagans." (Col 1:25–27).

Hence the mystery about Jesus is only magnified—the conclusion unavoidable: The New Testament dealt with at least two Jesuses. The two are irreconcilable. One or the other was the true Redeemer, the other was false. Or they were both the creation of profane writers who created literary falsehoods.

Chapter 28

The Doubts

1. If there is one event critical to the narratives and miracles of Jesus it is his "Ascension," the transfer of his body to heaven, his final glorification, his exaltation to the right hand of the Father. One would expect the Gospels recording Jesus' supreme triumph and realization of his dominant prophecy to be effusive in describing the event. For if the Ascension was of the body of Jesus, he must also have been bodily (not only spiritually) resurrected. What a grandiose way to cap the earthly activities and to make instant converts of the most "hostile" Pharisees, for an ascending Jesus would have been seen by a great multitude and the talk of it reached every corner of the country. But the Gospels that even mention the event are extremely restrained in their description and some texts were tampered with. To start, Mark stated: "And so the Lord Jesus, ... was taken up into heaven: there at the right hand of God he took his place, ..." (16:19–20). Mark's Gospel ends with 16:8, and verses 19–20 were added anonymously; they are not in the Vatican Codex and the Codex Sinaiticus. In other words, Mark does not mention the Ascension at all. The Gospel of Matthew speaks only of an appearance in Galilee and no mention is made of the Ascension. The Gospel of Luke narrates the appearance to the eleven disciples in Jerusalem: "Now as he blessed them, he withdrew from them and was carried up to heaven" (24:51–52). The Gospel of John does not mention the occurrence of the Ascension at all; its only reference is before the Ascension when Jesus spoke to Mary: "But go and find the brothers, and tell them: I am ascending to my Father ..." (20:17). Of the four Gospels, only Luke makes reference to an Ascension that took place and did this in the skimpiest of terms: five words! Luke does not even report that the Ascension was witnessed by the disciples or by anybody, but simply, as if embarrassed to discuss it, "and was carried up to heaven" (Luke

24:51–52). Three Gospels do not report the event at all and Luke does not report any witnesses! This is the literary treatment the Gospels accord the most climactic and glorious event in the earthly life of Jesus. Could three of the Evangelists have been ignorant of the event? And the fourth one barely mention it? For surely had the three known about it they would have mentioned it and the fourth author would have mentioned witnesses and give the event more than five words. The occurrence of the Ascension simply is not credible and must be treated as a non-event.

2. The Pentateuch, epicenter of the Old Testament, the work credited to Moses as the only revealed word of God, is historically inaccurate. As shown in previous chapters, the Exodus and the conquest of Canaan are not credible; the authorship of the Pentateuch by Moses is not credible, but written much later by unknown authors to whom no revelation by God was indicated. The canon was compiled by fallible men who included and excluded works to suit their preconceived notions. On the same Old Testament foundation the Christians placed the foundation of the New Testament and, as such, cannot carry more validity despite claiming to have replaced it. Jesus was born a Jew, believed in the law of Moses, Psalms and prophets, had no intention of founding a new religion and died a Jew. The Gospels tried hard to back away from Jewish form, present a confused picture of Jewish messianic tradition, Wisdom literature and prophecies; were tampered with by early Christian Church interpolators who, by then, were well conversant with Pauline and other Epistles. Paul who preceded the Gospel authors, despite insincere protestations, laid the foundation of a new religion to replace Judaism, but still could not break away from the messianic idea and eschatology, which were Jewish concepts. Paul needed to retain ties to Judaism in order to confirm Jesus as the long expected Messiah; Paul believed in Jesus' Davidic descent. Christianity became the religious heir to Judaism. The break was completed by early Church Fathers to whom Jesus became the pre-existent cosmic principle, unbegotten, part of the Trinity and of one substance with the Father; to them the Crucifixion, Resurrection and Ascension became the central dogmas of the new faith; the doctrine of the Eucharist the central mystery of the Church. Christianity, in many respects, resembled heathen mysteries and its esoteric doctrines were not original. Mithras was a redeemer of mankind; so were Tammuz and Adonis. But the Christians claim the salvation which they celebrated occurred only

once in the history of mankind and is therefore unique. But the bulk of Jews could not accept the divinity of Jesus Christ since they treated the idea as a subversion of monotheism and therefore blasphemous; it was a subversion of the real teaching of Jesus.

3. The enforced messianic secrecy and the speaking in parables are the most puzzling components of the Gospels. The Gospel of John makes no reference to the messianic secrecy. Jesus had not been held by the multitude to be the Messiah because, in the Synoptic Gospels, he never made such a claim publicly. Oddly, the signs of the Messiah were bound to miracle-making and curing the ill; there were many miracle workers and faith healers before Jesus and since, who did not earn the title "Messiah." Whenever Jesus performed a healing miracle he commanded that this be told to no one. When he cured the two blind men, he "sternly" warned them: "Take care that no one learns about this" (Matt. 9:31); when he restored the daughter of Jairus from death to life, he ordered them "strictly" "not to let anyone know about it ..." (Mark 5:43); "Devils too came out of many people, howling, 'You are the Son of God.' But he rebuked them and would not allow them to speak because they knew that he was the Christ" (Luke 4:41). The prohibitions against talking about the cures made no sense since some were witnessed by a multitude of people, who could not be silenced. And so with his twelve disciples. When they witnessed his transfiguration, Jesus gave them this order: "Tell no one about the vision until the Son of Man has risen from the dead" (Matt. 17:9–10). When Peter, in answering Jesus' question who he thought he was, said to him: " 'You are the Christ.' And he gave them strict orders not to tell anyone about him' " (Mark 8:30). In Luke 9:36, when the disciples witnessed the transfiguration, "The disciples kept silence, at that time, told no one what they had seen." And in Matt. 16:20, "Then he gave the disciples strict orders not to tell anyone that he was the Christ." To the question why Jesus spoke in parables he responded to his disciples: "Because the mysteries of the kingdom of heaven are revealed to you but they are not revealed to them ... that they look without seeing and listen without hearing or understanding" (Matt. 13:11–14). The people were taught only in parables, so the Gospel says, to fulfill the prophecies of Psalm 78:2.

Jesus performed miracles and healings to be recognized as the Messiah and then he forbade those cured to tell anyone and to keep it secret. This did not help his cause. He strictly forbade the Twelve to reveal what they knew about him. This messianic secrecy is not comprehensible; the concealment, the intentional secrecy, the idea of a secret which had to remain a secret—until the Resurrection implies that nothing was known about the messianic claims of Jesus. He referred to himself as the "Son of Man" (which, as mentioned in a previous chapter, had no messianic or divine connotation, meaning only "Man") making no messianic references to himself as in: "Anyone who says a word against the Son of Man will be forgiven" (Matt. 12:32). Jesus speaking of the prophecy of the Passion: "The Son of Man is going to be handed over into the power of man, ..." (Matt. 17:22–23); "... so will the Son of Man be in the heart of the earth for three days and three nights" (Matt. 12:40–41). The teaching in parables contains the same mystery: an intentional obscurity and obfuscation. It was an effort not to instruct the multitude clearly and to conceal the truth from them. Any claim to teach the "Good News" and reveal the mysteries of the kingdom of heaven is false: It is fiction. The messianic secret of the Synoptics is in complete contrast with the revelations in the Gospel of John. This contrast itself is a mystery; there was one Jesus and two "sacred" contradictory interpretations. In John, Jesus is bold and fearless with the language about himself, uses poetic and lengthy expressions to announce his mission and hides from no one. Testifying on his behalf: "I am the light of the world; ..." (8:12); "I am from above ... I am not of this world" (8:23); "If God were your father, you would love me, ..." (8:42). Identifying the Son of Man with the Messiah, Jesus said: "Do you believe in the Son of Man? ... You are looking at him; he is speaking to you" (9:36–38); "I believe that you are the Christ, the Son of God, ..." (11:27); "... out of fear of the Jews, who had already agreed to expel from the synagogue anyone who should acknowledge Jesus as the Christ" (9:22–23). In short, there is no messianic secrecy in John. In a 1984 review of a book by the Swiss theologian Hans Kung in The New York Times Review of Books, Thomas Sheehan wrote: "In Roman Catholic seminaries, it is now common teaching that Jesus of Nazareth did not assert any of the Divine or Messianic claims the Gospels attribute to Him, and that He died without believing He was Christ or the Son of God, not to mention the founder of a new religion" (National Review/November 7, 1986). In view of the messianic secrecy, this is the only conclusion that can be arrived at.

There is not a single date in Jesus' life that can be determined with certainty. On the matter of Jesus' historicity, there is no non-Christian evidence worthy of the name. His existence is not linked to any document that originated before 100 A.D. There is no first hand record of any writer who knew Jesus. Here are some additional reasons which weaken the case of the historical Jesus:

Paul's persecution of Christians is not credible.

The Jesus of Paul and of the Gospels do not reconcile.

In 1 Co. 9:5,Paul refers to "brothers of the Lord" and not to blood-brothers of Jesus; the reference is to a brotherhood.

Paul's ignorance of the life of Jesus is incomprehensible: he was his contemporary.

The differences among the Gospels, none of whose authors were eye-witnesses.

Paul's ignorance of Pontius Pilate.

Pontius Pilate's willingness to release the "King of the Jews" and finding no fault with Jesus despite this appellation.

The need for the betrayal by Judas since Jesus was so well known to the High-Priest and Pharisees.

The idea that a Messiah had to perform miracles, and that calling him "Christ" added to his divinity.

Error of Jesus in predicting the imminent coming of the Son of Man to establish the kingdom of God.

The need for the fulfillment of Old Testament prophecies which did not apply to Jesus.

The acceptance of Old Testament prophecies as "sacred" and without error.

The Gospels are not biographical.

The Gospels present no valid reason for which Jesus was crucified; neither blasphemy nor political crime.

The delay of the Parousia, the "Second Coming."

At Jesus' trial he had not been held by the multitude as the Messiah.

The myth of the "Messianic Entry" into Jerusalem.

The myth of the cleansing of the Temple.

Jesus nowhere defined the kingdom of God.

Jesus' disciples were ignorant men because it suited the authors of the Gospels.

The Book of Daniel, written in the 2nd century B. C., does not belong to the Old Testament prophetic writings.

At the time of Jesus there was no general expectation of a Messiah among these people.

Jesus told the Twelve: "Now we are going up to Jerusalem, and the Son of Man is about to be handed over to the chief priests and the scribes. They will condemn him to death …" (Mark 10:33–34). This was a clear prophecy. But when the hour was near, Jesus prayed to his Father: "Take this cup away from me. But let it be as you, not I, would have it" (Mark 14:36–37), a perfectly normal human reaction but not consistent with his divine plan.

4. The search of the biblical and non-biblical records of Jesus can find no grounds for supposing that he ever existed as a historical figure. The internal evidence is badly constructed, the various authors so at odds with each other, the reasoning so reflected the immaturity and intellectual weakness of the authors as to give up any hope for finding the historical Jesus. The enforced messianic secrecy; the speaking in parables to confuse the multitudes; the shabbily rigged trials before the High-Priest (and Sanhedrin) and Pontius Pilate; the half-learned content of the parables, suggesting limited intelligence of the authors or interpolators; the lack of agreement among authors about the unity of his biography relatively soon after the events, when some records should have been preserved; the absence of dates of birth and crucifixion and lack of any dates for that matter; the never ending mistaken reliance on prophets and Scripture to add credibility to the events; the lack of originality and copying from other religions; the total absence of anything written by Jesus or his disciples—all these make the existence of a historical Jesus improbable. Albert Schweitzer must have agonized when he wrote (12–398): "The Jesus of Nazareth who came forward publicly as the Messiah, who preached the ethic of the Kingdom of God, who founded the Kingdom of Heaven upon earth, and died to give His work its final consecration, never had any existence … This image has not been destroyed from without, it has fallen to pieces, cleft and disintegrated by the concrete historical problems which came to the surface one after another, … He will be a Jesus, who was

Messiah, and lived as such, either on the ground of a literary fiction of the earliest Evangelist, or on the ground of a purely eschatological Messianic conception." Where does this leave Christianity? It could have come about—and it did—even had there been no historical Jesus. In the eventful 1st century A.D., when Jewish religious forces and sectarians were rebelling against the strictures of the Temple and priesthood; when the animosity between the Pharisees and the Sadducees was tearing the nation apart; when the class struggle in Judea between the rich and poor reached its climax; when apocalyptic and eschatological ideas were in the air feeding the hopes and aspirations of the people; the times were certainly ripe for new religious ideas to have attracted a following. At first totally within Judaism, but with the disintegration of the Jewish State and the destruction of Jerusalem, trends developed for a total break with Judaism towards an independent religion, theology and rituals. Christianity was founded in opposition to Judaism as a "New Covenant," replacing the Covenant between Yahweh and Israel. For the Christian leaders felt quite justified in interpreting the destruction of Jerusalem and the Temple as God's punishment and abandonment of the Jewish people. The Christian movement grew in numbers and flourished two to three generations distanced from Pontius Pilate; they came to believe there lived a Jesus, the Christ, the Messiah, part of the Godhead, who was crucified; the founder of Christianity.

Modern biblical criticism inevitably arrived at the only conclusion possible: that Jesus of the New Testament does not belong to history.

Chapter 29

The Messiah

1. The Torah (the five books of Moses) is the only document in the Hebrew canon that can claim divine revelation, i.e., God communicated directly with Moses ("I speak with him face to face, plainly and not in riddles, ..." (Numb. 12:8). To others, including the Hebrew prophets, God spoke in a vision, in a dream, not plainly but in riddles (Numb. 12:6). How are we to know that a prophet truly speaks in the name of God? Only when a prophet speaks in the name of God and the prophecy really happens, i.e., the "thing does not happen ... then it has not been spoken by Yahweh ..." (Deut. 18:21). All other books included in the Hebrew canon were inspired, i.e., written by profane hands in contemplation of the Divine Presence.

2. All agents of God, i.e., kings, priests or a specially selected man had to be made holy, i.e., sacred oil daubed on his head. Then he was called the anointed, or Messiah (Mashiah in Hebrew), or Christ (Christos in Greek). The term "Messiah" or "Christ" simply designate one who has been anointed.

3. There were Jewish messianic pretenders in the 1st century A.D., not endorsed by the God of Israel or the prophets. They were politico-military leaders, self or publicly proclaimed Messiahs, who aimed by force of arms to free the Jews from Roman oppression: Judas of Galilee (6 A.D.); Theudas (44 A.D.) and Benjamin the Egyptian (60 A.D.). They sparked the fire of revolt against Rome, were defeated, killed in battle or crucified— God's hand could not be forced. They were false Messiahs.

But the God of Israel proclaimed to Moses his own criteria for choosing a Messiah, an anointed King, who would bring back from Exile the scattered people of Israel and lead them back to the land their fathers once possessed (Deut. 30:2–5). The Hebrew prophets Tobit (13:5), Jeremiah (29:14), Ezekiel (11:17), Amos (9:14), Micah (2:12), Zachariah (8:7–8), Isaiah (43:5–7), proclaimed and corroborated in unmistakable language their own understanding of the mission to be undertaken by God's chosen Messiah, i.e., to gather the children of Israel from all the places to which they were dispersed and bring them back to the land of their fathers from which they were exiled, and rule as King over them. This was the Messiah's only proclaimed mission. Any other representation of the mission of the Messiah based upon the fulfillment of the Old Testament and the message of its prophets is pure imagery, i.e., fictional portrayal.

4. Using more poetic language, the Hebrew prophets continue to pour forth encouragement for the suffering sons of Israel, pointing out that their God will not forsake them and in their darkest hour Lord Yahweh will gather them together from everywhere and bring them home to their own soil where his "servant David will be their prince for ever" (Ezekiel 37:15 ff). Similarly, Amos (9:11–12); Isaiah (11:10); Hosea (3:5). The prophetic books do not literally assume a personal Messiah, nor do they identify him. Some of the Rabbis expected a resurrected David, others a Messiah named David, but these are pure speculations.

5. The Old Testament (including the prophetic books) contains no references, express or implied, to the messianic activities of Jesus of the Gospels or Paul—all claims that Jesus displayed attributes and functions foreshadowed in the Old Testament are forced and mistaken. The profane writers, who laid the foundation to Christianity, diligently searched the Old Testament for suitable verses to knit together the needed experiences and stories in the life of Jesus, to give his mission a messianic character and convincingly treated these as the prophecies foretold and the Old Testament fulfilled. Reference is made to selected applicable quotations from the Old Testament books of Prophets, Psalms, Lamentations and Wisdom cited above in Par. 8 of Chapter 26. A few of the compelling verses are repeated:

> "And I saw him coming on the clouds of heaven, one like a son of man … On him was conferred sovereignty, glory and Kingship, and men of all peoples, nations … became his servants." (Dan. 7:13–14).

Copied by the Gospel writers–Matthew 24:30, 26:64 ff; Mark 13:26, 14:62; Luke 21:27.

"Do you take this Temple that bears my name for a robbers' den? (Jer. 7:11).

Copied by the Gospel writers–Matthew 21:13; Mark 11:17; Luke 19:46.

"... They divide my garments among them and cast lots for my clothes." (Ps. 22:18).

Copied by the Gospel writers–Matthew 27:35; John 19:24.

6. There is no affinity between the Old Testament concept of a Messiah and the Jesus portrayed by the New Testament; there is no attribute of the former expressed in the latter. For the Old Testament preaches a human Messiah chosen by God, probably a resurrected David or his descendant, whose avowed mission was to seek the ingathering of the scattered men and women of Israel and lead them to the land their fathers once possessed and rule over them as King, dispensing justice to all. That was all to the Old Testament Messiah. Instead, we are confronted with the concept of the New Testament Messiah, Jesus Christ, the heavenly sent Redeemer who died on the cross and shed his blood for the sins of mankind so that those who believed in him may have salvation and everlasting life, the Son of Man, Lord, Saviour, Word of God, a mystery beyond man's comprehension, Son of The Father equal with him in divinity, preexisting as the only begotten Son of God born from the Father before all times, a heavenly being who sits on the throne of glory, passing judgment on all mortal and spiritual beings, consubstantial with the Father and consubstantial with man, one sole being with two natures, the differences in natures are not suppressed by the union but the meeting of divinity and humanity produces one sole Christ.

From where and from whom did the New Testament writers, the Christian sages, derive the idea of a dying Messiah shedding his blood for the sins of mankind? Many previous historical counter-culture extremists were crucified without others claiming they had redeemed the world. Many men claimed to have cured the ailing and even raised the presumed dead for whom no one claimed divinity. Many spoke wise words, parables couched in wisdom, moral aphorisms and preached justice, for whom no one claimed possession of supernatural powers. It was Paul of Tarsus, the first New Testament writer, author of five, possibly seven, authentic Epistles, who gave the world a Christology according to which the suffering Messiah, Christ Jesus, hastened to shed his blood on the cross to give his life as a ransom for many, so that the believing sinners could have redemption—as foretold in the Scripture (Old Testament). But this is pure mythology—it was not foretold in the Hebrew Scripture. Paul was mistaken.

7. Paul grew up in Tarsus, the center of the Mithraic mystery religion. He absorbed the impact such beliefs had on impressionable and resourceful minds. As a result, his creative and perceptive mind generated an innovative and unique creed which was a blend of the Old Testament and the mystery religions, with greater weight given to the latter. He taught that Christ Jesus, the Messiah, had been crucified and had risen from the dead so that those believing in him would gain salvation and everlasting life. A few of the pertinent verses from his Epistles are cited:

> "Both Jew and pagan sinned … and both are redeemed in Christ Jesus (the Messiah) who was appointed by God to sacrifice his life so as to win reconciliation through faith." (Rom. 3:23–25).
> "God dealt with sin by sending his own Son (Messiah) in a body as physical as any sinful body, and in that body God condemned sin." (Rom. 8:3–4).
> "Christ (the Messiah) died for our sins, in accordance with the scriptures; …" (1 Cor. 15:4).
> "… and there is one Lord, Jesus Christ (the Messiah), through whom all things come and through whom we exist." (1 Cor. 8:6).
> "Christ (the Messiah) redeemed us from the curse of the Law (Mosaic) by being cursed for our sake, …" (Ga. 3:13).
> "We believe that Jesus (the Messiah) died and rose again, and that it will be the same for those who have died in Jesus: God will bring them with him." (1 Th. 4:14–15).

8. Christianity was not a sudden and miraculous transformation. Long before its onset, the Greco-Roman world was one of diverse mystery religions in which sacrifice and resurrection were common themes, from Orphism to Gnosticism. Antioch was one of the earliest seats of Christianity where the celebration of the death and resurrection of the god Adonis took place annually. Adonis suffered a cruel death, descended into

Hell, rose again and ascended to Heaven. In another mystery religion prevalent in Egypt, the death and resurrection of Osiris was celebrated annually. Osiris was slain by the powers of darkness, arose from death and was enthroned in the world of souls to judge mankind. The greatest of the mystery cults, Mithraism, was centered in Tarsus (Paul's birthplace, he was raised among mystery religions which featured dying and resurrected saviours), where Mithras was recognized as the "God of Light" and the "Protector of Truth"; shrines and images of Mithras abounded there and after performing his deeds (sacrifice and resurrection), was said to have ascended to Heaven to become the intercessor for the human race among the gods. The sacrifice and blood motif of Mithraism is evident in the "Paulist doctrines," the basic Christology which preaches that God's love compelled him to sacrifice his only son, so that our sins could be forgiven, washed in the saviour's blood, and the ritual eating of the flesh and drinking the blood of God. These concepts influenced Paul's authentic Epistles and the Gospel writers. Early Christianity converted pagans by absorbing their religions and beliefs.

9. Where did the story of a dying Messiah originate? Right in Judea. There were three Jewish political revolutionaries before Paul and the Gospel writers. They claimed the title of Messiah, were defeated, killed in battle or executed:

(a) Judas of Galilee (6 A.D.)
(b) Theudas (44 A.D.)
(c) Benjamin the Egyptian (60 A.D.)

These three were false Messiahs, contravened the divine and prophetic mission assigned to a Jewish Redeemer, i.e., the ingathering of dispersed Jews. God's hand could not be forced.

10. How have Christian biblical scholars traversed the seemingly unbridgable chasm between the Hebrew Scripture concept of the Messiah and the one triumphantly heralded by the New Testament—Let us hear the version from a very knowledgeable source—the New Catholic Encyclopedia (Volume 9, Pages 719–720, Copyright 1967 by The Catholic University of America, Washington D.C., Reprinted 1981):

"The New Testament writers never raised the question whether the Old Testament prophecies envisaged Christ's mystery literally and in every detail; they simply situated Christ's words and actions in the context of sacred history and thereby brought out the richest meanings of the ancient texts, which they then reapplied to the Christian mystery ... The Apostles' message was living and organic; it grew and adapted itself to various needs under the guidance of the Holy Spirit and in the secure awareness that they had been sent by Jesus to proclaim His mystery to the world. The validity of their use of prophecies rests not on an accurate and erudite knowledge of the Old Testament but in their divine commission as the new spokesmen for God and His Anointed; they were the new scribes, ... who brought forth from their storeroom of memory and understanding, strengthened and enlightened by the risen Lord and His Spirit, things new and old."

The above quoted exposition is anything but lucid and intelligible. It does not bridge the gap. The author/authors are guilty of sophistry.

11. It would be appropriate to conclude with a verse by Isaiah, a major Hebrew prophet, born ca 765 B.C., more than eight centuries before the earliest New Testament writer wrote his first Epistle:

"I, I am Yahweh, there is no other saviour but me, ...—it is Yahweh who speaks—and I, I am your God, I am he from eternity, ..." (43:11–12).

Chapter 30

The Jews Falsely Accused

1. Why the pursuit of doubts of the Christian dogma? What difference does it make to non-Christians whether Jesus was historical? The thoughts which Christian theology evolved, developed and completed—a theology which gave solace and comfort to millions of followers and believers is not dependent on any historical confirmation. Christianity let loose a powerful spiritual force which, in proper hands, led to the uplifting of man's soul, his moral and ethical guidance, piety and purpose in life—all totally independent of the historicity of its founder. Paul, the Gospel authors and other early Epistle writers, depicted a life and activities of Jesus which ended in foreordained crucifixion. There was no need to place the blame for it on the Jewish people in order to enhance its efficacy. Paul originally attributed the crucifixion to evil forces, but later chose to place the blame on Jews; the tenor of early Christian writing is strongly tilted and anti Jewish, nay anti-Semitic, for the Jews are depicted as an evil force whose father is the devil himself. It suited their purpose to do so. Whether Jesus was historical or not makes, however, a radical difference to Jews because they were accused of "deicide"—the killers of Christ, the murderers of the Lord—which accusation is at the root of Christian hostility to Jews, from antiquity to the present day and responsible for rivers of innocent Jewish blood. The charge of deicide against the Jews is a deception. The Rabbis and Jewish elders carry the burden of guilt for being too dull-witted and too immersed in the minutiae of the Law to fully grasp the tremendous historical implications of the false charge of deicide; so with the Tannaim and Amoraim, who were too occupied with the Mishnah and Talmud to pay attention to the potential danger of the Christian charges. Early on they paid no more attention than to any of the many Jewish sects. All this should have changed after the middle of the 2nd century A.D. when the Gospels became known and the Church

319

Fathers began to write—especially that arch-vilifier Bishop Chrysostom (The Jews have assassinated the Son of God); but more about him in a future chapter. Instead they busied themselves with absurd chatter like: "May we produce no son or pupil who disgraces himself like Jesus the Nazarene" (Ber 17b; Sanh 103a), or trivial statements in Toledot Yeshu (The life of Jesus), a tract written in the Middle Ages by various authors all of which was pure fiction. The Rabbis uncritically accepted Jesus' historical existence from the Gospels in the 2nd century A.D. and failed to protect the interests and safety of the Jewish people.

2. The story of Jesus was not original; Paul and the Gospel writers drew from well known pagan sources, the closest to it was the Mithra cult, by no means the only one (Adonis, Attis, Osiris and Dionysus also suffered and died to rise again). Long before the onset of Christianity, the Mithra cult developed in Persia the Sun-God, the deity of light and truth, Judge and Savior, a suffering God, slain and rising again, victorious over death. The Christian Fathers saw in Mithraism the great rival of their own worship, transformed and absorbed it into the Christian religion in due time. It was a test of the survival of the fittest. Christianity copied every one of its rivals and developed special features of its own. A Mithraist could feel well at home with the Christian mysteries of communion, divine sacrifice and resurrection, the mystic rock of Petra (presented as the rock of Peter), the foundation of the Church, the doctrine of the purgatory, the Virgin Mother, the doctrines of the Holy Spirit and Trinity. When Christianity became the religion of the Roman Empire it suppressed Mithraic worship in about 377 A.D.

The Mithraic priestly establishment (nor for that matter any other pagan priesthood) did not make it an article of faith to cast the blame for the divine sacrifice and slaying of their god on any people; they left it as a mystery just like Paul originally did. It was the genius of Christian theology to be the first and only such accuser, but then the Mithraists were not jealous proselytizers.

3. The accusations of Hebrew prophets read like the most acerbic and evil spirited attacks of the enemies of Israel. The early Christian writers and Evangelists, ranging over the Old Testament in search of causes and explanations for the divine rejection of Israel, found a veritable fount: the

worst excesses of anti-Jewish hysteria could find justification in God's curses of the children of Israel, their condemnation and vituperation at the hands of prophets. It was taken as axiomatic that God cursed the children of Israel because they deserved it: "I will inflict terror on you ... I will turn against you ... I will punish you sevenfold for your sins ... I will keep these plagues on you ... I will let wild beasts loose on you ... I will send pestilence among you ... You shall eat the flesh of your sons ... I will pile your corpses on the corpses of your idols ... I will reduce your cities to ruins ... And I will scatter you among the nations ... you shall perish among the nations ..." (Lev. 26:17–38). Who but the Hebrew priests could write such vitriol? Who but the Hebrew priests would subdue the nation into obedience with such terror? With all the tampering and corruption the text of the Pentateuch was subjected to, how could the scribes leave the curses in the text and the Rabbis consider such writings uncorrupted and place them in the canon? They did their share of damage but it did not compare with the bitterness and malevolence hurled by the Hebrew prophets, whose syntax was much superior: "A sinful nation, a people weighed down with guilt, a breed of wrong-doers, perverted sons" (Isaiah 1:4); "Yes, in wickedness they go to any length, ..." (Jer. 5:28); "I am going to scatter them throughout nations unknown to their ancestors ... I am going to pursue them with the sword until I have exterminated them" (Jer. 9:15); "You, you are the burden of Yahweh; ..." (Jer. 23:33); "... I mean to satisfy my fury against them" (Ezk. 6:13); "He is now going to remember their iniquity and punish their sins; ..." (Hos. 8:13); "I mean to break their heads, everyone, and all who remain I will put to the sword; ..." (Amos 9:1); "... I will send the curse on you and curse your very blessing" (Malachi 2:2). Did these prophets speak with the voice of Yahweh who appeared to them in a vision or in a dream? Were they true or false prophets? Were they lying prophets? Can true prophets speak with such unredeeming contumely? Yet the Jews, a "people of the book," have suffered the indignities of their rantings! No wonder the authors of the Gospels, Paul and early Church Fathers considered the Hebrew prophets their vindication of accusations against Jews and their abandonment by God; no wonder they treated the prophets as divinely inspired men, "true Christians," whose prophecies condemned a whole nation as pariahs, outcasts to be trampled on and abused. The Christian writers had an easy time extolling the superiority of Jesus' teaching over the Old Testament and quoted extensively the vilifications of the prophets in their writings, sermons and proselytizing. Did the Jewish people deserve the condemnation of the prophets? Were the charges uttered by angry and embittered men responding to slights or ill-treatment? Why did there not arise anyone to answer them? Why was there no one to point out that the prophets, who claimed authority from God, totally contradicted God's laws on sacrifice as outlined in Leviticus? By not answering the criticism, the Rabbis and sages thoughtlessly placed the writings into the canon without paying any attention to the consequences and this at a time when a defense was still feasible; no response was an implied admission to the veracity of the charges. The prophets gave Christian Jew-haters all the ammunition needed to justify their animus against Jews. Later on, when Christians possessed political power and Jews were dispersed, the latter were powerless to defend against these charges.

4. Ant-Semitism existed long before the onset of Christianity. The events in Alexandria which culminated in 38 A.D. were the most vivid examples. Anti-Jewish feelings were so severe as to result in bloody pogroms. The Jews by virtue of the religion they practiced—a religion that was more suitable to their own country—and living among non-Jews, had to ask for privileges and exemptions so they could comply with the religious requirements, a fact of life that led to resentment. As a consequence of following the ordinances of the Torah, Jews were exclusive; asserted their superiority; were intolerant; quick to take offense; unfriendly to non-Jews; boastful; did not intermarry with non-Jews; did not socialize with non-Jews and kept themselves apart—traits which made them odious. The Jesus sects were known earlier as the Nazarenes, the Galileans and the Brethren, whose followers were Jews. The Nazarenes taught the idea of a divine resurrected Messiah who would return to rectify the injustices of this world, a teaching which appealed to some Jews. The Nazarenes, the early Christians, convinced many Jews to follow their teaching. The Jesus sects were harassed by the Jewish Establishment and it was these excesses that gave impetus to Christianity. When they began converting pagans, they drew on a ready-made reservoir of ill-will which they harbored against Jews from before and facilitated proselytizing after the destruction of the Temple. As Christian proselytizing gained momentum, the hostility to the Jewish Establishment increased to the point where it became irreversible. Paul, the Gospels and the early Church Fathers set the tone of

antagonism toward Jews. Since Jews practiced conversions of their own among Gentiles, the early Church Fathers reacted with bitter opposition and conflict. They generated views, such as, Jews were a people cursed as punishment for their deicide; that they were a people rejected and dispersed for denying Jesus Christ, the Redeemer; that they were outcasts condemned to suffer humiliation and indignities; that they were a people rejected by their God. The hatred of Jews was well established from pre-Christian times. The early Church Fathers were convinced they were the possessors of the only true religion—the Old Testament fulfilled—supported by the Hebrew prophets whom they considered "Christian"; the Law of Moses was replaced, made obsolete and that they were the beneficiaries of a New Covenant with God. Since power, success and growth were on their side, this only reinforced their convictions; the Jews fell on hard times and later completely under the political domination of the Christians. Of all the accusations leveled against the Jews the most damning was the charge of deicide. It was the rallying cry of all Church actions against the Jews; it was unfailing, unredeeming, unforgivable, forever cursing the Jews; it brought forth such accusations as, that the Jews were condemned to eternal slavery as punishment for the death of Christ; they were to find no peace for all times as a consequence of their horrible deed; all violent outbursts against them were justified on the ground of their culpability in crucifying Christ.

The attitude of Gentiles toward Jews was already inclined to be hostile so that Christian proselytizing was made easier. This only increased the animosity between Christians and Jews. The Christians resented any interference in their conversion efforts, in particular, loss of their converts to the Jewish faith; they had to be protected from apostasy. The vilification of Jews by Christians does not exceed that of the Hebrew priests and scribes pronounced in the name of God, which was not challenged; the vilification does not exceed that of the Hebrew prophets pronounced in the name of God, which was not challenged. The Jews were in no position to complain against Christian anti-Semitism (except for the charge of deicide) because these sentiments were expressed before against them by their priests and prophets. The Jews raised no objections against such curses and condemnations. So the tragedy of Jews is this: The Torah, which was foisted on them, made them a peculiar people following peculiar laws. The Laws of the Torah were applicable in their Second Commonwealth when they enjoyed full freedom and the Temple in Jerusalem. Upon the loss of freedom and expulsion, obedience to the Torah adversely affected their conduct, relations with and attitudes toward non-Jews, which generated hostility toward them. The Christian Church, in opposing Judaism, made use of the defamation and condemnations of the Jewish people found in the Torah and prophets which charges had, by appearance, the stamp of divine approval. The charge of deicide was added to give the hostilities between them an aura of incontrovertibility, a nucleus of hate, a rallying point of religious fanaticism.

Summary

(a) For Jews, the Torah is the problem of first instance.
(b) For Jews, the condemnation voiced by priestly writers and prophets and bearing the divine stamp of approval, was the problem of the second instance.
(c) For Jews, the anti-Semitism to which they have been exposed by the charge of deicide, whose meaning and purpose is beyond their comprehension, is the problem of third instance.
(a) For Christians, the false charge of deicide is the problem of first instance.
(b) For Christians, the concept of deicide itself exposed them to assimilating pagan ideas of the death and resurrection of a god and thus committing a deception, is the problem of second instance.
(c) For Christians, the charge of deicide, based upon dubious authenticity which caused rivers of innocent Jewish blood to flow, is the problem of the third instance.

5. The Jerusalem Church disappeared after the destruction of Jerusalem in 70 A.D.; their leaders and members were branded heretics by the Church in Rome because they refused to dissociate from Judaism. They had no part to play in the formulation of Christianity; they had the sole right to the claim of apostolic succession because some of its founders and leaders claimed to be the disciples of the living Jesus. Instead Paul, who separated from them, whose only claim to recognition as apostle was his own version of Jesus' appearance to him (this was his only credential) and who was

determined to bring the Good News and salvation to the Gentiles; who countermanded Jesus' teaching, either deliberately or more likely through ignorance, is regarded the founder of Christianity, par excellence. He rightly realized early on that his evangelizing mission stood to succeed more among the Greek Gentiles than with Jews; his pragmatism was apparent as he aimed to dissociate Jesus' teaching from Judaism, so as to keep it free from Jewish political aspirations; a military Messiah—which was the only one understood by the Jew of his day—meant nothing to Gentiles. Christianity ("It was at Antioch that the disciples were first called Christians" Acts 11:26) was weak in the beginning, disorganized, short of needed funds, pulling in many directions; it needed a rallying cry, a dramatic challenge to its arch-rival: Judaism. Doubtful of its survival and facing an ancient competitor, an established antagonist financially much stronger, found in the anti-Judaism among Greeks and Romans easy converts to Christianity. As an organizational tool, the idea Paul conceived and later followed by the Gospel writers was brilliant: Instead of blaming supernatural evil forces for the death of Jesus—an idea which was of no benefit to anyone and carried the stigma of a pagan mystery—blame was placed on the Jews. Ignored was the previous conception that it was part of a divine master-plan which foreordained the crucifixion and resurrection of Jesus, with all kind of sacrificial blood connotations. The Jews were accused of deicide, murder of Christ, conspiracy in the killing of the Lord. As long as Paul was preaching to the Jews he could not voice such accusations. It was a unique idea in the history of civilization to accuse a whole people, generation after generation, men, women and children, of a crime that was unredeemable, unforgivable and forever cursed the accused and reduced them to suffering and degradation. Paul had no fear of making the accusation—even though he knew it was a deception—since he wrote and preached in countries distanced from the power of the Sanhedrin. Likewise, the Gospel authors (of whom Matthew and John excelled in these accusations) wrote long after the destruction of the Jewish State and in countries where they were free to express anti-Jewish views. As for the early Church Fathers, they enjoyed free reign in magnifying the charges against Jews because the latter were powerless to answer effectively. In short, the Gospels' and Paul's anti-Semitism influenced the early Church Fathers and later became routine up to the present day:

"Then the chief priests and elders of the people assembled in the palace of the high priest, whose name was Caiaphas, and made plans to arrest Jesus by some trick and have him put to death" (Matt. 26:3–5).

"After this Jesus stayed in Galilee; he could not stay in Judea, because the Jews were out to kill him" (John 7:1).

"... in suffering the same treatment from your own countrymen as they have suffered from the Jews, the people who put the Lord Jesus to death, and the prophets too. And now they have been persecuting us, and acting in a way that cannot please God and makes them enemies of the whole human race, because they are hindering us from preaching to the pagans and trying to save them. They never stop trying to finish off the sins they have begun, but retribution is overtaking them at last" (1 Th. 2:15–16).

"Men of Israel ... Jesus the Nazarene ... was put into your power by the deliberate intention and foreknowledge of God ... You killed him, but God raised him to life ..." (Acts 2:22–24).

"... Jesus Christ the Nazarene, the one you crucified, ..." (Acts 4:10).

"From that time Jesus began to make it clear to his disciples that he was destined to go to Jerusalem and suffer grievously at the hands of the elders and chief priests and scribes, to be put to death and to be raised up on the third day" (Matt. 16:21).

"From that day they were determined to kill him. So Jesus no longer went openly among the Jews ..." (John 11:53–54).

"Now we are going up to Jerusalem, and the Son of Man is about to be handed over to the chief priests and the scribes. They will condemn him to death ..." (Mk. 10:33–34).

From the original charge of deicide, the inventive Christian theologians developed rivers of additional charges to satisfy every whim of hatred. The ensuing Church struggle for self-preservation was brutal, the fruits belonged to those who could wield power and use it ruthlessly; it was light-years removed from the spiritual teaching of Jesus, from the Sermon on the Mount. The Church which emerged, the Catholic Church, confirmed the accusation of deicide against the Jews as one of the central themes of its dogma. The historicity of the incrimination was irrelevant.

Chapter 31

The Response of the Church to the Charge of Anti-Semitism

1. The charge of "deicide" was the foundation for the formulation of an unlimited number of false accusations levelled against the Jewish people by the Church and ecclesiastics. The Christians were unhindered by any authority from charging Jews with all manner of crimes nor were they hindered by any moral scruples from doing so, Christian charity notwithstanding. Why should the Christians be charitable towards a people whose own prophets hurled the most outrageous and scurrilous attacks against them? The Jews are forever saddled with their prophets (they thoughtlessly included them in the canon) and have to carry the burden of their verbiage. As for example (in addition to the many cited previously):

> "And death will be preferable to life to all the survivors of this wicked race, wherever I have driven them—it is Yahweh Sabaoth who speaks" (Jer. 8:3).
>
> "Your hands are covered with blood, ..." (Is. 1:15).
>
> "And I will smash them one against the other, father and son together ... mercilessly, ruthlessly, pitilessly, I will destroy them" (Jer. 13:14).

Aware of the fulminations of the prophets, Christian propagandists were aided by these mouthings to rouse hatred of Jews for whom they wished to make life as unbearable as possible so they would accept baptism. The stimulation of hatred suited a purpose: It served as a unifying force for the disparate groups of Christians, whipping up their passions by clerics and strengthen their faith; combat wavering allegiances and inclination towards apostasy; to serve as "scapegoat" for the release of social enmity; but most and above all to show their contempt for and condemn the crucifiers of Christ. To this end, the Jews were the people of the devil, for their father

was the devil and the father of lies, and they worship the devil; their synagogues belong to Satan; they seek to destroy mankind; they are condemned
to perpetual servitude, to be humiliated, condemned to roam from country
to country never to find a home or rest; to be kept in a degraded condition
suitable to a people who no longer enjoy the favor of God, an inferior and
condemned people, a people hated by God; by their suffering a "witness"
to the truth of Christianity, the Old Testament fulfilled, attesting to the triumph of Church over synagogue.

2. The perpetuation of Christian hostility toward Judaism, from generation to generation, is proof of its usefulness in the preservation of faith and
proof of its doctrinal need in demeaning the Jews and thereby elevating the
Church and reinforcing its Creed. Jesus' Passion is the most spell-binding
article of faith of the Christian. For the calumny of Jews in connection with
Jesus' crucifixion, as taught by the Gospels which are infused and perme-
ated with damning ill-will towards Jews, taught to generations of
Christians from early childhood on and up by the Church, are bound to
leave ineradicable feelings of animosity toward Jews; however deeply hidden, will float to the surface without much provocation and do their damage. Thus are Paul and the Gospels interpreted up to the present time; they
are the foundation of theological anti-Semitism. Pope John Paul II declared
in 1990 anti-Semitism "a sin against God and humanity." In 1991 he said,
"In the face of the risk of a resurgence and spread of anti-Semitic feelings
… we must teach consciences to consider anti-Semitism and all forms of
racism, as sins against God and humanity … condemned the wickedness
which made you (the Jews) suffer"; he added ominously, "Unfortunately,
the church can be blamed for this to a certain extent." He admitted that
some aspects of Catholic teaching had in fact fostered anti-Semitism. In the
"Declaration on the Relations of the Church to non-Christian Religions"
promulgated by the Vatican Council II (1965), it is stated: "… The Church
… decries hatred, persecutions, displays of anti-Semitism, directed against
Jews at any time and by anyone." A priest wrote in a Polish newspaper
Gazeta Wyborcza recently that anti-Semitism in Poland (a country with no
more than 5000 Jews out of a population of 35 million, but strongly under
the thumb of peculiar and mind-perverted Polish-bred Catholic priests to
whom anti-Semitism is endemic) is being abetted by the "prejudices and
anti-Jewish propaganda of some nuns, priests, preachers and theologians"

(*New York Times* 11/7/90). Pope John Paul II, a well intentioned good man, is not going to mitigate the fury of anti-Semitism by calling its practice a sin against God; he is closer to the truth by admitting that the Church can be blamed for it "to a certain extent"; he is even closer to the truth by admitting some aspects "of Catholic teaching had in fact fostered anti-Semitism." It cannot be possible that the Pope is unaware of the anti-Semitic content of Paul, the Gospels and the teaching of the early Church Fathers. Is he condemning them all as sinful? Is he condemning some aspects of Catholic teaching taught over 1900 years as improper and sinful? The Polish Catholic priest came much closer to the truth when he blamed "some" Catholic nuns, priests, preachers and theologians, for abetting anti-Jewish propaganda. It will take much more than removing from the Latin liturgy the word "perfidia" (in reference to "perfidious" Jews), because of its mistranslation (should be "unbelieving" Jews),as the well-meaning Pope John XXIII did (Vatican Council II, 1965)—he meant to be more assertive but found great opposition among some of the Cardinals. The Church cannot institute the required reforms which are called for in order to achieve the results desired; it would rock its foundation. As long as Paul, the Gospels and Acts are preached, the problem will be with us; and they will be taught as long as there are Christians. Cardinal Bea and the Secretariat for Christian Unity, delivered themselves of the following declaration (October 28, 1965), citing certain excerpts only: "… True, the Jewish authorities and those who followed their lead pressed for the death of Christ; still, what happened … cannot be charged against all the Jews without distinction then alive, nor against the Jews of today … the Jews should not be presented as rejected or accursed as if this followed from the Holy Scriptures." One must remind the Cardinal that the rejection of Jews and their accursedness does follow from the Holy Scriptures! There is no reassuring hope for improvement in the relations between Christians and Jews when a Vatican placed Cardinal—in the twentieth century—portrays the events of the Passion as an uneducated parochial priest did a thousand years ago. The Cardinal continues: "… in her rejection of every persecution against any man, the Church … (is)… moved … by the Gospel's spiritual love, …."

According to the Cardinal, "all" of the Jewish authorities pressed for the death of Christ, but what happened can only be charged against "some" of the Jews then alive (other than the authorities) and the Gospel's spiritual love did not suffice, historically speaking, to reject "every" of the persecution of the Jews; the Cardinal is guilty of a gross misuse of language and his statement is so shabby as to be beyond criticism; the Cardinal should be made aware that this kind of preaching and logic are no longer in good taste after 19 centuries of Catholic history; Pope John Paul II showed some remorse. The Catholic Church and the Popes are no longer powerful, politically and financially, no longer possess the long arm of the Inquisition, the torture chambers where victims were forced to testify against themselves, the dungeons where prisoners accused of lesser trespass against the Church were left to rot; no longer possess the right of expropriation, the right to declare, denounce and punish heretics at will, sell indulgences, accumulate wealth through fraud, extortion or murder, install or depose monarchs, authorize Crusades, place books on the "Index" of prohibited books the possession of which was considered a mortal sin punishable with death; can no longer control the thoughts of scientists and forbid free speech; can no longer master-mind punitive and murderous expeditions against dissenting Christians (Albigenses, Huguenots, Cathars, Jansenists) against whom they directed the utmost cruelties and total lack of mercy; can no longer order the wholesale burning of Jewish books including the Talmud. These are some of the activities they engaged in for nearly 17 centuries, completely unaffected by "the Gospel's spiritual love". Today, having lost practically all power and influence, the Catholic Church and Popes speak sparingly and softly; affect compromising attitudes and socially proper views; talk of understanding and compassion; of sins against humanity. This is a far cry from the conduct of the Church and Popes in the not too distant past. I shall catalogue their deeds in a later chapter.

3. Christian theologians appropriated the Hebrew Scripture (which they considered divinely revealed and the word of God because they foretold the coming of Christ) as their own since the new faith accepted the Ten Commandments, some of the Law of Moses, the Prophets, the Proverbs and Psalms. The Jews were the Chosen People and had an exclusive Covenant with God; both were based on the faith of Abraham, the first Hebrew Patriarch, to whom God made promises of reward ("your reward will be very great" Gen. 15:1) and was told by God to "Bear yourself blameless in my presence, and I will make a Covenant between myself and

you, ..." (Gen. 17:1–2), a covenant in "perpetuity." In return for God's election and special favors, Abraham was to fulfill the commandment that "all your males must be circumcised" (Gen. 17:11) and that was binding on all of Abraham's descendants; this was an obligation in perpetuity.

The Christians called themselves the "real" Israel, the Covenant with Abraham was replaced by a "New Covenant" ("See, the days are coming— it is Yahweh who speaks—when I will make a new covenant with the House of Israel ... but not a covenant like the one I made with their ancestors ... deep within them I will plant my Law, writing it on their hearts" (Jer. 31:31–34) and the Laws of Moses were replaced by the sacrifice of Christ on the Cross and by the salvation it brought to those who believed in him as the Redeemer. "Christ redeemed us from the curse of the Law by being cursed for our sake ..." (Gal. 3:13); "But now we are rid of the Law, ..." (Rm. 7:6). Justin Martyr, one of the Church Fathers, wrote ca 150 A.D.: "The Church is the true Israel, vindicated against rival sects by being the object of persecution" (57–95 Vol. 8); "He (Christ) has overridden the Law, and cancelled every record of the debt that we had to pay; ..." (Col. 2:14–15). Abraham was declared the first "Christian" because, according to Paul, "Abraham drew strength through faith ..." (Rm. 4:21). The sacrifice of Christ on the Cross replaced the need for all ritual Temple sacrifices. Abraham became to the Christians "our father" (First Epistle of Clement, ca 100 A.D.), his Covenant replaced by a "New Covenant." The Laws of Moses were made unnecessary and abrogated; ritual sacrifices were abolished. The prophets were declared "Christian." The Old Testament was "Christian." Paul, mindful that circumcision was an obligation in perpetuity, was part of the old Covenant, proceeded to dispense with the ritual since it was the greatest impediment to the conversion of Gentiles. Although circumcision is plainly described by God in Genesis 17:11, Paul drew on a verse that was not responsive to the issue of circumcision: "Circumcise your heart then and be obstinate no longer" (Dt. 10:16); similarly, Paul drew on Jeremiah's poetic rendering: "Circumcise yourselves for Yahweh; off with the foreskin of your hearts ..." (4:4). Taking a great leap forward in the art of sophistry, Paul reasons: "The real Jew is the one who is inwardly a Jew, a real circumcision is in the heart ..." (Rm. 2:29). His leaps in thought get progressively longer until he finally concludes: "... if you allow yourself to be circumcised, Christ will be of no benefit to

you at all" (Gal. 5:2–3) and "… since in Christ Jesus whether you are circumcised or not makes no difference …" (Gal. 5:6).

The Hebrew Scripture was the only work the Christians treated as sacred
until the end of the 2nd century A.D., it was their only Bible. They treated
the work as their own, freely purloined excerpts from it, appropriated ideas
from it that suited their cause and claimed it foretold the suffering, crucifixion and resurrection of Christ. The Jews, whose colorful history helped
create the Scripture which they rightfully claimed as their own, were condemned by Christians as incapable of following the commandments and
leaned towards apostasy despite divine threats and warnings by prophets.
The conclusion Christian theologians reached was simple: The Jews just
did not understand their own Bible, misinterpreted its true meaning and
were incapable of following its commandments. The Church Father
Tertullian wrote ca 200 A.D.: "When was there a time when the Jews did
not transgress the Law?" (56–492). In an allusion to Moses' veil (Ex.
34:33–35), Paul explains: "And anyway, their minds had been dulled;
indeed, to this very day, that the same veil is still there when the old
covenant is being read, a veil never lifted, since Christ alone can remove
it" (2 Co. 3:14–15). They misunderstood its hidden meaning in that many
laws including animal sacrifices and circumcision were symbolic; that
Jesus Christ was the answer to the mysteries and messianic prophecies and
that they were rejected by God on account of their apostasies. Even Moses
is declared hostile to the Jewish people: "You place your hopes on Moses,
and Moses will be your accuser" (John 5:45). According to the Epistle of
Barnabas (composed ca 130 A.D., obviously a forgery, but the meaning is
clear and its acceptance by the Christian community total) the Jews never
properly understood the Law or the prophets; in regard to sacrifice, circumcision, and food, they erred from beginning to end. They made the fatal
mistake of a gross literal interpretation of what was meant to be lived spiritually and have been, therefore, justly rejected (57–103 Vol. 2). They ran-
sacked through the Hebrew Scripture, took what suited them, called it
"Christian inspired," discarded and abrogated the rest. The Jews, who
according to the Christian Fathers, lacked the capacity of understanding
their own Scripture because of their pagan hearts: "You stubborn people,
with your pagan hearts and pagan ears. You are always resisting the Holy
Spirit, just as your ancestors used to do … you who had the Law brought

to you by angels are the very ones who have not kept it" (Acts 7:51–52). Why was it necessary to charge them with not keeping the Law, the Law the Jews are said to have misunderstood? Because "In the past they killed those who foretold the coming of the Just One, and now you have become his betrayers, his murderers" (Acts 7:52–53). The fog has lifted. The convenient and ever useful charge of "deicide" is again milked for all its worth. They talk of having abrogated the Law. Did they abrogate the Ten Commandments, prohibition against molesting the stranger, the widow, or the orphan, laws against false testimony, laws for tithes for the support of priests and sanctuary, laws honoring old age, love of neighbor and stranger, laws against sacred prostitution, usurious interest, laws protecting newly married couples, exploiting a hired servant who is poor and destitute? Of course they have not abrogated that part of the Law of Moses.

They appropriated from Scripture those passages that helped them construct their system of ideas, sometimes the connection was illogical just as in the case of the prophetic predictions; they wanted to prove their case and in the process trampled all over the facts. The charge can be made much more justly that the Christians did not understand Jesus' message, for they ignored it over the past 1900 years as the tree they planted began to bear fruit.

4. Jews were persecuted by Christians because they were viewed as a spiritual menace; until the Jews convert to Christianity there can be no "second coming" and until they become Christians there can be no messianic peace in the world. Those who believed in Jesus as the Messiah were the only "true" Jews. But the Jews as rival claimants to the "true" faith would not go away, disappear. The Church and the Christians imposed the harshest measures possible in their path of survival; placed tremendous obstacles in their survival as human beings; destroyed their ability to earn a living; dehumanized them by enforcing the wearing of distinct badges and apparel; made them live in overcrowded segregated parts of the city with limited sanitation; organized murderous punitive pogroms against them on an all too regular basis; imposed confiscatory taxes and levies; imposed obligatory loans and expelled them from the country when they came due; restricted printing of prayer books and building of new synagogues; periodically abducted their children for purposes of baptism, never to be returned to their natural parents unless they also converted; forced

them to attend church services on a regular basis and listen to proselytizing sermons; exposed them to an unpredictable fate depending on the mood of the clergy; expedited the process of baptism by inflicting upon them ever greater suffering; the Church and its clergy invented totally false new accusations of ritual murder, desecration of the consecrated host and image desecration, which required the accusing finger of only one lying scoundrel to set the punitive machinery in motion. The list is endless. And when all these attempts did not accomplish the desired result, the gloves were taken off and the Jews bluntly given the choice: Baptism or death, or in more "humane" cases, baptism or expulsion from the city, county or country; Christianity became an intolerant, a murderous religion. And still the Jews pressed on, their survival instincts not muted, their perseverance not muffled; they found solace and comfort in their prayers, rituals and religious teachings, inspiration in the Torah and Talmud, consolation within their restricted community and synagogues. True, there were conversions, voluntary or under pressure; Jews who for the sake of their family chose baptism or who lost the will to withstand the harassment and did the expected. During the periods of persecution, very few indeed succumbed to sweet persuasion, very few indeed saw the light of the Christian dogma and creed open their eyes to the blessings of the new faith. It was difficult enough to lure Jews away from their familiar community for social and economic reasons, but what faith could Christianity offer them in exchange? That belief in Jesus would destroy death; that salvation was by faith alone; that Jesus, the Messiah, died on the Cross for the sins of mankind; that through his suffering and death on the Cross the Torah was abrogated; and belief in the Trinity—that mystery of mysteries? As a faith, Christianity had very little attraction for Jews who were asked to abandon a religion rich in ritual, antiquity and tradition and the religion of their forefathers. What it could offer them was respite from persecution, murder, expropriation and degradation. But were the benefits real? For as long as he was a Jew and did not attempt to proselytize or blaspheme Christians, he was free from the clutches of that Church-created murderous institution: The Inquisition and the Holy Office. As a convert his views were suspect, it took only one skulking accuser—who may have held a grudge against him—to denounce him, his wife or child to the Inquisition for him to encounter a whole new set of horrors: Imprisonment, loss of property, degrading trials and recantations, undergoing penance; or it could mean the fiery stake. Those Jewish converts, who had second thoughts about Christianity and who showed signs of apostasy, defiantly went to their death by burning. The great pressure put on Jews to accept baptism was not a favorable recommendation for its acceptance since one need not be forced to receive salvation and forgiveness of sins: the compulsion betrayed insincerity. On the other hand, had there been no persecution or degradation, the Jews probably would have converted freely on their own, if for no other than economic reasons, in the struggle to survive and to preserve themselves. Had real Christian charity been shown them, most of the Jews would have long ago merged with other nations and disappeared from the scene as a separate race. For it is a well known maxim that anti-Semitism helped preserve the Jewish nation because it kept them together and in togetherness there is strength; the Jews owe their survival to it as Jews. In the 20th century, despite the Holocaust, "Reform" Judaism has gained greatly in popularity because it removed the strictures of the Law of Moses and also most of the rituals of the Mosaic laws. It is a station of last resort prior to abandoning Judaism, either to another faith or to agnosticism. In the United States, 50% of Jews intermarry with a partner of another faith, and either abandon their religion or pay only token recognition; in a generation or two they will be completely removed from Judaism. In a few generations only the hard core Orthodox Jews will remain faithful to Judaism, a group that is greatly splintered even today and at odds with other segments of the community. In any event, it would constitute a comparatively small percentage of today's Jewish population.

5. The theologically inspired Christian hatred and persecution of Jews aimed at forcing their conversion to Christianity had the opposite result: It preserved the Jewish nation despite millions of forced baptisms and Christian converts and millions of martyrs. But it left its mark also on the persecutors.. It is thankfully a law of human nature that the brutalizer becomes in time himself brutalized by his deeds; the same applies to thoughts. From the Church's axiom that the Jews were made to suffer for their crime of deicide, the teachings of the Church about Jews were justified, there followed rivers of anti-Semitic teachings and deeds which had a dehumanizing, irrational and savage effect upon the Church and the total Church hierarchy; the same ruthlessness they applied against the Jews they let loose against non-conforming Christians. The need of the

Church's elimination of differing views and creeds (starting with the Jews) was rooted in the quest for absolute power. Any opposing views threatened absolute power and, as such, were treated as heretical and enemies of the Church. A power that is absolute must eliminate opposition in order to preserve itself. And what was there to preserve? The Catholic Church created its own aristocracy, maintained by sumptuous wealth and living in luxury which was a reflection of its power; any means of increasing its wealth was considered in accordance with its doctrine and the opposite as the word and work of the devil and condemned as heretical. The Catholic Church was brutalized by its quest for power; became oppressors; persecuted believing Christians just as it did Jews; split the Christians into many sects, each claiming to hold the key to truth; forging, destroying and corrupting documents to establish supremacy. Using the weapon of excommunication and papal ban on whole segments of populations meant the accused could be killed, expropriated, banished and outcast from society with impunity and their persecutor receive the blessings of the Church and total absolution. The future belonged to those who best utilized the concept of mass conversion and mass propaganda, for therein lay power; the papacy had become a means to power and those who sought the office were power-seekers. Greed, rapacity, jealousy, violence and venality were the dominant vices.

6. The Catholic Popes and clergy enjoyed an ascendancy of power and prestige from the 2nd century to the Thirty Years War (1618–1648), which was a religious war until 1635 between the Catholics and the Calvinists; the Catholic Church was on the defensive and tried to prevent the secularization of ecclesiastical property. The end of the war marked the end of the Counter Reformation which was the Church's response to Luther's Reformation (ca 1500). The prestige of the papacy continued to decline from 1648 until the outbreak of the French Revolution in 1789. The conduct of the Popes and clergy from the 9th century to the 16th century was so appalling on religious, moral and ethical grounds as to raise serious doubts in the minds of religious-minded observers—who thought of the Church as sacrosanct—whether it represented the spirit and teaching of Jesus Christ or some evil aberration. The Crusades (1095–1291) which, despite high promises and religious hopes, ended in total disaster, degradation of participants and a large loss of Christian lives, were abetted by

the Popes to embark upon them. Some religious-minded observers began to doubt the validity of the Popes' claims to be God's representative on earth. The Popes and clergy, who were brutalized by the persecution of Jews and all the fabrications of anti-Semitism, applied the same brutality and fabrication of charges against Christians who did not toe the line; some of the pious Christians, exposed to all the greed, pompous luxury, rapacity, violence and venality they observed around them, began to long for a simpler faith without all these impediments, a faith that was more in line with the message of Christ; they began to doubt and to resist; most importantly, they were emboldened in their actions by noticing that the Catholic Church was losing the power it once possessed.

7. The Catholic Church, through its many councils and convocations, was unmolested in inventing suitable fables about matters of faith, creed and dogma because the layman was not given any choice of reading the Bible. First of all, the official Catholic Bible was written in Latin, a language accessible to few laymen, but its reading in any language was expressly prohibited to the laity since about the end of the 11th century; the reading of the Bible by the laity was treated as treason and the punishment death by burning. Those who managed to read the Bible found that it contradicted papal and clerical teachings. With the introduction of printing in the 15th century, the prohibition against reading the Bible in any language was moot; it .was read and a whole series of papal inventions stood naked: indulgences, pilgrimages, masses for the dead, veneration of images; the function of the Popes and priests; the corruption of the papacy began to be noticed. In the 12th century a founder (Waldus) of what was to become a heretical sect of Waldensians, read the Bible diligently and came to the conclusion that it contained no warrant for the purgatory, prayer for the dead, adoration for the crucifix. They rejected all priesthood; repudiated indulgences, transubstantiation and prayers to Saints. The Waldensians were mercilessly persecuted by the Catholic Church with all the means at papal disposal; the harshness of their treatment produced a reaction of sympathy for their martyrdom from among the population and a feeling of revulsion directed against papal oppressors that was to have lasting consequences. Doubts were raised as to the validity of the Pope's claim to be God's representative on earth. The Waldensians were simple Christians who espoused poverty, as Christ preached in the Bible. In Acts 7:52, we

read: "Can you (Jews) name a single prophet your ancestors never perse-cuted?"; again in Matthew 23:34: "... I am sending you prophets ... some you (Jews) will slaughter and crucify. ..." They tried to show that the "evil" Jews persecuted and killed their own prophets because they object-ed to the "Christian" messages they preached. This is not a truthful state-ment. But can one imagine how papal authorities would have treated an Isaiah, Jeremiah or any other prophet who would excoriate them for their moral degradation? They would have pronounced eternal anathema upon them, declared them heretics and handed them over to the Inquisition to be dealt with; not one would have survived.

8. The Christians had many "prophets," those who exposed the perfidy and corruption of Popes and priests, their deviation from the true faith, and exposed the growing contempt for the Church by laymen. These were exceptionally brave men who risked all for the true teaching of Christ, as they perceived it. I shall name a few.

Arnold of Brescia (1100?–1155)

He combatted the corruption of the clergy; demanded that the clergy renounce wealth; attacked the Cardinals for their avarice and hypocrisy, and their Church of God as a den of thieves; attacked the Pope as a man who was concerned with looking after his own wealth. The Pope excom-municated him as a heretic; Arnold refused to renounce his views and met death on the gallows in 1155.

John Wycliffe (1324–1384)

He developed a systematic attack upon the hierarchical system; consid-ered the Church unfaithful to its true mission; opposed vehemently the power of the priests; attacked the papacy as corrupted by power and a blasphemous institution because it did not follow Christ's humility; strongly opposed the doctrine of transubstantiation; denied priestly power of absolution; power to enforce confessions; rejected penances and indul-gences; taught that the Church had no right to worldly power and wealth but was subordinate to the State. He envisioned the time when the priest would devote his task to serving fellowmen. A fatal stroke saved him from the clutches of Rome. Nevertheless, in an act of macabre symbolism, the Council of Constance in 1415 ordered that his bones be exhumed, burned and thrown into the river.

John Hus (ca 1370–1415)

A professor of philosophy at the University of Prague, he discovered Wycliffe through his books and became his follower. He preached that the Pope was not infallible and if he lived in sin he had no right to be one; to rebel against a sinful Pope is to obey Christ; that the Popes have become executioners who burn faithful Christians; he preached against papal simony; he denounced the sale of indulgences; that the Western Church had deviated from its original course. In a book he authored "The Treatise on the Church" he wrote: "No pope is the manifest and true successor of Peter, the prince of the apostles, if in morals he lives at variance with the principles of Peter; and if he is avaricious, then he is the vicar of Judas,.. the cardinals are not the manifest and true successors of the college of Christ's other apostles unless the cardinals live after the manner of the apostles … if he (Christ's faithful disciple) truly knows that a pope's command is at variance with Christ's command or counsel … then he ought boldly to resist it lest he become a partaker in crime by consent … It is clear a pope may err.., he may sin more abundantly … than others, …" Hus was excommunicated and forbidden to preach, but he disobeyed. He was asked and agreed to appear before the council in Constance in 1414 to defend himself and he carried a safe-conduct guaranteeing his return. He was betrayed, abandoned by his patron, convicted of heresy and burned at the stake in 1415. The Church extinguished the voice of a fearless prophet whose martyrdom had far-reaching consequences in the anti-Catholic movement; his martyrdom later caught the attention of Martin Luther: The rest is history.

Girolamo Savonarola (1452–1498)

He entered the Dominican novitiate at Bologna and soon felt a deep distress at the prevalent moral corruption in the Church. He later delivered powerful sermons which betrayed a strong "prophetic" trait. He preached that the Church would soon be terribly chastised for its sins; that the widening corruption of the clergy spread to the highest levels of Church hierarchy. He was sent to Florence, attacked the Roman Court in his sermons and made reference to the Pope's (Alexander VI) scandalous private life. After the Medicis were driven out he became master of Florence; he introduced a democratic government, the best the city ever had. His triumph gave rise to jealousy and the Pope called him to Rome; he found excuses for delay. But his fate was sealed; the papal commissioner came from Rome to

Florence and after an ecclesiastical trial he was handed over to the secular arm to be hanged and burned. The sentence was carried out in 1498.

When the Catholic Church was all powerful, not one critic who dared denounce the licentiousness and depravity of the Popes and clergy managed to escape the executioner, except Martin Luther, By a stint of good fortune and clever political machinations, his friends helped him avoid the tentacles of Rome. But what a critic of Rome he proved to be. Here are some excerpts: "... he ascribes the corruption of the world to the clergy, who delivered to the people too many ... fables of human invention and not the scriptural word of God ... He blamed the preachers of indulgences for taking advantage of the simplicity of the poor ... called a heretic by those whose purses will suffer from the truth ... in the first centuries of Christianity the Roman See had no more authority than several other bishops of the Church ... Rome is a sea of impurity ... a bottomless sink of iniquity ... he (the Pope) is the greatest thief and robber that has come ... and all in the name of Christ ... The Roman Church has become the most licentious den of thieves, the most shameless of all brothels, the kingdom of sin, death and hell ..." (4–345 ff, Vol. VI).

The common trait to all was their perceived corruption and power of Rome, Popes and priests and their abuse of power in the procurement of wealth; resistance against their oppressive rule and rules and irritation with their deviation from the teachings of Christ by the Church hierarchy. The Catholic Church brutalized by its power, persecuting believing Christians for showing any form of dissent whether it represented the teaching of Christ or not. The Pope, like God, could not err and this was dogma; except the Pope was not God. The five named theologians were expertly versed in the New Testament, the teaching of Jesus about love of neighbor and enemy, judging others and observing the golden rule. They lived from the 12th through the early 16th centuries, the period of Dark Ages for Jews, a time of their endless persecution and mistreatment, when outrages were committed against a whole people by Catholic institutions, hierarchy and ordinary Christians which could not have escaped the attention of even the most disinterested observer. We heard murmurs about the wealth of clergy, laments about the Popes not following Christ's humility and mutterings about the scandalous morals of them all. But we heard not one word condemning the maltreatment of Jews as being against the teaching of

Christ—Luther made some friendly remarks early in his life but he made up for it later—not one word of compassion out of their rebellious mouths protesting the humiliation of a people (women, children, elderly, lame and sick) who have done no wrong other than be accused of that accursed "deicide" which washed all humanitarian feelings away. When they remembered the verse in Matthew 27:26 "His blood be on us and on our children!," and in what context it was said, that monstrous invention of Matthew or some forger, their eyes were averted from the misdeeds of the Church; their voices stilled because they espoused causes for which the backing of the papacy and the clergy were essential. Speaking out on behalf of Jews would have firmly aligned the people against the Church, which fostered the ecclesiastical anti-Semitism in the first place. So hypnotized were they all by the homicidal narrative of the crucifixion that they fixed their imagination on just one phase of the dramatic story to the exclusion of all others. The significance of Christ? His parables, curing the infirm, speaking out for the poor, announcing the coming of the kingdom of God? No, just this: He was unjustly condemned by evil Jews, suffered at their hands, was tried, condemned and crucified by them. The "deicide" plays a pivotal role in Christology. So pervasive was the need of the "deicide" episode, so corrupted by it was the spirit of Christ, so totally dependent on it was the story of the Gospels that one can take the following statements as axiomatic:

(a) Christianity cannot be viewed without deicide as taught by the Gospels.
(b) The Jews will always be viewed guilty of deicide.
(c) The Christians will never forgive the Jews for the deicide.
(d) The charge of deicide will always be the core of Christian anti-Semitic hatred of Jews, in varying degrees.
(e) As long as there are Christians, this state of affairs will never change.

No ecumenical council goodwill will alter that; no papal efforts condemning anti-Semitism as a sin against God will alter that; no change of wording in Church liturgy will alter that; no well meaning meetings between Christians and Jews to reach an understanding about mutual problems will alter that. The only course that will alter that is to change the wording in the New Testament to reflect the truth—and that can never happen.

9. Martin Luther, a world-class theologian, a religious reformer, an initiator of the Reformation movement against the Catholic Church, a founder of the Protestant religious movement of immense importance and influence, who championed the cause of spiritual freedom, aware during his lifetime of the vital role he played in this drama and all these world-shaking achievements, could nevertheless unburden himself of anti-Jewish feelings which, in their ferocity, had no precedent:

> "Verily a hopeless, wicked, venomous and devilish thing is the existence of these Jews, who for fourteen hundred years have been, and still are, our pest, torment and misfortune ..." (quoted from 22–167).

> "First their synagogues should be set on fire, and whatever is left should be buried in dirt so that no one may ever be able to see a stone or cinder of it. Jewish prayer-books should be destroyed and rabbis forbidden to preach. Then the Jewish people should be dealt with, their homes smashed and destroyed and their inmates put under one roof or in a stable like gypsies, to teach them they are not master in our land. Jews should be banned from the roads and markets, their property seized and then these ... should be drafted into forced labor and made to earn their bread ... In the last resort they should be simply kicked out for all time" (6–242).

> "It is incomprehensible that Luther ... could repeat all the ... tales about poisoning of the springs, the murder of Christian children, and the use of human blood ... All prayer-books and copies of the Talmud and the Old Testament were to be taken from them by force ... and even praying and the use of God's name were to be forbidden under penalty of death ... Christians were not to show any tender mercy to Jews" (54–550, Vol. IV).

In one of his last sermons he urged his countrymen that if the Jews refused to be converted, they ought not suffer them any longer.

The Catholic Church accepted Jewish converts into its fold; Luther did not. He wanted to be rid of Jews, not to show them any mercy and have them expelled for all time. He could not shake off what he acquired in his youth and lay dormant within him nor the contagion of burning hatred of his milieu and peers. They floated to the surface without much provocation. How warped must be the tree that bears such poisonous fruit.

Chapter 32

The Sayings of Jesus

1. In the New Testament the word "Gospel" does not refer to the written Gospel but to the "good news or good tidings." It is acknowledged by biblical scholars that the canonical Gospels were not intended to be biographical, but a compilation of material which already existed in a set form of popular narratives. Earlier written collections containing both canonical and non-canonical sayings of Jesus were found in papyri in Egypt, dated around 200 A.D. In December 1945, a unique archaeological discovery in Upper Egypt (Nag Hammadi) came upon some fifty-two texts of writings from the early centuries of the Christian era. This collection included early Christian non-canonical Gospels most of which were previously unknown. Although some fragments of a Gospel of Thomas were discovered in 1890, this time, in addition to the full text of the "secret" Gospel of Thomas, there were discovered the Gospel of Philip, the Gospel of Truth and the Gospel to the Egyptians, among others. The Gospel of Thomas was compiled ca 140 A.D. and is said to include tradition that pre-dates the written Gospels of the New Testament. As suspected, these newly found Gospels were suppressed in the early Christian struggle for identity, authenticity and supremacy. "The Nag Hammadi texts, and others like them, which circulated at the beginning of the Christian era, were denounced as heresy by orthodox Christians in the middle of the second century. We have long known that many early followers of Christ were condemned by other Christians as heretics" (58–xvii). In the Gospel of Thomas there are found non-canonical sayings of Jesus, such as:

> "Let him who seeks continue seeking until he finds. When he finds, he will become troubled. When he becomes troubled, he will be astonished, and he will rule, over all things" (32.14–19).

"Jesus said to his disciples, 'Compare me to someone and tell me whom I am like.' Simon Peter said to him, 'You are like a righteous angel.' Matthew said to him, 'You are like a wise philosopher.' Thomas said to him, 'Master, my mouth is wholly incapable of saying whom you are like.' Jesus said, 'I am not your master. Because you have drunk, you have become drunk from the bubbling stream which I have measured out'" (34.30 ff). Note how it differs from Mark 8:27–30!

These verses were ignored by the canonical Gospels which were written by unknown authors who were not witnesses, who did not know Jesus nor anyone who knew Jesus, and who had no first-hand experience with the content of their narrative. Yet Irenaeus, Bishop of Lyons (ca 120–200 A.D.), who was the first Church Father to recognize in 180 A.D. that the Acts and the Gospel of Luke were by one and the same author, made the following astounding statement: "What proves the validity of the four gospels ... is that they actually were written by Jesus' own disciples and their followers, who personally witnessed the events they described" (58–20). Irenaeus was totally mistaken; the Gospels were not written by Jesus' own disciples nor followers. St. Augustine (354–430 A.D.), recognized as the greatest thinker of Christian antiquity, had the following to say about the credibility of the canonical Gospels, "Truly, if it were not for the authority of the Catholic Church, I would attach no credibility to the Gospels" (56–137). St. Augustine therefore based the trustworthiness of the Gospels not on the authority of internal evidence but on the authority of the Church. Porphyry (233–304 A.D.), a Neoplatonic philosopher who also wrote books on Christianity, could not be convinced of the truth of Christian teaching. He wrote a 15 volume work "Against the Christians"— which work was burned by Church authorities as soon as Christianity became the official religion of the State—known to us through quotations and excerpts from his critics. He accused the Evangelists of lying and forgery, of producing a myth and pointed to their numerous contradictions.

2. We can view the Gospels (for that matter the New Testament) from knowing the greater totality of documents not available to earlier theologians or Church Fathers like St. Augustine, a logical thinker of first impression, who begged the question, however, when on the one hand he tried to

prove the Gospels from the authority of the Church and on the other hand tried to prove the authority of the Church from the veracity of the Gospels. The newly discovered Gospels in Egypt have hundreds of sayings of Jesus which were left out of the canonical Gospels, and sayings which were related differently in them. An invisible hand guided the compiler/compilers to the source material from which the first Evangelist (Mark) drew upon; a definite purpose guided them to include some and leave out other sayings of Jesus. According to the Gospel of Thomas, the sayings of Jesus were "secret" and "whoever finds the interpretation of these sayings will not experience death." This is a very strange statement indeed and does not fit into anything we know about Jesus' teaching. Apart from the sayings of Jesus in the Gospels as not being in full agreement with each other, there arises also the question whether they are in agreement with the personality of Jesus as projected and in conformity with the vision modern theologians hold of him. One thing becomes clear: The personality of Jesus as presented by the Synoptic Gospels does not agree with the one presented by the Gospel of John and that various personalities of Jesus emerge from the Gospels which do not harmonize with each other; they are inconsistent and present Jesus' public ministry as not of the same man.

3. A "Jesus Seminar" based in Sonoma, California, formed to counteract literalist views of the Bible, consisting of about 200 members of Christian biblical scholars from all over the country, concluded six years of voting on what the Jesus of history most likely said and did not say. They first met in 1985, met twice a year examining Jesus' sayings in the Gospels and based their conclusions on their own studies and scholarship. This Seminar claimed no divine inspiration but was simply a consensus of expert theologians who were facing troubling questions. In an article in the Los Angeles Times, March 4,1991, some of their conclusions were revealed. They attributed most of the sayings to the theological bias of the Gospel authors or to the beliefs of early Christians. They rejected the authenticity of most of the sayings of Jesus in the Gospel of John except 4:44—that a prophet has no honor in his own country. They accepted as authentic 20% of all the sayings of Jesus in the Gospels, 30% were termed as doubtful and 50% were rejected outright as not authentic. Among the sayings rejected were the following:

"And then they will see the Son of Man coming in the clouds with great power and glory ... I tell you solemnly, before this generation has passed away all these things will have taken place" (Mark 13:26–31).

"Happy are you when people abuse you and persecute you and speak all kinds of calumny against you on my account" (Matt. 5:11–12).

"Now we are going up to Jerusalem, and the Son of Man is about to be handed over to the chief priests and the scribes. They will condemn him to death and will hand him over to the pagans, who will mock him and spit at him and scourge him and put him to death; and after three days he will rise again" (Mark 10:33–34).

This last saying is the third prophecy of the Passion. There are in each of the Synoptic Gospels three similarly worded prophecies. Mark 8:31–32, 9:31, 10:33–34; Matthew 16:21, 17:22–23, 20:18–19; Luke 9:22, 9:44 (somewhat different), 18:31–34; it is assumed that the authenticity of them all is rejected. These are the main sayings of Jesus declaring that he was to be rejected by the elders, chief priest and scribes (all Jews) and put to death; the sense is that it was the responsibility of the Jews. This saying was rejected as not authentic by the Sonoma Seminar; it follows that similar Passion prophecies in Mark, Matthew and Luke were also rejected. They repudiated the authenticity of these verses in a detached manner and failed to draw the significant conclusion: That the failure of the cited verses to pass the test of authenticity could be the first chink in the armor of the sacrosanct deicide accusation and that the Jews, throughout history, were perhaps falsely accused because of discredited Gospel verses. The Sonoma Seminar carried no theological imprimatur; but it did admit some daylight upon ignorance. There is no hope that these verses will be changed or omitted, but the thrust of their work went further than the recent ecumenical message of the Vatican or the apology of Pope John Paul II was prepared to make.

Chapter 33

The Sins of Popes and Church

1. The Old Testament itself could be taken to supply the evidence for the rejection of Jews; that idea is reinforced by the destruction of the Jewish State, Jerusalem and the Temple in 70 A.D. and the total defeat of Bar Kokhba in 135 A.D.; this seemed to the rabbis the end of the road. They lost all their privileges in Jerusalem, the city where their God dwelt and were truly exiled. The only road open to them was the immersion in the study of their sacred Scripture, compose the Jerusalem and Babylonian Talmud and related works to hold the Jews together, and to find secular rulers in the Diaspora who would allow their studies, religious and communal life to find roots until the day of the ingathering of Jews to the Promised Land would take place, as a sovereign people in their own land, their own Third Commonwealth. Unlike during the Babylonian Exile, there were no prophets to secure divine guidance and the Jews rightly felt abandoned. They read and reread God's curses spelled out in Deuteronomy 28:15 ff which were punishment for not obeying the voice of Yahweh and ask themselves to whom, if anyone, was the torch passed who would observe all those commandments and statutes that he enjoined? The curses threatened had been fulfilled; the Jews were accursed, exploited, continually plundered, facing ruin and destruction, scattered among all the peoples from one end of the earth to the other, finding no repose amidst nations and only a handful of Jews were left. There was a new faith gaining ascendancy, which boldly claimed divine revelation, to be the new "Israel" and the beneficiary of a "New Covenant," that claimed and inherited the ultimate test of God's favor: Success. Did the people of the new faith observe Yahweh's statutes faithfully? They claimed that the Jews misunderstood these statutes and therefore could not follow them according to God's wishes. Did they also misunderstand the moral statutes, the Ten Commandments? The followers

of the new faith, the Christians, claimed that Jews spitefully disobeyed the moral statutes, which were clear and distinct in their nature and only reinforced the reason for their rejection. Did the Christians, their religious orders and Church hierarchy, distinguish themselves by displaying an exemplary compliance with God's sacred commandments and moral statutes to justify his favor and their remarkable growth? Did the ecclesiastical branch of the Christian movement distinguish itself sufficiently to set an example to be emulated by the people in general? Did the Jews look with envy at the moral accomplishments of their self-proclaimed successors? Did the Christians adhere to the teachings and precepts of their affirmed Redeemer, Jesus Christ, through whom they sought salvation? All these questions must be answered in the negative. Never in the history of any religion have its functionaries been so far removed from the faith they proclaimed. Never in the history of any religion have its functionaries shown such utter contempt for the tenets of the faith they claimed to profess and in whose name they claimed the right to the office they held. The Church hierarchy mixed faith with power politics and the result was the crassest struggle for power and preservation of the emoluments of office. Anything that stood in their way had to be destroyed; anything that challenged their authority was cynically silenced. No cost was too high, no method too brutal and no violation of rule too extreme to be beyond their call. The Popes, Cardinals, Bishops and priests, not all but too many to count, were guilty of misconduct; of greed, gross moral perversion, wickedness, venality and brutal exercise of power; this went on most spectacularly from the 9th to the 17th centuries. It was only the Church's loss of power that placed a restraint on this activity. For it is only the less powerful facing a greater power who play by the rules, invoke the discipline of conduct and appeal to the sense of decency and lawful conduct; it is only in this modified behavior they seek and find their self-preservation.

2. The Jews, who lived through these turbulent centuries, had to ask themselves how God, who punished them severely for disobeying his voice, could countenance such blasphemies and reward the perpetrators with success and prosperity, a Jewish sign of grace. Was the torch passed to these people? A people whose conduct was far removed from the ordinances of their Redeemer and whose only claim to him was the self-proclaimed right of apostolic succession by which they possessed the Holy See? The Jews

suffered religious persecution at the hands of the Christians for nearly 1800 years; they suffered mostly helplessly, in silence and could only ease the pain through financial means (the importance of wealth was quite evident to them as a means of survival), by bribing the oppressors, the persecutors, and buy some respite till the next time. They had ample opportunity to observe and judge how the new "Israel," who claimed a "New Covenant"—whose founder promulgated the rule of love of enemy, the golden rule, who spoke about the danger of riches, taught compassion for fellowmen, not to judge, not to condemn and to grant pardons—followed the commandments. The Catholic Popes have occupied center stage after the 4th century in the development and history of Christianity and of Catholicism after the Reformation movement of Martin Luther. With the object of rooting out abuses in the Church and freeing it from lay control, there appeared on the scene a man of exceptional ability, Pope Gregory VII (1073–1085), who with his Dictatus Papae, a decree setting forth twenty-seven propositions (1075), a programme of action that was to influence the development and history of the Church for many centuries to come. Here are some of his propositions which proclaimed the autocratic powers of his office:

(a) The Pope can be judged by no one
(b) The Roman Church has never erred and never will err till the end of time
(c) The Roman Church was founded by Christ alone
(d) That no chapter and no book shall be considered canonical without his authority
(e) That a sentence passed by him may be retracted by no one, and that he himself, alone of all, may retract it

These were to set the Church and Pope on a collision course with secular powers. The rest is history.

3. **The Donation of Constantine**

It may seem proper to begin the discussion of the worst abuses of the Church with a forgery. It purports to be a letter written by Emperor Constantine to Pope Silvester I (March 30, 315), wherein Constantine records gifts to the Vicar of St. Peter, among others, of the imperial insignia, the Lateran palace in Rome, the transfer to the Pope of the imperial. power in Rome, in Italy, and all the provinces of the West. As a result of the

Donation, the Pope was supreme temporal ruler of the West. The forged letter was written by Pope Stephen II (752–757) and promptly changed fiction into a world of fact. The forgery was accepted as genuine and was acted upon accordingly. The Donation made the Pope not merely independent of the emperor but in fact his superior. The effect of the forgery was to make the Pope a feudal lord placing great financial value in his office and holding the keys to many revenue producing cities in Italy. Had the forger been clever, his forgery would not have been detected. But he was ignorant. A papal official by the name of Christophorous, the forger, committed two major blunders: (1) He referred to St. Silvester, Bishop of Rome, as "Pope Silvester," nearly 200 years before the title was limited to his office. (2) He made Constantine refer to himself as the "conqueror of Huns," nomadic pastoralist invaders, fifty years before they made an appearance in Europe. A Latin linguist discovered the letter to be a forgery around the middle of the 15th century, but by that time all the damage was done.

4. From the 3rd to the 5th century the name "Pope" (from the Latin Papa) was applied to all Bishops. The title was restricted to the Roman Bishops since the 8th century. The Pope, successor of Peter in his primacy, is the supreme pontiff of the Catholic Church. The Pope can vacate the papacy by resigning, death or loss of reason; he can never be deposed. From the 4th to the 11th centuries temporal rulers exercised their influence and attempted to control the selection of Popes. They sometimes forcibly deposed a Pope not to their liking or forcibly imposed one who met their preference. From the 11th to the 16th centuries the selection was by gradual development of the conclave, the Cardinals doing the voting, with the rest of the clergy and the laity approving the selection. From the 16th century to the present, the method remained the same except the conclave, during the selection, was secluded and the secular influence gradually eliminated. The election of Popes is based on a system of Church canon law.

5. In the following pages I have attempted to give a short outline of the history of the Popes from 891 A.D. to 1045 A.D., when the first converted Jew reached the highest office of Christendom; an outline which presents the papacy as completely detached from the teachings of Christ. Here is Christ's representative on earth fighting brutal primitive battles devoid of any moral and ethical considerations.; treating his fellow Christians with utter contempt; hiding degeneracy and all sorts of crimes behind a facade of pomp,

ritual and ceremony; practicing deception upon the common people. The Church and papacy lay claim to the direct line of apostolic succession, a divinely ordained pastoral mission to preach, baptize, forgive sin and teach men to observe all that Christ had commanded, for Christ promised that he would be with them " … always; yes, to the end of time" (Matt. 28:20).

Pope Formosus (891–896) The only fault alleged against him was ambition and he made many enemies. He died of heart attack or was poisoned; was subjected after his death by Pope Stephen VII to the most macabre humiliation.

Pope Boniface VI (April 896) Prior to his election was twice defrocked for immorality by Pope John VIII; was assassinated within 15 days by orders of Agiltruda, an ambitious aristocratic woman of Spoleto. She installed her own candidate.

Pope Stephen VII (896–897) He suffered from uncontrollable rage. His hatred for former Pope Formosus caused him to organize a mock trial after he had his body disinterred, clad in full papal vestments and propped up on a throne, solemnly arraigned on charges of perjury. The corpse was then stripped, the three fingers of benediction hacked off, his body dragged through the palace and then thrown into the river Tiber by the mob. The mob turned against Stephen, stripped him of his papal insignia, had him imprisoned and strangled.

Pope Romanus (Aug.–Nov. 897) He was Pope for 4 months only, was deposed by pro-Formosan faction.

Pope Theodore II (Nov. 897) Pope for only 20 days; the cause of his early death is unknown.

Pope Benedict IV (900–903) Murdered after 3 years in office.

Pope Leo V (Aug.–Sep. 903) After a reign of only 30 days, there was a palace revolution; he was thrown in jail by Cardinal Christopher. Cardinal Sergius also aspired to be Pope. With the assistance of Theodora, a woman of the powerful family of Theophylacts, he imprisoned Pope Christopher and had both Leo and Christopher strangled in prison and also those Cardinals who opposed him.

Pope Christopher (903–904) Murdered by Cardinal Sergius.

Pope Sergius III (904–911) Arranged for the murder of Pope Leo and Pope Christopher. Took as mistress the 15 year old Marozia, Theodora's daughter, by whom he had a son, the future Pope John XI.

Pope Anastasius III (911–913) Chosen by Theodora. Two years later she had him murdered.

Pope Lando (913–914) Chosen by Theodora. One year later she had him murdered.

Pope John X (914–928) Theodora installed Bishop John of Ravenna, her lover of many years, as Pope John X. He was deposed, imprisoned. and suffocated by a pillow at the instigation of Marozia.

Pope Leo VI (May.–Dec. 928) He owed his election to Marozia who within a few months arranged for his disappearance.

Pope Stephen VIII (928–931) He owed his appointment to Marozia. In 931 he disappeared.

Pope John XI (931–935) Son of Marozia and Pope Sergius III, a youth in his early twenties, installed through the influence of his mother; in 932 Marozia's other son Alberic II gained control of Rome, had both his mother and his step-brother imprisoned.

Pope Leo VII (936–939) He owed his elevation to Alberic II, prince of Rome. He appointed Archbishop Frederick of Mainz apostolic vicar and legate for all of Germany and encouraged him to expel Jews who refused to be baptized.

Pope Stephen IX (939–942) He owed his elevation to Alberic II. Participated in a conspiracy against Alberic II, was imprisoned, brutally mutilated and died of his injuries.

Pope Marinus II (942–946) He owed his elevation to Alberic II. Never dared to do anything without the prince's instructions.

Pope Agapitus II (946–955) He owed his promotion to Alberic II. When Alberic lay dying, anxious that all power in Rome spiritual as well as temporal should be concentrated in his family, he assembled the nobility, clergy and the Pope, and made them swear that after Pope Agapitus II's death, they would elect his bastard son Octavian as supreme pontiff and that the papacy would become a hereditary dynasty.

Pope John XII (955–964) Became Pope at the age of 18, the bastard son of Alberic II, he showed disinterest in spiritual matters, addicted to boorish pleasures and uninhibited debauched life, surrounded by boys and girls his own age; the Pope's palace frequented by prostitutes and gossip had it that he turned the Lateran palace into a brothel. Deposed by Otto I, Emperor of Germany, who appointed Pope Leo VIII as his successor.

Pope Leo VIII (963–965) A layman, appointed Pope by Otto I, rushed through the lower orders in a single day under revised rites introduced by Otto I; Pope John XII was deposed but not yet dead, so Leo VIII's legitimacy was contested. When the emperor and his forces left Rome, violent disturbances forced Leo VIII to seek refuge in the imperial court; this enabled Pope John XII to resume the reign of authority. He deposed and excommunicated Pope Leo VIII as a usurper of the Holy See, guilty of perfidy. John XII took his revenge by mutilating and beheading some of the clergy and nobility.

Pope Benedict V (964–966) Emperor Otto I preferred Pope Leo VIII; marched on Rome and laid siege to the city notwithstanding the anathemas Benedict V hurled at the besieging army from the walls. Benedict V was forced to yield, condemned as a usurper, stripped of his pontifical robes and insignia and had the pastoral staff broken over his head by Pope Leo VIII himself as he lay prostrate; he was exiled to Hamburg.

Pope John XIII (965–972) Elevated by Emperor Otto I; he was hated by the faction-riven city and it revolted. John XIII was assaulted, imprisoned and banished to Campagna. He was restored by Otto I.

Pope Benedict VI (973–974) He was seized by the rebels and imprisoned to await trial. A newly elected (June 974) and consecrated Pope Boniface VII promptly had Pope Benedict VI strangled.

Pope Boniface VII (June–July 974) Horror at his murder of Pope Benedict VI turned the populace against him and he soon had to take refuge in a Roman stronghold. The stronghold was stormed but Pope Boniface VII escaped to south Italy with part of the papal treasures.

Pope Benedict VII (974–983) He excommunicated Pope Boniface VII. Boniface VII carried out a coup in the summer of 980 which compelled Pope Benedict VII to leave Rome. With the help of the emperor, Benedict VII was restored.

Pope John XIV (983–984) Pope Boniface VII returned with the help of the powerful Roman Crescentii family, seized Pope John XIV, brutally assaulted him, formally deposed him and flung him into prison, where he died four months later of starvation.

Pope John XV (985–996) His installation was supported by the powerful Crescentii family. When his support waned, he was persecuted by Crescentius and hated by his clergy for his avariciousness and nepotism. He was forced to seek refuge.

Pope Gregory V (996–999) He was a 24 year old relative of Otto III, the first German Pope formally elected; when Emperor Otto III left Rome, resentment aroused in Rome by the appointment of a foreign Pope caused a revolt and drove Pope Gregory V, stripped of everything, out of the city. On the pretext that the papal throne was vacant, Crescentius and his adherents had their protégé elected and installed as Pope John XVI. The emperor had Pope Gregory V restored and Pope John XVI, already mutilated, was deposed and imprisoned in a monastery. His unexpected death in 999 started rumors that he had been poisoned.

Pope John XVI (997–998) Allowed himself to be elected and installed Pope while another Pope Gregory V was still installed. He was excommunicated after he fled under pressure, was captured by forces of Gregory V, blinded and badly mutilated in his nose, lips, tongue and hands. He was then paraded around the city, sitting back to front on an ass. A formal trial was held under Pope Gregory V, he was condemned, deposed, degraded from his priestly rank. Broken and humiliated, he was shut up in a Roman monastery.

Pope Silvester II (999–1003) The first Frenchman to become Pope; he was an intransigent champion of the traditional rights of papacy, denounced simony and nepotism and called for celibacy. He was murdered.

Pope John XVII (May–Nov. 1003) He was poisoned within 7 months.

Pope John XVIII (1003–1009) Forced to abdicate shortly before his death.

Pope Sergius IV (1009–1012) A violent political upheaval took place in Rome at that time; the disappearance of both Pope Sergius IV and Crescentius, his sponsor, from the scene within less than a week of each other and the immediate election of a Pope of the rival Tusculan family, gave rise to the suspicion that neither man died a natural death.

Pope Benedict VIII (1012–1024) In a struggle between two rival families, the Crescentians elected one Gregory and the Tusculans elected a layman who assumed the name Benedict VIII.

Pope John XIX (1024–1032) A layman, obtained succession by lavish bribery; elevated from layman to Pope in a single day.

Pope Benedict IX (1032–1044), (March–May 1045), (1047–1048) A layman in his twenties, his personal life was scandalously violent and dissolute; he practiced bisexuality and sex with animals. He was the only Pope to hold office at three different times. An insurrection at Rome and resentment at his loose life forced him to abandon the city. Pope Silvester III was installed. Benedict IX, who had never been deposed, promptly excommunicated Pope Silvester III, expelled him from. Rome and resumed the papacy, which lasted less than two months. In May 1045 he made out a deed of abdication in favor of John Gratian, a Jewish convert to Christianity (1030), by accepting a large sum of money which was represented as an inducement to step down. John Gratian was then elected and took the style of Gregory VI.

Pope Gregory VI (1045–1046) An elderly man respected in reforming circles, son of Baruch Pierleoni (his name before his conversion), the founder of a wealthy Jewish banking family which lavishly supported the Church financially, became Pope after a huge sum of money changed hands and the people of Rome had been bribed. A synod accused him of simony, he acknowledged his culpability and voluntarily laid down his office.

There were then three consecrated Popes living in Rome: Gregory VI, Benedict IX, Silvester III.

In the above short history, the Popes may appear as solitary figures who acted and fought their disputes without much assistance. That impression is wrong. The papal Curia, in the early stages of its development, was quite complex. The Popes exercised their rule through synods, composed of the clergy of Rome, where senior priests "cardinals," priests and deacons assisted in the administrative functions and were consulted; they numbered in the thousands. The Lateran palace teemed with factions, plots and conspiracies, some of them subdued, others violent.

6. Salvian of Marseilles, (ca 400–ca 480) an ecclesiastical writer, inveighed against avarice which he saw widespread among Christians, adding: "Besides a very few who avoid evil, what is almost the whole body of Christians but a sink of iniquity? How many in the church will you find that are not drunkards, or adulterers, or fornicators … or robbers, or murderers …?" From one who was favorably disposed to the interests of the Church this was serious criticism. After the early centuries of Christianity things did not get better. Salvian's criticism would be appropriate for most of the Popes between the 9th and the 11th centuries, and then some. Christianity, the Church and clergy, did not get off to a good start. After appropriating and arrogating to themselves the Hebrew Scripture and plagiarizing from the Jews their ethical teachings; after the writing of Paul and

the canonical Gospels under mysterious circumstances and after locating the tomb of St. Peter on the Vatican Hill under even more mysterious circumstances, they proceeded systematically to destroy and burn pagan records which could trace the source of their theology, records of other Christian sectarians or heretical sects, so as not to "confuse" the faithful and obliterate all opposition; they burned libraries, irreplaceable collection of books, as the one in Alexandria, so as to eradicate any traceable record of conflicting ideas; and when in the early 4th century they became the exclusive religion of the empire, they proceeded to eliminate their opposition by brute force so as to gain and maintain sole primacy. They resorted to fraud and forgery of documents on a massive scale to give their doctrines and history a sense of credibility that was not there. The Popes and Curia, while concerned with creed and dogma, showed greater concern for the emoluments of office; obtaining and maintaining wealth and power; fighting for the exclusive use of it and preserving the rich gifts and rewards the office offered in the aristocratic standard of living. The Holy See was constantly in turmoil, it injected itself as prime mover in the political struggle and machinations of the day; arranged and rearranged emperors and kings and, in time, became consumed by the power struggles which ensued. It could play the game of checks and balances for only as long as it took the secular rulers to become aware of the power of their own armies and the emptiness of the Popes' curses, anathemas, interdicts and excommunications. As the secular rulers' power increased and the Popes' diminished, they had to play the political game of shifting alliances, all to the detriment of the Christian faith which suffered as a consequence of needing to satisfy an insatiable thirst for money. Understandable to secular rulers as the name of the game, it was nevertheless degrading and annoying to the faithful adherents who were mostly poor people and were asked to furnish the bulk of the money. The privileges, which the Catholic Church and clergy claimed for itself, could not be justified in the light of the teaching of Jesus and in the light of the ever more noticeable moral degradation of the Popes, the Curia, Bishops and priests. The schism and opposition which developed were treated as a prime threat to its very existence and opposed forcefully and ruthlessly with every means at its disposal. Armies of secular rulers were used to obliterate opponents; the office of the Inquisition was set up to control and punish those who strayed from dogma and in the process enriched the Holy See with the properties confiscated from the condemned. The Spanish monarchy was able to finance the expeditions of Columbus in 1492 with funds expropriated from Jewish-Christians whom the Spanish Inquisition condemned for their "relapse." But nothing, absolutely nothing, exceeded the evil and monstrous deeds of Popes as the order to burn witches (300,000 of the unfortunates were ultimately executed), totally innocent people as we assuredly know today, who died for nothing and were sacrificed on the altar of Church stupidity, vindictiveness, corruption and sheer terror to keep the laity in check. While increasingly preoccupied with keeping Christians under control, and watching zealously and with suspicion any movement which questioned the authority of the Church so as to extinguish the flame of dissent before it could spread, the Popes, Church, Bishops and priests never relaxed or eased up in their efforts to make life for Jews as miserable as possible, leaving no stone unturned in devising new means of persecution and suffering for the "murderers" of Christ.

7. In the realm of money, the Church was pre-eminent for everything in it was sold for money: The papacy, indulgences, pardons, masses, ceremonies, benefices, bishoprics; bishoprics were anxious to increase their income and so were priests through the sale of "holy remains" of which there was a never-ending inventory. Except for the few of the clergy who led an ascetic life dedicated to Christ, the great majority aimed for the good life—wine, women and song—and that required money; money, lots of it, was also required by the Popes to play power politics, pay or bribe armies and fund construction programs behind which to hide their pained existence. Papacy reached the very bottom of the pit with Pope Alexander VI. In his early forties, Cardinal Borgia was one of the richest men in Europe. By bribing 15 Cardinals with what was for them a large fortune, he secured the papacy for himself. He was Pope from 1492 to 1503. As Cardinal, he lived an openly licentious life, which he continued after he became Pope. He fathered seven children by two mistresses (alleged to be mother and daughter), two of his children were to gain notoriety: Cesare Borgia and Lucrezia Borgia. A major Italian historian, Francesco Guicciardini, commented on Pope Alexander: "But these virtues were bound up with far greater faults. His manner of living was dissolute. He knew neither shame nor sincerity, neither faith nor religion. Moreover, he was possessed by an insatiable greed, an overwhelming ambition and a burning passion for the

advancement of his many children who, in order to carry out his iniquitous decrees, did not scruple to employ the most heinous means" (59–173).

He had a consuming passion for gold, women and the enrichment of his relatives, especially his children; his papacy had become a means to power and wealth. The ambitions of Alexander and his son Cesare, which involved the crushing of great Roman families, required enormous sums of money which were raised by assassinations (poison was the favored means), and imprisonment of opponents followed by seizure of their property and by the creation of Cardinals who paid a high price for their elevation. The College of Cardinals was now dominated by Spaniards of whom eight were related to Pope Alexander VI. In a clash with his Florentine moral critic, the Dominican friar Savonarola, who severely castigated his debauchery, Alexander had him excommunicated (Savonarola responded that anyone who accepted his excommunication as valid was a heretic); was later tried in Florence since he refused the Pope's invitation to come to Rome, sentenced to death, hanged and burned. In a possible ironic ending, Alexander and Cesare met their death by mistakenly taking the poison intended for their next victim. Despite Alexander's seeming effort to outstrip any of his predecessors in villainy and sex perversion, he was unable to do so in the case of the piratical adventurer Baldassare Cossa, who became Pope John XXIII (Antipope 1410–1415). He was an "unblushing libertine," engaged in "dubious" money-raising schemes before he became Pope; he seduced no fewer than 200 women in what was said to be his "harem." When brought before the Vatican Council in 1415, after a trial at which he was accused of simony, perjury, fornication, adultery, theft and murder, he was deposed and held in strict confinement. Machiavelli commented: "We Italians are more irreligious and corrupt than others ... because the Church and its representatives set us the worst example ..." (8–23).

The Popes and clergy were consumed by the passions of this world, in league with secular rulers and guided by secular rules of the game; for a time in possession of a monopoly of power and privileges, surrounded by riches just for the asking, no different in morality than their secular counterparts, a world kept under control by bluff, fakery and deception. The world was in vain thirsting for spiritual guidance to come out of Rome.

Chapter 34

The Church Horrors

1. The Crusades: The First Crusade (1095–1099)

The Crusades were military expeditions organized by the Church for the liberation of the Holy Land from the infidels, who were interfering with Christian pilgrimages to the Holy Sepulcher of Christ in Jerusalem and for the liberation from the dangers and molestations experienced by pilgrims and the desecration of the holy places. Pope Urban II (1088–1099) launched an appeal to Christian knights to cease fighting one another and to deliver Jerusalem from Moslem domination. The war to defend Christian society was a holy enterprise, so to this end the Pope granted plenary indulgence to those who undertook to aid the Christian cause in the East, granted freedom to the serfs for the duration of the Crusade, freed prisoners, exempted the people from taxes, death sentences were commuted, granted debtors moratorium on payment of debts and interest, granted the participants a license to steal, rob and plunder the Moslem wealth for which deed he exonerated them in advance. Another cause advanced for the Crusades was more mundane: it was the Venetians' and other Italian port cities' desire for expanding their shipping trade, secure eastern Mediterranean markets for their export and to increase their commercial power. The port cities conducted profitable trade and the holy Crusades were another vehicle that could be used to penetrate the newly opened markets. Another more cynical cause advanced for the Crusaders was the Pope's desire to rid the West of turbulent knights, to stop their wanton pillaging and slaying of each other and instead channel their energy to do God's work. The Pope also saw an opportunity of uniting the Christian forces and strengthening his own standing. He did not foresee that failure of the Crusades would seriously damage the prestige of the Church and raise the prestige of another religion. If before the Crusades

359

"The love of God and of fellow Christians had proved an ineffective deterrent to aggression" (18–167), the lifting by the Popes of restraints on the behavior of knights and peasants in fighting the infidel would most assuredly bring out in them the worst case of barbaric conduct. Ill equipped, short of provisions, they lived off the land moving like a swarm of locusts among Christian communities, cursed and condemned by them. Impatient to wait for the slaying of the Muslim till they reached Jerusalem, they recognized the infidel close by in the Jew and before they got out of France and Germany, the worst part of the mob led by some demented clerics raised the cry "The Jews have crucified our Savior, therefore they must acknowledge him or die", and proceeded to commence with the Jews the holy work of plunder and murder. Thousands of Jews were slain or converted to Christianity at the point of the sword and their property plundered. Some of the citizens tried to protect them from the mob by hiding them in their homes till the locust passed. After many tribulations, the Crusaders led by Count Bohemund and Duke Godfrey conquered Jerusalem in 1099, and the scene was described by an eyewitness priest, "… wonderful things were to be seen. Numbers of the Saracens were beheaded … others were shot with arrows, or forced to jump from the towers; others were tortured for several days and then burned in flames. In the streets were seen piles of heads and hands and feet. One rode about everywhere amid the corpses of men and horses" (4–592, Vol. IV). They were "wonderful" things indeed! "Other contemporaries contribute details: women were stabbed to death, suckling babes were snatched by the leg from their mothers' breasts and flung over the walls, or had their necks broken by being dashed against posts; 70,000 Moslems remaining in the city were slaughtered. The surviving Jews were herded into a synagogue and burned alive. The victors flocked to the church of the Holy Sepulcher … they wept with joy … and thanked the God of Mercies for their victory" (4–592, Vol. IV).

The Second Crusade (1146–1148) was led by the rulers of France and Germany, who made an unsuccessful attempt to capture Damascus; they failed in the attempt and returned home without accomplishing anything.

The Third Crusade (1189–1192) was led by three sovereigns of Germany, France and England. Their sole achievement was a five year truce with Saladin, sultan of Egypt and Syria (capturer of Jerusalem), who allowed Christian pilgrims free right of entry into Jerusalem. They also freed the town of Acre.

The Fourth Crusade (1202–1204) was demanded by Pope Innocent III (1198–1216); it was meant as a campaign against Egypt and towards Jerusalem. He enlisted the aid of the Venetians for transport of the troops and horses, but the Venetians had no intention of fighting Egypt with whom they had trade alliances. It was, in fact, no Crusade at all but a fight of Christians against Christians through the conspiracy of the Venetians and the business stupidity of the Crusaders' leadership who were maneuvered into what turned out a total side-show for them, but the main show for the Venetians. The Venetians were eager to complete the conquest of the Dalmatian port-city of Zara which had recently passed into Hungarian possession and was competing with Venetian navigation. When Pope Innocent III had learned that the conquest was in defiance of his strict orders to the contrary, he managed to excommunicate the whole expedition, including the Crusaders! When he realized that the Crusaders had been the victims of blackmail, he forgave them but did not lift the excommunication of the Venetians, so little did the latter care about the Pope's doing when it was a matter of business priorities. The Venetians originally demanded a payment of 85,000 marks of silver to furnish the required shipping. This the Crusaders were unable to raise; thereafter, the Venetians could call the tune and they did. They lusted for the conquest of Constantinople which would enlarge and strengthen their trading privileges throughout the Byzantine Empire. There were some murmurs among the Crusaders about fighting Christians not Moslems, but hefty Venetian bribes took care of that. The Crusaders reflected on the riches of Constantinople and looked forward to the loot. The Venetians had the finances and were therefore in control. When the Pope objected to the prospect of Christian fighting Christian, he was quickly calmed by the expectation of submission of the Church of Constantinople to Rome. The victorious Crusaders, after some delay due to power-politics, passed like consuming animals through Constantinople. Parties of drunken Crusaders constantly pillaged Christian villages, the leaders and Venetians divided the city and empire among themselves, leaving only one quarter to the newly installed emperor. Constantinople had made no provisions for a defense since the reigning emperor did not expect an attack from his Christian brethren. But the Crusaders and their

Venetians (who were masters at picking the right loot) told their soldiers they might "spend" the next three days in pillage: "The sack of Constantinople is unparalleled in history … It was filled with works of art that had survived from ancient Greece and with the masterpieces of its own exquisite craftsmen. The Venetians … wherever they could seized treasures and carried them off to adorn the squares, churches and palaces of their town. But the Frenchmen and Flemings were filled with a lust for destruction. They rushed in a howling mob down the streets and through the houses, snatching up everything that glittered and destroying whatever they could not carry, pausing only to murder or to rape, or to break open the wine-cellars for their refreshment … Nuns were ravished in their convents … Wounded women and children lay dying in the streets. For three days the ghastly scenes of pillage and bloodshed continued, till the huge and beautiful city was a shambles" (60–123, Vol. III). Christian fighting Christian. Needless to say, not a word was thereafter said about fighting Moslems in Egypt or Jerusalem. In spite of all this, Pope Innocent III made the title of Vicar of Christ current, given not only the Universal Church to govern but the whole world.

The Fifth Crusade (1217) left Germany, Austria and Hungary under the Hungarian King Andrew. They got as far as Egypt; the war went badly for the Crusaders and an eight-year truce was signed. The Crusaders were required to leave Egyptian soil.

The Sixth Crusade (1228–1229) was led by Frederick II, Emperor of Germany and Italy (while excommunicated). Succeeded in signing a treaty with al-Kamil, leader of the Saracen army (1229) by which the latter ceded to Frederick Acre, Jaffa, Sidon, Nazareth, Bethlehem, all of Jerusalem except the Dome of the Rock enclosure. After Frederick's departure, the Christian nobility of the Holy Land waged war against Egypt, lost in 1244, the Egyptians and Turks recaptured Jerusalem, plundered it and massacred a large number of Christians.

The Seventh Crusade (1248–1254) was led by Louis IX of France. He did not reach Jerusalem; was defeated at Mansura (Egypt); fled in rout; 10,000 Christians were captured and later slaughtered or enslaved.

2. The Crusades, after resulting in considerable loss of life, achieved nothing; they were total failures and their theological effect was negative.

The undisputed leadership and wisdom of Popes in matters of spiritual guidance were justifiably questioned; the superiority of Western Christian emperors blessed by the Popes in their enterprise over infidel warriors was debunked. Christians recognized painfully that there were non-Christian civilizations second to none; that they did not hold a monopoly of divine guidance and that the followers of another faith could possess "Christian" values of humanity and loyalty. The Popes learned from the Crusades the collection of levies on clerical incomes. Lastly, the Fourth Crusade and the destruction and plunder of Constantinople so enraged the Greeks that any union or rapprochement between the Eastern and Western Churches was no longer possible. The Crusades demonstrated that the Pope can be lied to with impunity; that excommunications so often used against Christian rulers had lost their efficacy; that an excommunicated monarch could lead a Crusade; that the Venetians could blackmail a Pope and their countrymen excommunicated en masse without any ill-effects.

3. **The Albigensian Heresy**

The failure of the Crusades brought doubt to the fore about the divine support of the Christian Church. It was not a matter of Latin liturgy, which was not comprehensible to the layman or the intricate ecclesiastical theology that was beyond his understanding, but the simple fact of an army of men on a Church-blessed mission utterly failing in their enterprise; a set of facts the ordinary illiterate peasant could understand and draw simple conclusions from. What were the conclusions? At first tentative and subdued, only a glimmer of doubt that perhaps all the sacerdotal pomp and Latin mumblings were just that. The wealth flaunted by the prelates was viewed with suspicion by the laity as not being apostolic and therefore not Christian; most sectarian movements began as a protest against the riches of the clergy. In the early 13th century in southern France, getting its name from the town of Albi, the Albigensian sect of Christians gained prominence. It was based on the doctrines of the Cathari whose beliefs were founded, in part, on the yearning to return to early primitive Christian beliefs. There was something sanctified about poverty because Christ preached its virtues. The Albigenses believed in Neo-Manichaean dualism that professes two principles—good (God, spirits) and evil; all matter was identified with evil, including the consecrated Host of the Eucharist; all sexual relations were sinful; they rejected the sacraments, the Mass; taught love of their enemies; care for the sick and poor. Since matter was evil they did not believe in hell and purgatory; the soul had to be purified on earth to be saved, and every soul would be saved in time, if need be, after several transmigrations. Pope Innocent III (1198–1216) used persuasion in the beginning—unsuccessfully—and when a papal legate was slain by a knight belonging to the sect by then declared heretical, the Albigenses became the target of a ruthless Crusade commissioned by the Pope and undertaken in 1209 by a Simon de Monfort. He conveniently combined allegiance to the Pope and the Cross with the more mundane greed for land the Pope offered him as a reward. In pursuit against the declared heretics and in furtherance of the orthodox Christian faith, the Crusaders slew 20,000 men, women and children; blinded and otherwise mutilated all prisoners, all Christians, in the town of Beziers; assaulted town after town and the same fate awaited all inhabitants, devastating the whole country-side with death and destruction, slaying indiscriminately all without making any distinction between the hunted heretics and those of true Catholic faith who lived among them peacefully; many thousands of the latter were slaughtered because the marauding troops were told not to make any distinction between them. In the end, the orthodox Church succeeded in extirpating by brute force its Christian opponents. But the Albigenses did not die in vain. The "heretical" ideas were not eradicated but the flame was lit to advance the sectarian ideas at another time. Bible reading in the vernacular by the laity without the benefit of a priest was not too far away. The Church as it was constituted, had not much choice in the matter; had to preserve itself against forces that threatened its very existence and had no choice but to proceed with brutal force to extirpate the dissenters. The Pope, like any other secular monarch, had to reward the arch-perpetrators of this evil deed by distributing to them the confiscated properties of the murdered victims.

4. **Witchcraft and Witches**

Witchcraft is defined as the practice of sorcery and association with the devil in order to commit acts of evil. The human brain must have sunk to the depth of its reptilian complex to have come up with beliefs in the existence of witches; in nocturnal witches' sabbaths; in sexual intercourse with the devil and in witches casting evil spells on innocent humans. It strains one's credulity to contemplate whether the death-dealing witch-hunters and Inquisitors really believed their accusations or whether they were extending the field of the Inquisition, adding another human activity to its surveillance by identifying witchcraft and witches as opposing Christian belief and, therefore, with heresy. It is difficult to understand how the Jesuits, an order of highly intelligent men, were associated with the most savage campaign of extermination of witches. When Pope Innocent VIII (1482–1492) issued his Bull against witches in 1484 and ordered the Inquisition to investigate the accused, he placed the stamp of approval of the papacy on the valid foundation of the charges. As a result, two Dominicans wrote a commentary on witchcraft "Hammer of Witches" in 1487 to act as a guide in recognizing, procedure of investigation and tattle-tales about witches. That a book, written by two obvious lunatics, could have gained such notoriety and acceptance is sorry testimony of the power of Church terror exercised over Christians. For example, this guideline to witchcraft and witches refuted all skepticism by asserting that anyone who admitted the slightest doubt of the belief in witches was guilty of the charge of heresy and was to be hauled before the Inquisition examining heresy; that women were much more inclined to be witches than men; that female witches could cause impotence in men, barrenness in women, hail-storms and crop failures. Others accused female witches (married women) of engaging in sex orgies with devils, casting spells for getting a husband, casting an evil eye thereby able to injure or kill, change men's mind from love to hate and from hate to love. Those "convicted" of witchcraft faced one inevitable fate which was unavoidable: death by fire. Why this certainty? Because the Bible said so. "You shall not allow a sorceress to live" (Ex. 22:18) and "Any man or woman who is a necromancer or magician must be put to death by stoning; …" (Lev. 20:27). These were priestly laws aimed at protecting not the faith of Israelites but the turf of priests who wanted no competition and interference in their exclusive wonder-making activities. It is incredible what havoc and agony the biblical laws caused, although misapplied and misunderstood by the Church and their appointed witch-hunters, for to them a witch worshiped the devil and not Christ and was therefore guilty of rank heresy. This witch-mania was not limited to a particular country but was a European (later also a limited American) phe-nomenon. In France, Germany, Italy, Poland, Spain and England, witch burning took place; the 15th and 16th centuries were the most active. In 1623, Pope Gregory XV (1621–1623) commanded that persons who had made a pact with the devil should be given the death penalty but he never offered an opinion how this "pact" had to be documented. Protestants (Luther also thought that witches should be burned for making a pact with the devil; so much for the voice of reform!) were as guilty as Catholics, each of them had their own scores to settle, rid themselves of "heretics" or other opponents and trouble-makers as the charge of witchcraft was easy to prove. The victim, once accused, was always found guilty under torture, for if some hardy person did not break down under the pain of torture (as most did) and confess in order to alleviate the agony, the resistance to pain was itself taken as proof of an alliance with the devil and resulted in condemnation. Everywhere it found support; no one was safe from its clutches and accusations; the interpretation favored the accuser. Some repentant officials who dragged their feet or wanted to be merciful, or conscience-stricken priests who whispered protests, however slight, became victims themselves, subjected to torture and burned at the stake. Without the use of torture, specially authorized by the papacy, no person would have ever admitted the accusation, nor implicated others, whether the person was a cripple, one-eyed, ugly, long-nosed, hunch-backed, stupid or, intelligent—such criteria gave rise to accusations. In the age of sectarianism and incipient free-thinking, the laity terrorized by the Church and Protestant leadership had to toe the line, attend Church regularly, be silent on issues and give no cause for notice; wives had to be careful not to alarm their husbands; even women 90 years of age or children as young as 9 years were not safe from the acts of men with brain-damage. Over 300,000 totally innocent victims died a horrible death after they were brutalized by torture and other humiliations; they protested their innocence to the end. "All of them bewailed with heart-rending lamentations the malice or ignorance of the judges … and in their last agonies they cried to God to witness their innocence" (61–284). Once torture was banned, witch-hunting gradually ceased. It is to the everlasting credit of Frederick the Great (1712–1786) that he prohibited the use of torture in Prussia. "If all of us have not confessed ourselves witches, that is only because we have not all been tortured" (62–311).

How could Christianity respond, as it did, to the phenomenon of witch-craft which never existed and was a myth and deception from beginning to end? The thousands upon thousands of false and fraudulent accusations, trials, tortures and burnings of innocent men, women and children? Christians doing this to Christians in the name of Christianity, the "Religion of Resplendent Love"? It is to the everlasting shame and disgrace of the papacy and Protestant clergy who were the instigators of terror and murder against innocent Christians, and not to have apologized for their criminal acts. They are totally unmoved, feel no remorse and offer no special prayers for the victims. For unlike the 20th century Holocaust when they stood on the sidelines claiming ignorance (this claim will be put to a severe test in a future chapter), the witch-burning madness and the use of torture on accused victims were all done at the instigation and with full knowledge of the papacy and Protestant clergy; this at a time of the full flowering of Catholicism and Protestantism during centuries of their maximum power. They feared no one, not even God. Here and there, on the rarest of occasions, a solitary figure raised his fist in defiance against these atrocities, like the Lutheran theologian (Johannes Matthias Mayfort) who issued this warning to the Inquisitors: "... The day will come when you shall have to give an accounting for every order you have given to trap, to scourge and behead and burn; for every mockery you poured upon the poor tormented creatures; for every tear they wept; for every drop they bled!" (61–285). For it could be asserted with much justification that it was the Popes, the Protestant clergy and the Inquisitors who made a pact with the devil to spread evil among Christians.

Mercifully, the last witch-burning took place in Catholic Poland in 1793, years after the American and French revolutions.

5. **The Knights Templar** In this chronicle about the Templars, a religious military order of knighthood established at the time of the Crusades, a drama of conflict between the king of France and the papacy will illustrate the dealings and the brutal assertion of power of a secular ruler and a double-dealing, selfish, duplicitous and cowardly Pope, who was more interested in protecting papal rights than seeking justice done. The Templars were destroyed not only because of the greed of both king and Pope and vengeance of the king, but also because the Pope feared for his life and wellbeing like any other ordinary man. The order of Templars was formed ca 1120 during the early years of the Kingdom of Jerusalem to protect the Christian pilgrims from marauding Muslims and to serve as their guides. They performed courageous service and added to their duties the

obligation to fight all infidels threatening Christianity. They promised to observe the three monastic vows of poverty, chastity and obedience. Their numbers increased rapidly and further diversified their activities by engaging in the field of finance, acquiring considerable wealth; their properties were scattered all over Europe. They developed into an efficient military organization and adopted absolute secrecy to cover all their internal activities. No member of the Templars could be excommunicated and their sole lord on earth was the Pope. They became influential and this created many enemies for them. The Templars were the defenders of the Church; they were exempt from paying tithes and the order formed an ecclesiastical organization directly subject to the Pope. They were about to become a standing international mercenary force at the disposal of the highest bidder. The French King Philip IV the Fair (1268–1314) was very strong-willed and resourceful; he had continual problems with the Popes as he resented their interference. Pope Boniface VIII (1294–1303) empowered the king to tax the clergy in case of need without consulting Rome, even though he occasionally dressed up in imperial insignia claiming he was emperor and Pope. Difficulties with the king led him to emphasize papal supremacy over secular power. Philip challenged Boniface's right to be Pope and the latter excommunicated Philip. In 1303 Philip's soldiers tried to kidnap the Pope and bring him to France to answer charges of sodomy, sorcery, heresy and blasphemy, but the plan failed. The Pope died from shock. Philip was desperately in need of money; thought the easiest way of filling his coffers by arresting all the Jews in France in 1306. He expropriated their goods and money and expelled them from his dominions with only the clothes on their backs; no Christian raised any protest. The new Pope Benedict XI (1303–1304) was determined to maintain the right of the Holy See, but died suddenly after experiencing harassment from Philip.

6. Philip's wife died in 1305 and he was greatly grieved by the loss. To console himself he applied for membership with the Order of Templars and intended to abdicate in favor of his son. What an honor for the Order; it was indicative of their power, wealth and prestige that they refused his application. This act was tragically ill-advised as Philip was greatly insulted by this snub and planned their demise after this rejection. In 1305 the Templars had no Crusades to fight and did not engage in acts of charity; they were bankers who earned interest on loans and acted as money depos-

itory to the wealthy; for a time, the French royal treasury was housed in their Paris Temple. But they provided a good life for their brethren and all this was shrouded in secrecy, a good bait for the cynics. The new Pope Clement V (1305–1314) was elected at Lyons, formerly archbishop of Bordeaux, a Frenchman, who later resided in Avignon, France (the beginning of the "Babylonian Captivity" 1309–1378). His depth of humiliation was reached when he collaborated with the king in his suppression of the Knights Templar; lusting for the Templars' wealth, suspicious of their intentions (a State within a State) and still resentful of being rejected by them, Philip told the incredulous Pope Clement about a long list of accusations against the Templars involving blasphemy, heretical ideas and immoral practices. The king told the Pope that every brethren denied Christ, spat on his image, stepped on the cross, kissed each other on the mouth, the navel and the anus, engaged in homosexual orgies and bowed before an idol in the shape of a human head which they adored as their god, and all kinds of other heretical practices within the Temple. Philip demanded that the Pope conduct a full inquiry. The Master of the Temple, Jacques de Molay, in a meeting with the Pope emphatically denied the charges. The king's charges were all bubbles and lacked any credibility; the king was well known for his mendacity and fabricated accusations. Even though the Pope referred to the Templars as the "brave Knights of Christ," he promised Philip to begin an inquiry; he approved a double inquest into the affairs of the Templars, one on the individual members, the other on the Order itself. On October 13, 1307, every one of the five thousand or so Templars in France was arrested on the orders of King Philip; he was determined to conduct his own inquiry, using the services of the general Inquisitor for France and prove his accusations by using the reliable method of the Inquisition: torture. And this was done without papal approval and in direct contravention of their ecclesiastical immunity. There was no resistance.

7. The Inquisition was a Tribunal of the Catholic Church for the discovery and punishment of heresy and other offenses against the Church or Catholic religion. Treated at length in the next chapter, suffice it to say here that everyone who came as an accused before the Inquisitors was deemed guilty and had to prove his innocence; this was impossible when the instruments of torture were applied. The strongest men broke down

and confessed to falsehoods just to be spared further agony; the imprisoned Templars were placed under torture and confessions of guilt extracted from them including that of the Grand Master de Molay. Pope Clement issued a Bull commanding the neighboring kings of Christian lands to arrest the Templars in their countries in the name of the papacy. For the Pope to issue such a proclamation without one scintilla of evidence of their guilt marked him as a man damned and guilty of the crime of false accusation. He should have been strengthened in his resolve to see justice done when news came back from countries where the examination did not include torture—such as England, Scotland, Ireland, Aragon, Castile and Germany—that the Templars were found innocent. He should have been even more doubtful of his hasty judgment when he sent two Cardinals to Paris to interview over sixty of the Templars (including de Molay) and they had all revoked their confession. It is to Pope Clement's credit that he gathered some strength of character and had the Inquisition in France suspended pending review of evidence. The king accused the Pope of siding with the Templars, that he took bribes from them and that therefore he would have him deposed. The king had seventy-two Templars brought to the Pope who confessed to him their crimes; the Pope believed them despite evidence of torture. All the Pope cared about was protecting papal rights, not justice. In 1310, fifty-four Templars were burned alive and all of them professed their innocence to the end; the Pope did not care. In 1311 "Pope Clement was still sending out orders to the places where the brethren had been unequivocally acquitted, orders saying that such acquittals could not be correct and that torture should be used everywhere to find the truth" (63–302). So much for the seeker of truth. Speaking of the Pope: "He himself had decided that the Order should be dissolved, its goods reserved for the Holy See … His one abiding wish over the previous four years had been to preserve papal power and by 1311 he was past caring for the technicalities of justice and law" (63–303). He had come to accept the Templars guilt because it was convenient for him to do so. De Molay was now seventy years old, for 6½ years prisoner, tortured and confined to the dungeon, a shadow of his former self; betrayed and abandoned by the Pope, went to the stake unrepentant, withdrew his confession in his last act of defiance, stating: "I gave the declaration demanded of me only to escape torture and suffering, and move to pity those who made me suffer" (63–17). He was chained to the stake still shouting his innocence.

Pope Clement V, who formerly referred to the Templars as his "dearest sons", fearful for his prerogatives and playing the coward in the face of heroic Christian men, accepted the confession of guilt of the brethren who were accused of monstrous crimes even though he knew it was obtained under torture; where acquittals were obtained he insisted that torture be used to "find the truth"; commanded neighboring countries to arrest Templars without any assertion of guilt and in the end proved just as greedy to divide the property of the Order as the secular ruler. Papal sanctity was beginning to lose its splendor; secular rulers were beginning to see through the provincialism of Popes and lose respect and fear.

Chapter 35

The Inquisitions

1. The Catholic Church did not have to invent the concept of "inquisition": It arose as a logical consequence of its prior conduct and views. It viewed itself as "universal," the supreme and only valid religion established directly by God; brimming with the spirit of evangelism; ready to absorb one and all when it acquired power; ready to dispatch "infidels" with utmost ferocity, showing little patience with Catholic heretics. The Church saw itself as the only arbiter in the matter of faith, ruling with finality, completely unopposed and guilty of distorting Christianity in its efforts of ridding itself of enemies. The divine mission of the Popes was placed in doubt by the failure of the Crusades; their style of living and that of the clergy contributed to the atmosphere of apprehension facing the believer; the non-believers and skeptics increased to the point where the Church felt threatened and, as a result, had to take steps to protect its interests. The Church, which previously punished heretics (those Christians who diverged from orthodoxy) with excommunication, took more drastic steps; by the 13th century it considered heresy as meriting capital punishment. There were sporadic burnings of heretics in France, Goslar and Milan, but Pope Innocent III (1198–1216) laid the foundation for the severe prosecution of heretics. The Second Lateran Council (1139) required lay princes to prosecute heretics under pain of anathema; Pope Gregory IX (1227–1241) in 1231 established the Inquisition as a papal Tribunal and published its fundamental constitution. Limited at first to Germany, extended to Aragon in 1232, the Inquisition became general in 1233; the Spanish Inquisition—the most notorious—began its operations in 1481 and was not permanently suppressed until 1834. The Italian or Roman Inquisition, called the Holy Office (Sanctum Officium), was active up to the 19th century; the Holy Office—only a relic from its powerful past—was finally abolished in 1965.

The Spanish Inquisition followed the Conquistadors to the New World, wherever the Catholic Church gained foothold.

2. From the darkest recesses of the human mind, from the vilest catalogue of man's cunning, from the crafty instincts of a Neanderthal hunter, completely contemptuous of Christ's teaching, drunk with arrogance of power and cynical disdain for human suffering, from common robbers and murderers in ecclesiastical vestments, from these there emerged a set of rules and regulations for the Inquisition which forever soiled Christendom and especially the Catholic Church. These instigators would have been condemned as common criminals by any court of law. The Dominicans (also aptly known as the 'Black Friars"), an order following strict military discipline and an uncompromising orthodoxy in faith, were up to their chosen task of ably serving as "inquisitors," the task of servicing the newly created courts of Inquisition. When it became apparent that even under the established corrupt system confessions were sometimes hard to extract, Pope Innocent IV (1243–1254) came to the rescue in 1252 with his Bull permitting torture of prisoners; the Inquisition could extract a "confession" under torture from most prisoners, so long it was determined to do so. For the hardy prisoner able to withstand torture and escape the incriminating confession was convicted anyway: He was accused of being in league with the devil and thus of witchcraft—and condemned to death on that account. Under that system even Jesus Christ would be convicted. The Hebrew Scripture has been justly blamed for originating the idea for the death penalty for heresy. "Any man who curses his God shall bear the burden of his fault. The one who blasphemes the name of Yahweh must die; …" (Lev. 24:16); apostasy invited the wrath of Yahweh and the punishment was death, "… all the followers of Baal of Peor have been wiped out from among you by Yahweh your God; … " (Deut. 4:3). Yahweh speaking to the Israelites: 'Be sure that if you forget Yahweh your God, if you follow other gods, if you serve them and bow before them … you will most certainly perish" (Deut. 8:19–20). "If a prophet or a dreamer of dreams arises among you … and if he then says to you, 'Come, then, let us follow other gods … and serve them … That prophet or that dreamer of dreams must be put to death, for he has preached apostasy from Yahweh your God …" (Deut. 13:2–6). "You must keep the sabbath, … The man who profanes it must be put to death; …" (Ex. 31:13–14). The same if your brother, sister, son,

daughter, wife or friend, secretly tried to entice you to serve other gods, he or she must be shown no pity, he or she must be stoned to death (Deut. 13:7–11). As in the case of witchcraft, it is again the Holy Scripture, the Torah, that book of Israelite rapacious priests, that sounded the clarion call for the death penalty for blaspheming or cursing God; for apostasy and following other gods; for violating God's covenant and for profaning the Sabbath. This narrow definition of violations, however, was greatly expanded by the Popes and the Inquisitors so as to condemn and expropriate the property of any man or woman who happened to be their target; they discarded the Torah ordinance that in case of the death penalty, the testimony of one witness was insufficient, but that of two or three witnesses must be obtained (Deut. 17:6–7); they made a mockery of that ordinance.

3. To keep the Inquisition proceedings out of public view, for centuries nothing was permitted to be written about it. The powers of the Inquisitor were unlimited and those who came under the control of the Inquisition were doomed in most cases. The accused was guilty until proven innocent; was ignorant of the charges against him until the day of sentencing; never faced his or her accuser nor was informed of his or her identity; not versed in legal proceedings which were conducted in Latin; could not be defended by a lawyer and any favorable witness testifying on his behalf was liable to be hauled before the Inquisition; was thrown in jail and kept incommunicado and in chains; his property was sequestered and in most cases with finality, depending on the severity of the charges; when examined on the charges brought against him, he had to take an oath to answer all questions truthfully and therefore be his own accuser; to obey all commandments of the Church and to reveal to the Court under oath the existence of other heresies or heretics known to him. When confession could not be obtained, torture was applied and the accused was broken in body and spirit. No mercy was shown by the Inquisitors, their sentences were harsh and pitiless; they had a vested interest in death sentences and life imprisonments, for under the rules they benefitted from the confiscation of the accused's property which was to be divided among the Inquisition authorities, secular States and the Holy See. No one was safe from their tentacles except the Pope, Bishops, papal legates and the Inquisitors themselves. It was the duty of all Christians to support the Inquisition and failure to report heresy or identify the whereabouts of a heretic could land one before the Inquisition.

This order extended to members of one's immediate family; a son or daughter, even a minor, was expected to denounce his or her family—incognito—a wife her husband and a husband his wife; the family and close neighbors of a suspect were themselves suspect. Anyone who spoke in defense of the accused came under suspicion of heresy. The Inquisitor Konrad Von Marburg, showed no mercy to suspects and followed a simple, albeit brutal, rule in passing out death sentences to all even remotely accused of heresy, stating "… God knew whether in fact he was guilty or innocent and would himself decide on how he would spend eternity …" (64:43–44). Under the rules of the much harsher Spanish Inquisition, those who refused to confess their guilt (or if they were tardy in doing so) were given the death sentence by burning; their only recourse if their accusation did not merit the death penalty by definition—was to plead guilty, recant and ask the Court for mercy, in which case they might receive a lesser sentence: penalties and or imprisonment. The decision was final and there was no appeal. For those judged "obstinate" heretics the penalty was death by burning. The condemned was turned over to secular authorities for the execution of the sentence. It was the height of cynicism and sophistry for the Church to assert that it shed no blood and burned no heretic. Death by burning was the punishment following John 15:6, "Anyone who does not remain in me is like a branch that has been thrown away—he withers; these branches are collected and thrown on the fire, and they are burnt." Some condemned were shown "mercy" if they repented before execution of the sentence: They were strangled and then burned. Their ashes were scattered so that on the day of the "Resurrection of the Dead" they would not share the blessings of the Kingdom of God. Even the dead were not spared. On the accusation of an anonymous informer who possibly bore a grudge against the decedent or wanted to share in the rich reward offered, in most cases 50% of the property inherited by his family—the Inquisition after condemning the decedent as a heretic—sometimes years after his death—had his bones exhumed and ceremoniously burned; all the property passed on by the decedent was confiscated without regard to the hardships caused to his or her heirs. The naked greed of the Church and Inquisition knew no limits. How could the dead threaten the Church? How could the Church presume to save them from "hell" years after death? Was divine judgment suspended pending the finding of guilt by the Inquisition? The dead (who left a lot of wealth to their heirs) were dug up for one reason only: to confiscate their property.

4. In the Spanish Peninsula, the Jews from early on were threatened with a choice of death, expulsion or conversion to the Catholic faith; they had been numerous there as far back as the Roman Empire. As early as the 7th century (under the recently converted Catholic Visigoths), an edict was issued ordering the baptism of all Jews or suffer expulsion and the loss of property. Of the thousands who converted to Catholicism most reverted back to their former religion when opportunity arose. During the Spanish Reconquest of the Peninsula from the Moors, the Jews were to suffer even more hardships at the hands of the Christian population whose passion was continuously whipped up by inflammatory sermons from the pulpit by priests and higher clergy. In 1391 matters came to a head with the whole-sale sacking of Jewish quarters in the cities of the Peninsula; whole Jewish communities were exterminated; a great part of the Jewish population opted for baptism to save their lives; it is estimated that the number of Anusim (those Jews who converted under duress) exceeded 200,000. After 1391 matters went downhill for the Spanish Jews; the converts called "New Christians", to distinguish them from "Old Christians", did not buy their freedom from persecution, discrimination and harassment which they experienced formerly as Jews. Despised for their economic success and social position, the population and authorities treated them with contempt and suspicion; they questioned the displayed sincerity to their new faith and found cause to do so since clusters of renegades were discovered who secretly practiced Judaism: These were called "Marranos", a degrading epithet. The persecution of New Christians by the Old Christians caused the former to defend themselves aggressively and pitched encounters were fought between the two, all to the embarrassment and chagrin of the Church authorities who were powerless to stop the bloodshed. Finally, the Judaizing practices of the renegades reached a level where tolerance by State authorities was no longer possible and the Spanish sovereigns—who employed many New Christians in high places and were dependent on their services—requested the Holy See for the establishment of an Inquisition to deal with the problem. The first Tribunal was established in Seville and its first burning, Auto-de-Fé, took place in 1481. In 1483, the Spanish Inquisition consolidated its various Tribunals under one Grand Inquisitor to which post it named Tomas Torquemada, whose jurisdiction extended over the entire kingdom. Thus was established the Spanish Inquisition, the most thoroughgoing, enduring and infamous of all Inquisitions, directed by

ruthless, implacable and pitiless men who brooked no interference, were beholden to no one, a State within a State and who made their own rules and regulations.

5. The Jews were left unharmed by the Inquisition as long as they did not interfere in matters of Christian faith. The Inquisition considered baptism a sacrament that could not be withdrawn. The voluntary and forcibly converted Jews thus came under the jurisdiction of the Inquisition whose major task and mission was to deal with New Christian renegades, who were suspected of relapsing into heresy. Thousands upon thousands were hauled before the Tribunal by often unfounded and flimsy accusations—many anonymous—of vindictive Old Christians who had scores to settle, or who gave satisfaction to their religious hatred of Jews whom they considered to be masquerading as Christians to preserve their economic and social benefits which they could not retain as Jews. Practicing Jews were forcibly baptized as Catholics, a religion which was new to them and about which they knew nothing, only to be accused shortly of flimsy transgressions: changing linen on a Sabbath, abstaining from eating pork, lighting candles on Friday. Not performing any work on a Sabbath could land the "trespasser" before the Inquisition accused of Judaizing; if the accused admitted his guilt and was penitent, he could get off by performing public penance and be fined a considerable sum of money, depending on his wealth. This relief was available only once and any offense committed thereafter marked the accused as a relapsed heretic to be dealt with harshly: The penalty was death at the stake and confiscation of property, even if the offense related to an infraction of rules about the clothes to be worn by the penitent.

6. The Inquisition was unrelenting in its pursuit, doggedly followed up every lead, could not be deflected from its course of pursuing those suspected of heresy, took its time bringing them to trial while the suspects languished in prison in chains—incommunicado—sometimes for years not knowing what they were charged with. The New Christians attempted to minimize the fury of the Inquisition by offering substantial bribes to Spanish high ecclesiastics; even the Popes accepted large sums on various occasions, but all was of no avail. The office of the Popes was ignored by the Spanish Inquisitors. To stamp out heresy, all heretics and their sympathizers had to be destroyed. This was true Church policy for its survival was threatened by the rising dissent. This was also the sole aim of the

Inquisitors despite their overtly stated aim of saving the heretic's soul from burning in hell forever. The Spanish sovereigns sought unity of faith in their kingdom which would assure them of political unity and effective rule over their subjects. If, in the process, the empty coffers of their treasury were replenished on an ongoing basis with the property of condemned heretics, this was a blessed event not without anticipation, satisfaction and an important source of revenue.

7. While the Inquisition became wealthy from the confiscated property, the Marranos suffered economic privations from newly imposed curtailment of trades and occupations which were closed to them. The Inquisition added a new torment to the difficulties of the conversos, a racist element, that of Limpieza de Sangre (purity of blood). Those Christians who could claim they had no Jewish blood in their veins were given Certificates by the Inquisition which attested to this "purity" and, as a result, could enjoy social and economic advantages denied the New Christians; the latter became second class citizens, shunned by the rest of the people, living in ghetto-style segregation, objects of unprovoked physical attacks on their person and property and severely discriminated against. The clergy had transformed the people into malefactors and the object was repression and violence against what they perceived as Crypto- Jews. The authorities and Church decreed that it took six generations for New Christians to wipe away any impediment of Jewish blood and for them to lose the discriminatory burden imposed on them on that account. In imposing these debilities, they did so purely in response to the continuous civil unrest caused by the tensions between the Old and New Christians and to pacify the unruly element of the former, whose hatred of anything Jewish—abetted regularly from the pulpit—knew no bounds and who found competition with Crypto-Jews on level grounds too tough to take. Could the Jews, who embraced Christianity or were forcibly baptized, have anticipated what lay in store for them? Could they have foreseen that the curse which haunted them as Jews would stay with them as Christians for six generations? Could they have predicted that they would be treated no better than they were formerly as Jews with the added curse of the Inquisition? The answer is an emphatic "no" but no other choice was open to them; they were painted into a corner from which there was no escape except to throw themselves upon the mercy of the Church. Most of those converted quit

Judaizing after a few generations, partly from exhaustion and fear and partly from the conviction that God abandoned the Jews, and that Christians succeeded them to divine favor despite the cruelty of their missionaries and the blood-stained hands of their baptizers.

8. The Church was able to fight its battle against heresy because it still had the power to do so; it fought the battle restrained by no moral or religious considerations; displayed no compunctions of conscience and trampled on all humane criteria. In this, it displayed a short-term view of the problem in the belief that by sheer terror and cruelty of the Inquisition it could subdue, eliminate and frighten its enemies and regain conformity speedily. But the days of enforced compliance were coming to an end. The conduct of the papacy, which originated the worst crimes of the Middle Ages, was responsible for the onset of bloody religious wars which, by their nature, destroyed the unity of Christendom, opened the way to belligerent sectarianism and exposed the nature of the Catholic Church and papacy. The Inquisition was the instrument fathered by the Catholic Church to crush its enemies who were powerless to resist; displayed the cunning of a beast of prey to ensnare its targeted victims by setting up monstrous rules and procedures and cynically stripped the victims of any possible defense. It dispensed with the dictates of the divine law as outlined in Scripture and with Roman trial jurisprudence as practiced at that time. The New Catholic Encyclopedia, in trying to justify what it admits to be "one of the darkest chapters in the history of the Church," states it disingenuously (57–537, Vol. 7): "The inquisitorial procedure was a departure from traditional forms of accusation or of denunciation, which had been ill suited to the repression of heresy." This is a sorry apology for the crimes committed.

Chapter 36

Anti-Semitism

1. Deicide

There is nothing in monotheism to make it superior to polytheism. Monotheism created intolerance, persecution and forcible conversions; it created hatred for people of different beliefs, all manipulated by power-seeking priestly sects. Just as the Hebrew Scripture contains vilification of alien peoples and idolators, so do the Gospels and Paul's writings condemn non-believers in Jesus' divine mission. The Jews were foreclosed by historical necessity after the last uprising against the Romans from asserting defenses against this condemnation; the Christians, on the other hand, suffered no restraints and, in time, their condemnations raged with full fury, the main thrust was against Jews. The Jews suffered the full brunt of Christian hatred and malice nurtured on theological grounds mainly by the concept of deicide, which accused the whole Jewish people unforgivingly and without any time limit of the murder of Jesus Christ. No thought was ever given to the veracity of the accusation, to any mitigating factors or to the fatal contradictions in Paul and the Gospels. The deicide was dogma and the Jews were to pay the bloody price. In previous Chapters, I have outlined doubts about the historicity of Jesus and his crucifixion. The mythical Jesus was crucified by mythical Jews without sparing the Jewish people the slightest burden of guilt of the charge, a favored subject of preachers to whip up passions of congregations, keep them in turmoil, to be forever reminded of the foul deed blamed on the Jewish people. The hatred of Jews, then, is the work of the Church, and the tendentious manner in which it chose to interpret the accusation. It is the foundation of hostility embraced by the collective term "anti-Semitism." But anti-Semitism existed before the Christian era, before there were any Christians to charge the Jews with deicide. Besides theological anti-Semitism, there are political, racial, economic and social causes—all reflecting a hatred and dislike of Jews.

2. By following the precepts of the Torah and its commandments, the Jews were bound to come into conflict with their neighbors, particularly if they resided outside of Palestine. The criteria have been covered at length in prior chapters; suffice it to say that strict Torah observance (which was not required outside of the land of Israel) could not help but result in the demand of privileges, exceptions, exclusions and exemptions not accorded the native population; this placed a stigma on Jews as a people separate and apart from others, specially favored. Compliance with special dietary laws, strict observance of the Sabbath, prohibition against intermarriage and the right of communal self-government, could not help but arouse the envy and dislike of their neighbors, which, in time, turned to hatred and violence. The Jews did not moderate their demands and lifestyle, on the contrary, retained their pugnacity and obstinacy. The Roman Emperor Hadrian was the first to publicly recognize the cause/effect relationship between the Torah teaching and the hatred of Jews aroused by their rebelliousness; after the defeat of Bar Kokhba, he decreed the severest punishment for those who followed the Jewish Law in the future.

3. Anti-Semitism is a term used to signify hostility toward the Jewish people based on theological, political, racial or social grounds. Pre-Christian anti-Semitism was political and racial in its treatment of Jews. All a Manetho, Molon, Apion, Cicero or Tacitus could complain about were their misanthropy and unsociability, their exclusivism, that they were hateful to the gods, that they refused to become part of the surrounding cultures, that the religion of the Jews was "superstitious"; all random shots without any pattern, method or cohesion. Except for occasional disturbances or bloodsheds—which in most cases also reflected Jewish contributory guilt and except for the Seleucid wars which were spurred on by Hellenized Jews who betrayed the Jewish cause—their hatred and antagonism were confined to oratory, literary efforts, some discrimination and political actions. The Jews could adapt to and cope with this kind of anti-Semitism.

But nothing, absolutely nothing, prepared the Jews for an onslaught of monstrous lies and crude fabrications so comprehensive, a hostility so colossal and unbending, an ill will so unyielding as that which the Christians and their unique theology rained down upon the Jewish people. The Church made it its sacred mission to corrupt Christians with poisonous lies about the Jewish crime of deicide—which is still preached to this day—about their rejection by God, a people accursed for their crime forever to roam upon this earth in suffering and rejection and yet, by the miracle of baptism—forced or voluntary, it did not matter—have their sins washed away in an instant; become good Christians; be accepted into the Christian community without any blemishes; gain eternal salvation and all their accusations to become non-accusations. But if Jews rejected baptism, were too obstinate to see the truth preached by their tormentors, then those who were spared death had to remain alive to provide constant proof of their crime, condemned to a life of perpetual torment and allowed to live only by Christian sufferance.

4. Who were the originators of this theological anti-Semitism? When did it arise? We have to go right to the beginning to the letters of Paul in the 1st century A.D. and the four Gospels in the 1st and 2nd centuries. Paul was the creator of the Christian myth and the Evangelists, who authored the four Gospels and related the primitive traditions of the birth, ministry and death of Jesus. It is in these writings that we find the theological roots of anti-Semitism. Roman Emperor Hadrian's persecution of Jews, after the defeat of Bar Kokhba, also included the Christians since Roman authorities could not distinguish between the two faiths. In a petition to Hadrian, Church representatives gave convincing evidence of the separation of the two faiths; since that time they became two hostile camps. Christian proselytizing activities, essential to the survival of the new faith, came on a collision course with Jewish interests. Christians who had the curses against Jews spelled out in the Torah and Prophets, in addition to the calumnies of the Greeks and Romans, had all the tools necessary to conduct a campaign of defamation against the Jewish people which, in its ferocity, was without precedent. I refer the reader to the many citations from the Bible enumerated before. I shall quote one excerpt from the New Testament (quoted in a prior chapter) which epitomizes the brutality, permanence and finality of the charge of deicide, so essential to the Christian dogma and so punishing to Jews, who to this day wear the stigma of Christ-killers, murderers of the Lord:

"You stubborn people, with your pagan hearts and pagan ears. You are always resisting the Holy Spirit, just as your ancestors used to do. Can you name a single prophet your ancestors never persecuted? In the past they killed those who foretold the coming of the Just One, and now you have become his betrayers, his murderers" (Acts 7:51–53). The New Testament will always be read in this manner; the leaders of the Church will always manipulate the believers into accepting these untrue charges. This false education starts at an early age with children who are taught how their Christ was crucified by the Jews and this conviction colors the rest of their living days; the stain will never be eradicated. A whole Christian civilization grew up from the 2nd to the 21st centuries never to question the truth of the charge of deicide, the guilt of a whole people, the curse it brought on them, the deserved punishment by God which would endure forever, on which account Jews were reduced to a life of disrepute on earth and condemned. This false charge, central to the Christian doctrine, brought untold persecutions, suffering and massacres to the Jewish people who, in the past, had to endure the havoc in silence, for to have raised even the slightest doubt about the accusation meant certain forfeiture of life. And so it was, as will be seen, with other false charges. The teaching of the Gospels is essential for the view of Jewish guilt, for the charge of deicide will exist as long as Christianity and for as long as Christians read the Bible; this state of affairs will never change, the guilt will never be forgiven for the Christians will never change the message of the Gospels.

5. The specific periods in which the damaging effects were felt are not important; what is important is that they occurred and spelled brutal massacres of the innocent. The participants of the First Crusade in 1096 A.D. did not wait till they made it to the Holy Land to fight the infidel; the Jews were nearby, defenseless and propertied. As they made their way through the Rhine valley, they were determined to punish "the murderers of Christ" and avenge the crucifixion. It is estimated that 10,000 Jews were murdered in Northern France and Germany (1096 A.D.), other bands slaughtered 12,000 Jews near Cologne (1096 A.D.), many thousands more were given the choice between baptism and death—most chose death; all the way from Mainz to Trier, Regensburg, Metz, Worms, Spier, Prague and Strasburg, the story was repeated and thousands of Jews lost their lives to avenge the Lord's crucifixion for which they were blamed. And so it went on for cen-

turies. Bishop Chrysostom's (4th century A.D.) cry "... The Jews are odious assassins of Christ and for killing God there is no expiation possible, no indulgence or pardon ..." was heard loud and clear by the malefactors and murderers, especially the clergy, who urged them on.

6. The Christian charge of deicide against the Jewish people is the most difficult to refute, because the accuser has no proof except what is written in the New Testament and repeated a thousand times over by every cleric; it refers to seemingly historical events and yet recorded history of those times is inexplicably silent about Jesus. Despite the total fabrication and myth of the charge (I refer the reader to Chapters 24–32 of this book), events of seeming consequence were tied to it to make it appear that heaven grieved and cried at the betrayal and crucifixion of Jesus; mapped proper retribution and punishment of Jews. The Second Temple and Jerusalem were destroyed, the priesthood vanished, the Jewish people decimated in the wars against the Romans and ultimately exiled to suffer oppression, privation and persecution; all, we are told, as damning testimony of guilt. Further, we are told that God abandoned the Jews, no longer listened to their prayers and cursed them. This is Christian proof of Jewish guilt. For in their view, if the Jews prospered and led a normal existence, the guilt of Jews would be in doubt. Therefore, they have the enviable advantage of their own judgment of participating in its fulfillment by making the life of Jews a suffering on earth, fabricating all sorts of lies and false accusations, causing uncountable murder of innocents, and happily claim these to be "proof" and a divine sign of the guilt of Jews.

7. The Ritual Murder and Blood Accusation

The ritual murder and blood accusation are another form of Christian anti-Semitism based on deliberate lies propagated mostly by the Catholic clergy in localized situations to instigate hatred of Jews, blacken and vilify their rituals. The accusers were without proof or facts, did not need any, relied on torture of the accused to extract confessions of guilt, and also relied in some cases on malevolent baptized Jews and their hostile testimony which, coming from former Jews, was deemed sacrosanct. Whenever civil authorities or the papacy investigated the charges, they concluded there was no foundation or truth to them, strongly condemned the vilifiers and absolved the Jews of guilt. The papacy, in particular, came out vehemently in condemning the accusations and forbade the clerics to tolerate the rumors. Whereas the clergy dealt with the common people, mostly ignorant, about the finer points of ritual and theology, the Popes knew better and did not wish to risk the reputation of Christendom on account of falsehoods, fabrications and all too obvious ignorance. But the clergy did not honor the dicta of the Popes, continued to incite the common people and, in the process, caused the torture and massacre of generations of Jewish men, women and children in many parts of Europe.

8. What was it about Christian blood, particularly that of children, which was said to have made Jews so bloodthirsty? It was not based on Holy Scripture; it was not based on any direct observer or spy who infiltrated Jewish circles; it was not based on any written document or confession without applying torture; it was totally repudiated by the papacy. It was based on efforts by the clergy in the 12th century, and after, to terrorize the common people into obedience and submissiveness when the first signs of schism and sectarianism appeared; to permanently preclude the possibility of a rapprochement between Christians and Jews, and to add a new dimension to the reliable standby charge of deicide in that the Jews were accused of torturing, killing and crucifying innocent Christian children as a sign of their enmity toward Jesus Christ. We are told that Jews needed the blood of a Christian—particularly of innocent children, because they were not corrupted by sin and therefore more efficacious—for baking unleavened bread for Passover, for medicinal remedies and healing purposes; to daub their bodies to prolong their lives; to alleviate the wound of circumcision; for its fragrance to offset their smell; for use as balm in labor pains and childbirth—all fairy tales to amuse children with, very young children at that. A Jewish convert of Canterbury "… who obligingly came forward with the explanation that Jews were required to sacrifice a Christian child annually at Easter …" (23:130). This statement was made by a former Jew, obviously to please the clergy and crowd, yet the believers reacted with violence against the perceived culprits. The claim was made "… that the Jews crucified Christian children usually during Passion week, in order to reenact the crucifixion of Jesus, mock and insult the Christian faith" (23:131). Shades of deicide. The accusation was expanded that Jews were in league with the devil in their acts of child torture; that Christian children were murdered while curses and evil spells were pronounced and that Jews made use of magic and sorcery to commit the foul acts, all consonant with their diabolical effort to destroy Christendom.

9. The reader will suppose that these accusations so closely tied with medieval superstitions ceased with the beginning of the Age of Reason; it would be a gross mistake. Malcolm Hay quotes Dr. James Parkes, "among both Roman Catholics and Eastern Orthodox Christians ... there are almost more examples of blood-libel accusation between 1880 and 1945 than in the whole of Middle Ages" (22:310–311). In Central and Eastern Europe, the dissemination in modern times of blood-libel slanders was encouraged by "an ecclesiastical anti-Semitism in Rome" (22:311) and the agitation of Greek Orthodox monks. The Jesuit priests rank high in the field of intellectual endeavor. It is therefore incredible that one of them writing in the semi-official journal of the Vatican—La Civilta Cattolica—between the years 1881 and 1882, could dispense for posterity to read such diatribe: "It remains therefore generally proved ... that the sanguinary Paschal rite ... is a general law binding the consciences of all Hebrews to make use of the blood of a Christian child ... In order that the blood be effective, the child must die in torments ... Some hold that the blood of a child is essential, others ... think that the blood of an adult is sufficient ... In the Hebrew Jubilee years, the fresh blood of a child is essential ..." (23:311–312). Although this journal was read by Catholic ecclesiastics all over the world and Pope Leo XIII (1878–1903), subsequent Popes must have been informed about the controversial content of a semi-official Vatican journal, the articles were not withdrawn, the writer was not reprimanded, his opinions were not questioned or rejected, nor was anyone offended; instead, they were handed down to future generations, uncontroverted, to serve as fodder for vilifiers and slanderers.

10. In the end, it was the Jewish martyr who knew of his innocence and that his accuser subverted the truth. He knew further that it assuredly was not part of Judaism to drink human blood or use it for ritual purposes. His opposition to Christians was fortified by the use they made of false accusations which he himself knew to be contrived. The Jewish people knew that the monstrous fabrications about blood-rituals were to serve only the spread of hatred and blacken the reputation of Judaism.

11. Desecration of the Host
The desecration of the Host is one other charge that was heaped on Jews by the Catholic Church who preached that Christ was bodily present in the wafer which, through consecration and transubstantiation, is changed into

the whole substance of the body of Christ. This is one of the most important sacraments of the Church, part of the Eucharist, necessary for the salvation of Church followers. The doctrine of transubstantiation was officially recognized at the Fourth Lateran Council in 1215, which also decreed, among many other restrictive measures, that Jews must wear on their clothing a distinctive badge. We are told that Jews were accused of Host desecration by making use of it for magical purposes; by stabbing and mutilating it till it bled; by shedding their anti-Christian feeling upon, what was recognized as, the body of Christ and that in some instances the desecration took place in a synagogue where they made it part of their ritual. Whole Jewish communities were implicated and suffered the consequences. "But not unusually the criminals were represented as acting for the group, distributing pieces of the host far and wide, or inviting the leading Jews of the country to assemble and participate in the act of desecration" (23–113). Jews reenacting the crucifixion by piercing the Host with knives and nails? Jews using the consecrated wafer to perform magic and sorcery? Jews using the blood of the consecrated wafer to cure their ailments? This is tantamount to saying that Jews believed in the central Catholic dogma of the Real Presence of the body of Christ in the consecrated Host, possessing the miracle- making properties of the miracle-dispensing Jesus! Jews were treated as greater believers in the dogma of transubstantiation than most Christians! If Jews acted on this—which is wholly antithetical to Judaism—then they believed like Christians, seek baptism and avoid the terrible fate awaiting them when apprehended in the act. This is another clerical myth, a total fabrication invented not only to strengthen the animosity toward Jews by the common people—and to help relieve Jews of their properties—but also to reinforce the belief of Christians early on in the 13th century in the efficacy of the consecrated wafer and the presence of the body of Christ in the Eucharist. If Jews were guilty of desecrating the Host and suffered the ultimate punishment for this act—most of the confessions were obtained under torture—then Christians had every reason not to doubt the dogma.

12. The punishment of the accused Jews was so severe and the publicity of the alleged misdeed so widespread, that they had to be on guard not to cause the slightest offense to Christians in a matter to them so wholly devoid of substance and reality. But the punishment for the supposed

wrongdoing was real: Beelitz near Berlin 1243, all the Jews of the city were burned; Prague 1389, 3000 Jews lost their lives; Bohemia 1338, a large number of Jews put to death; Paris 1290; Brussels 1370; Bavaria 1337–1338; Knoblauch (Berlin) 1510; Segovia 1415; as late as 1761 in Nancy (France), an Alsatian Jew was executed; and in dozens of other cities and towns scattered throughout Europe between the 13th and 17th centuries. A few Jews confessed under torture and that was sufficient evidence to put to death whole communities or banish them from the city and steal their properties; all the result of greed, superstition, ignorance, that special inclination to bear false witness in matters of theology and crass anti-Semitism. In the background looms the charge of all charges: Deicide.

13. **The Black Death**

It was the belief of common people in the Middle Ages, inspired by anti-Semitic preaching from the Church pulpit, that when Jews prayed they hoped for the destruction of Christians; that Jews were the personification of evil; that they committed the ultimate crime against the founder of Christianity; that they were destined to be allied with the devil and do his work willingly, for did not the Gospel of John say of them that their father is the devil? The Jew was feared by Christians who saw him as stubbornly rejecting Christ against all Old Testament evidence; that they saw him as adept in the art of magic and sorcery, and master in the use of poison to serve his evil designs on Christendom. Even Jewish physicians, sought after by Christians of all ranks for their superior knowledge of medicine, were not beyond suspicion of poisoning some of their patients to act out their hatred against Christians. Mysterious deaths called for an explanation and the Jew conversant with magic, sorcery, the preparation and use of poison was a ready target of suspicion. Thus, when the bubonic plague, the Black Death, devastated the European population between 1348 and 1351 (estimates range from a third to one half perished), the charge that Jews poisoned the wells in order to destroy the Christian population of Europe hit them with a vengeance. The disease was mysterious and no medical explanation was available; it started in the East and the bacillus was progressively carried to the Black Sea, Venice, Central Europe, Germany, France, Spain and England; the infection was silent and deadly; healthy people died within a day or two; family life and morals were disrupted; no segment of society was spared; the despairing population was first told it was divine retribution for immorality, until reports began to circulate accusing the Jews of poisoning the wells and causing the plague. From the accusation of masters in the use of poison it was no great step to the accusation of poisoners of wells; the population reacted with extreme fierceness and targeted the Jews with wholesale massacres, expulsions, and confiscation of property. About 300 Jewish communities throughout Europe felt the impact and never fully recovered from the onslaught. Using confessions obtained from Jews by torture—they always confessed, as any other people would, after torture was applied—the marauders felt justified in burning alive thousands of Jews, men, women and children and engaging in plunder. Pope Clement VI (1342–1352) in a Bull defended the Jews from the accusations, but his effort had practically no effect since the majority of the population, who were ignorant, chose to believe in the guilt of Jews.

14. But what of the guilt? If reason had been restored, it would have become clear that Jews also suffered from the devastating scourge like other members of the community and no magic protected them; that in poisoning the wells they would have destroyed their own water supply; that the tens of thousands of wells would require an amount of poison that was beyond the competence of any group to produce in those days ("… compounded of spiders and lizards, of frogs and flesh, and of the hearts of Christians mixed with the dough of the sacred host" 5–201); that the epidemic was just as virulent in England even though Jews were expelled from the country (1290) before the outbreak of the plague and that, in some cities in Germany, Jews were punished for their crime by the terror-stricken population before the outbreak of the epidemic. Although the bubonic plague subsided in Europe after 1351 (killing over 25 million people),it reappeared in 1361–1362, 1478–1480, and there were sporadic outbreaks until the 17th century. The attacks upon Jews continued for the same charge, particularly in Germany, where the plague reappeared although it must have occurred to Christians that there were fewer Jews around and that they surely learned a lesson from the devastating punishments meted out to them. The plague broke out locally in 1382, 1397, 1401, 1448, 1453, 1472, 1475, 1500, 1541, 1543, and later years, with the predictable result as far as Jews were concerned.

15. The Black Death helped to reinforce the hostile attitude of Christians toward Jews which, by now, was pervasive throughout Europe,

especially in Germany, where Luther's preached anti-Semitic diatribe fell on receptive ears—such as if the Jews could kill all the Christians they gladly would do so.

16. **Usury: The Accusation**

Excluded from all other professions by the Church and hostility of Christians, the Jew, in order to eke out a living, had to resort to money-lending, or usury, as labeled by Scripture; not excessive interest but any interest. Moneylending filled a popular need, an activity sternly prohibited to Christians by the Church, a position later moderated by changing economic conditions; Popes Alexander III (1159–1181) and Alexander IV (1254–1261) issued decrees against usury to buttress the opposition of the Church in ill-considered decisions, which confused the issue and was ignored by Christian moneylenders when they entered the field, such as the Lombards, Cahorsins (who became agents of the papacy), The Knights of Templar, and later on the Fuggers. The Church and authorities just barely tolerated the Jews as moneylenders as long as they derived some benefit from their activities. The debtors of whatever stripe, when faced with the inability of loan repayment targeted the lenders, the Jews, with all kinds of abusive charges from usury to heresy, including all the standby fulminations commonly heaped on Jews. They were accused of oppressive usury, exposed to bitter hatred, and finally expulsion from the country when royalty or nobility were unable, or unwilling, to repay the loans. The stigma of "usurer" attached strongly to Jews even after Christian moneylenders entered the field (charged much higher interest rates), supported by the Church and replaced Jews as principal moneylenders.

17. Why was the Catholic Church so bitterly opposed to lending at any interest? Reliance was claimed on Deut. 23:20–21, "You must not lend on interest to your brother … You may demand interest on a loan of a foreigner. …" Ex. 22–24 states, "… to any poor man among you, you must not play the usurer with him: you must not demand interest from him." Also Lev. 25:35–37, "If your brother falls on evil days … do not take any interest from him … you are not to lend him money at interest. …" These were the laws of the Israelites applicable to their society only and not to be viewed as having universal application; charity was the key guide and no profit was to be earned from the impoverished and needy. The Church appropriated these laws and was mistaken in the interpretation and application. The reward to

the Israelites for keeping these laws was Yahweh's blessing. Even the Church, at first, considered the taking of any interest as only "reprehensible" (Council of Carthage, 345), but strictly forbade the practice in the Middle Ages (the third Council of the Lateran, 1179; the second Council of Lyon, 1274; the Council of Vienne, 1311). "Yet nowhere is it stated that interest is in itself and under all conditions a violation of Justice" (57–499, Vol. 14). The Holy Office totally withdrew the prohibitions against the taking of interest in the 19th century, yet one cannot help noting that the last three above cited councils took their stand at a time when the Jews were most active in their moneylending business. To be a lender of money is to have power over the borrower; in some communities over one half of the population was indebted to Jews; that meant real power, much to the chagrin of the Church and clergy. The Jews, after all, were to be tolerated only as long as they lived in modest circumstances (i.e., in poverty) at the mercy of Christian authorities and suffered humiliation for their crime. For them to have power over Christians was intolerable, and the Church and clergy did their utmost to stir up hostilities and repudiation of the debt, followed by persecutions, expropriations, and expulsions; for in practicing usury the Jews were guilty of heresy, as ruled by the Council of Vienne, 1311. Nothing could please the debtors more, nor could the Church perform a more pleasing service for them, than canceling their debt and punishing the lenders.

18. The Jews can thank their ancestor priests and scribes for placing in the Torah socially worthy laws about not charging interest on loans to the poor and needy of their brethren and for using muddled language in Deuteronomy (23:20–21) which was devoid of economic reality, was resisted, subverted and also misinterpreted. Exodus, Leviticus and Deuteronomy are clear that the poor of Israelites' brethren had to be protected from the rich and that this restriction did not apply to foreigners who could be charged interest. This led to enmities with Christians who considered this biblical relaxation against usury, as to them, the crassest of discriminations and the work of the evil spirited and conniving Jews. Violations of this law were considered in the nature of moral transgressions only; the law was ignored; infractions were continuous, particularly in view of the economic conditions. The Babylonians (the code of Hammurabi contained laws which regulated the rate of interest that could

be charged), the Assyrians, the Egyptians, the Greeks and Romans, all permitted interest on loans and appreciated the economic necessity of lenders. The Jews of Egypt (in the region of Elephantine), as far back as the 5th century B.C., charged interest on loans, ignored the biblical prohibition against it as if it did not exist (were they aware of it?), for they did not make any effort, nor deemed it necessary, to evade the law by artificial means. In Jerusalem—already during the time of Nehemiah—much worse abuses were taking place by lenders than the charging of interest: Debtors pledged their children who were enslaved when the debt was not paid. It is evident, therefore, that the charging of interest was regular and widespread; that it was considered a necessary compensation to lenders; that lending at interest was viewed a profession like any other; that the ancients regulated interest that could be charged; that the Israelites were well acquainted with that ancient custom as were their neighbors; that the biblical prohibition was based on socially necessary considerations alleviating the plight of the poor; that due to economic realities, the biblical injunction was ignored and that observant Jews contrived every conceivable sham transaction for the purpose of evading the spirit of the prohibition.

19. Fate destined the Jews to be financiers, experts in commerce, adept in banking and skilled in the profession of moneylending. Deprived of the benefits of a country to call their own, prevented from owning land and engage in other professions or useful occupations by anti-Jewish legislation directed by papal authorities, allowed to practice as physicians by virtue of their expertise, but against great Church opposition (except in the case of Popes) and that of the common people who looked upon them as magicians, sorcerers and poisoners; the hostility of the town burghers closed the trade guilds to them and thus the right to engage in any of the covered trades; living without security and dependent on the whim of the rulers and the Church for their safety, existing without rights except the power to offer bribes to lenient officials, the Jews of the Middle Ages and up to the French Revolution were active in the one profession open to them: Moneylending. Faced with expulsion at any moment, Jews kept their wealth in a readily movable state, such as cash, coins, precious metals and negotiable instruments, which were also required tools of the moneylending business. They could read (at a time when most people were illiterate), spoke several languages useful for translators and in

international commerce. Study of the Talmud sharpened their mind and gave them a legal background. And most importantly, their brethren also lived in various far away countries and Hebrew was their language of communication which made for easy correspondence; there was a mutual trust among them based on common observance of Torah laws. In the days which marked the beginning of commerce, the use of letters of credit and bills of exchange depended on mutual trust as an essential requirement. Everything was in place pointing to success; it was not to be. Necessity made them usurers; the rulers and nobility made excessive demands on them for taxes, gifts and loans (the latter were seldom repaid in full), forcing Jews to charge higher interest on other loans to recoup losses. This led to Jew-hatred by the people, particularly since Jewish lenders frequently had Christian delinquent debtors imprisoned to force compliance. Jewish moneylenders were protected by the rulers as long as they were a source of profit to them. When Christian moneylenders—with the help and blessing of the Church—began to compete with Jews, they lost their importance to the rulers and also the protection extended to them: they faced expropriation and expulsion. And so the cycle continued.

20. Christian moneylenders were notorious for charging higher interest rates on loans than Jews, the Lombards in particular, who among other loans supplied money to the debtors of the Church for cash payments to the Vatican, with the assurance, that excommunication threatened any delinquent debtor who refused repayment, including the usurious interest. The Vatican, when in need, found ways to circumvent its prohibitions; they faced economic realities just like common debtors had to. It is noteworthy that in the Gospel of Matthew 25:27 (also Luke 19:23–24) in the "Parable of the talents", the earning of interest is looked upon with favor. A servant is chided by his master for not investing his master's talent with bankers so that, "… on my return I would have recovered my capital with interest." Banks, of course, take depositors' money and invest it at interest, and it is Jesus himself speaking.

21. The horrors of the church were visited upon the Jews; almost every means of earning a livelihood was closed to them by Church design; every conceivable difficulty was placed in their path to make earning a living— so natural for Jews—a nightmare until Pope Paul IV (1555–1559), wanting to starve the Jews of Rome out of existence, decreed "rag picking" the

only economic activity open to them. The Church erred in identifying interest with usury and usury with heresy; the Church erred in preaching hatred of Jews for pursuing the moneylending occupation and the Church erred in the negative biblical interpretation of usury. The Church did not acknowledge its errors nor apologize to the Jewish people for all the hardships it caused on account of false beliefs. Yet in the 20th century, the Vatican did become one of the larger institutions with investments in interest bearing securities, happily collecting the income which, at times, borders on excessive interest, i.e., usury.

Chapter 37

The Road Led to Auschwitz

1. And so it went on and on in never ending cycles of more oppressions of the Jewish people followed by lesser oppressions, repeating the myths and fabrications of the deicide blood-libel, and other favored charges of Christian bishops and priests, supported by papal functionaries and the not always visible hand of the Popes. Theologically inspired hostility toward Jews—which is the real basis of anti-Semitism—grew more sophisticated as the Enlightenment cut into the influence of the Church and Christian doctrine; economic and political anti-Semitism gained a steady following among all classes of people because they were based on an individual's magnified fears of the unknown. The accusations of Host desecration was easily punctured by Christian laymen who probably conducted experiments on their own to satisfy their curiosity and prudently remained silent. But in later centuries, the 19th, the charge that Jews were specially advantaged competitors in business because of their financial power (resentment of their economic success); that they would always be outsiders politically, and that, during the period of awakening national movements, they would not, and could not, be nationals first and Jews second (they were an alien element within human society); these charges were based on incomplete, although pragmatic, observations exasperated by anti-Semitic propaganda. Mistrustful of Jewish activities and suspicious of their secret intrigues, they were viewed as a challenge to the national aspirations of Christians. When towards the latter part of the 1890s, a Russian writer authored a book "Protocol of the Elders of Zion" in which he alleged a general Jewish conspiracy to dominate the world through secret financial speculation, it aroused a wave of anti-Semitism throughout the civilized world even though critics, without exception, considered the book rank forgery (Henry Ford believed it). Jews were, after all, dominant in the banking

community, they probably met in secret and certainly would not reveal their aim for domination to an outsider; to the closet anti-Semite, this was credible commentary and the book caused serious damage to Jewish reputation in general, the effects are felt to this day. The latent anti-Semite, if provoked enough, would snicker with self-satisfaction at the secret knowledge gained about a covert Jewish conspiracy for financial world domination.

2. The mood of the Catholic, Protestant, and other Churches toward anti-Semitism was contrite after the Holocaust. Perhaps, but only perhaps, a small spark lit up their collective conscience that their preaching of hatred against the Jewish people in past centuries and their anti-Judaic doctrines contributed, to some extent, to the events which led to the Holocaust and made it possible. Pope John Paul II declared that anti-Semitism was a sin against God, called for special training for priests to combat anti-Semitism and reform of discriminatory allusions in Catholic texts and liturgy. The Pope acknowledged that, in fact, some aspects of Catholic teaching had fostered anti-Semitism. Encouraging words, but things remain pretty much as before. After World War II, the World Council of Churches—an umbrella organization of Protestant, Anglican, and Orthodox Churches—passed a resolution strongly condemning anti-Semitism. They recommended that Christians should repudiate the idea of collective guilt of the Jews for the crucifixion of Jesus. The Lutheran and Episcopalian Churches' resolution contained expressions of regret for past persecution of Jews fomented by the Churches. Resolutions were passed to examine the religious literature, teaching manuals of the Church and prayers to excise from it material liable to create hatred of Jews. Encouraging words, but things remain pretty much as before. Pope Pius XI (1922–1939), a well meaning man, was guilty of totally untrue statements—perhaps senility took its toll—that the Vatican always protected the Jewish people against unjust oppression (16–293); that the Holy See disapproved of all hatred and animosity between people; that it specifically condemned the hatred against the people who once were chosen by God (16–457), and that anti-Semitism was a repugnant movement in which Christians could have no share (16–347). All three statements are totally false, the opposite are the facts; it was perhaps wishful thinking on the part of one who was unable to confront the horrors of Vatican history. Perhaps it was an effort to camouflage the sor-

did remote past, as his successor, Pope Pius XII (1939–1958), was obliged to falsify events of his most immediate past. According to historians, the Jews should have vanished from history a long time ago. Anti-Semitism is considered the cause of Jewish survival in the past in that it stimulated resistance and a sense of identity. In the darkest hours of their bloodstained history, when all seemed lost, there always appeared a small light at the end of the long tunnel, a ray of hope, which reinvigorated the Jews and gave them strength to continue.

3. Martin Luther's anti-Jewish polemic had a disastrous impact on the treatment of Jews in German countries and the attitude towards them grew harshly more anti-Semitic, culminating in the events of the Nazi era. When a powerful and respected religious leader of a people preached that the synagogues of the Jews should be set on fire, their homes destroyed, that they should be banned from the roads and markets, their property seized, drafted into forced labor and kicked out of the country for all time, then a hatred—grim and bewildering—was preached for all to take notice. The nature of German anti-Semitism owed a great deal to the peculiarly harsh and direct pronouncements of Luther, whose strong influence can be detected in the language and thoughts of succeeding generations. Beginning in the 19th century, German anti-Semites broached the subject of the extermination of Jews. In intellectual circles the idea found adherents, such as sending Jews to the front as cannon-fodder, predicting a German-Jew Armageddon, advocating campaigns against Jewish "vermin" which are to be exterminated as quickly and thoroughly as possible, and that the "Jewish question" should be solved by killing and extirpation (6–393 ff). This was spoken not by ignorant and illiterate masses but by German intellectuals. In 1922, already before he gained power, Hitler was quoted as saying that if he gained power, "the annihilation of the Jews will be my first and foremost task ..." (6–483). "In November 1938, the SS newspaper The Black Corps called for 'the extermination with fire and sword, the actual and final end of Jewry in Germany.' Hitler made speeches in that month attacking Jewry, prophesying annihilation of the Jewish race ... The year is significant. The fact of systematic extermination of Jews was public knowledge in Germany, in the democracies of Europe and America, and in the Soviet Union" (66–385). The Vatican did not back the ideas of disposing of Jews, but never openly contradicted them or spoke

out against them; it gave impetus (by its silence) to the storm gathering around the fate of Jews, culminating in the Nazi Holocaust by a thousand years old propaganda of hatred and abuse, first by targeting Jews as enemies of Christ and later as exerting a pernicious influence on civilized society. The unbending papal hostility toward Jews was briefly lifted when Pope Gregory XVI (1831–1846) became financially obligated to the banker Rothschild. Similarly, Pope Pius IX (1846–1878) dispensed with the requirement that Jews attend weekly proselytizing sermons after he received a substantial loan from Rothschild. The centuries old preaching of Christian clergy against Jews was epitomized in 1819 in the predominantly Catholic City of Würzburg (Germany), which experienced extensive anti-Jewish pogroms. A characteristic call to action, recalling the ghost of Luther, by one of its leaders displayed all the venom injected in the spirit of the time by the clergy: "Brothers in Christ! ... Rise up, gather yourselves, arm yourselves with courage and strength against the enemy of our faith, the time has come to suppress the race of Christ murderers, so that they do not become your rulers and of our posterity, since the Jew hordes lift their heads with pride ... down with them before they crucify our priests, before they desecrate our sanctuaries and destroy our churches, we still rule over them ... death and ruin for all Jews, you must flee or die!" (56–506 ff). Those who carried out Hitler's Final Solution advanced but a small step from the pogrom leaders of Würzburg.

4. The German Catholic and Protestant clergy supported Hitler with only minor exceptions; the support was unflinching, to the bitter end and never wavered despite obvious signs that the war was lost. The clergy were German nationalists first and Christians second. The quotations cited do not reflect any concern that Christians were fighting Christians, that Germans were using the most brutal and inhumane methods to suppress the freedom of other Christians and that Jews were persecuted, deprived of all rights and exterminated. The quotations are from "Abermals Krähte Der Hahn" (56) by the German Church historian Karlheinz Deschner. Speaking of the attitude of the German Churches to the Nazi movement, after Hitler assumed power in 1933, in a pastoral letter of all German Catholic Bishops: "We German Bishops are far removed from interfering with this national awakening ... Under no circumstance is it our intent to remove from the State the strength of the Church" (590).

"Archbishop Gröber of Freiburg in April 1933 adjured the German Catholics that they must not reject the new State but positively accept it and must cooperate with it. And later in August 1933 ordered ... to place the flags and insignia of the National Socialist Workers Party in the Catholic Churches" (592). "Bishop Bornewasser of Trier stated 'we entered the new Reich erect and with firm stride and are prepared to serve it with the pledge of all strength of our body and soul' " (593). As stated by Bishop Burger: "The objectives of the Reich government have for very long been the objectives of the Catholic Church" (593). All the complaints of Churches were directed toward alleviation of damage to their interests. "The Bishops never objected to ... Hitler's attack on Austria, Czechoslovakia, Poland ... France, the Soviet Union, a war which they welcomed. They never protested against the persecution and gassing of the Jews ..." (596). Bishop Graf Galen, praised for his resistance, never complained against Hitler's instigated war but against persecution of religious institutions and the killing of inmates of insane asylums, "... the Catholic Bishops of Germany never condemned the Nazi regime as long as Hitler was in power" (597). "When in March 1936 Hitler occupied the demilitarized Rheinland ... the Catholic Churches held thanksgiving services ..." (599). When Hitler invaded Austria in 1938, Cardinal Innitzer of Vienna celebrated the occasion "... with Church bells pealing and swastika flags fluttering from Churches and instructed his clerics to hold thanksgiving services ..." (599). "When in the fall of 1939 German bombardment of Warsaw caused massive loss of life of Polish Catholics, the German Catholics—abetted by their Cardinals and Bishops—prayed for the protection of the Nazi Reich" (601). After the invasion of the Soviet Union in 1941, the army's Catholic Bishop directed a pastoral letter to the German Catholic soldiers, "... as so often in history, Germany presently became the savior of Europe ..." (602). After the defeat of Poland, "the Evangelical leaders thanked God and Hitler ..." (607). After the invasion of Norway in April 1940, Pope Pius XII (1939–1958) was urged by many to condemn the aggression, but remained silent. "Only through the Osservatore Romano did he indicate that Norway had 2619 Catholics, but Germany had 30 million" (617). In 1943, the leaders of the Evangelical Church called for a total and ruthless war, a war without sentimentality and without shame. In support they cited Luke 9:62 (607). The verse from Luke reads, quoting Jesus, "Once the hand is laid on the plough, no one who looks back is fit for the kingdom of God." In their support of the Nazis, the

German clergy went well beyond the call of duty; they were for Nazi power and were exhilarated by it. It relieved their inordinate fears of the public exercise of the freedom of religion, freedom of speech and freedom of the press, values which were not of the "old Christian tradition" and values which the Nazis totally suppressed.

5. The Jewish people, whose history stretches across a span of thousands of years, the survivors of unsuccessful uprisings against Rome, the Crusades, the expulsions from England, France and Spain; the fires of the Inquisition; the horrors of the Black Death; the humiliation of the ghettos; the pogroms of Eastern Europe; hundreds of years of papal provoked hostility; over a thousand years of Christian persecutions; the accusation of deicide which condemned a whole people as murderers of the Lord—all of these the Jews survived with heavy losses and a bitter price for the right to be a nation apart from other nations. But survive they did. The forced separation of children from their parents, husband from wife, the arbitrary confiscation of properties, expulsion from homes and from cities where they lived for centuries, the ruthless and senseless killing of family and friends, the uncertainty of the future—all these the Jews survived with painful memories. The Christian false accusations of Jews were a bitter pill to swallow; they were not permitted to defend themselves against the charges and had to suffer the humiliation in silence. From Germany, ranked among the most civilized countries of Europe, there evolved forces which took advantage of the economic despair and political unrest; unified by the most pervasive and racist anti-Semitism which drew on, and combined with, past Christian determined hatred of Jews. Nothing that happened in the past history of Jews prepared them for the events which were to befall them, events which struck the Jews of Nazi Germany and Nazi controlled countries with a vengeance. It started before the war of 1939, like many persecutions, expropriations and expulsions which Jews experienced many times before; no statesman, politician or a person of knowledge from other countries predicted anything more serious than brutal and hoodlum-style Jew-beatings, although they should have been forewarned by Hitler's threats and other reverberations about the annihilation of Jews. After the invasion of Poland, there were the first signs of the mass-murder of Jews by shooting which aroused only negligible protest from the rest of the world; the Nazis were emboldened. It was not until the invasion of the

Soviet Union in June 1941 and after the German disastrous winter retreat from Moscow in 1941 (the first German army defeat of the war), that the Nazis—overwhelmed by the millions of Jews under their control—prepared the groundwork for the Final Solution—the total annihilation of European Jewry—at a secret conference held on January 20, 1942 in a suburb of Berlin. The conference, in fact, was really nothing more than an announcement of the decision to top Nazi officials; the gassing of Jews had already taken place at Chelmno (Poland). With the zest of Crusaders, the Germans constructed a chain of extermination camps, mostly in Poland, with specially designed gas chambers and crematoria (German firms were eager bidders for the construction work) and organized a network of railway facilities to transport the victims to the camps. The largest of these camps was at Auschwitz-Birkenau where the capacity for gassing and crematoria was almost 10,000 victims per day at its peak. In the Soviet Union, where great distances overwhelmed the Germans and extermination camps were not feasible, the employment of Einsatzgruppen units (murder groups) did the mass-killing of Jews by shooting. The operations were efficient, staffed by unusually committed and competent men and women; total secrecy was maintained so as not to alarm the victims and keep the mass-murders secret from the outside world. This was a State operation, utilizing considerable manpower, railway rolling stock, trucks and maintenance equipment, at a time when the German war effort was desperately short of transportation equipment. This situation existed at a time when it was known that Germany was losing the war and that there would be swift retribution for the murderers; the Nazis displayed a dogged determination and tenacity to pursue the murderous course relentlessly (most of the camp staff attended Sunday Church services regularly) and to the bitter end. The shortage of army tailors and shoemakers in the occupied East (work performed by Jewish conscripts) was rectified by the murder of the craftsmen—such was the determined zeal of the Nazis to annihilate the Jews. The murder process was brutal, pitiless, full of guile to confuse the victims, using a special double-speak (such as calling the murder process "Special Treatment," transport to the extermination camps "Resettlement," gas chambers "Showers") and brute force was used when necessary. The worse the war went for Germany, the more determined they were to complete the extermination process, so they could claim at least one war achievement: The Final Solution of the Jewish problem. A few heroic Christians tried to save the Jews—children in particular—from the round-up for transports and certain death by taking them into their homes and caring for them for the rest of the war; this they did at great risk to themselves and their families, for they faced death, if caught. In the midst of the greatest horrors committed by the Nazis, all of whom were Christians, a few heroic Christians of another kind saw it the other way. And so it was with some countries. Finland and Bulgaria refused to turn over a single Jew to the Nazis. Little Denmark, the most heroic of them all, transported most of its Jews to Sweden when word got out that a Nazi round-up of Jews was imminent. Fascist Italy protected its Jews; Fascist Spain was helpful in saving Jews by permitting entry and transit; even Hungary refused Nazi requests for Jewish round-ups as long as Horthy was in power.

6. The secret did not remain a secret for very long. Allied governments received intelligence reports of wholesale Nazi murder of Jews in 1942. In early 1943, the Polish government-in-exile in a report by eye-witnesses confirmed the mass extermination of Jews by gassing; in 1943, escaped concentration camp prisoners confirmed the horrors taking place in extermination camps. The Allies, engaged in a total war with Germany, were in no position to give effective help without compromising the war effort. Most Jews living in German occupied lands could not believe the reports from the extermination camps that reached them in 1942 and 1943—it just was not possible that such things could happen, total incredulity! But such things did happen, 6 million Jews were slaughtered (4 million by gassing, 2 million by shooting), most Jewish families suffered the loss of loved ones. European Jewry would have vanished had Hitler won the war. The gas ovens of Auschwitz-Birkenau continued to operate until October 1944, when they ceased operations because of approaching Soviet army units. British and Palestine Jews pleaded with the Allies to bomb the three rail lines leading to Auschwitz from Bohumin, Cracow and Sosnowice and thus interdict the transports; the Allies refused to divert personnel and aircraft. The Allies did bomb the I.G. Farben Buna works (a synthetic oil and rubber plant), located immediately to the east of Auschwitz, on August 20, 1944 (the first raid), but the purpose was Allied war effort and not saving Jews.

7. The Jews were expendable and nothing short of total Allied victory would stop the carnage. The Jews mostly went to their death quietly; the well-fed and cared for Germans plotted continuously to deceive the ill-fed

and ill-cared for Jews, hiding their barbarity behind a screen of well planned and coordinated misinformation; the closely-knit family unit of Jews was not suited to frivolous and hopeless resistance, particularly when there seemed no escape from the terrible fate and all was lost; resistance would only postpone the inevitable and create frightful scenes among women and children. There were, however, some desperate and fore-doomed uprisings by Jews willing to risk all and not be slaughtered like sheep. The most noteworthy was the Warsaw ghetto uprising on April 19, 1943, with pitched battles between German soldiers and Jews; the saga of that epic resistance was related in a prior Chapter. There were also smaller uprisings throughout the eastern territories and in the camps, the most note-worthy were at Treblinka (August 2,1943) and Auschwitz-Birkenau (October 7, 1944); the results were predictable.

8. Heroic Jews, men, women and children (far too many children) were tortured, starved, dehumanized, ill-treated, and finally murdered. They suf-fered unspeakable grief, tears, anguish, and cries in their ordeal. Never in the history of mankind has such a tragedy occurred on such an immense scale. The Jews of the Holocaust died for nothing, in vain, their death served no purpose. Their death did not stop hatred, anti-Semitism, and other mythical accusations of Christians. Their sacrifice was no more than a caprice of history, a bloody page, a confluence of distorted and foul events which were compressed into a twelve year period. The odious anti-Semitic message of the Christian Scripture accusing Jews of deicide, mur-derers of Christ as its central theme, reproduced a hundredfold throughout history as its main dogma, reached the inevitable destined conclusion and culmination at Auschwitz-Birkenau.

Chapter 38

Pope Pius XII and the Holocaust

1. Pope Pius XII was condemned for remaining silent during the Nazi era when the extermination of Jews was in full operation; contrary to his claims and the claims of the Curia, the Pope did not speak out on behalf of Jews, specifically or generally; instead, he made use of superficial references to suffering, offenses against morality, the right to live for all men of whatever race or to whatever religion they may belong. This was language that the German Ambassador to the Vatican characterized as "richly meandering and unclear." The Pope did speak out on behalf of Jewish converts to Catholicism, but that was in defense of Catholics. For some reason he did not speak out on behalf of courageous Catholic priests in German concentration and extermination camps. For the claim was made that to be specific would make matters only worse for the victims. Why should the Pope have spoken out on behalf of Jews to slow down or stop their extermination? Does not the whole history of the papacy point to an unmitigated hostility toward Jews? The Popes did speak out in the past when Jews were mercilessly slaughtered by Christian mobs and protested their innocence, such as, when they were falsely accused of poisoning the wells and murdering Christian children for ritual purposes. Their protests had little effect on the mobs but they did strengthen the fabric of Christian society by showing spiritual leadership. Pius XII had his own very good reasons for remaining silent, Jewish hopes of intervention were totally misplaced. The pleas of non-Jews for Pius to speak out against the suffering of Christians under Nazi domination were equally wasted; they should have done their homework. For that stern, authoritarian, and phlegmatic Pope was an out and out Germanophile—the Jews were declared enemies of Nazi Germany and Christians who suffered under the Nazis did so because they were opposed to them.

2. Born on March 2, 1876, Eugenio Pacelli, he entered papal service in 1901. In April 1917, he was appointed nuncio in Munich and in June 1920, he was named nuncio to the new German republic; named Cardinal in December 1929, succeeded to the post of Secretary of State on February 7, 1930, and as such was responsible for concordats with Austria (June 1933) and with National Socialist Germany (July 1933). He was elected Pope on March 2, 1939. He served in Germany from 1917 to 1930, and during those 13 years had occasion to develop a close friendship with the German people, a friendship which would develop, in time, into an admiration for Hitler and the Third Reich to the apparent exclusion of all other nations. There was nothing held back or camouflaged in his expressions on the subject of Germany. On the occasion of the New Year reception (1940)—after the outbreak of World War II and the defeat of Catholic Poland, which had more than 30 million Catholics but could never match Germany's contribution of 1 billion marks yearly to the Catholic Church—Pius XII was heard to say that, "… His great affection and love for Germany continued undiminished … and perhaps he loved it all the more … in these grave times" (67–40). Pius in a speech to German travelers in Rome on April 25, 1939, said (speaking in German): "… we rejoice in the greatness of Germany, at her resurgence and her prosperity …" (67–16). German foreign minister Ribbentrop, in a letter written February 15, 1941, quoted Pius that he had expressed extreme optimism about the prospects of a German victory and spoke even of certain victory for Germany (67–71). On October 4,1941, a German diplomat wrote, "… Pius XII had friendly feelings to the Reich. He had no more ardent wish for the Führer than to see him gain victory over Bolshevism …" (67–85). A German diplomat quoting the Spanish Ambassador to the Holy See in a letter dated November 17, 1941, "…(the) Pope replied … he had always felt, and still felt, not only the warmest sympathy for Germany, but also admiration for the great qualities for the Führer" (67–86). After the defeat of Holland, Belgium and France, Pius "directed the German episcopate to hold thanksgiving services for the Führer" (56–617). After the occupation of Bohemia and Moravia on March 15, 1939, Pius totally ignored the aggression after he was asked to speak out against it, declaring to all, "how he values Germany and that he is prepared to do a lot for Germany" (56–610).

3. Pius was not neutral in World War II, he took up the cause of Germany whenever and wherever he could. His ardent hope was for a German vic-

tory, notwithstanding what Nazi Germany stood for, as long as the Soviet Union—the "Bolsheviks" as he called them—would be obliterated from the face of the earth. He deflected requests for speaking out against German atrocities and extermination of Jews with statements that to do so could affect the loyalties of German Catholic soldiers as they fought for Germany, and the morale of German Catholic civilians and their support for the German war effort. He was opposed to anything non-German, anything which could result in a German defeat and which would not bring about the defeat of communism. The Pope expressed the view that "a powerful German Reich is quite indispensable for the future of the Catholic Church" (67–191). His protests at the 1940 German attack on Belgium, Holland and Luxembourg—they were among the largest contributors of money to the Vatican—were limited to paternal affections and regrets that the countries became involved in a war; not a word about invasion or the aggressor. In the case of France (a predominantly Catholic country), the Vatican advised the French to sign a separate peace treaty with Germany or capitulate to the Germans. Early in the war, England and France requested Pius to declare Germany the aggressor—the Germans invaded Poland: he refused. His refusal to take sides against Germany was in accordance with his assurance given to German diplomats. When reports of atrocities against Polish Catholics reached the Pope, he issued an Encyclical on October 20, 1939, which expressed, among others, "… The blood of countless human beings … has been shed and cries out to heaven, especially the blood of Poland, …" (67–36). No reference to the culprit. After the collapse of Poland, the long-time Polish foreign minister Beck (who escaped from Poland) declared: "One of those most responsible for the tragedy of my country is the Vatican. I realized too late that we conducted a foreign policy in the interest of the Catholic Church" (56–615). The assistant to the American Special Envoy to the Vatican, in a talk with Pope Pius (before Germany's invasion of the Soviet Union) related his view that war between Germany and Russia was imminent and that the Vatican would do everything to hasten the outbreak of that war, even to the point of encouraging Hitler with a promise of moral support (67–75). That titanic conflict was regarded by Pius as in defense of Christian culture which he declared was the foundation of European civilization; the misery and suffering of the Russian people was by "the will of Providence." Already as early as December 25, 1939, in his Christmas message, Pius played the role of mediator trying to bring together the Christian belligerents: "Let us end the war of brothers and join our forces against the mutual enemy, against Communism" (56–616). When in 1943 it became apparent that Germany was losing the war, the Vatican again made several efforts to mediate a rapprochement between Germany and the Allied Powers for the purpose of combatting Bolshevism; the Pope even sent a messenger to the United States (August 1943) to explore this aim. Pope Pius XII—the representative of Christ on earth and the leader of 800 million Catholics—played a crude political game during the war and lost; he was convinced that Nazi Germany was the way of the future and he was mistaken. He was not humble enough to admit his error, nor did he apologize to those who in desperation sought his help but were rebuffed.

4. Pius was meticulous during the war period not to mention the extermination of Jews by name in any of his public pronouncements. Although he was repeatedly asked to condemn Nazi atrocities against Jews and asked to do so specifically, he responded that to do so would make matters even worse for the victims, and that his protest could not be specific since by doing so the loyalties of German Catholics might waver. He did speak out as Cardinal Secretary of State on April 17, 1937, when he preached a sermon in Rome against "the God-murdering nation of the Jews" (35–16). Pius was given too much credit for his ability to influence the course of events. Amidst all the seeming panoply of moral strength, amidst the decorum, stateliness and the calming facades of the Vatican, amidst the pretense of fair dealing and evenhanded dispensation of justice, Pope Pius XII was perceived to stand above the tumult of the times, radiating divine confidence to an immoral and dispirited world. But his appearance was a delusion, a deception, a carry-over of the mystique of the Holy See from centuries ago, kept alive by ardent Catholics and sentimentalists. For in reality, Pius had no power to influence the course of events before, during and after the war, power in the sense of persuasion and moral leadership—this is clear from the reading of history. The Axis Powers could not be influenced by appeals to the decorum of man—they were fighting the battle of survival. Even with the best of intentions Pius could not interfere and his appeals would have been of doubtful value despite German internal memos—probably written by Catholics—counseling caution in dealing with the Pope for the duration of the war; they were low-level diplomats

out of step with Nazi bigwigs. But the intentions of the Pope were not the best; far from being evenhanded, he was partisan to a fault; professed without hesitation and prompting his love for Germany and an admiration for Nazi achievements on many occasions when a subdued or muffled voice would have sufficed. He faced with equanimity the prospect of a Nazi Europe which he equated with a Christian Europe, a Europe only for Aryans, a Europe from which the Jews were eliminated. To the increasing clamor coming from concerned Catholics for Pius to speak out against German barbarities—to raise his voice—he responded like a coward, his troubled mind seeking shelter behind statements which would not offend nor help anybody, or withdrew into silence. "... the Holy See was unable to denounce publicly particular atrocities ..." (67–125).

5. In view of the above, why is so much significance attached to the Pope's silence? Could his character have reacted differently? Should we have expected him to react contrary to his nature? Should he have spoken out and risked a martyr's death as the future Pope John XXIII probably would have had he been Pope instead of Pius? We shall never know. But we do know that the Vatican did not tell the truth about what it did and when it knew. We do know that the statement (December 1942) "that everything possible was being done privately to relieve the distress (sic) of the Jews" (67–125), attributed to Pius by the Vatican Secretary of State, was false and that the immediately following statement of same date and attribution," that the Holy See was unable to verify Allied reports as to the number of Jews exterminated ..." (67–125) was equally false. The statement made after the war and attributed to Pius XII that "... the Pope was responsible during the war for saving tens of thousands of Jewish lives" (16–438) is false. Jews did find protection in Italian Catholic Churches and convents during the Nazi occupation as a result of efforts of courageous individual priests; the claim of Pius XII, that they were acting on his instructions was denied by the priests involved—another false claim of Pius XII. The Vatican information that a great number of Jews found shelter in the Vatican is false, "... neither the chief rabbi of Rome, nor any other important members of the Jewish community along the Tiber have ever heard of a single Jew (not converted) who had been hidden inside the Vatican itself" (16–426). On August 3, 1942, the American representative at the Holy See stated that he had on numerous occasions warned the

Vatican for the Pope to speak out against Nazi atrocities in German-occupied areas, but without success. On September 26, 1942, the same spokesman informed the Vatican of the continuing liquidation of the Warsaw ghetto; of the mass executions of Jews in newly constructed extermination camps; of wholesale deportations of Jews from other parts of occupied Europe to the East for mass-murder purposes and general information about the Nazi plan for the "Final Solution." On December 17, 1942, "all the Allied nations officially condemned the extermination of the Jews by the Nazis ..." (67–124). The Holy See was unable (December 1942) to verify the number of Jews exterminated and that was given as an excuse for not speaking out? Did it matter to Pius whether the number was 100,000 or more? Verify the numbers with whom, the Nazis? Under the circumstances, is it credible that Pius meant to speak out if he could verify the number of Jews murdered? The question deserves no answer. On January 2, 1943, the President of the Polish government-in-exile in a letter to Pius: "The extermination of Jews ... has only been a test for the systematic application of scientifically organized mass murder ... Hundreds of thousands of people are killed ..." (16–141). Pius XII responded with silence; if he spoke out it might make matters worse; would cause greater evil; would result in violent death of more people and he could be reproached later by the German people "in bitterness of their defeat." When on October 15, 1943, Jews were seized in Rome under the Pope's very nose and 1007 deported to Auschwitz, Pius could not be moved from his attitude of silence; the German Ambassador was able to report to Berlin that the Pope "... has done everything he could ... not to injure the relationship between the Vatican and the German Government of the German authorities in Rome" (67–207).

6. Pope Pius XII never condemned Nazi terror; never condemned military aggression against other countries; never condemned the oppression and exploitation of conquered nations; the starvation of whole segments of the population; the murder of Catholic priests and never uttered a single protest against the extermination of Jews. His conduct during the war was a disgrace to the Catholic Church, an embarrassment to individual Catholics some of whom put their lives on the line to ease the suffering of the persecuted. After the end of World War II when the extent of Nazi bestiality was revealed for all to see, this weakling Pope, this man with a

strange ideology unfit for the Bishop of Rome, who placed a distorted and cynical twist on his public pronouncements during the war, unburdened his soul to the College of Cardinals on June 2,1945, when he said: "During the war we have never stopped ... to oppose ourselves to the ruinous and relentless applications of the National-Socialist doctrines, which made use of the most refined scientific methods to torture and to do away with people who often (sic) were innocent" (16–409), a brave statement (after the war) but false; this from a man who proudly proclaimed in late 1943, that a powerful German Reich was indispensable for the future of the Catholic Church. This Pope was a friend of the Nazis to the bitter end. "He interceded on behalf of German war criminals at the Nürnberg trial" (56–641) and many German war criminals found temporary or permanent asylum at the Vatican (56–641). Pius XII showed his dark and sinister side when as Cardinal Secretary of State in a speech in 1937—reacting to the Kingdom of Yugoslavia's revocation of the Vatican-Yugoslav Concordat, he threatened: "The day will come when the number of those will not be small who will greatly regret to have rebuffed the magnanimous and benevolent work of the Vicar of Christ offered to your country" (56–621). The "regret" was not long in coming; Nazi Germany invaded Yugoslavia on April 6, 1941, followed by crimes "which equaled the vast crimes of the Christian Middle-Ages" (56–621).

Pope Pius XII, this man of God, shamed the honor of his Catholic followers. On them falls the burden of sharing his guilt.

Chapter 39

Epilogue and Conclusion

1. In this book I have tried to examine the causes of anti-Semitism and other problems peculiar to Jews which led to their persecution and martyrdom throughout history. I have examined the question of what could be done to remove that scourge from the shoulders of the Jewish people. In that connection, I have analyzed the origin of the Israelite religion and Judaism, and their influence on the psychological make-up of Jews by the Bible; the influence of prophets and the stranglehold priests, scribes and rabbis held upon the Jewish mind through the written word. It was apparent that until the discovery of a Book of Law during the reign of King Josiah (640–609 B.C.), monotheism was unknown and pagan worship, idolatry, human sacrifice and polytheism were the religious practices of the Israelites; they were indistinguishable from the practices of their neighbors. The influence of the biblical injunction not to be ruled by a foreign king or ruler led to many unnecessary and frivolous revolts which resulted in devastating defeats for Jews and their dispersion. The Jewish version of the history of the Maccabean wars (167–160 B.C.); the death of Judas Maccabeus; the revolt against Rome (66–70 A.D.), and the Bar Kokhba uprising (132–135 A.D.) will have to be rewritten.

2. I have examined the influence Christianity had upon the Jewish people, the writings of Paul and the four Gospels. Although anti-Jewish sentiments were known before Christianity, it was from the teaching of the New Testament that a virulent new kind of anti-Semitism evolved; the false charge of "deicide" was invented which became one of its central dogmas, according to which Jews conspired in the death and crucifixion of Christ for which they earned eternal condemnation and punishment. This accusation is at the root of theologically inspired anti-Semitism, the most unbending and radical hatred of a people.

415

Immeasurable suffering and rivers of innocent Jewish blood flowed as a result of that false accusation and others which followed from it. At the hands of Christians, during the Middle Ages the Jews were reduced from a once fiercely proud nation to a physically stooped, compliant, fearful, cowering people, segregated in ghettoes, and forced to wear a piece of clothing which marked them off from the rest; all to the great satisfaction of Christians who regarded the continuous plight of Jews as foretold in Scripture to be punishment for their crime. The Church hierarchy ruled with an iron hand and the treatment of non-conformists—all Christians—was just as severe or worse. The Fourth Crusade against Constantinople, the massacre of the Albigenses, the burning of witches—all of them totally innocent—the fagots of the Inquisition and the history of some of the most disreputable and murderous Popes reveal a strain in Christianity unworthy of its founders. The Popes, Curia, and Bishops mixed faith with power in order to preserve the prestige and emoluments of office.

3. Throughout the history of Christendom, its ecclesiastics knowingly perpetuated doctrinal falsehoods as a means of strengthening the faith of adherents; all religions, by their very nature, fabricate events and myths to dress up their creed and beliefs to appear superior and more convincing—this is to be expected. But when Christianity measured its success in direct proportion to the failure of Judaism; when the suffering and humiliation of the Jewish people—mostly at the hands of the Christians themselves—was declared a measure of the truth of its teaching and the claimed fulfillment of Old Testament prophecies; when the degradation of Jews—all at the hands of Christians—was deemed a punishment for their crime of crucifying the Lord; when the guilt of Jews can never-be removed as long as the Gospels preach it despite efforts by the Vatican Ecumenical Council of 1962 (Pope John XXIII) to limit the accusation to a "few" Jews living in the time of Jesus—then one must regretfully conclude that not only did the preaching of hatred against Jews for 19 centuries and the anti-Judaic Christian doctrines make the World War II Holocaust possible, but that nothing has changed to prevent the repetition of similar tragedies.

4. But what claim can Christianity assert for the cogent basis of its theological foundation? That it was the fulfillment of the Old Testament? That the mission of Jesus, the Messiah, was predicted by the Hebrew prophets? This presupposes that the Old Testament—or at least the Torah—was the revealed

word of God and that the Hebrew prophets proclaimed the divine message which foretold the coming of Jesus, the true Messiah. However, based upon the account made known in this book, the Christians will find little encouragement and support that such reliance advanced their cause, for the genesis of the early religion of the Israelites was inauspicious: pagan worship; pervasive idolatry and polytheism; worship of golden bulls and calves; pillars of stone on high places; sacrifices of children; the worship of Baal (the storm-god) and Astarte (the goddess of fertility); the obligatory sacrifices of bulls and spilling their blood on the altar—that from antiquity until the Babylonian Exile (587 B.C.), with two minor short-term exceptions (during the reign of Kings Josiah and Hezekiah), monotheism was unknown and nothing but idolatry practiced; that the Torah was not revealed to Moses but redacted by priests and scribes (principally Ezra) during the Babylonian Exile and the religion of one God, Yahweh, of monotheism, was literally forced upon recalcitrant Jews (formerly Israelites) by Ezra and Nehemiah after the return from Exile in 537 B.C.; that the God of the Israelites proclaimed his own criteria for choosing the Messiah whose divinely ordained mission would be the ingathering of the scattered tribes of the Israelites and lead them back to the land their fathers once possessed, as also proclaimed by the major Hebrew prophets (Jeremiah, Isaiah, Ezekiel)—and not a Christ Jesus, a Redeemer, destined to die on the cross to shed his blood for the sins of mankind, so that those who believed in him earned salvation and everlasting life.

The Torah was not revealed to Moses but written and redacted more than 700 years later by profane hands; Christ Jesus was not the Redeemer (Messiah) foretold by the Torah and the prophets. Given the idolatrous and polytheistic antecedents of the religion of the ancient Israelites; given the unambiguous mission of the chosen Messiah as made known by the God of the Israelites and further amplified by the Hebrew prophets, it would be calamitous for Christians to predicate the validity of their religion on the fulfillment of the Old Testament and their dying and resurrected Saviour as the Messiah foretold by the Hebrew prophets.

5. I examined the claim made by the head of the Catholic Church, Pope Pius XII, the Vicar of Christ on earth, that he helped save the lives of Jews during the Nazi era—that claim I found to be false. True Catholics will find his cynical conduct and duplicitous rhetoric during World War II a disgrace and hard to live down.

6. Today there is no unified Jewish outlook of any kind—the Jews are deeply divided according to their religious views; there are the secular, Reform, Conservative, Orthodox and ultra-Orthodox; other sects are forming leading the Jews totally away from any pretense of belief in Judaism. The secular and Reform Jews define their "Jewishness" in their own individual styles which have little to do with Judaism; the memory of orthodox grandparents and perhaps fathers is fading and the children are assimilating to the gentile surrounding to make them indistinguishable; inter-marriage is rampant as well as apostasy from the faith. The Conservative, Orthodox and ultra-Orthodox Jews—the true believers in the Torah and its commandments—are proud of their Jewishness and religious tradition, make every effort to continue the process by guiding the education of their children; are faithful-bearers of the spiritual heritage of their ancestors and most willingly shoulder the burdens anti-Semitism imposes on them. They have a cause to suffer for. If anti-Semitism and gentile hatred can be said to be the major factors in the survival of Jews, given a free choice, how much are the Reform Jews willing to suffer? Is it reasonable to assume they would suffer for a religion they did not really profess or have the required belief in? It is against human nature to do so. But the attachment they enjoy with like-minded Jews is not religious but economic and social. Judaism is a communal religion and institution, as such, communal economic and social bonds constitute a powerful cohesive force and incentive to remain loyal to the "Jewish" community; they are willing to suffer the abuses of anti-Semitism because they enjoy economic and social advantages as "Jews" which would otherwise be denied them as non-Jews. The Orthodox regard the Reform as apostates beyond redemption; the Reform regard the Orthodox as fanatical fundamentalists, unfit for the world of today; there is nothing common or mutual between them except that both groups alike are collectively the target of anti-Semitism. The charge of "deicide" does not distinguish between believing and non-believing Jews, between fundamentalists and agnostics. The only way for a Jew to lose the "stigma" is to undergo the sacrament of baptism or dissolve his bonds with Judaism and let posterity completely efface any links.

7. What can be done to remove the scourge of anti-Semitism? Nothing! The baselessness of the charge will not deter the accuser, nor will it daunt the accused; for the Orthodox will see it as the ongoing intervention of the

divine hand to keep them holy and apart and the Reform will have to weigh the pain against the economic and social benefits of belonging to a communal religion. But nothing, absolutely nothing would explain away an accusation which deteriorated to murder, massacres, pogroms or a Holocaust of the recent past. The standby explanation of the Orthodox justifies it as divine punishment for abandoning the commandments of the Torah; the Reform Jews have no explanation. Millions of Jews of every kind of belief—men, women and children—done away in cold-blooded and methodical murder as divine punishment? The mind is not capable of grasping such abnormalities, let alone offer an explanation—there is none.

The religious foundations are cracking, the ghost of the witch of En-Dor (1 Sam.28:7ff) stirred and cried, "why have you deceived me?" It was not Moses, the man who is said to have spoken with God "face to face" who wrote down the divine Law but unknown profane hands; it was not Moses, the man whom God is said to have selected to lead the Hebrews out of Egyptian slavery, who authored the Torah, but ignorant defilers of the word and corrupters of the spirit who conspired to put forth a law and curses over 600 years after the events described. It was these imposters who gave standing to their work by pretending a facade of divine revelation—they blasphemed the name of God. The Torah, therefore, cannot claim to be a divinely revealed work (the only work in the Old Testament capable of putting forth such a claim) and violation of its commandments and ordinances—some of which are praiseworthy and utilitarian—therefore could not invoke divine condemnation and punishment. The Jews suffered for nothing and were slaughtered for nothing. God remained silent.

From the trembling earth containing the mass-graves drenched in blood, the slaughtered innocents, the martyred Jewish men, women and children, their restless spirit finding no deserved eternal repose till the avenging angels palliate the contrived and baseless accusation resulting in the crudest form of anti-Semitism—a curse hurled against them— voices proclaiming to all the living that their sacrifices were for nothing, victims of a lie concocted by a cabal of fallible artificers combining messianic ideas derived from the Old Testament and existing pagan mythologies and superstitions—no atonement is acceptable. Men corrupted by an evil agenda invented the execrable and unique accusation of deicide, which was unhistorical. The related crucifixion of Jesus of the Gospels had no earthly existence, and did not need one, for the fabled depiction of the Passion, his suffering, to enhance the core of Christian beliefs.

8. The Conservative, Orthodox and Ultra-Orthodox still believe in the God of the Torah, never wavered in the faith of their fathers; they found profound inspiration and dedication in the study of the Tanak and Talmud, perceived the essence of Judaism as a continuous learning process about the Torah, unraveling its mysteries and conforming to its guidelines. This brought them happiness and peace of mind. But their religion is not a social force. For while they perform good deeds for like-minded Jews, they keep themselves separate and apart, consider all other Jews (let alone non-Jews) unclean and polluted, treat others with disdain bordering on contempt, show an unforgiving and intolerant attitude toward others. They are a hardy people, resist change and are unaffected in their personal lives by the reciprocated hostility of their neighbors; harbor deep within them understandable resentments against Christians for centuries of slights and torments suffered at their hand. They treat other Jews as apostates who abandoned the religion of their ancestors and prostituted themselves to other gods. Any thought of rapprochement between Orthodox Jews and Christians in matters of religious accommodation is out of question; their lives and relations will go on as before, with peaks and lows in tolerance and hostility in never-ending cycles.

Conclusion

9. It is the essence of Christian theology to be anti-Judaic and anti-Semitic, it cannot be otherwise; the Gospels and other writings of the canon derive their polemic from it. Any effort to remove these writings are bound to fail since they are foundational to Christian theology.

10. The Torah, in preaching exclusivity, separateness, special election and holiness of Jews to the exclusion of all other peoples, bears a contributory responsibility for the anti-Judaism and anti-Semitism to which Jews have been exposed throughout history.

11. The priestly sects of the Jews, the Apostolic See and hierarchy of the Catholic and other Christian Churches, were full of venality, rapacity and cupidity; derived their divine authority from self-generated edicts. In their struggle for self-preservation and preservation of privileges, they created

an aristocratic power base which, at times; accumulated great wealth. They set the course of history by fomenting political action furthering their interests, made and unmade kings and rulers, started and concluded hostilities responsible for uncountable millions of deaths, suffering and degradation; authored and interpreted laws and commands they styled divine, all as manifestations of their prerogatives.

12. The validity of anti-Semitism as reflected in Paul and the Gospels presupposes their divine revelation. The peculiar Laws and Commandments of the Torah binding on Jews throughout and making their conduct execrable and odious to their neighbors, presuppose their divine revelation. If it can be shown, by examining the internal evidence of the Hebrew and Christian Scriptures, that their guiding hand was not divine revelation, then the Laws and Commandments which made the Jews hateful to their neighbors, and the narratives of the Passion and Crucifixion of Christ which inspired theological anti-Semitism, were authored by fallible men corrupted by their earthly designs, motives and instincts. The author went to great length to demonstrate that such conclusions could be drawn from the Old and New Testaments and were in fact drawn.

13. There are no Jews with authority to effect changes in the Old Testament text that would please Christians; there are no Christians with authority to effect changes in the New Testament text that would satisfy Jews. I refer to changes that would fundamentally alter the status of their hostile and contradictory theological positions and make a dialogue between them possible. Hence, the curse of anti-Semitism will not abate. The claim of Jews to be the Chosen People, privy to an exclusive Covenant with God and to special election to fulfill God's purpose on earth will not square with the Christian claim that Jesus was the divine Messiah, Christ crucified, who died for the sins of mankind, was resurrected and ascended to Heaven. No dialogue is possible.

14. As a result of religious persecutions, wars, atrocities, murders and massacres, Jews and Christians died for nothing. No purpose was served by their death and sacrifice.

15. The shedding of blood, the suffering and privation inflicted upon the Jewish people for ostensibly theological reasons, can be laid at the doorstep of the Catholic and other Christian institutions, their functionaries, their

representatives, their firebrands, their various monastic orders, their unholy alliances with scheming secular potentates for crimes against humanity and responsibility for inventing the baseless charges of:

Deicide

Ritual Murder

Image Desecration

Desecration of the Consecrated Host

Sorcery and Magic

Blood Lust

Sin of Usury

Anti-Christian Practices

Select Bibliography

(1) *Exploring Exodus*. Nahum M. Sarna (Schocken Books, 1987)

(2) *Jews, God, History*. Max I. Dimont (Simon & Schuster, Inc., 1962)

(3) *Archaeology and the Old Testament*. Pritchard

(4) *The Story of Civilization*. Will Durant/Part I (Simon & Schuster, Inc., 1963)

(5) *A History of the Jews*. Sachar (Alfred A. Knopf, 1964)

(6) *Jews*. Paul Johnson (Harper & Row, 1987)

(7) *The Early Church*. Henry Chadwick (Penguin Books Ltd., 1967)

(8) *The Reformation*. Owen Chadwick (Penguin Books Ltd., 1972)

(9) *The Middle Ages*. Southern (Penguin Books Ltd., 1970)

(10) *The Church and the Age of Reason*. Cragg (Penguin Books Ltd., 1970)

(11) *The Church in an Age of Revolution*. Vidler (Penguin Books Ltd., 1971)

(12) *The Quest of the Historical Jesus*. Schweitzer (Collier Books/ Macmillan Publishing Co., 1968)

(13) *Popes from the Ghetto*. Prinz (Dorset Press, 1966)

(14) *The Mythmaker (Paul)*. Maccoby (Harper & Row, 1986)

(15) *Jesus in History and Myth*. Edited by R. Joseph Hoffman and Gerald A. Larue (Prometheus Books, 1986)

(16) *The Pope's Jews*. Waagenaar (Open Court Publishers, 1974)

(17) *Pagan Christs*. Robertson (Dorset Press, 1966)

(18) *Disciples of Destruction*. Sutherland (Prometheus Books, 1987)

(19) *Back to the Ghetto*. Huppert (Prometheus Books, 1988)

(20) *Deceptions and Myths of the Bible*. Graham (Carol Communications, 1975)

(21) *The Transformation*. Domb (Hachomo, 1989)

(22) *The Roots of Christian Anti-Semitism*. Malcolm Hay (Freedom Library Press, 1981)

(23) *The Devil and the Jews*. Joshua Trachtenberg (Yale University Press, 1943)

(24) *Some Mistakes of Moses*. Robert Ingersoll (Prometheus Books, 1986)

(25) *Who Was Jesus*. G.A. Wells (Open Court Publishing Company, 1989)

(26) *The Historical Evidence of Jesus*. G.A. Wells (Prometheus Books, 1982)

(27) *Did Jesus Exist?* G.A. Wells (Goodwin Press Limited, 1975)

(28) *Atheism—The Case Against God*. George H. Smith (Prometheus Books, 1979)

(29) *The Unknown History of the Jews*. E.E. Jessel (Watts & Co., 1914)

(30) *Bible, Religion & Morality.* Steve Allen (Prometheus Books, 1990)

(31) *Chutzpah.* Alan M. Dershowitz (Little, Brown and Company, 1991)

(32) *From the Maccabees to the Mishnah.* Shaye J. D. Cohen (The Westminster Press, 1989)

(33) *The Ruling Class of Judaea.* Martin Goodman (Cambridge University Press, 1987)

(34) *Justice Not Vengeance.* Simon Wiesenthal (Grove Weidenfield, 1989)

(35) *Every Day Remembrance Day.* Simon Wiesenthal (Henry Holt and Company, 1986)

(36) *History & Ideology in Ancient Israel.* Giovanni Garbini (Crossroads Publishing, 1988)

(37) *Out of the Desert?* William H. Stiebing, Jr. (Prometheus Books, 1989)

(38) *On the Gods and Other Essays.* Robert G. Ingersoll (Prometheus Books, 1983)

(39) *The Religion of the Semites.* W. Robertson Smith (Meridian Books, 1957)

(40) *The Early History of God.* Mark S. Smith (Harper & Row, 1990)

(41) *Britain and the Jews of Europe.* Bernard Wasserstein (Oxford University Press, 1979)

(42) *Hebrew Religion—Its Origin and Development.* Oesterly & Robinson (S.PC.K., 1957)

(43) *Yahweh and the Gods of Canaan.* WF. Albright (Doubleday & Company, 1968)

(44) *A Theologico-Political Treatise.* Spinoza (Dover Publications, 1951)

(45) *A History of the Babylonians and Assyrians.* G.S. Goodspeed (Charles Scribner's Sons, 1902)

(46) *History of the Jews.* Simon Dubnov (A. S. Barnes and Company, 1967)

(47) *The Age of Reason.* Thomas Paine (Citadel Press, 1974)

(48) *Who Wrote the Bible.* Richard Elliott Friedman (Summit Books, 1987)

(49) *Physicians of No Value.* Miles R. Abelard (Reality Publications, 1979)

(50) *History Begins at Sumer.* Samuel Noah Kramer (The University of Pennsylvania Press, 1981)

(51) *Cultural Atlas of Mesopotamia.* Michael Roaf (Equinox–Oxford, 1990)

(52) *The Outline of History.* H.G. Wells (Garden City)

(53) *Encyclopaedia Judaica.* Fourth Printing 1978 (Keter Publishing House)

(54) *History of the Jews.* Graetz (The Jewish Publication Society, 1981)

(55) *Antiquities.* Josephus (Holt, Rinehart and Winston)

(56) *Abermals Krähte Der Hahn.* Karlheinz Deschner (Econ Verlag, 1980)

(57) *New Catholic Encyclopedia* (The Catholic University of America, 1967)

(58) *The Gnostic Gospels.* Elaine Pagels (Random House, 1979)

(59) *The Bad Popes.* E.R. Chamberlin (Dorset Press, 1969)

(60) *A History of the Crusades.* Steven Runciman (Cambridge University Press, 1951)

(61) *The Heretics.* Walter Nigg (Dorset Press, 1962)

(62) *A History of Christianity.* Paul Johnson (Atheneum, 1976)

(63) *The Knights Templar.* Stephen Howarth (Dorset Press, 1982)

(64) *The Inquisition.* Hroch/Skybova (Dorset Press, 1988)

(65) *The Causes and Effects of Anti-Semitism.* Paul E. Grosser and Edwin G. Halperin (Philosophical Library, 1978)

(66) *A Man Called Intrepid.* William Stevenson (Ballantine Books, 1976)

(67) *Pius XII and the Third Reich.* Saul Friedlander (Alfred A. Knopf, Inc., 1966)

(68) *They Dare To Speak Out.* Paul Findley (Lawrence Hill & Company, 1985)

Index